ALEXANDER
PATERSON

PRISON
REFORMER

ALEXANDER PATERSON

PRISON REFORMER

HARRY POTTER

THE BOYDELL PRESS

First published 2022
The Boydell Press, Woodbridge

ISBN 978 1 78327 667 7

The Boydell Press is an imprint of Boydell & Brewer Ltd
PO Box 9, Woodbridge, Suffolk IP12 3DF, UK
and of Boydell & Brewer Inc.
668 Mt Hope Avenue, Rochester, NY 14620–2731, USA
website: www.boydellandbrewer.com

A CIP catalogue record for this book is available
from the British Library

The publisher has no responsibility for the continued existence or accuracy of URLs
for external or third-party internet websites referred to in this book, and does not
guarantee that any content on such websites is, or will remain, accurate or appropriate

This publication is printed on acid-free paper

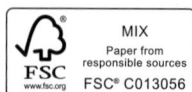

MIX
Paper from
responsible sources
FSC
www.fsc.org   FSC® C013056

Printed and bound in Great Britain by TJ Books Limited, Padstow, Cornwall

CONTENTS

PART IV
CROSSING THE BRIDGE: 1945–1947

ILLUSTRATIONS

All illustrations are from the author's or the family's collection unless otherwise attributed.

The author and publisher are grateful to all the institutions and individuals listed for permission to reproduce the materials in which they hold copyright. Every effort has been made to trace the copyright holders; apologies are offered for any omission, and the publisher will be pleased to add any necessary acknowledgement in subsequent editions.

ABBREVIATIONS

Attlee	*As it Happened*
Bailey (1987)	*Delinquency and Citizenship*
Bailey (2019)	*The Rise and Fall of the Rehabilitative Ideal*
Baron	*The Doctor*
BEF	British Expeditionary Force
Benney	*Low Company*
BJC	*British Journal of Criminology*
Booth	*Life and Labour*
Clayton	*The Wall is Strong*
CO	Commanding Officer or Colonial Office
Cronin	*The Screw Turns*
Diary	Paterson's own war diary
Darwall-Smith	*University College*
Eagar	*Making Men*
EPBS	Fox, *The English Prison and Borstal Systems*
Forsythe	*Penal Discipline*
Gordon	*Borstalians*
Gore	*The Better Fight*
Grew	*Prison Governor*
Gutman	*Seven Years' Harvest*
H&B	Hobhouse and Brockway, *English Prisons Today*
HC	House of Commons
Henriques	*Indiscretions of a Warden*
HJ	*Howard Journal*
HL	House of Lords
HO	Home Office
Hood	*Borstal Reassessed*
IJSL	*International Journal of the Sociology of Law*
Ingham	*Altrincham and Bowdon*
IPC	International Prison Commission
IPPC	International Penal and Penitentiary Commission
JCLC	*Journal of Criminal Law and Criminology*
Letters	Paterson's correspondence during the Great War
LLGJ	Llewellin's Lowdham Grange Journal
Macartney	*Walls Have Mouths*
Maude	*History of the 47th Division, 1914–1919*

Merrow-Smith	*Prison Screw*
Moseley	*The Truth About Borstal*
Neale	*Prison Service People*
OBC	Oxford and Bermondsey Club
OBM	Oxford and Bermondsey Mission
OMM	Oxford Medical Mission
Paterson	*Across the Bridges*
Phelan	*Jail Journey*
PJ	*Probation Journal*
PPA	*Prison Problem of America*
Radzinowicz	*The Emergence of Penal Policy*
Report (date)	Reports of the Commissioners of Prisons or reports on prisons
Rich	*Recollections of a Prison Governor*
Richter	*The Politics of Conscience*
Ruck	*Paterson on Prisons*
Scott	*Your Obedient Servant*
Snape	*The Back Parts of War*
T&M	Teagle and Midgley, *The Unitarian Congregation in Altrincham*
THJ	*Toc H Journal*
TNA	The National Archives
Univ.	University College Oxford
Vidler	*If Freedom Fail*
War Diary	47th Division, 142nd Brigade
Watson (1939)	*Meet the Prisoner*
Watson (1969)	*Which is the Justice?*
YMCA	Young Men's Christian Association

For full references to those sources listed here please see the Bibliography.

PREFACE

A GOOD AND USEFUL LIFE

May we become masters of ourselves that we may be the servants of others.

Alexander Paterson

With Paterson the springs of action lay deeper than the desire for fame. He believed that his work must consist in the service of his fellow men, and that it was the most dejected who had most need of that service. He had faith in the ultimate value of the most apparently worthless individual, and was possessed of greater power of evoking the best from the worst than is given to most men.

Sidney Ruck

Alexander Paterson ('Alec' to his friends, 'Pat' to his comrades, 'A.P.' to his colleagues) was an extraordinary man who made a deep impression on everyone he met, and whose achievements in penal reform and especially in the development of borstals were celebrated not just in Great Britain but in many other countries wrestling with the problems and purpose of incarceration. A contemporary said of him that he had 'left the mark of his wisdom and compassion on every aspect of progressive prison administration' and was 'as famous in the world of prison reform as Elizabeth Fry and John Howard.'[1] Yet, now, he is almost forgotten. Who today knows that Paterson Park, a small and undistinguished area of greenery in South London is named after him? He appears in the *Oxford Dictionary of National Biography* and in *Who Was Who*, and there are short biographical sketches in a number of works. Sources are rarely cited and detail is sparse. I became fascinated by this elusive figure when researching a book on the history of incarceration in the British Isles. I looked in vain for a full and comprehensive biography. There is none, an extraordinary lacuna given his significance. It was time to rectify the omission.

---

1   Reginald Goodwin, 'A Matter of Faith' (Toc H archives, 1973), p. 3.

Embarking on a biographical trail along which no one has ventured has its challenges as well as its rewards when some or other fact is unearthed or connection made. The following is based upon all I could glean from his writings, including his various reports, articles and book prefaces, as well as from birth, marriage and death certificates, census returns and land registry entries, college archives, newspapers recording his success at the Oxford Union, letters he wrote during the Great War, personal and regimental war diaries, Prison Commission, Home Office and Colonial Office deposits, and books by his contemporaries, friends, colleagues and others. The extant material spans his adult life from his time as an undergraduate in Oxford to his death in 1947, although there is minimal correspondence before 1914 or after 1918. His childhood and teenage years are less well-documented, but it is still possible to paint a picture of his family, his upbringing and of the influences that would have worked on him in his youth. Fortunately, snippets from his later writings and letters illuminate aspects of this period.

As my researches progressed it soon became evident that apart from his later work as a Prison Commissioner, his whole life was one of remarkable interest and importance, sufficient in itself to justify a biography. Not only did he interact with some of his most substantial contemporaries – Churchill, Attlee, Galsworthy, Temple, Kitchener – he was at the forefront of the settlement movement, wrote an influential best-seller, recorded in detail his experience of the Great War, and became a leading figure in Toc H. His story illuminates many aspects of late Victorian Cheshire, Oxford at the turn of the century, and Edwardian Bermondsey, as well as the social, political and penological concerns of inter-war Britain. The influences that acted upon him in the first half of his life, the experience of living intimately with working-class people both in South London and Flanders Fields, the convictions he formed in youth and which he matured over the years, and an enduring Christian faith, all help to explain the compulsion he felt to identify with the less privileged, the motivation for his transformatory work on prisons and borstals, and the energy which drove him on right up to his dying days.

Thus I have incorporated a great deal of the family's material, and have described in detail those aspects of his life that have been practically untouched: his childhood and youth, his university years, his time in Bermondsey and in the army, and his involvement with Toc H. Much more is known of his career as a Prison Commissioner, and documentation for that period is readily available in the National Archives. Many aspects of his prison and borstal work in England have already been covered by others, in particular William Forsythe and Victor Bailey. Although I have traversed the same ground, I have not given it as detailed an appraisal as I should have liked: otherwise this biography would be even longer. I have instead devoted considerable space to those aspects of his professional career not previously considered, such as his foreign missions (after one of which he persuaded the French to close Devil's Island and for which I have his wife's diary), his expert evidence before a number of committees, his involvement with the International Penal and Penitentiary Commission culminating in his confrontation with the Nazis in 1935, his decisive intervention on the part of internees in Canada, his arduous last years, death and commemoration. Strict chronology in the earlier chapters has perforce had to yield to a more thematic approach in the later ones. As Churchill put it:

> Chronology is the key to narrative. Yet where a throng of events are marching abreast, it is inevitable that their progress should be modified by selection and classification. Some must stand on one side until the main press is over; others, taking advantage of any interlude, may haste forward to periods beyond the general account.[2]

There remain gaps. Without diaries, personal correspondence or records of his conversations we can only surmise how he reacted to the great events between the wars, such as the General Strike, the rise of totalitarianism, the Great Depression, the deaths within days of each other of Kipling and King George V, the Spanish Civil War, the Jarrow March, the destruction of the Crystal Palace, the Abdication Crisis, and the Munich Agreement, or to such notable trend-setters as T.S. Eliot, Ezra Pound, the Sitwell siblings, the Mitford sisters, Charlie Chaplin or Agatha Christie. We also know nothing of his views on the Battle of Britain, the attack on Pearl Harbour or the bombing of Dresden and Hiroshima. He may have been so all-obsessed with his job as to have little time for anything else, but this is unlikely for a voracious reader and ready writer, especially as he had time on his hands when undertaking many, lengthy voyages. Almost all the existing material from 1922 to 1947 relates solely to his prison and borstal work, and may not be complete.[3] His personal life lies in shadows. It can only be hoped that further material will surface that may shed light into the recesses.

I have many people to thank for the assistance they have given. The Unitarians showed me around Dunham Road Chapel and provided information on its history and the major role the Patersons played over the years in its worship and administration. Dr Darwall-Smith of University College Oxford gathered material from the archives, and the College granted permission to use its photographs. Michael Selby gave me the journal of Alec's acolyte, Bill Llewellin. Dorothy Butters proof-read and dissected an earlier draft.

2   Winston Churchill, *The World Crisis*, vol.2 (Folio Society, London, 2007), p. 214.

3   In particular the 'Paterson Papers' provided by Kenneth Neale to Victor Bailey for his book *Delinquency and Citizenship* cannot be reconstituted. They are either lost or deposited in the National Archives with their contents dispersed among the many Home Office and Prison Commission files.

Above all my gratitude must go to the descendants of Alec Paterson: his niece, Katharine Draper, granddaughter Jennifer Rendell, and grandsons Tony and David Stedham. They responded with enthusiasm to my inquiries, gathered together all the material that the family hold, including the unpublished typescript of *Over the Walls*, a sequel to his best-selling *Across the Bridges*, that their grandfather was writing up to his death. They have also kindly granted permission for the text of this manuscript to be produced as an appendix to this book, housed on the Boydell & Brewer website.[4] In Katharine's case she mined her memories of Alec himself, his brother Willis (her father), his wife Frances and his daughter Margaret (her childhood friend). Katharine is custodian of many of the family photographs and of the Allingham portrait of the Paterson children reproduced in this book.

Biographies frequently depict their subjects as tortured, damaged and fault-ridden individuals, split by contradictions, and often harbouring dark and abhorrent secrets. Alec Paterson was neither a tortured soul nor a tarnished one. There are many references by his contemporaries to his outstanding qualities, very few to his faults. I have included all the criticisms I have found, but even cumulatively they amount to little, and often come from tainted or embittered sources, or arise out of the cynicism of ideologues, or are a result of simple error. Discontented governors of 'the old school' were outraged to see the overturning of long-held nostrums, and dissident prisoners were contemptuous of what they considered to be cosmetic changes. Contemporary critics such as Playfair blamed Paterson for working within the system rather than condemning it from without, the usual argument from 'purists' who achieve nothing, and carp at those who try to do something. 'Revisionist' historians, with an ideological axe to grind, have disputed the sincerity or denigrated the integrity of humanitarian reformers in general, and Christian ones in particular. Liberal reformers have always been a target for radicals of a Marxist persuasion since the latter rightly perceive that implementing reforms and ameliorating conditions delays or prevents revolutionary change. Revisionists have little conception that people may be motivated by anything other than economic benefit and class-interest. For them, humanitarian sentiment cloaks Machiavellian intent. This is patently untrue, and they in turn have had their arguments comprehensively demolished by more exacting scholars and by the facts. Let them lament with Voltaire, who said '*malheur aux détails, c'est une vermine qui tue les grands ouvrages*' [a curse on details; they are vermin which kill great works].

4   https://dhjhkxawhe8q4.cloudfront.net/boydell-and-brewer-wp/wp-content/ uploads/2021/11/15102344/Alexander-Paterson-Online-Appendix.pdf.

As for error, one of his critics, J.E. Thomas, repeatedly claimed that Paterson hardly ever consulted ordinary prison officers and excluded them from 'the socially approved work of rehabilitation'. Neither is the case, as the facts show. In one egregious instance Thomas completely misunderstood and misrepresented the evidence. He drew attention to an ominous statement advocating covert surveillance on suspect prison officers made by Alexander Paterson, 'the most influential and important Prison Commissioner of the century', in his book, *Our Prisons*. It is, however, neither Alec's book nor his sentiments. It was written by his uncle Arthur, who in any case is quoted out of context by Thomas. His concern was about bullying, not 'work performance'.[5]

Even the more sympathetic William Forsythe falls into error. In a passage on Paterson, he refers to Major Blake taking advantage of the relaxed ethos of the Commission after Evelyn Ruggles-Brise had gone. The governor, in some trepidation, informed his superiors that a man he had released without authorisation on day-parole had absconded. There was some sympathy and no repercussion. However, this incident took place in May 1919 when Ruggles-Brise was still chairman and Alec not yet a Commissioner.[6]

Roger Hood charges Paterson with timidity, pointing out that open borstals were the preserve of boys with good prospects, and concluding that his 'belief in the innate trustworthiness of the British lad obviously did not extend to those with bad records', and that 'those who were considered untrustworthy were simply beyond being trusted'.[7] The same could be said of open camps for men where careful selection took place. Such a conclusion is too cynical. Certainly Paterson preserved open camps in England for the better bets, but this was in the early days when he had to ensure public acceptance, and build up the experience of the staff. When he inaugurated his first open borstal in 1930 he was well aware that road camps in Burma, established four years earlier, had been largely abandoned because of police protests about dangerous criminals being at liberty within a few months of receiving long prison terms. He had to ensure that risks were minimised. The borstal system itself was still in its infancy. Had its growth been allowed to continue unabated, had more and more open borstals proved their worth, he would have improved and extended the scheme as he intended. His expressed aim, for adolescents and adults, was to substitute camps for walled prisons and closed borstals, and he predicted that no more 'walled

5   J.E. Thomas, *The English Prison Officer since 1850* (London, 1972), pp. 139f., 151 n.32; Arthur Paterson, *Our Prisons* (London, 1911), p. 49.

6   Forsythe, pp. 202f.; Wallace Blake, *Quod* (London, n.d.), pp. 173, 226–231. Blake thoroughly approved of the transformation of prisons into 'moral hospitals' during the Paterson era (p. 320).

7   Hood, p. 120.

establishments for penal purposes' would be built in England.[8] Don't judge a long-distance runner by the first mile.

While a few of those who worked under Paterson found him impetuous, difficult, arrogant or brusque, most found him visionary, friendly, kindly and charming. While he liked people, he detested snobs. To a modern sensibility some things he said and wrote may jar. He was a man of his time, and occasionally in his use of language betrays an imperial condescension that was prevalent among many of the most advanced figures of his day. On the other hand, in his promotion of the training and employment of natives in the colonies he was ahead of his times. Similarly, his qualified support for the retention of both capital and corporal punishment was unexceptionable in the first half of the twentieth century. The case of Harold Jones, for which he has recently been taken to task, has a chapter in this book to itself, putting the facts in a rather different perspective and drawing on records not utilised by his critics. There was one criticism made in his own day and repeated thereafter that has some traction. For people to 'benefit' from training they could be sentenced to longer periods in detention than their crimes warranted. Though true, that is not a blot on Paterson's character or a questioning of his sincerity or integrity, but a comment on the most controversial consequence of his penal ideology. He believed, and may have been right, that a period of prolonged training in youth would prevent prolonged periods of imprisonment thereafter.

The unexplained neglect of his sick brother, and the effective disregard of the needs of his frequently abandoned daughter, are the worst that can be said against a man who put duty before family. All the rest is on the positive side. Like those other pioneers of prison reform, John Howard and Elizabeth Fry, Alexander Paterson led a life that was both good and useful.[9] The more I learned about him the more admirable I found him to be, as a man, a soldier, a friend, a husband, and a reformer. On the available evidence, and its cumulative effect, that is an objective assessment for which I make no apology. It is for readers, considering the evidence, to judge if I am right.

---

8   CO323/1344/3: Letter, 31st October 1934.
9   Alec may have coined this phrase. It certainly resonated with him.

The Paterson Family Tree

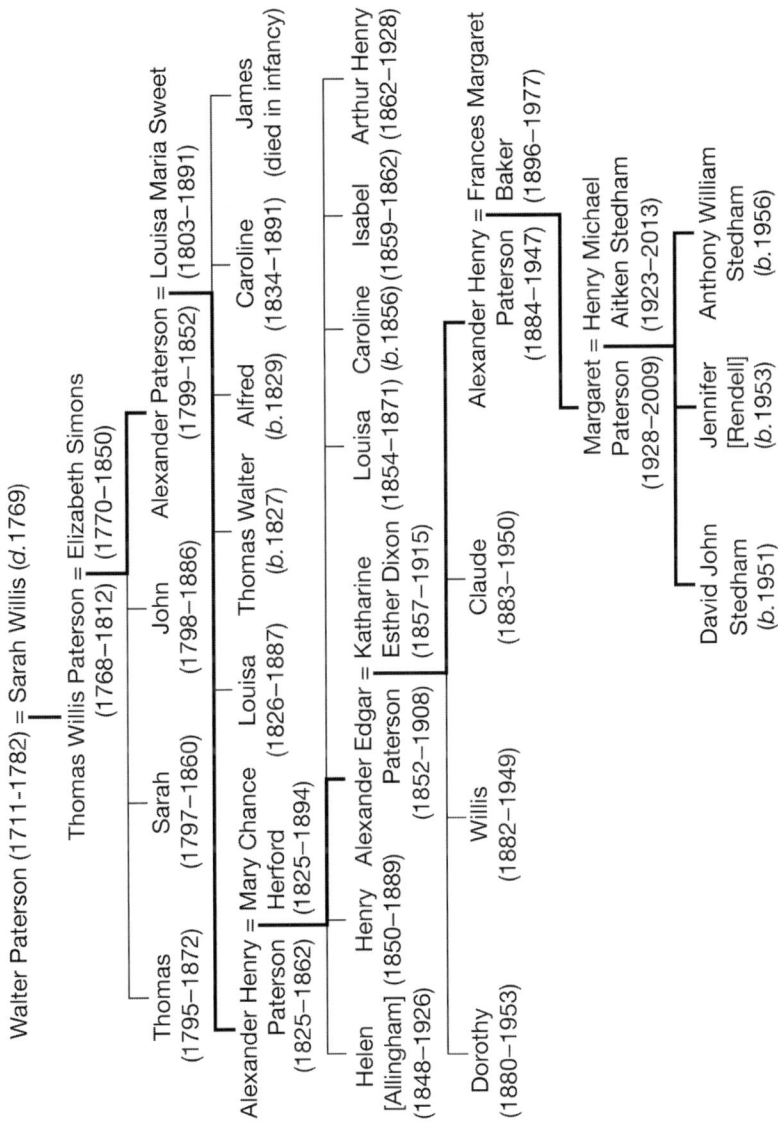

Walter Paterson (1711-1782) = Sarah Willis (d.1769)

Thomas Willis Paterson = Elizabeth Simons
(1768–1812) | (1770–1850)

Thomas
(1795–1872)

Sarah
(1797–1860)

John
(1798–1886)

Alexander Paterson = Louisa Maria Sweet
(1799–1852) | (1803–1891)

Louisa
(1826–1887)

Thomas Walter
(b.1827)

Alfred
(b.1829)

Caroline
(1834–1891)

James
(died in infancy)

Alexander Henry = Mary Chance
Paterson | Herford
(1825–1862) | (1825–1894)

Henry Alexander Edgar = Katharine
[Allingham] (1850–1889) Paterson | Esther Dixon (1854–1871) (b.1856) (1859–1862) (1862–1928)
(1848–1926) (1852–1908) | (1857–1915)

Louisa   Caroline   Isabel   Arthur Henry

Helen

Willis
(1882–1949)

Claude
(1883–1950)

Dorothy
(1880–1953)

Alexander Henry = Frances Margaret
Paterson | Baker
(1884–1947) | (1896–1977)

Margaret = Henry Michael
Paterson | Aitken Stedham
(1928–2009) | (1923–2013)

David John
Stedham
(b.1951)

Jennifer
[Rendell]
(b.1953)

Anthony William
Stedham
(b.1956)

Part I

The Young Idealist: 1884–1914

CHAPTER 1

EARLY YEARS AND INFLUENCES: 1884–1902

The rich man in his castle,
The poor man at his gate,
God made them high and lowly,
And ordered their estate.

Cecil Frances Alexander, 'All Things Bright and Beautiful'

Alexander Henry Paterson came into this world on Thursday the 20th November 1884, the fourth and last child of Alexander Edgar and Katharine Esther Paterson of Bowdon in the county of Cheshire.

The new-born's father was a thirty-two-year-old solicitor, the son of an Altrincham surgeon after whom Alec was named. His mother was a Dixon who, although she hailed from Hampshire, traced her roots back to both the northwest of England, as her own mother was from Cheshire, and, more distantly, on her father's side, to Scotland. She was a quiet and compassionate person, adored by her children.

The eldest of Alec's siblings was his sister, Dorothy, who at the time of his birth was four years old. His two older brothers were Willis, aged three, and Claude, who was still a toddler, just sixteen months old. With little difference in age the four youngsters would have been playmates and friends, although there may have been some sibling rivalry between Claude and Alec as the latter had displaced his infant brother as the baby of the family. Judging from later life, it seems he was closest to Dorothy, or 'Dor' as she was called by Alec, 'Dorkin' by Claude, and 'Dodo' by others. He was 'her baby'. We first set eyes on the children in a watercolour by their aunt Nellie, by then a celebrated artist.[1] There they are, her niece and nephews painting at a table, Alec second from the left,

---

1   Helen Paterson married William Allingham in 1874. She would go on to become a renowned watercolourist, and in 1890 was the first woman to be granted full membership of the Royal Society of Painters in Water Colours. The children called her 'Aunt Nellie' (*Letters*, 2nd January 1918).

I

FIGURE 1. The Paterson Children painted by Helen Allingham

'a small boy with a big head', probably about five years old.[2] They are neat little children, well-cared for and well-nourished.

Theirs was a comfortable, cosy and Christian household, but it was certainly not conformist, religiously or politically. Their parents were in faith Unitarians and in politics Liberals (a large portrait of William Ewart Gladstone, the 'grand old man', dominated their dining room) when many of their neighbours in Bowdon were Anglicans and Tories.

Alec's family, though presently pillars of society, were pedigree Dissenters. Paterson is a Scottish name and his father's family's roots lay in what Victorians would call North Britain. Like so many other Scots, after the opportunity afforded by the Union and the disruption caused by the '45 rebellion, his great-great-great-grandfather Walter Paterson had migrated to England, perhaps owing to a certain reticence about staying in the land in which he had served as chaplain in the British army that had routed the Young Pretender, Charles Edward Stuart, at Culloden. It was not until 1757 at the age of forty-six that Walter married a Sarah Willis of Dorset whose surname was long preserved in the Paterson line. Eleven years later their only child, Thomas Willis, was born in

2   *Letters*, 4th September 1915.

Bristol, the city where the couple had settled. Thomas became a Unitarian minister, as did his own youngest son, Alexander, a graduate of Glasgow University.[3]

Alexander's oldest son, Alexander Henry, after studying medicine at Aberdeen University, married Mary Chance Herford of Altrincham. She too came of staunch Unitarian stock. Her father, John, was a wine merchant. Her younger brother, Brooke, became a well-respected minister. Her mother, Sarah, who was clever and artistic, kept a school for girls. Initially the newly-weds lived in Swadlincote in Derbyshire, where their first child, Helen, was born. Following her birth the Patersons moved to an opulent part of Altrincham and lived at 16 The High Street (now Market Street), where the father set up his medical practice and where their first son, Henry Walter, was born. The Patersons were sufficiently well-to-do to have their own house built on the hills of neighbouring Bowdon, and in April 1852, shortly after the birth of their second son, Alexander Edgar, they translated to The Downs. There, three more daughters were born, the last in 1859. The girls grew up in an enlightened middle-class family environment, surrounded by their mother's Herford relations, whose connections included the Gaskells and other prominent Unitarians, and were educated at their maternal grandmother's school. Then disaster struck when diphtheria, contracted on the assiduous doctor's rounds when a dying child coughed in his face, and transmitted to his youngest daughter as she sat on his knee, carried off both father and child in 1862, the same year the youngest son, Arthur, was born. Mary Paterson and her remaining children, now much less well-off as a result of this calamity, moved to stay near relatives in Birmingham.

Alexander Edgar survived his childhood traumas, married Katharine Dixon in 1879, and became a solicitor in Manchester. Thus established, he could afford to move back to his birthplace. Initially he and his growing family lived in West Bank, before finding a permanent residence at Dudley House, The Firs, a substantial Victorian dwelling in fashionable and affluent Bowdon. Alec, the youngest of the brood, was the only child born there. It would remain his home throughout his childhood and youth. Within a few years the family were joined by the maternal grandmother, Sarah Dixon, a widow of independent means, but ailing health – she would die in 1901. The household was augmented by two servants: Kate Healey, a domestic nurse or nanny, and Lizzie Downes, a housemaid. Both were single. Kate, a lifelong spinster, would become a fixture in the family, but the much younger Lizzie would leave her post after a few years to be replaced by Fanny Thomason. An older woman, Frances Sumner, was appointed as nurse when Kate was elevated to the status of cook.[4] In this affluent milieu in this upper-middle-class area of Bowdon, the young boy would grow up.

3   Detailed records of Alec's paternal ancestry are held by the family, but there is little on the maternal side.
4   Census returns, 1891 and 1901.

Dating back to Anglo-Saxon times or earlier, the parish of Bowdon was extensive, encompassing a wide area of Mercia and incorporating the market town of Altrincham. Bowdon was particularly well-favoured, as its name suggests, deriving as it probably does from two Old English words: 'Bode' meaning dwelling or habitation, and 'Don' or 'Dun', a plain upon a rising hill or down.[5] Built on elevated land affording fine views of the rich Cheshire plain and the Bollin river valley, it was surrounded by farms, market gardens and Dunham Massey, the seat of the earls of Stamford, and its deer park. By the seventeenth century picturesque timber-framed thatched cottages and fine houses enclosed the stone-built Norman parish church of St Mary the Virgin. Around the hamlet were farms with sturdy barns and large houses. The Bridgewater Canal, which opened in 1776, and the improvements made to the main Chester road when it became a turnpike, proved a spur to the growth of both industry and population, but it was the coming of the train that had the biggest impact on tranquil Bowdon, making it easily accessible to those who worked in the nearby smoggy 'Cottonopolis'. The original railway line, finished in 1849, ran for eight miles from Manchester to Altrincham, but was soon extended to a terminus at the foot of The Downs. This marvel of the industrial age allowed well-heeled professionals and commercial entrepreneurs to live in the far more salubrious, semi-rural environment that Bowdon afforded. That is so long as accommodation of sufficient quality was available.

Money soon talked. Rural landowners could make a killing by selling to the *nouveaux-riches*. Thomas Smith led the way when, in the early 1840s, he sold part of the southern downs for residential development. His success persuaded George Grey, 7th Earl of Stamford and Warrington, to follow his lead and make available some of his agricultural land for prestigious dwellings. By dictating the quality, type, density and rental value of housing through covenants in the deeds, Lord Stamford ensured that he would have prosperous and genteel neighbours. There was no shortage of takers, and building went on apace. Balshaw's 1850 *Guide* stated that in the previous decade 'the proverbial salubrity of the air has caused great numbers of neat villa residences to be erected by the merchants of Manchester', and that the houses, constructed of yellow or red bricks, or stuccoed, had 'a remarkable light, clean and elegant appearance'.[6] That the rich had come to stay was obvious and proved the impetus for further enhancement. Seventeen parishes were carved out of the original vast parish

<hr />

5   George Ormerod, *History of Cheshire*, 3 vols (2nd edn, London, 1882), I, p. 392. Alternatively, Domesday Book's 'Bogedon' denotes a down or hill by a bog. Ormerod noted that 'towards Ashley lieth a great deep bog'.

6   Charles Balshaw, *Stranger's Guide and Complete Directory to Altrincham, Bowdon Dunham, Timperley, Baguley, Ashley, Hale, and Bollington* (Altrincham, c.1850), p. 45.

FIGURE 2. Dudley House, The Firs, Bowdon

and between 1857 and 1860 St Mary's was rebuilt on a much grander scale in High Victorian Gothic. The fact that gas lighting had been introduced into the church, onto the streets and inside some commercial and domestic properties, a complete system of sewerage was well underway, and a supply of pure water from the Manchester reservoirs could be ensured, were added inducements.[7] Others would soon follow: in 1880 Stamford Park, a place of recreation for the local inhabitants, was created on land in Hale Moss given for that purpose by the earl; and in 1894 the Altrincham Electric Supply Company began generating power for the inhabitants of Altrincham and Bowdon.[8]

Certainly by the time of Alec's birth Bowdon had become a rather superior suburb of Altrincham, an oasis safely secluded from any industries that would spring up in the Broadheath area on the far side of the Bridgewater Canal, and characterised as 'studded with the many commodious and handsomely designed villas and terraces of a large and flourishing community, chiefly composed of those who every evening seek a healthy and pleasant retirement from the toils of business.'[9]

7   Ingham, pp. 209, 214f.
8   *Ibid.*, pp. 219ff.
9   Nicolas Pevsner (*The Buildings of England, Cheshire* [London, 1971], p. 110) attributed this quotation to the second edition of Ormerod's *History of Cheshire,*

As a result, the lovely village became a rather exclusive refuge for Lancashire mill-owners known as the 'Cottontots', and other industrialists fleeing the urban squalor that they had created in and around Manchester. If that great industrial city 'glittered like a slag-heap stuck with brilliants', Bowdon was a genuine gemstone nearby, a nirvana for millionaires and tycoons who 'relished conformity and ostentation'[10] and for professionals who relished non-conformity and ornamentation. Life was leisurely as well as luxurious. Each afternoon at 2 o'clock the Bowdon medical fraternity could be seen biking off to the golf course, their working day over.[11] At the same time, Altrincham's middle-class residents, increasingly concerned about the deteriorating environment and the increasing influx of poor people into their town, bringing with them, so it was feared, disease, dirt and bad odour, were upgrading to Bowdon. Fresh air and select neighbours were what was wanted and what was on offer only a mile or two away. The finest mansions were built on the high ground of Bowdon to house the most affluent, the largest and most opulent being the magnificent mock-Elizabethan Erlesdene and the Flemish-style Denzell, both on Green Walk. Within a short time more millionaires, it was said, were to be found on Green Walk in Bowdon than in Park Lane in London. They brought in their wake upmarket retailers, coffee shops, fine craftsmen, and emporia for luxury goods. In 1881 The Polygon was built in Bowdon village to provide the sort of shopping facilities the new residents required. Alongside a pharmacist and a grocer, a photographer, with an eye or lens for upmarket portraiture or weddings, set up his studio.

In Bowdon the new rich could add polish to their pile by hobnobbing with the long-established landowners of the 'Cheshire set' and socialising with, or perhaps even marrying into, the local aristocracy. But it was not just brash money on display, for many of those who moved into Bowdon were luminaries of science, literature, education, architecture and music. Both the beneficiaries of capitalism and the doyens of high culture graced the pavements of this earthly paradise, and they did so in ever-increasing numbers. Whereas in 1841 Bowdon's population was under 600, by 1891 it was nearing 3,000, and its rateable value had increased in the same period from under £2,000 to over £25,000.[12] The recently-created Altrincham constituency, of which it was a part, became a much-coveted parliamentary seat and from 1892 until 1906 its MP was none other than Coningsby Disraeli, nephew of the famous prime minister.

---

although he gave no volume or page number. In fact it cannot be found in those volumes, and since Ormerod wrote the first edition in the first half of the nineteenth century, and the second was published after his death, this is hardly surprising. Whatever its source, the characterisation is accurate.

10   Ronald Blythe, *The Age of Illusion* (London, 1963), p. 23.

11   *Letters*, 30th March 1917.

12   Ingham, p. 323.

The Patersons were part of the middle-class society that had sprung up in this select area, even though the arrival of newcomers in such numbers heralded the destruction of aspects of the bucolic idyll that they sought. Take the road in which Alec lived, for instance. Where were the great conifers its name portended? The Firs was the name Victorian developers, anxious to increase its allure, had bestowed on the erstwhile Burying Lane, so-called because it was the *via dolorosa* along which the dead were carried from Altrincham to the parish church for burial. That 'the lane lay deep in the shadow of some tall firs that had weathered a century's storms' merely aggravated its doleful aspect.[13] Ironically the building work necessitated felling most of the very firs after which the road was renamed, and transforming an unpaved track lined with unruly bushes and venerable trees into an avenue of suburban neatness and orderly gardens, Victorian decorum eradicating Gothic romance. Perhaps nature tamed was better than nature red in tooth and claw, and there was something to be said for domestic comfort, if you could afford it. The new white-brick houses that were built on the road were capacious and elegant, befitting the status of the mercantile and professional classes for which they were designed, and well beyond the means of tradesfolk. Dudley House was a five-bedroom semi-detached property, with an extensive garden large enough to boast tennis courts, befitting a man with a solicitor's income and a large family. If the Patersons were comfortably-off by any standards, they were not particularly well-to-do by Bowdon standards. Nearby in their smart villas on The Downs lived the really rich: entrepreneurs and industrialists such as Joseph Sidebottom of Strines Mill near Stockport; Henry Lee, co-founder of the textile firm of Tootal, Broadhurst and Lee; and the Crossley brothers who were manufacturers of the Otto Gas Engine. Yet it was a matter of degree, not of substance, and solicitor and industrialist could be at ease with each other. They were genteel.

The divide between them and the lower orders was stark and obvious. To accommodate the growing number of parishioners, and to ensure that the poorer residents would not embarrass the rich congregants of the new and modish St Margaret's church on Dunham Road, a satellite, St John's, was built in 1866 to serve the spiritual needs of the working class. Private schools sprang up to provide for the children of parents who were prepared to pay handsomely for an education in an exclusive, homogenous and congenial environment where their offspring would not have to hob-nob with the children who attended the church, charity and state schools. Even the watering holes were kept separate. To serve the monied newcomers the Stamford Arms was rebuilt. Their servants and the less well-off had to make do with the unrenovated Griffin nearby. Similarly, Bowdon Vale, an ancillary village for non-resident employees, was constructed

---

13   Charles Nickson, *Bygone Altrincham* (Didsbury, 1935), p. 168.

lower down the hill from the swanky villas of the affluent they served.[14] The rich man in his castle, the poor man – unless a domestic servant – well outside his gate, even if the accommodation and amenities, such as the clubhouse and allotments, with which they were provided were of a high standard.

There was the one extraordinary and exemplary exception to this rule of keeping the less fortunate at arm's length, and one that may well have been an inspiration to the young Alec while still at an impressionable age. Francis Crossley, a very wealthy engineer and devout Congregationalist, had long 'determined', as he put it, 'to leave this respectable neighbourhood and go right down among the poor folks' which 'is where a church should be'. Even when he proposed marriage he had told his future wife that once his business had prospered he would devote his wealth as well as his person to the cause of the poor. He remained true to that pledge. First he joined the ranks of the Salvation Army, becoming its 'Paymaster' as General Booth put it, bankrolling the new order to the sum of £100,000. Next he gave up Fairlie, his mansion in Bowdon, to live among the wretched of Ancoats, the densely-populated and squalid industrial suburb of Manchester. There in 1889 he built a mission hall and a maternity hospital to cater for the spiritual and physical needs of the desperately poor inhabitants. He also pioneered work among the children of the slums. After his death in 1897 a bronze portrait plaque was erected to 'A Friend of God, A Friend of Man'.[15] His missionary zeal and social commitment stood in stark contrast to those solely intent on making money and enjoying themselves. Having succeeded in the former they could indulge in the latter in well-appointed Bowdon.

The Patersons were not of that ilk, even if they fell short of the self-sacrifice of Crossley. Engagement with those less well-off was integral to both sides of Alec's family. Their consciences were pricked by the unregulated industrialisation of which they were beneficiaries. Nagging social anxiety was a prevalent force in the stratum of Victorian society from which young Alec had sprung.

His maternal great-uncle, Brooke Herford, had made his name ministering to the working class in Sheffield, and his empathetic understanding of the needs and aspirations of the urban poor was a trait passed down the generations.

---

14   Bowdon History Society, *Bowdon and Dunham Massey* (Stroud, 1999), p. 55.

15   E.K. Crossley, *He Heard from God* (London, 1959), pp. 16, 43, 63. It is likely Alec knew Francis, the youngest Crossley, who was also born in 1884, but Waldo Eagar states that it was not Crossley but Charles Russell who first interested the young Paterson in working boys and juvenile delinquents (Eagar, pp. 357f., 383 n.1). If that is so, and I can find no corroboration for it, their paths must have crossed when Russell, in the 1890s, was working at the Ancoats Settlement and other 'lads' clubs' in the Manchester area. He certainly shared Paterson's interests. Between 1905 and 1910 Russell published *Manchester Boys, The Making of a Criminal*, and *Young Gaol Birds*. He also became chairman of the borstal committee at Strangeways prison.

Alec's mother, in particular, had inherited it and hoped that her children would carry it on. Alec certainly would. He was devoted to her and, as his letters to her revealed, remained so in adulthood. Perhaps, as the baby, he was her favourite. Perhaps she saw in him the realisation of her own ideals.

Alec's paternal uncle, Arthur Paterson, must also have inspired the growing boy and certainly did the grown man, when the parallels between them became evident. Educated at University College School in London, Arthur left in 1877 at the age of fifteen to work his passage to Australia as an able seaman. At sixteen he was in New Mexico and within a year owned his own ranch. Eventually he returned to England, rich but restless. He took to his young nephew Alec, letting him stay with him in Winchfield, Hampshire, and teaching him to ride horses.[16] Eventually Arthur found his true vocation. From 1896 he engaged in social work in the Hoxton area of London's East End. He grew to believe that the lot of the poor could not be improved by charity, but only by a growth in mutual understanding between employers and employees. The former had to learn that their employees were not machines, the latter that their employers had burdens and responsibilities unknown to workers. He founded, and became secretary to, the National Alliance of Employers and Employed. Arthur also became a writer and journalist, and in 1907 his loosely autobiographical novel about social work in London, *John Glynn*, was published.

Four year later came *Our Prisons*, a collection of articles on prison life and administration originally printed in *The Times*. In the chapters on young offenders, he praised the new 'borstal system' which had been inaugurated in 1902 when 'Fort Borstal' near Rochester in Kent became the first penal reformatory for 'juvenile adults'.[17] It was a considerable 'departure from ordinary prison standards of life and discipline'. While boys transferred from prison to Borstal were 'lumpy, slack, sometimes defiant and generally out of condition', a transformation soon followed their arrival.

> In Borstal they have created the atmosphere and practice of continuous vigorous doing ... Merely to see the lads drill is a revelation, ... the brisk energy that they put into their labours, their greater freedom of action, ... the difference in carriage and bearing.

Borstal boys, he concluded, 'come in as criminals' but leave, in most cases, 'better men than when they entered it'. While 'the Institution has justified its own existence' he hoped it would 'prove the beginning of much more'. Another vital adjunct which also received his approbation was the Borstal Association.[18]

16   *Letters*, 8th October 1915.
17   Wherever possible, to avoid confusion and the clumsiness of 'Borstal borstal', I use the alternative name, Rochester.
18   Arthur Paterson, *Our Prisons* (London, 1911), pp. 30–35.

FIGURE 3. A Family Holiday

Thus Arthur's interests, observations and views foreshadowed those of his nephew. In personality they were also alike. The uncle was described by a contemporary as 'a man who "gets hold" by sheer personality, vivid, compelling, irresistible'. He was a veritable force of nature:

> The fierce torrent of his own enthusiasm carries along with it not only himself but all with whom he comes into contact. It is utterly impossible to be lukewarm about any project he advocates. He is a human Niagara. He sweeps you off your feet before you have time to think whether it is good for you to be so swept or not ... Unity, concord, brotherhood, and co-operation for the commonweal is a gospel and Arthur Paterson is its apostle. His faith

is unbounded, his enthusiasm is unquenchable. He has visions of a new social and industrial England, and he knows it will come.[19]

All this could and would be said equally of the nephew. Neither espoused charitable paternalism, but nor did they espouse socialism, let alone communism. Their vision was of a commonwealth based on class co-operation not class conflict. It was a vision that time would hone in the man, but had its origins in the boy's privileged upbringing.

And privileged it was. Heaven lay about him in his infancy. The high society of the town was a rich mixture of the monied, the intellectual, the musical and the artistic. Elegant soirees were a common feature in their grand houses, where hosts vied to outdo each other with the notable guests they could attract, amuse and impress with their manicured croquet lawns and even the private observatories and telescopes which some had incorporated into their properties to take advantage of the wondrously unpolluted air. And Bowdon was portal to much more, being strategically placed for the sort of holidays the Victorian middle and upper classes relished: to the seashores of North Wales, the highlands of Scotland, or the fells of the Lake District. Back home and on their doorstep was every fashionable facility they could desire: a hydro, bowling greens, tennis courts, a cricket pavilion, a croquet club, golf links, cycling parties, photographic clubs, and exclusive dining circles. Of the last the most prominent was the Roundabout Club, which had started up in the early 1860s for twelve *bon-vivants* who took it in turn to host its monthly meetings, remarkable for their 'qualities of geniality and unrestrained liberty of expression of opinions'. It could enlist as after-supper speakers such well-known members of parliament as John Bright and musicians as eminent as Charles Hallé. One of its founders was the Scotsman, Alexander Ireland, the erudite proprietor of the advanced liberal newspaper, the *Manchester Examiner*, who had personally known Wordsworth, Lamb, de Quincey, Leigh Hunt and Elizabeth Gaskell, and was a close friend of Ralph Waldo Emerson and Thomas Carlyle. Alec would certainly have been acquainted for a time with the elderly Ireland's youngest son, John, the future composer, who had been born five years before him at Inglewood, the family mansion in the adjacent St Margaret's Road. The Irelands, like the Patersons, as well as being of Scottish origin, were Unitarians, and both families were devout congregants of Dunham Road Chapel until the departure of the former from Bowdon in the late 1880s.[20] Another musical luminary who was also a near neighbour was Hans Richter, Wagner's devotee and the former conductor of the Vienna Philharmonic Orchestra. In September 1900, after his appointment as

---

19   *Unity* (June 1920).
20   T&M, p. 12. Although her husband was a friend of Carlyle, it may have been through the Irelands that Helen Allingham first met the 'sage of Chelsea', whose portrait she would famously paint.

director of the Hallé Orchestra, he took up residence in The Firs. His lead violinist, Adolph Brodsky, a friend of Tchaikovsky, Grieg, Elgar and Brahms, shortly thereafter moved into a fine house on nearby Laurel Mount. It is likely that Alec, whose family was musical, knew both, and he certainly heard them perform when he attended concerts in Manchester.[21]

For those with keen intellects and enquiring minds there was also the Literary and Scientific Club which had been formed sometime after 1870 by Theophilus Hall, Alec's future headmaster, and the 60 Club which provided entertainment and talks.[22] For those of an adventurous nature and with deep pockets new-fangled motor vehicles proved irresistible. The first automobile was registered in Bowdon in 1896, and it was on the Chester Road and Bowdon Hill that Henry Royce would test-drive new models of his luxurious creation. Soon the rich could be seen with their wealth on display in their chauffeur-driven limousines, while their sons would disport themselves on motorbikes. This was the rarefied social milieu in which the young Alec grew up. From infancy he was accustomed to associating with the literary, artistic and political elite. Family photographs show an intense little boy of obvious intelligence.

He was a voracious reader, and from an early age was borrowing books from the Altrincham Free Library. Novels were a favourite. He certainly devoured works by Wilkie Collins, Walter Scott and Charles Dickens, and it is likely that he encountered those of Charles Kingsley, the Anglican Christian socialist, whose repute was then at its height. In particular, *Alton Locke*, the 'chartist novel' about a young tailor-boy with aspirations beyond the normal expectations of his working-class background, would have struck a chord and, in its depiction of Jacob's Island in Bermondsey, given a foretaste of his future.[23]

For him family holidays to the seaside at Pensarn in North Wales or to the Lake District were enchanting, especially the latter. There he could walk over the fells, musing on Wordsworth and Coleridge, row, fish and swim in the translucent lakes, Windermere, Coniston Water and Ullswater being favourites, or when it rained, as often it did, read in the pastoral tranquillity of Fold Head farmhouse at Watendlath which his family had rented for the summer. He also holidayed with them in Italy and Austria, where they skied at the Alpine resorts of Trent, Innsbruck and Ampezzo.[24]

Mens sana in corpore sano, a healthy mind in a healthy body. Alec did not just like to read and think and talk. He was a keen sportsman, frequenting the Bowdon Cricket, Hockey and Squash Club to enjoy its facilities and social life.

21   *Letters*, 23rd March 1916.
22   Bowdon History Society, *op.cit.*, p. 58.
23   *Letters*, 15th June 1917.
24   *Letters*, 3rd and 25th May, 12th June 1915. Alec loved the Lake District and would often return there, usually with university friends in tow.

FIGURE 4. The Siblings

He took part in all three sports. He was, in particular, a keen tennis and hockey player, a keen swimmer and a keen cyclist. He was also a keen Christian.

In late Victorian England Christian denominations of all sorts abounded and churches were well-attended. The wealthy who had moved into Bowdon were just as determined to get into heaven. The parish church was enlarged and improved, and non-conformists built substantial and imposing chapels for their growing congregations. Mammon could embrace Methodism. Bowdon had a plethora of places of worship, not just Anglican and Catholic but Congregationalist, Methodist, Presbyterian and Unitarian too. The Patersons were, like so many of the professional class, Unitarians, and by the mid-nineteenth century Altrincham and Bowdon were major centres of that confession. The local Dissenting tradition dated back to the Civil War period when Presbyterians

FIGURE 5. An Intense Youth

built a church in the hamlet of Ringway in nearby Hale. They worshipped there for many decades until their minister, Mr Waterhouse, was forcibly ejected by the lord of the manor, bent on restoring the chapel to the Established Church. Waterhouse, taking most of his flock with him, in 1733 erected a chapel for non-conformist worship in the nearby hamlet of Hale Barns. By the end of the century the congregation, although still ostensibly Presbyterian, had largely adopted Unitarianism, Hale becoming the mother chapel of the surrounding area. In 1814, a year after the sect ceased to be illegal, an avowedly Unitarian daughter chapel was built in Shaw's Lane, Altrincham.

In the coming decades such was the surge in the number of Unitarians coming into the area, in particular the ingress of the better-off to Bowdon, that more substantial provision was needed. Thus in 1872, to complement Hale Chapel and to replace the smaller one in Shaw's Lane,[25] a new larger chapel in Dunham Road, north-west of Bowdon, was erected, the preacher at its first Sunday service being William Gaskell, the novelist's widower. The exterior of the building was 'plain but substantial', faced with brick, and with stone dressings around the entrance porch on the south side. 'The west end has two gables, and the roof is carried round the east end, having a large cross at the apex of the apse', the windows of which were 'filled with stained glass, illustrating by means of flowers, the emblems of Faith, Hope and Charity.' The interior was furnished with pitch-pine seating for about 250 adults and forty children.[26]

The Patersons were prominent and very active members of Dunham Road Chapel. Throughout Alec's childhood and teenage years his father was both secretary and treasurer, posts he held for the last twenty-five years of his life.[27] The Paterson family pew – for which they paid rent – was at the very front of the chapel, next to that of the minister's family.[28] Alec regularly attended with his parents and grandmother for Sunday services and with his siblings for Sunday school classes. He did so on many other occasions as well, such as for the 'Lads' Club' held on two evenings a week. He may have been too young to have heard, or at least understood, the preaching of his parents' great friend, the Revd James

25 The remains of those interred in the Shaw's Lane burial ground were 'reverently removed and re-interred in the quiet God's acre of the parent chapel at Hale' (Nickson, *op.cit.*, p. 145). It was there that Alec's ashes would be interred with his forebears.

26 Ingham, p. 158. In 1896 these windows were moved to the south wall and replaced with depictions of biblical personages as well as the symbolic figures of Faith and Hope. Charity was omitted (T&M, p. 27).

27 Willis would succeed his father as secretary, his thirty-nine-year tenure likewise ending with his demise. Both father and son have commemorative plaques prominently displayed on the chapel wall, while the children's corner is dedicated to the memory of the latter.

28 T&M, pp. 12, 18, 21. The Ireland family pew was second from the back.

Odgers, who, on his appointment to the lectureship in ecclesiastical history at Manchester College, Oxford, resigned as minister of the chapel in 1893 when Alec was not yet nine.[29] The teenage boy, however, would have heard his next but one successor preach and teach. This was the Revd Denby Agate, who took over the ministry in 1898 and was in post for eighteen years. An early innovation of his was to start a Sunday morning Bible class with the aim of getting to know and influence the young people in the congregation. The teenage Alec was one. It is probable that he heard and was impressed by Agate's lectures. One which may have had particular resonance was on 'John Howard and Practical Philanthropy', Howard being the noted eighteenth-century Dissenter who, following the biblical injunction to visit the imprisoned, did so much to uncover the deplorable condition of British gaols, and inspired the prison reform movement which dominated the first half of the nineteenth century. Thus at Bowdon Chapel, as at home, Alec imbibed a commitment to social activism alongside a strong Christian faith. This combination was the essence of nineteenth-century Unitarianism.

Unitarianism in Europe dates back to the Reformation period, but in England, as with the Quakers, it had its origins in the ferment of the Civil War. It gained such popularity in the wake of the Enlightenment that in 1774 Theophilus Lindsey created Essex Street Chapel in London to accommodate the first avowedly Unitarian congregation in the country. In their quest for social justice and in their moral influence on society, Unitarians stood alongside Quakers. Both were small, committed sects whose impact was hugely disproportionate to their numbers. Joseph Priestley in the eighteenth century and James Martineau in the nineteenth were the most eminent Unitarian thinkers and apologists, while Mary Carpenter was deeply involved in the Ragged School movement, as well as writing extensively on prisons, convicts and juvenile delinquents.[30] Mrs Gaskell was an outstanding success as novelist and chronicler of the northern industrial towns. And, of course, there was looming over the last quarter of the nineteenth century the towering political figure of Joseph Chamberlain with his electoral slogan of 'Each for All and All for Each', a very Unitarian sentiment.

Despite the eminence of some of their membership, Unitarians were considered heretical by mainstream denominations since they rejected the doctrines of the Trinity, the divinity of Jesus, and the sacrificial atonement. For them Christ's saving work was his ethical teaching and example of service. Jesus was

---

29   The Patersons maintained close contact with the Odgers, Alec visiting them on many occasions while an undergraduate at Oxford, feasting on their cook's cakes (*Letters*, 11th May 1915).

30   *Juvenile Delinquents* (London, 1853); *Our Convicts* (London, 1864); *Reformatory Prison Discipline* (London, 1872).

'an expression of God in terms of Man.'[31] The incarnation was not an event that happened once in Galilee. 'God is always manifesting Himself in the lives of men, is becoming incarnate.'[32] Some agreed with their orthodox detractors that Unitarians were not Christians, though many in Alec's childhood and church considered themselves to be so. With no formal creed, and no adherence to the inerrancy of the Bible, reason and conscience were the final arbiters of truth and morals and the wellspring of belief and practice. They held that there could be 'union for worship and fellowship without uniformity in theological belief'. Just as scientific inquiry had to be based on logic and evidence, so too did spiritual. The quest for truth in religion and morals could not be hampered by restrictions imposed by some external authority – Holy Scripture or the Church. Thus neither the theory of evolution nor other attacks on the inerrancy of scripture had any adverse impact on Unitarian belief. Central to their faith was the doctrine of unity – 'the unity of God and the unity of Man', and 'the unity of God with Man'. Two generally held tenets were the abiding goodness of human nature and the universality of divine love. In sum, to serve humanity was to incarnate the divine.

Agate's teaching and preaching merely reinforced these long-held convictions in his flock. The time was ripe for dynamic social involvement. The other churches towards the end of the nineteenth century, faced with the growth of inner-city slums and the needs of a burgeoning urban working class, were beginning to take social reform or even societal reform seriously. The Cadburys in Birmingham and the Rowntrees in York, wealthy Quaker manufacturers, did much to evaluate and alleviate the lot of the poor. The new-born Salvation Army sent its noisy legions onto the streets and into the slums, preaching salvation and bringing succour to soul and body. Christian Socialism was asserting itself in all the denominations, and Anglicans were not exempt. In 1896 Frederick Temple, an open advocate of the social gospel and father of a more radical son, became Archbishop of Canterbury.[33]

Unitarians, with their long-standing tradition of social engagement, were to the fore in this trend. Men and women alike were encouraged to take a positive part in public affairs and in philanthropic endeavours. The worshippers in Dunham Road Chapel were no exception. Most members of the congregation were involved in charitable activities and were spurred on by a succession of ministers to do what they could 'to remedy the unhappy conditions in which so large

---

31   The Unitarian ministers, J.L. Hines and P.P. Perry, quoted in Tresham Lever, *Clayton of Toc H* (London, 1971), pp. 154f.

32   Alexander Birkmire and Henry Michelmore, *Toc H at the Crossroads* (private circulation letter, 1928), para I, p. 2.

33   The son, William, the leading Christian Socialist thinker of the twentieth century and a friend of Alec, would also become Archbishop of Canterbury.

a proportion of this land live'. They became active in all sorts of social work, in particular supporting 'domestic missions' in the deprived Hulme and Collyhurst areas of Manchester as well as nearer to home. Katharine Paterson put her faith into practice by doing charitable work among the poor who dwelt in Altrincham's squalid and insanitary backstreets where filthy privies and manure heaps germinated disease, rubbish heaps swarmed with vermin, cold and damp killed off the elderly, and measles and mumps readily infected the children.[34] Alec's father, as deeply involved in wider society as he was in the church, served in the volunteer militia, and developed an interest in young offenders, culminating in his appointment to the role of inspecting the workings of the Children's Courts throughout the country.[35] This was the activist ethical creed and culture of moral earnestness in which the young Alexander was brought up. Despite his later apostasy to orthodox Anglicanism, it was the creed by which he would live his life, and an earnestness that would never leave him.

The secular education of the children of the élite was also important, and the young Paterson followed his brothers in attending Bowdon College, a privately-run school for boys aged eight to eighteen, owned by family friends, the Pikes.[36] Their venture had a rapid growth. The school had been founded in 1857, originally in a house in Stamford Road, near The Firs, but so successful was the enterprise in eclipsing the local grammar school that its second headmaster, Theophilus Hall, could afford to have an imposing – if ugly – edifice built in South Downs Road to accommodate the demand for places, although rarely did the number of boarders and day pupils exceed a hundred and thirty. When Hall left the school at the end of 1891 he bequeathed a strong legacy. Not only was he a distinguished classicist who had demanded the very best from his pupils academically, he was a moralist who had expected them to utilise their privileged upbringing and education for the betterment of the underprivileged. His 'kindness, broad-mindedness, the power to put himself in another's place' continued to pervade the school long after his tenure of office had ended. It prided itself on creating a common understanding between 'masters and boys' and between older pupils and younger, and above all on instilling a sense of social responsibility

---

34   T&M, p. 29. One of the worst was Chapel Street, a Georgian cul-de-sac housing the labouring poor. It would later achieve fame as 'the bravest little street in England', after 161 of its residents volunteered to serve during the course of the Great War. For them at least life in the trenches would be no great shock.

35   *Manchester Evening News*, 3rd January 1906. Coincidently, this appointment came shortly before Alec began his long involvement with the boys of Bermondsey. The previous year Dorothy had been asked to assist the Social Questions Committee set up by the Manchester District Association of Presbyterian and Unitarian Churches (T&M, pp. 90f.).

36   Dorothy went to school in nearby Culcheth (*Letters*, 27th April 1916).

in its charges and a strong '*esprit de corps*'.[37] Such an ethos would reinforce the impact of Alec's Unitarian background and his family's tradition of service.

It was to Bowdon College that he was sent as a small boy. His mother sped him off to school each day with 'a clean handkerchief and the other impedimenta of a suburban scholar', and the injunction to come straight home ringing in his ear.[38] There he would be well-grounded in Latin and Greek, mathematics, history and English. From there he gained a place at University College Oxford to read *Literae Humaniores*, the Oxford name for the Classics, a degree in two parts and taking four years. Alec remained proud of his old school, and it of him, not just for getting a place at Oxford but for his adult achievements. Many years later, when he was invited to award prizes at Speech Day, he was described in the school magazine as the college's most eminent alumnus.[39]

Alec was not the only Bowdonian to aspire to Oxford, two of his fellow pupils getting places at the same time, one of them, his friend Arnold Boyd, to read history at the same college.[40] The other, Philip Oliver, a future Liberal MP, having left Bowdon College to attend Manchester Grammar School, went to Corpus Christi College. Alec was the only one of his siblings to go to university, Willis having followed in his father's footsteps by becoming an articled clerk in a solicitor's firm, and Claude being articled as a pupil to an architect. While his elder brothers stayed at home, entering safe, staid middle-class professions, Alec left Bowdon for good.[41]

37   *The Bowdonian*, XIX/1 (December 1928), pp. 16–19; Bowdon History Society, *op.cit.*, p. 75.

38   *Over the Walls*, p. 23. Where cited, the pagination for this work is based on my transcript which may be found on the Boydell & Brewer website (https://dhjhkxawhe8q4.cloudfront.net/boydell-and-brewer-wp/wp-content/uploads/2021/11/15102344/Alexander-Paterson-Online-Appendix.pdf).

39   *The Bowdonian*, XX/1 (December 1929), p. 16. It was one of the last such occasions. The college, as had been predicted by an inspector in 1927, became unviable and closed in 1936 (TNA ED109/337).

40   *Bowdon Guardian*, 4th August 1906. Boyd, 'a cheery red-faced' single child idolised by his mother, was a welcome guest at Dudley House, and would stay with Alec in Bermondsey from time to time. He was killed in May 1917 (*Letters*, 16th May 1917).

41   Willis continued to live in Dudley House with his widowed mother and sister (*Bowdon Directory*, pp. 189ff.). By 1910 he was a solicitor in Altrincham, clerk to the Rural District Council, and a prominent 'Old Bowdonian'. In partnership he set up the firm of Denby and Paterson in Manchester. In 1923 he married Marjorie Runton, with whom he had three children: Thomas, born in 1924, would become another solicitor (at Holmes Son and Pott, London EC2); Katharine, born in 1927; and Barbara ('Bunty'), born in 1929. Marjorie predeceased her husband, dying at the age of thirty-six in 1936. Willis remarried, this time to Margaret Vaughan. He

He may well have had an inkling that Bowdon was too small a stage for him when he took the train to Oxford, an earnest young man with very decided views about politics and social justice and with a burning sense of duty. As he journeyed south perhaps he thought about the lectures his minister had recently been giving on 'The World as it Might Be – the social question in the light of the Teaching of Jesus'.[42] This was a world he wanted to help bring into being.

---

died in 1949, aged sixty-seven. His son died in 2010, but his daughters are still alive, the sole survivors of those who knew 'uncle Alec'. Claude, traumatised by his experiences in the Great War, spent twenty-seven years in the Warneford Asylum in Oxford. While Willis, then head of the family, visited him regularly, as did Dorothy, breaking the journey by staying overnight with the Odgers, Alec never did. No one knows why, and it is surprising since Alec mentioned him fondly in his letters written during the Great War. Perhaps it was guilt, since he had been enriched by a war that destroyed his brother. Claude died suddenly on 19th December 1950. He too was sixty-seven. Dorothy, a spinster, was principal beneficiary of Claude's will. She outlived her siblings, if not for long, dying in 1953, her seventy-third year.

42   Alec had considerable regard for Agate. 'Glad there is a body of opinion felt in England to protest against the bullying of the tribunals', he approved of a sermon the minister preached in 1916 defending the rights of conscientious objectors (*Letters*, 8th July 1916).

CHAPTER 2

ALMA MATER: 1902–1906

From its unique length of 360 feet of frontage abutting on the much coveted High Street, University College is able to boast possession of, perhaps, the finest site in Oxford. Two massive towers link together a long range of weather-worn Jacobean stonework, and the whole presents to the eye a picture of dignified solidity.

William Carr

If the majority of [Univ. members] can hardly be described as intellectual, they are at all events, good fellows.

'A Graduate', The National Review, 1907

University College, or Univ. as it is commonly called, is the oldest collegiate foundation in Oxford, dating back to a bequest made in 1249. Its founder, William of Durham, hailed from the north-east of England, and it was from there that most of its early scholars came. As the centuries passed other colleges were created, and many eclipsed in grandeur and in achievement the first-born, although the kudos of its primogeniture was unassailable and its fortunes fluctuated. By the beginning of the nineteenth century it was respectable if unremarkable. Between 1850 and 1881 the winds of change swept over Oxford and Cambridge. Most significantly, the religious test which prevented entry to those who refused to subscribe to the thirty-nine articles of the Church of England, thus excluding Catholics and Dissenters, was removed. By the time Alec Paterson was ready to go to Univ. his Unitarian background proved no problem. His four years there would reinforce all that he had been brought up to believe, and would open a door of opportunity to put his beliefs into practice.

Paterson, still seventeen, matriculated as a commoner of the college in October 1902, towards the end of the long tenure of James Bright. Bright had been a Fellow since 1874 and became Master in 1881. He would retire the same year that Paterson graduated. Bright was liberal in his theology and Liberal in his politics. Others among the Fellowship were more radical, some even espousing the novelty of socialism. The Bursar, Charles Faulkner, who had caused a sensation by inviting his friend William Morris to give a lecture which had amounted to a public avowal of the cause, had relinquished his post in 1882 and gone on to create the Oxford Socialist League. Another eminent exponent was Alexander Carlyle, who was a college lecturer in politics and economics and chaplain during Paterson's time. Clement Attlee said of Carlyle that he was one of the few men in Oxford who kept the light of socialism burning.[1] In his position he could exert a considerable influence over the young men he taught and to whom he ministered.

Another Fellow who involved himself in undergraduate life was Arthur Farquharson. 'Farky' or 'the Fark' was a classics Fellow from 1899 to 1942. He was a philosopher, an eccentric, and an officer in the Territorial Force.[2] The other leading classicists in the college were Arthur Poynton, a Balliol man who was elected to a Fellowship in 1894 and who taught Greek and Latin language and literature, and Reginald Macan, the 'heretic of Christ Church', who had been a Fellow and praelector in ancient history since 1884. Poynton would supervise Paterson for his first five terms; Farquharson and Macan for the last seven. All three must have had an influence upon him. Macan certainly did.

In the year of Alec's matriculation, a young man who would add to that influence was awarded a prize fellowship at Univ. Having attended a Unitarian school and Charterhouse, in 1897 William Beveridge had gone up to Balliol where he became close friends with William Temple and Richard Tawney. A brilliant scholar who was studying law, Beveridge would renounce a stellar career in academia or at the Bar to become sub-warden of Toynbee Hall, enabling him to turn his analytical mind to social problems and their resolution. Coming from a similar background and with similar interests, Alec knew him at Oxford and would encounter him thereafter. They were both compassionate, quixotic and funny.

As a result of many reforms and a series of reforming Masters the reputation of University College had risen considerably by the end of the nineteenth century. It had become one of the foremost in the university and one of the most progressive. It had also become more socially exclusive, drawing its intake largely from the major public schools. It was emerging as a smart and more intellectual place, but it retained a reputation for being friendly 'regardless of background, wealth (or lack of it), and academic or athletic ability'.[3] To cater for the growing number of more select undergraduates, living conditions were improving. Electric lighting was installed in 1893, and more and superior

1   Darwall-Smith, p. 410; Attlee, p. 15.
2   A part-time volunteer force created in 1908 for home defence.
3   A.D. Gardner, *Some Recollections* (typescript, 1975), pp. 64f., quoted in Darwall-Smith, p. 433.

accommodation was provided. A Junior Common Room, established by 1892, became a popular venue for undergraduate meetings and debates. A fitted bathroom was installed in a basement, mainly 'to benefit muddy sports players'.[4] Most bizarrely the college in 1893 had agreed to house an androgynous memorial to its most infamous matriculand, Percy Bysshe Shelley, who had been expelled in 1811 for atheism.

Student life in late Victorian and Edwardian Oxford was varied but leisurely. Undergraduates were awakened at quarter to seven every morning by their 'scout' beating the stairs with a heavy stick.[5] Scouts were college servants who served meals, made beds, cleared up after the slovenly, and cleaned their rooms. Breakfast, served in those rooms, was a major social event. It was followed by academic work in the mornings and sport and recreation in the afternoon. Tea would be taken in individual rooms but dinner was a formal and communal occasion in hall. In the evenings various college societies, the membership of which included some Fellows, would meet, or there would be dramatic or musical entertainments put on by the undergraduates themselves at 'smoking concerts'.[6]

This milieu would suit the competitive, self-confident and gregarious Paterson. After dinner on his first day, he and some other 'freshmen' were invited to take coffee in a senior's rooms. Although he was the youngest of them all, he neither looked nor acted it. One member of his year thought him thirty. Although his social and educational background was less elevated than many of his peers, no one was contemptuous or condescending.[7] They were impressed.

Out of necessity, or thrift, he occupied one of the cheaper rooms – no.1 on staircase XII – paying £2 16s a term. A close friend there, and thereafter, was Barclay Baron, who was also on the same staircase but in room 3, which cost four guineas, while another lifelong friend, Clement Attlee, was grander still, paying five guineas for room 3 on staircase III.[8] Attlee could well afford it as his father gave him an allowance of £200 a year.

After the tranquil rusticity of Cheshire, Oxford was breathtaking and exhilarating. Its buildings, its spires, its characters, its traditions and its history all conspired to captivate the new arrival. Protestant martyrs had been incinerated in its centre, Cranmer extending his culpable hand into the purifying flames.

4   *Ibid.*, p. 418.
5   William Carr, *University College* (London, 1902), p. 226.
6   For instance, in 1905 a recital was given by Saki's cousin, Cecil Mercer, an undergraduate who went on to write thrillers. Smoking was universal, even at concerts. Some undergraduates indulged in smoking cannabis and, unlike a later noted alumnus, inhaled (Darwall-Smith, p. 434).
7   Baron, 'Across the Bridges', *Four Men* (London, n.d.), pp. 30–40, at p. 32.
8   In his last year (1905–1906) Alec upgraded to a more expensive room nearer to Barclay.

FIGURE 6. A College Room, 1901, by permission of the Master and Fellows of
University College Oxford

Behind its walls Charles I had set up his headquarters during the Civil War. In
these quads Gibbon had grumbled and Jowett had discoursed. In its churches Newman and Pusey had worshipped uneasily and yearned for past glories.
Along these streets Peel and Gladstone had walked and talked, ambition and
determination sharpened by an exquisite and incisive education. Poets, phi-
losophers, politicians had dreamt or mused or conspired in its meadows or on
its river. Nor had its glory days dried up; they were in full flood. Everywhere
was talent, everywhere was learning, everywhere the products of pedigree and
public schools were being primed to assume the highest ranks in academia, the
Church, the State, and the Empire. Yet everywhere there was a certain unease
and a nagging doubt.

This was the magical realm into which the young man from Bowdon had
been lured. For him it would not be a snare eviscerating his nascent radicalism, but a stage upon which he could display it. Alec loved every minute of his

Oxford days. There was 'no spot like it in the world', and Univ. was its epicentre.[9] He was gregarious, and extrovert, and accommodating, and was one of the first to welcome the Rhodes Scholars freshly come from Germany. 'Nice fellows, most of them', they would one day be enemies.[10] More immediately he made friends who would last a lifetime; he seized opportunities that would change his own life; he took to writing and public speaking; and he made a name for himself as a champion of righteous causes.

The lifestyle to which most students aspired was costly, and Paterson, early in his Oxford career, wrote an article in which he blamed the heavy expense of undergraduate life on the 'avarice of the colleges'. The 'average undergraduate' had to pay £10 a year for college club subscriptions whether or not he 'indulged in the athletic enjoyments of university life'. Yet all, even the sportsmen, had to pay 10 per cent more for every item of food purchased in town shops, and over the top for breakages or the use of electricity in college. In addition they had to pay their scouts 'handsomely', as well as remunerating porters and other college staff. Those who indulged in extra-collegiate activities had to fork out even more, especially as dining and drinking accompanied membership of almost every literary, social, political and sports club, and if, as a result of a good night out, undergraduates got back to their colleges after midnight they had to pay a fee to the porters to gain admittance.[11] Even the pastime of punting proved a costly luxury. Only lectures were cheap and that was because they were sparsely attended.[12] An outraged bursar from one of

9   He often referred fondly to Univ. in his letters, would keep a photograph of it by him in the trenches along with that of his mother, and write wistfully, 'there is not an inch of Univ. nor a yard of the High that has not some memory' (*Letters*, 19th May 1915, 2nd April, 30th August 1916). It was his *alma mater*.

10   Alec noted wistfully that 'this strange war has caught our generation badly and on both sides of the water'. The German scholars whom Britain had benefited would 'still be of military age, and therefore fighting against us' (*Letters*, 19th May 1915).

11   Paterson joined the Palmerston Club, becoming its secretary, and proposing the toast to the Liberal Party at its annual junket (*Oxford Times*, 2nd December 1905).

12   *Oxford Chronicle*, 22nd May 1903. Andrew McFadyean, who matriculated in 1905, kept a detailed account of his expenses, down to tips, cab-fares and haircuts. Clothes were a major item, especially sports gear, and chilblain lotion was a winter necessity. Yet he managed to subscribe to the Oxford Mission in the East End and to Toynbee Hall (Darwall-Smith, p. 427). Coming-of-age birthday dinners were especially extravagant affairs where young men in dickie-bows supped turtle soup and quaffed champagne. Alec was unlikely to celebrate his twenty-first with such a display. He did have an *ad hoc* birthday breakfast on his twentieth (*Letters*, 16th June 1916).

FIGURE 7. A 21st Birthday Dinner in Alec's time, by permission of the Master and Fellows of University College Oxford

FIGURE 8. The College Hockey Team: Alec sits second from the left on the front row, by permission of the Master and Fellows of University College Oxford

the colleges who called Paterson's claims 'mendacious' got it in the neck when Alec answered him point for point and concluded that the bursar had better 'have left me unanswered than belittle his authority by challenging figures he has not the means to check'.[13] The young Paterson had a way with words, an independent streak and a need to make money, which he did by writing such articles as this. He would remain a regular correspondent of local newspapers throughout his time at Oxford.

Paterson was not an alumnus of a distinguished public school but of a recently-founded private one. Nor, despite his obvious intellect, was he a star student academically. He got a fourth in his first public examinations (known as 'Honour Moderations' or 'Mods' for short) in the spring of 1904, and a third in his finals (known as 'Greats') in 1906.[14] His successes lay elsewhere, in taking part in college sports, writing articles for the press, debating at the Oxford Union, and motivating his friends and peers to engage themselves in his schemes. Many fell under his spell and some would remain enthralled for the rest of their lives. Attlee recalled that although Paterson was 'younger than most of those of his year he very soon became an outstanding influence in the life of the college' owing to 'the power of his personality'.[15] Others testified to his magnetism, humour, originality and determination. He was a moral whirlwind. He was a man who made a name for himself in wider Oxford, and even among such extraordinary talent as the university could boast at that time, he stood out.

Sporting ability was held in high regard even by the less athletic and more cerebral, and achievements on the field were more highly prized among Paterson's peers than those in the examination hall. He was always an avid tennis and squash player[16], but it was as a team sportsman that Paterson was most highly regarded, both for his prowess and his leadership. He played hockey for the university but never got a Blue. There are photographs of him in the college's hockey XI in 1904 when he was secretary, and in 1905 when he was captain. Physically he is depicted as a powerful, thick-set young man with broad

13   *Oxford Chronicle*, 12th June 1903.
14   This was not an unusual or even disappointing honours degree in the era before 'grade inflation'. In Paterson's time 'Firsts' were rare, and some Oxbridge undergraduates merely read for a pass degree, or did not bother to graduate. Greats was the most prestigious degree and to pass at all was an indication of a superbly educated mind. It was the portal through which those wishing to govern the nation or the Empire were expected to pass. The examination comprised lengthy translations into and from Latin and Greek, and essays on intricate historical issues or abstruse philosophical questions. It was assumed that those who had mastered this range of thought and theory could master anything. Often they could.
15   Paterson, p. 7.
16   Attlee, p. 14; Alec was playing squash in his late fifties (letter from Richard Fletcher, 28th December 1978, University College archives).

shoulders, deep chest, and a 'contemplative face'. He was five feet nine inches tall with penetrating blue eyes and flowing brown hair.[17] Not for long: the hair would dramatically recede.

He also penned match reports for the local rags. He was brain as well as brawn, and he had a brain that belied his modest academic achievements. His focus was not on examinations, nor was it confined to his own college. There were other arenas as well-suited to his talents as the sports field. In particular, in addition to his journalism, he took up debating and politics within the university, and visiting the outcast and destitute in the town. It proved a fertile combination.

Despite his intensity his contemporaries appreciated his capacity for enjoyment, ready wit and turn of phrase. He threw himself into whatever Oxford had to offer, including attending the Commemoration Ball in May 1906 when his companion was a young woman mysteriously called 'M'.[18] He liked to sing, round the piano and in chapel. He sang, when he could, as part of a chorus. Both its harmony and power of crescendo appealed to him. It was a metaphor for his life. In all his ventures he gathered around him a coterie of like-minded individuals who 'sang from the same hymn-sheet'. Many of them were remarkable young men in their own right. Some were at University College.

Barclay Baron – or 'Barkis' as Alec nicknamed him – was one. The son of an eminent throat surgeon, he was of Quaker stock but at the age of thirteen was, along with the rest of his family, baptized into the Church of England, a transition that Alec would also make. After an adolescent crisis of faith brought on by reading *The Origin of the Species*, Baron managed to reconcile science and Christianity, and throughout his life would retain a firm faith allied to a strong social conscience. They had met on the night of their arrival, soon became intimate friends and remained so until death divided them. They were close allies in a campaign against sweated labour in the clothing trade, and lobbied their friends to buy only from tailors on the approved 'white list', even though they were not the best in town. In this they had been much influenced by the Christian Socialism of Henry Scott Holland, whose trenchant views were expressed in his monthly periodical, *Commonwealth*, and the Christian Social Union which he had founded in 1889.[19]

Another contemporary was Charles Dodd, also a classicist, who would graduate with a first and go on to become a Cambridge professor, well-known for espousing the doctrine of 'realized eschatology', the belief that the Kingdom of God in Jesus's teaching referred to a present reality and not to some

17   Details from his passport 1929–1939, and Baron, *Once Upon a Time* (unpublished memoir, 1942), p. 8.

18   *Letters*, 29th May 1916.

19   Snape, p. 4. Scott Holland drew inspiration from Frederick Maurice, Charles Kingsley and Thomas Green.

post-apocalyptic utopia. Another young man much influenced by Paterson was Philip Fletcher, whose son Richard would also fall under his sway.[20] The seemingly unremarkable Clement Attlee, despite being politically Conservative at that time, and despite his shy and undemonstrative nature, soon grew to admire this young and charismatic Liberal. They had much in common. Both had fathers who were solicitors and families that were much involved in social work with the poor. Both had a strong sense of duty and of patriotism. Both saw no distinction between the classes, and both would have friends from the most diverse of backgrounds. Attlee would later pay tribute to his old chum, recalling that 'always as we talked there emerged his intense interest and sympathy for the individual', and concluding that 'his sympathy never degenerated into mere sentimentality. He was essentially wise and well-balanced in his outlook.'[21]

Determination accompanied charisma. Uneasy with what he called 'the spirit of lazy success' that permeated the air of Oxford, Alec persuaded the Senior Proctor to allow him and his friends to visit incognito (without the mandatory caps and gowns) the places in the town where conditions were at their worst. He, Barkis, and an unnamed undergraduate used to spend each Wednesday evening at 'Dolloway's doss-house', a common lodging-house near Oxford prison in the parish of St Ebbe's. It was their 'earliest, tentative incursion into the abyss of poverty', and would serve as an 'apprenticeship for later tasks'.[22] Paterson wrote a long article – later to be echoed in *Across the Bridges* – in which he described the first visit. The undergraduates received a welcome that was mixed with much surprise and a degree of suspicion from the down-and-outs 'from sixteen to sixty' whom they encountered there. They had not gone to 'preach sermons, compile statistics or foment political agitation', but to make friends, and so they played dominoes, drank tea and, while providing all the tobacco, smoked 'the pipe of peace and equality'. Despite their indigence none of the homeless asked them for money or even for food. Paterson was moved by the reception he had received, but still thought, echoing the received wisdom of the day, that while some of their 'new friends' were the victims of 'adverse circumstances', most were 'loafers' who had brought on their own misfortune by 'intemperance, moral weakness and inherent vice'. Drink was watering the roots of misery. It was also a catalyst for crime: on one occasion the undergraduates had to pin 'Fishy to the floor when he drew his knife in a drunken scrap'. Yet 'the blind charity of misguided philanthropists', or the sentimental compassion of passers-by, merely perpetuated the evil they were trying to alleviate. If such 'pampering' was counter-productive, the 'cold cautionary approach' of the state-sponsored Charity Organization Society ('Cringe or Starve'), while temporarily alleviating material

20   Letter from Richard Fletcher, 28th December 1978, University College archives.
21   Attlee, p. 15; Preface to Ruck.
22   Baron, *One Man's Pattern* (London, n.d.), p. 7.

need, alienated the recipients of such grudging benevolence and did nothing to alter or elevate character. If such work were supplemented by 'a spirit of friendliness and equality' far more could be effected. A friend was there to assist a man to stand on his own two feet, not just to prop him up until he fell over again. Paterson was also troubled by the sight of so many neglected children playing in the squalor of the surrounding streets. They were innocents deprived of any chance in life through no fault of their own. Surely something could be done for them?[23] He continued his forays into the shadow world of Oxford, and even as an undergraduate became somewhat of an authority on the subject. In 1905 his name in block capitals adorned a flier produced by Toynbee Hall advertising a debate at one of its 'Smoking Conferences', the subject being 'The Tramp'. He was deemed an expert on the issue and an engaging speaker.[24]

From his early days at Univ. Alec had begun writing anonymous articles for the *Oxford Chronicle*.[25] In his very first literary outing he championed the institution of a school of modern languages 'to relax the tyranny that classics have imposed for centuries upon their more unwilling students'. Perhaps, given his future results, he had himself in mind. Academic rigour, he insisted, would be maintained, and Oxford would never emulate the 'utilitarian and commercial' approach to modern languages taken by 'the younger universities'. Such an innovation would be a progressive move, the new complementing but not threatening the old.[26] He was a true Liberal and quoted his great hero, Gladstone, who had said that 'reform must always be gradual.' The pace of reform in Oxford had, however, been glacial.

At the same time he was reviewing ephemera, a book of verse by a Captain Adams and a 'Varsity Novel' called *Sandford of Merton* by 'Belinda Blinders' – which he guessed was the *nom de plume* of its supposed editor, Desmond Coke. The guess may well have been an educated one, since Coke was in his last year at Univ., and reading classics: the two must have known each other. The review of this parody of Oxford life sparkles with wry humour, Paterson indulging in Wildean paradox when he categorised the hero as hovering between 'pardonable vices and unpardonable virtues'. He could take a joke and run with it. On a more serious subject but one dear to his heart Paterson wrote a cogent appraisal of *Christian Difficulties in the Second and Twentieth Centuries* by 'an exponent of rational Christianity', the Cambridge don, Frederick Foakes-Jackson.[27]

23   'An Evening in a Tramps' Lodging House' and 'Out of Work in Oxford', *Oxford Chronicle*, 27th November 1903; Baron, 'Across the Bridges', *op.cit.*, p. 32.

24   Toynbee Hall flier. The debate took place on Thursday 14th December.

25   As was customary in those days they were attributed to 'a correspondent' or 'a contributor'.

26   'The Tyranny of the Classics', *Oxford Chronicle*, 1st May 1903.

27   *Ibid.*, 15th, 29th May, 12th June 1903.

FIGURE 9. Alec and Barkis in the Lake District, 1903

Reading was a passion that would never leave him. In the long vacation of 1903 he organised a reading party to his beloved Lakes. Barkis recalled

> Stepping out of the night train at Keswick, we walked with him beside Derwentwater for the first time in our lives. He opened a wayside gate, and led us across Ashness bridge into the enchanted hills. For a month we lived together in the old hidden farm at Watendlath ... We read every day, walked and fished a lot, undeterred by a fortnight's rain, laughed and talked enormously. There we learnt each other's minds and laid unsuspected foundations for the years to come.[28]

Foundations of lifelong friendships; foundations of emerging hopes and aspirations; and the reservoir of literature and laughter that would help them endure dark days ahead.

During term time the prestigious debating society, the Oxford Union, was the main arena for Alec's talents. They were soon on display. His first foray from the floor, devoted to refuting those who had opposed a motion censuring the French government's attack on religious liberty, was judged as being 'well-framed and well-delivered'. The next day, although he loved a tipple, he was back on his feet defending teetotallers. The verdict was that he had a 'good voice and [spoke] with conviction'. A month later he was one of the billed speakers, seconding the opposition to the motion that 'This Society [the Union] is in need

28   Baron, 'Across the Bridges', p. 33.

of drastic reform'.[29] He had been invited to speak either for or against the motion and so the choice was his. He was pugnacious in defence of the *status quo*. In May the following year he was to move a motion in favour of women's suffrage. While attendance at the debate was poor and the motion lost, Paterson's speech was deemed the best of the four, his 'arguments clear, concise and emphatic'. In contrast to the others, 'he was amusing but not flippant, he was serious and yet not dull.'[30] This was a refrain oft repeated in appreciations of his oratorical style.

From then on he always moved or opposed a motion, and nevermore played second fiddle. He spoke against restrictions on immigration in a speech which was very well-researched, 'quiet but impressive', and provoked the president himself to take to the floor to try to counter his arguments.[31] Paterson had become a star performer in debate, and the following month was elected secretary of the Union, overwhelmingly defeating the other candidates.[32]

It was at the Union that he made two other lifelong friends, both of whom were former presidents. William Temple of Balliol College, a brilliant classicist, was one. The other was Herbert Du Parcq, who studied Greats at Exeter College and law at Jesus. On one memorable occasion the trio travelled to Cambridge to 'battle with such Goliaths as Edwin Montagu, Maynard Keynes and Henry Harris'.[33] Another friend, and future president, was the grandson of his great political hero, Gladstone. Also called William, he was a year younger than Alec, but would not outlive him, as he was killed in April 1915 while serving in France.[34]

Paterson next took centre stage in February 1905 when called upon to stand in for John Gorst, the liberally-minded Conservative MP, who had been prostrated with influenza. Alec did not hesitate to propose a motion dear to his own heart, that 'the state should fund the feeding of destitute children in schools'. His 'clear enunciation and quiet eloquence did much to press home a powerful speech.' His 'power of advocacy' was not deployed for self-aggrandisement but in the service of others. This was no undergraduate tiro but a young man speaking with compelling sincerity. His speech was reported at length and to

29   *Oxford Magazine*, 13th May; *Isis*, 14th May; Oxford Union, 18th June 1903.

30   Oxford Union, 10th March; *Oxford Review*, 11th March; *Isis*, 12th March 1904.

31   *Oxford Review*; *Isis*, 29th October 1904.

32   Oxford Union Voting Paper, Michaelmas Term 1904. He would go on to become junior treasurer and then librarian, but was never president of the Union. Playing second fiddle while being first violin would be a lifelong trait.

33   Paterson, *Over the Walls*, p. 3. Montagu had been president of the Cambridge Union in 1902, while Keynes and Harris held that office in 1905. Montagu would become Secretary of State for India, Keynes a world-famous economist, and Harris the editor of *The Spectator*.

34   William was conscious that he lacked the ability to live up to his inheritance and was destined for failure. Paterson, discerning this, would opine that death in battle was 'the finest ending for him' (*Letters*, 19th April 1915).

widespread acclaim. He could be animated, eloquent and stylish, all at the same time. As one observer commented, 'he never can forget that things matter.' He was already recognised as someone of 'real conviction'.[35] Although he could be witty and was adept at raising a laugh, his forte was not to amuse but to inspire, not to show off his talents but to show up injustice.

He had established himself as one of the foremost debaters in the Union on matters of morals, social justice and politics. This became clear when later in February he led a debate in Birmingham on the necessity of a Liberal government taking power. His seconder was the president of the Oxford Union, supporting, not leading, his secretary. In the debate Paterson was caustic in his criticism of the Conservatives' paltry palliatives when what the country needed was social transformation. Although his team lost the vote, the party they supported swept to electoral victory in the New Year.[36] The following month he reverted to the vital importance of social reform when moving a motion that its claims were 'more urgent than those of any Imperial Policy'.

He made another sally against Balfour's government in a debate on its policy of importing indentured Chinese 'coolies' or 'pigtails' into South Africa. Needed to mine gold, they were forced to live and labour in the most servile conditions. In England billboards portrayed them in chains, being kicked and flogged, and cartoons depicted the ghosts of British soldiers killed in the Boer War pointing to the fenced compounds where the Chinese were corralled and asking 'did we die for this?' Paterson was sure they did not. It was a moral outrage. The Chinese had been deliberately duped and deplorably treated. The vaunted liberties of the English, which should have universal currency, were not being accorded to them. His peroration was condensed into one word: 'Liberty'. The verdict on the debate was that, while he had stated his case 'with lucidity and conviction', on this occasion he had been 'much more animated than usual, and the increased cogency of his argument was adorned with his usual elegance and style'.[37]

His next foray into the political arena was to urge that public money be used to support the growing number of the unemployed, the magnitude of the problem having overwhelmed charitable resources. In a passage of considerable eloquence and power, for which he received an ovation, he asked his audience 'to think of those poor figures to be seen day by day on all four corners of Carfax, with no money in their pockets, no tobacco in their pouches and in their hearts no hope.'[38] He was not being sentimental but inspirational. This was a man who could both

35   *Isis*; *Varsity, Oxford Review, Oxford Magazine*, 11th February 1905.
36   *Birmingham Daily Post, Birmingham Express*, 23rd February 1905.
37   *Isis*, 27th May 1905. Nonetheless it was Herbert Du Parcq, his friend, seconder and former president, who was deemed to have made 'the speech of the evening: logical yet ardent; funny but not flippant'.
38   *Isis, Oxford Review*, 21st October 1905. Carfax is the centre of Oxford.

convince the intellect and appeal to the emotions. When the Liberals came into office he was equally trenchant in defending their policies as he had been in denouncing those of the Conservatives.[39] Had Paterson decided on a parliamentary career within the Liberal Party his rise would have been meteoric.[40] His ability to appeal to both head and heart, a rare gift, explains how he managed to engage others in the causes he was espousing. It would remain with him throughout his life.

In his last few months at Oxford his college had a new Master, Reginald Macan. Macan broke new ground. He was the first lay master for 300 years. Times were changing. Chapel attendance on Sundays was still compulsory, but weekday services were not and were sparsely attended. Among many undergraduates religious sentiment was still strong, however. It was so for Paterson, although his faith was finding a new spiritual home. While at Univ. he began his slow migration from Unitarianism to Anglicanism. This may have been the influence of the chaplain, Alexander Carlyle, or of his friends, Barclay Baron, William Temple and Neville Talbot in particular.[41] Attending chapel would have allowed Alec to demonstrate another attribute: an ability to sing. There he would have heard Macan set out his vision of the College as 'a United Society: a Society free from divisions, sets, jealousies; a Society in which all work and play together, so far as may be, harmoniously, for the common good' and his invocation for all of its members to 'hold fast by that tradition'.[42]

For Paterson what was true of the College should be true of the wider community, throughout the country and beyond. Writ thus large, this call for the realisation of a society which was both cohesive and co-operative fitted well with the intellectual climate of the time, and had already found expression in the social work in London with which Oxbridge men were increasingly involving

---

39   Oxford Union Society, 1st March; *Isis*, *Oxford Review*, 3rd March 1906.

40   Guy Thorne (the pen name of Cyril Ranger Gull) certainly thought so. He asserted that Paterson's banning of his anti-Semitic novel, *When It Was Dark: The Story of a Great Conspiracy*, from the Union library would 'surely entitle [him] to a place in the Cabinet'. The 'regard for accuracy and feeling for public morals' which Paterson had displayed provided him with 'all the necessary equipment to be a Radical minister' (*Varsity*, 8th March 1906). Gladstone, in an angry riposte, denounced the 'patronising and offensive character of the letter as revolting to those who know the man against whom it is invidiously aimed' (10th March).

41   Neville was the son of Edward Talbot, the founder of Lady Margaret Hall who would become in 1905 the first Bishop of Southwark and in 1911 the ninety-third Bishop of Winchester. Neville was at Christ Church from 1903 to 1907, would rise to prominence in the Student Christian Movement, co-found Talbot House, and be consecrated Bishop of Pretoria. He died in 1943, and Alec attended his Requiem at All Hallows-by-the-Tower (*The Times*, 9th April 1943).

42   Darwall-Smith, p. 424. The quotation comes from the Michaelmas term of 1906, by which time Alec had graduated, but the sentiments will have been similar to the ones he heard expressed by Macan previously in chapel or tutorial.

themselves. Many public schools and colleges had created missions or settlements in some of the worst areas of the capital. Based in and around those outposts, 'old boys' and graduates volunteered to help the disadvantaged. Jocelyn Devas, for instance, set up University College House in Battersea in 1884, aiming to provide some education and training for local boys.[43] Haileybury College – Attlee's *alma mater* – had its own settlement in the East End, and one Dr John Stansfeld had created the Oxford Medical Mission in Bermondsey. Each Whit Monday the members of the boys' clubs associated with the university were invited to Oxford to be entertained by undergraduates. Paterson wrote about one such jaunt and concluded that 'the East has never been brought nearer to the West, and each has begun to realize, perhaps unconsciously, that there are chords of sympathy between them that only await the touch of generosity and love.'[44]

This social activism, or 'slumming' as some would have it, was very much of that time and place, and it served two needs: the needs of the beneficiaries and the needs of the benefactors. Many undergraduates were uneasy in their idyllic 'dreaming-spires' surroundings. They were uncomfortable about being too comfortable. They nursed a social conscience, one that was both pricked and nurtured at the heart of their university. Philosophical weight was given to, and could undergird, philanthropic sentiment. Christian, agnostic and atheist alike could all share the same idealism. This was the clarion call that still echoed in the cloisters of the colleges and reverberated in the hearts of so many who walked those cloisters. This call to conscience had come from a Fellow of Balliol, the dominant philosophical voice of his age: Thomas Hill Green.

Green had died in 1882, and now is all but forgotten, but the influence of his version of Idealist philosophy, in Oxford and further afield, persisted well into the twentieth century. Macan testified to this in 1918 when he wrote that Green was the unchallenged 'master mind in our spiritual building ... His whole philosophical influence and his ever-memorable personality – so intense, so sincere, so lofty – declare him a missionary of the Spirit.'[45] Green was an energetic Liberal, convinced that the extraordinary economic and imperial triumphs

43 *Ibid.*, p. 410.
44 *Oxford Chronicle*, 5th June 1903.
45 R.W. Macan, *Religious Changes in Oxford During the Last Fifty Years* (Oxford, 1918) p. 13. In a passage about the influence of one of Green's disciples, Arnold Toynbee, the political economist and Fellow of Balliol, who had wholeheartedly adopted his master's gospel of civic duty, Macan mentioned Paterson as one of the products of this teaching (pp. 36ff.): 'Toynbee set Good Samaritanism in a new light, gave it almost a scientific charter, brought it into connection with good citizenship, and established a special relation between the universities and the wage-earning masses. Directly or

of Victorian individualism had made many of the well-to-do, muffled in their conventional Christianity, indifferent to the effects of industrialisation on the social fabric. He was obsessed with the need to lead a 'useful life' by engaging in society, rectifying injustices, and eradicating inequalities. These were categorical imperatives. 'All things bright and beautiful' was not a hymn he relished. 'Who is my neighbour?' was the question he asked, and answered 'everyone'. Green, in short, was an early and influential exponent of what would be called 'New Liberalism', a political philosophy combining Christian 'communitarian' zeal for the common good with traditional Liberal concerns for the preservation of rights, justice and freedom.[46] A new and better kind of society was evolving, one that was ethical, harmonious and inclusive, within which the Darwinian struggle for survival would be mitigated. All could survive and all thrive. Individuals were not isolated. They could not, and should not, be extricated from the community within which they lived. To flourish they had to be nourished in the compost of community. Individual rights should be protected and respected by the community, but equally each individual had a responsibility for all in that community. Thus he sought to reconcile individuality with social responsibility, the rights and liberties of each with the common good, something Alec would always seek to do. Green also sought to extract the Christian ethic from dogma, something Alec, brought up a socially-conscious Unitarian, had already done.

Green's extraordinary impact on the minds of the young was down to the fact that his teaching met the needs of those who shared both his inheritance and his dilemma, as many of them did. The inheritance was evangelical; the dilemma doubt. His English adaptation of Hegelian Idealism attempted to provide an answer to the great contemporary challenge: how to preserve and harness the Christian social ethic, instilled in particular by the evangelical tradition, when the doctrines of Christianity were being challenged both by scientific discovery and biblical scholarship. Doubt raised by science and what was called 'the higher criticism' warred with the need to believe, and the desire to put belief into civic action. For many undergraduates brought up under the discipline of evangelical piety, as for many dons, the retention or rejection of Christian belief was of paramount importance. Some such as Henry Newman would seek refuge in the old securities of the Catholic Church, some would abjure the Christian faith entirely, but some would try to save the essence, or at least the ethic, from the wreckage. For those desirous of finding an intellectually respectable justification for the moral code and values of their parents Green was a 'godsend'. One of his Balliol students, Andrew Bradley, said that his mentor had saved his soul.

---

indirectly this movement has given us the university and college settlements in London and other slum-cities; it has sent Alec Paterson Across the Bridges.'

46   See Avital Simhony and David Weinstein (eds), *The New Liberalism* (Cambridge, 2001).

In mid-Victorian Oxford, as in all Great Britain, Christian believers who were also thinkers struggled with their faith, or rued their lack of it. Evangelicalism was postulated on the inerrancy of scripture. It was susceptible to literary or scientific disproof. The biblical foundation was subsiding, but the ethical superstructure remained intact. Evangelical homes instilled a belief in self-sacrifice, a dedication to a just cause, and above all a sense of moral imperative, of duty, that 'stern daughter of the voice of God'. These were traits that survived even a loss of faith. They constituted the common heritage of Green and his audience and which he attempted to preserve in his philosophical teaching. He sought to replace fundamentalism with a metaphysical system that would transform Christianity from a historical religion into an undogmatic faith, independent of the accidents of time and place, turning his followers from seeking personal salvation in the next world to improving the conditions of this one. The immanence of God replaced the transcendence of God. Salvation was to be found in service, in active involvement with the here and now, in good citizenship, in self-sacrifice. Duty replaced dogma as the main expression of this civic gospel. In ethics, as in theology, the doctrine of good citizenship and social activism developed by Green can best be understood as 'a surrogate faith appealing to a transitional generation'.[47] That generation was one deeply imbued with Victorian moral earnestness.

Paterson, brought up a Unitarian, was immune to any undermining of his malleable creed, and the Christian Socialist precepts of his friend Temple were in tune with his own, but he would have reacted with pleased recognition to the civic communitarianism for which Green contended.[48] For Paterson a strong religious faith and a strong commitment to social activism went hand in hand. To mix metaphors, belief in God and belief in Man were two sides of the same coin. Whether or not he ever read Green's books, he was the very embodiment of Green's ideal.

Asquith, a Balliol man and Green adherent, thought this liberal version of Idealism had superseded Utilitarianism as the most prominent philosophical school in the universities. And beyond. Green's influence was far wider than the lecture rooms of Oxbridge. Between 1880 and the outbreak of the Great War no philosopher had anything like his impact on public policy. 'He gave conscience a political and social meaning, and gave an outlet to the strong sense of duty, and obligation to serve' so characteristic of the generations of young men straddling the end of the nineteenth and beginning of the twentieth centuries.[49] He converted Idealism, which in Germany had served as a rationale for

47 Richter, pp. 1–19.
48 Temple was conversant with Green's teaching as his submission to the Select Committee on Capital Punishment in 1930 shows (*Minutes of Evidence*, pp. 375, 378).
49 Richter, p. 12.

conservatism, into something close to a practical programme for the radicals in the Liberal Party and later for the emergent Labour Party which, as was often said, owed more to Methodism than to Marxism. His politicised faith encouraged members of the upper and middle classes to see disinterested social service as a particular field for the exercise of Christian or post-Christian virtue. Robin Collingwood, not quite a contemporary of Paterson at Univ., testified to the continuing posthumous potency of Green's appeal:

> The school of Green sent out into public life a stream of ex-pupils who carried with them the conviction that philosophy, and in particular the philosophy they had learnt at Oxford, was an important thing and that their vocation was to put it into practice. Through this effect on the minds of its pupils, the philosophy of Green's school might be found, from about 1880 to about 1910, penetrating and fertilizing every part of national life.[50]

The immediate impact of his influence was apparent in the huge success of Mrs Humphry Ward's 1881 novel *Robert Elsmere*. Dedicated to Green, and containing a character – Professor Grey – directly modelled on him, it follows the fortunes of a young man going up to a thinly disguised Balliol College in the 1870s. There Elsmere comes under the sway of Grey, and after ordination, having encountered the writings of German rationalists, begins to doubt Anglican doctrines. He experiences a crisis of faith, but instead of succumbing to despairing atheism or taking refuge in Roman Catholic obscurantism, he adopts a 'constructive liberalism'.[51] He would subdue the chaos of his feelings in the discipline of social work. He resigns his living and goes to work with the poor in the East End of London, where he eventually founds a church, 'The New Brotherhood of Christ', which was dependent on neither miracles nor dogma, thus echoing Green's own theology. In the novel two themes dominate: the crisis of conscience and its resolution in a form that applies religious energies to the secular problems of modern life. Elsmere's new-forged faith is activist rather than contemplative.

Liberalism in theology led to radicalism in social and political life. Mrs Ward saw in political and social activism the realisation of the true meaning of

---

50 R.G. Collingwood, *An Autobiography* (Oxford, 1939), p. 44. Collingwood, an eminent philosopher and historian, matriculated in 1908.

51 The depiction of Elsmere may have been partly based on a near contemporary and namesake of the philosopher, the priest-historian John Richard Green. During his final year at Oxford he had fallen under the spell of the regius professor of ecclesiastical history, Arthur Stanley, whose doctrine of ennobling Christian service propelled Green into the Anglican priesthood. He worked in poor parishes in the East End of London and became an early exponent of the settlement movement, before writing his innovative *Short History of the English People*, first published in 1874. It is likely that Paterson would have read *Elsmere* and the *Short History*.

Christianity. In her memoirs she wrote of the central importance to Green of leading a 'useful life', a pregnant phrase Paterson would adopt.

> Mr Green was not only a leading Balliol tutor, but an energetic Liberal, ... a man preoccupied with the need of leading a 'useful life'... 'Usefulness', 'social reform', the bettering of daily life for the many – these ideas are stamped on all [the work of Jowett, Green, and Toynbee].[52]

Religion, she contended, 'if it was to have any reality, must begin its real task of working with genuine humanising effect upon the great mass of men living rural and deprived lives.' Its task, to use Green's phrase, was 'to moralise masses' and thereby transform society. It was a clarion call that many Elsmeres answered. Scott Holland remarked that Green 'gave us back the language of self-sacrifice and taught us how we belonged to one another in the one life of organic humanity. He filled us again with the breath of high idealism.'[53] The *Oxford Magazine* in 1883 put it thus: 'A new faith with professor Green for its founder, Arnold Toynbee as its martyr, and various societies for its propaganda, is alive amongst us.' Alive and growing fast.

From Oxford had come a stream of serious young graduates who had 'heard the "bitter cry" of the poor' and 'were conscious of something wrong underneath modern progress' but who did not believe that 'mechanical' philanthropy that was patronising and 'missions' that were sectarian were capable of bridging the chasm between different groups living in the same city. Many would spend their lives in improving the school system, working in adult education, re-organising charitable provision and – most of all – establishing settlement houses. Those who went off to live in such establishments in London's East End or 'across the bridges' in Southwark were determined to find 'words that unite', to make friends with and come to understand their alien and alienated peers. They wanted not merely to get to know, but to merge with, those they hoped to serve. At Oxford these young men had readily proved susceptible to 'appeals to their conscience, their generosity, their repugnance at the prospect of living in a society permanently divided into classes by birth or wealth'.[54]

---

52 *A Writer's Recollections* (London, 1918), pp. 133f. Benjamin Jowett was Master of Balliol from 1870 to 1893.

53 Richter, pp. 31, 35.

54 Samuel Barnett, 'University Settlements', in Will Reason (ed.), *University and Social Settlements* (London, 1898), pp. 11–26, at p. 12; Richter, p. 35. Attlee would opine that 'perhaps the most immediate influence in formulating the ideas that produced the Settlement movement was the teaching and practice of T.H. Green (*The Social Worker* [London, 1920], pp. 191f.). Perhaps 'perhaps' should be removed from this sentence.

Francis Bradley, Andrew's older brother, was at Univ. and Bernard Bosanquet was at Balliol during Green's heyday. They were, like Green himself, the sons of evangelical clergymen. They would reject the dominant Utilitarianism and Empiricism of Victorian England and become the leading exponents of British Idealism. While Bradley stayed in Oxford until his death in 1924, Bosanquet resigned his fellowship for a less purely cerebral life. He and three of his Harrow school friends had gone up to Oxford together intending to become clergy. None did. Because of Green's teaching and example, they gave another form to their original vocation by embarking on social work in London. Indeed, one of Bosanquet's friends, Robert Tatton, became the first warden of the Passmore Edwards Settlement in Bloomsbury, which had been founded by Mrs Ward to put into practice those ideas of Green she had fictionalised in her novel.

It was a path many Oxford graduates would follow, including the three friends, Attlee, Baron and Paterson. One serendipitous encounter early in their university career proved decisive for the latter two. John Stansfeld of the OMM had been invited by a third-year undergraduate called Herbert Pelham to give a talk about his work in Bermondsey. When he arrived, there was no audience. Uncharacteristically, Pelham, who was affectionately known as 'the slug', rushed around the college, knocking on doors to drum up support. Behind one such 'oak' he found Alec playing bridge with Barkis, Clem and Bertie Holland. Despite fearing this was yet another ruse to fleece them out of yet more money for yet another 'good cause', they were persuaded to attend the talk. It was delivered by a wiry human dynamo with a pointed beard and flashing dark eyes who remained perched on the edge of a chair throughout. He spoke so quickly and in such clipped sentences that what he said was hard to take in, but its overall effect had an immediacy unlike any other appeal for boys' clubs that they had previously heard. One phrase struck a particular chord. It was about 'coming to live the crucified life in Bermondsey'.[55] Attlee had already abandoned the Christian faith, which may explain his indifference to the summons he heard.[56] The three

---

55   Baron's memoir, *Once Upon a Time*, contains details not included in his later book, *The Doctor*. After Alec's death, Tubby Clayton would usurp this story and put himself centre-stage, claiming that while *he* was playing bridge with friends in a college room, Stansfeld swept in and invited them to 'come and live the crucified life in Bermondsey' (Melville Harcourt, *Tubby Clayton* [London, 1953], pp. 38f.; Linda Parker, *A Fool for Thy Feast* [Solihull, 2015], pp. 27f.).

56   Attlee, p. 15. The Christian ethic, however, never deserted him, and Green's secularising of that ethic greatly appealed to him (Frank Field [ed.], *Attlee's Great Contemporaries* [London, 2009], pp.xviii–xx). Attlee left Oxford interested neither in politics nor social work. Nevertheless, he did, at Alec's invitation, stay for over a

others, all of whom would remain staunch Christians for the rest of their lives, responded positively to religious language and were moved by this prophet's entreaty. They were also curious to see what he was actually doing in South London. Stansfeld invited them to help out with his mission, 'just for a fortnight'. Holland, Baron and Paterson would take him up on that offer during their first Christmas vacation. For them it would prove life-changing. Holland, a North Country man who would end up as a bishop in New Zealand, for years to come would return to Bermondsey whenever he could. Baron would spend the better part of twelve years 'on and off' in Stansfeld's company, become warden, and write his biography. Paterson would devote his young manhood to fulfilling Stansfeld's vision in Bermondsey, and would never lose touch with the area which 'the doctor' had made his own and with which Paterson so closely identified.

Yet this was no road to Damascus moment. Devoting many years of his life to Bermondsey was not inevitable. His Oxford days had just begun, and throughout his time there Paterson was doing more than evening social work with down-and-outs and vacation placements in boys' clubs. He was making a name for himself as an orator and was nurturing political ambitions. Even in his last year, with 'finals' looming, he had undertaken a hectic round of speaking engagements on behalf of the Liberals during the general election campaign in January and February 1906. This was not surprising given his family's party allegiance. His father went further, acting as the electoral agent for an up-and-coming young radical who was standing for the Manchester North-West constituency, which, in the event, he triumphantly took for the Liberals. The young radical was Winston Churchill. Alec must have met the future Home Secretary during the campaign, a connection that would prove invaluable to his own future.

After graduating from Oxford Alec began reading for the Bar at Inner Temple, to which he had been admitted two years previously when his political interests were paramount.[57] At the same time he accepted an appointment as

---

week at the Bermondsey mission in 1907 and, as a result of a chance expedition with his brother into *terra incognita*, he would go on to spend ten years in the East End, first at the Haileybury Boys' Club in Stepney and latterly at Toynbee Hall. The experience politicised him and gave him a sense of purpose. In 1920 he published *The Social Worker*, in which he wrote that 'work in a boys' club is one of the easiest ways of obtaining an introduction to social questions' (p. 211). Later he acknowledged that it was such work that had prepared him for the office of Prime Minister (Baron, p. 158, n.1).

57   Inner Temple Admissions Database; *Manchester Guardian*, 28th June 1906; *Bowdon Guardian*, 6th July 1906. Paterson would never be called to the Bar, and never practised as a barrister. Bermondsey put paid to that. He would have made an outstanding advocate, with his quick intelligence, melodious voice, and a temperament that was both fearless and commanding.

private secretary to Richard Cherry QC, the Attorney-General for Ireland.[58]
He was positioning himself for the brilliant parliamentary career his Liberal
friends in Manchester and Oxford had long predicted for this radical.[59] At the
time of their graduation in 1906 no one, least of all the man himself, would have
envisaged a political career for the bookish and unassuming Clem Attlee. Alec
Paterson as a cabinet minister, or even as Prime Minister, would have been quite
conceivable. Yet his life's trajectory would take an entirely different course. All
the diverse influences of his youth pointed in one direction: social service. And
then there was Bermondsey. Bermondsey had bitten him. Bermondsey was in
his blood. Bermondsey called.[60]

58   The following year a question was asked in Parliament about the cost of his
       appointment.
59   Baron, p. 162. When, shortly after graduating, Alec had the temerity to contra-
       dict Hugh Egerton, the first Beit Professor of Colonial History, on the issue of
       transportation to Australia, he was challenged to find documentary support for
       his condemnation. He proceeded to do so, digging out dispatches and reports in
       the British Museum which supported his contention that 'the system was ill-con-
       ceived, born of bad principles, and wrecked beyond hope by mal-administration'
       ('Transport the Gunmen?', *The Spectator*, 22nd May 1947, pp. 11f.).
60   In a 1918 sermon P.B. Clayton would refer to a 'brilliant Oxford man with a great
       political future, had he not renounced it, [who] threw up his career to cross the
       London bridges and to live where the ignorance was blackest and the need greatest'
       (*The Smoking Furnace and the Burning Lamp* [London, 1934], pp. 27f.).

CHAPTER 3

ACROSS THE BRIDGES: 1906–1910

I went to Bermondsey to teach and stayed to learn. I went to give and stayed to receive, and what I learnt and what I received were the three gifts of faith, hope and love ... In Bermondsey I have reaped a harvest of happiness and friendship I never hoped for.

Donald Hankey

At thirty a man has given up playing games, making love to his wife, reading books or building castles in the air. He is dangerously contented with his daily work. Promise perishes as a cramped manhood absorbs the fullness of youth.

Alexander Paterson

'The Doctor', as John Stansfeld was universally known, was ever ready to welcome Alec back to Bermondsey. They got on. They shared a vision, a vision which Stansfeld began to realise in 1897 when he set up a small medical mission near London Bridge. His Bermondsey venture would soon grow from a one-man endeavour into a university 'settlement' in all but name, one of the earliest in London and the only one south of the river.[1] Of the others the most notable were Toynbee Hall in Whitechapel, Oxford House in Bethnal Green, and the Passmore Edwards Settlement in Bloomsbury.

The settlement movement was the same age as Alec himself. Founded in January 1884 and opened before the following Christmas, Toynbee Hall was named after Arnold Toynbee, who had died prematurely the previous year at the age of thirty-one. It had the distinction of being the earliest of the university

---

1   It was soon joined by its Cambridge equivalent, another evangelical medical mission with a boys' club set up in 1907 and run by the Revd Harold Salmon in a refurbished building on Jamaica Road. Further land and new halls were added in 1910. A girls' branch followed in 1916. In 1922 the name changed to the Cambridge University Mission.

settlements. It was also the grandest. Established on a non-denominational basis by the Revd Samuel Barnett – 'in religious faith an idealistic Christian without dogma ... in social faith a Christian Socialist' – it was to be a place where richer students of diverse creeds and different political persuasions could live alongside, befriend, and contribute to the welfare of much poorer people. But it was to be more. Industrialism, and the growth of great cities that accompanied it, had riven society in twain. Toynbee Hall, it was hoped, might 'do something to weld classes into society'. In this it singularly failed. It appealed to Ruskinian aesthetes rather than Franciscan ascetics. The tasteful and elegant surroundings in which young university men lived – all Arts and Crafts and wood-panelling – were far removed from anything their Cockney neighbours had experienced, and the only depiction of them in the 'club-house' portrayed them as domestic servants.[2] It was more successful in another respect. From its inception it had a wider agenda than just dealing with the needs of the local area. Its residents and visitors displayed a predilection for 'studying problems or testing theories'.[3] It became a centre for research and the formulation of social policy. It was from there that Charles Booth, 'the perfect embodiment of the union of faith in the scientific method with the transference of the emotion of self-sacrificing service from God to man', helped by 'industrious apprentices' among whom was his cousin Beatrice Potter (later Webb), researched his magisterial *Life and Labour of the People in London*.[4] It was there that William Beveridge would gather material for his groundbreaking work on unemployment. It was there that Clem Attlee would be politicised.

The Passmore Edwards Settlement was established in 1897 to give a permanent and larger home to Mrs Ward's earlier venture which had occupied rented rooms since its foundation seven years before. It was named after its principal benefactor, the philanthropic newspaper proprietor and champion of the working class, John Passmore Edwards. It boasted a fine Arts and Crafts building in Tavistock Place, and devoted itself mainly to education and social improvement. Activities included lectures, readings, concerts, cookery classes, billiards, dance evenings, mother and toddler groups, legal advice sessions, and Saturday morning outings for children to museums, the Zoo, Westminster Abbey, and other places of interest. Modelled on Toynbee Hall, it was avowedly non-sectarian, although with a strong Unitarian background.

2   Seth Koven, *Slumming: Sexual Politics in Victorian England* (Princeton, 2004), pp. 245–248.

3   So thought a future Archbishop of Canterbury, contrasting the rather 'superior' persons who frequented the Hall with 'the greater simplicity and cheerfulness' of the acolytes of Oxford House (J.G. Lockhart, *Cosmo Gordon Lang* (London, 1949), p. 50.

4   Beatrice Webb, *My Apprenticeship* (London, 1926; Cambridge edn, 1979), p. 221.

The exception to these ecumenical or secular bodies was Oxford House. It had been set up by Keble College expressly as a High Church alternative to Toynbee Hall, which was not considered 'sufficiently religious' by Keble's Warden, Edward Talbot. It opened in October 1884 to nurture a celibate lay brotherhood devoted to serving the poor. The early leaders of this 'seminary' were pleased to be called 'abbot' or 'prior'. To some this medieval clericalism was mawkish, or at least mirth-making. It was not until 1892 that the money was raised to replace the first sparse and Spartan quarters with the substantial five-storey red-brick building that still stands today. It remained, however, 'a more genuinely monastic establishment than Toynbee', with more conformity and more uniformity.[5]

Whichever of the three settlements took their fancy, all the residents were fuelled by the same philanthropic impulse and ethical imperative to work among, and with, the poor, even if in their collegiate settlement houses they did not live like the poor, or in their religious retreats they did not live with the poor.[6]

By comparison South London had been rather neglected. In Bermondsey heretofore, with the exception of the Bermondsey Settlement established by the Wesleyan Methodist minister, John Lidgett, in 1891, there had been precious little philanthropic provision: no university settlement – Anglican or otherwise – no medical mission, and no boys' clubs other than those few attached to churches. Stansfeld would introduce both a medical mission and a boys' club within one facility (and shortly after entice Oxford men to help him make it a university cause), prescribing exercise along with enemas. By then he was a medical doctor. He was also a staunch evangelical.

Born in 1854, John Stansfeld was a gregarious Lincolnshire lad who left school at fifteen and within a few years had become a civil servant. He was bright and very determined and, while still working, became both an undergraduate at Exeter College, Oxford, where he studied Greek and theology, and, intent on taking Holy Orders, a student at Wycliffe Hall, the evangelical theological college. Money troubles precluded ordination at that time, so he embarked on another career in medicine, studying part-time and, after a stint at Charing Cross Hospital, qualifying in 1895. Two years later, under the aegis of the Oxford Pastorate, founded in 1893 by Francis Chavasse, the principal of Wycliffe Hall, he established, as a direct rival to Oxford House, the OMM in a small dilapidated house in Abbey Street, Bermondsey. It would have no such sociological pretensions as Toynbee Hall, nor grand buildings, but would have a

5   Henry Nevison, quoted in Koven, *op.cit.*, p. 261. 'Monastic' was a term often used of the settlements, but as monks sequester themselves from the world, 'friarish' would be a more accurate label for a community of men who engaged with it, as friars did.
6   On the early settlement movement see Will Reason (ed.), *University and Social Settlements* (London, 1898).

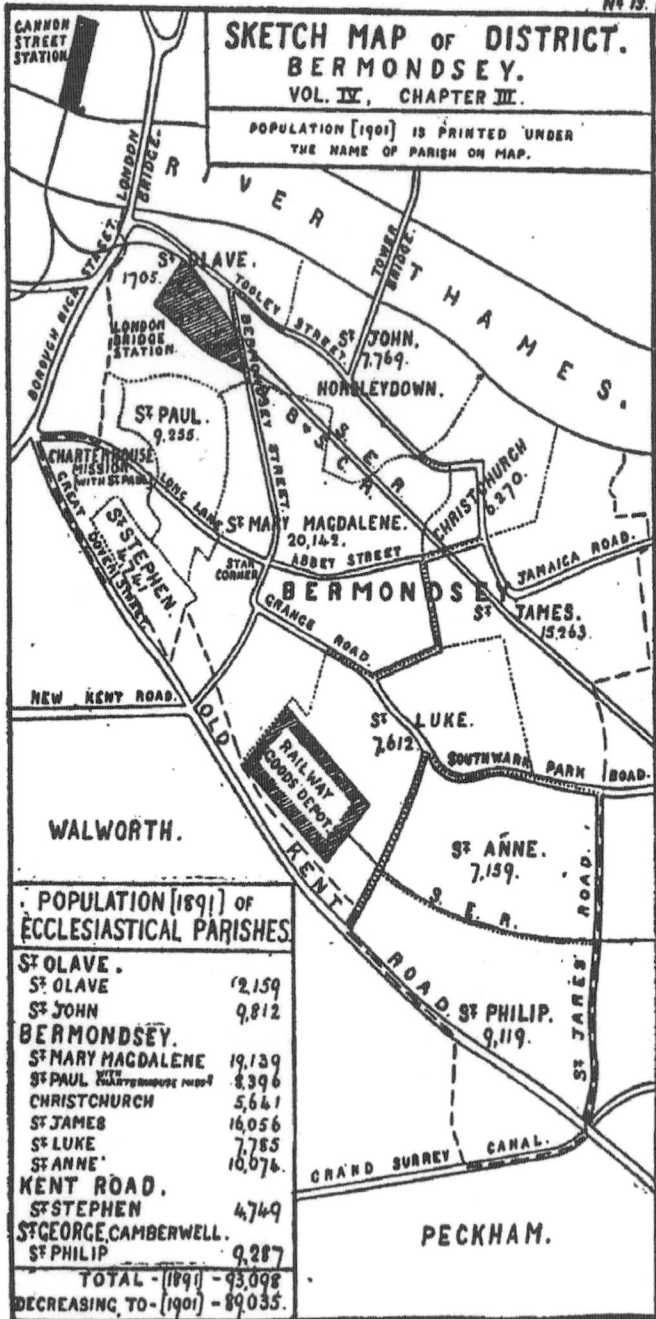

FIGURE 10. Sketch Map of Bermondsey in 1901

major impact on the riverside community within which it operated, and would foster, more than any other settlement, an ethos of equality and fraternity. It was something special. So too was Bermondsey.

Bermondsey occupies the land on the southern bank of the Thames running from London Bridge to Rotherhithe. In Roman times, Southwark, its next-door neighbour to the west, guarded the southern approach to the City while 'Beormund's eye' was a low island protruding from the marshy ground to the east. By the time it was mentioned in Domesday Book it had become a royal manor hosting a Cluniac priory (from 1399 an abbey) dedicated to St Saviour which had been built on the site of an Anglo-Saxon monastery. In the Middle Ages the two areas were the domain of the bishops of Winchester. In Southwark they built a palace and prison, around which brothels sprouted under episcopal control. Wanted criminals holed up in the 'liberties', players performed there, prostitutes known as 'the Winchester geese' and their customers haunted 'the stews', bordellos 'for the repaire of incontinent men to the like women' as John Stow put it.[7] Bermondsey, by contrast, remained an area of open fields, gardens and orchards where Londoners such as Samuel Pepys came for their cherries.[8] With the influx of Huguenot refugees in the sixteenth century it became the great tannery of England, with water aplenty, a reliable source of skins from the butchers of London, and easy access to oak bark from outlying districts such as Forest Hill, Norwood and Honor Oak. Industrial expansion in the nineteenth century further transformed the area. With its bustling docks, London's first railway line and terminus, and a ready workforce, by the reign of Queen Victoria many businesses had established themselves there, importers and exporters as well as manufacturers. Tooley Street, with its towering warehouses holding the bulk of the bacon, butter, cheese, tea and canned meat needed by the metropolis, became known as 'London's larder', while Bermondsey's position in the leather trade was consolidated by the building of the Leather Market and the adjacent Leather, Hide and Wool Exchange. Brewing and biscuit-making were other major enterprises.

It was a time of plfenty for entrepreneurs, but for their employees a time of persistent poverty. Jobs were onerous, hours long, and wages low. Merchants and industrialists had long since moved out of the area to leafier suburbs or further afield, leaving Bermondsey as the abode of the urban poor, many of whom were Irish unskilled labourers. They lived with their families in terraced houses

7   John Stow, *A Survey of London* (1603), 2 vols (Oxford, 1908), ii, p. 54.
8   Samuel Pepys, *Diary*, ed. Robert Latham and William Matthews, 11 vols (London, 1970–1983), v, p. 178.

or tenements in narrow back-streets; gardens had they none. The poorest slum properties of all were those nearest the river, housing casual dock-workers who moved out when work dried up, as it often did. The area around St Saviour's Dock, comprising Dockhead or Jacob's Island as it was formally known, was surrounded at high tide by the dirty flood waters of the Thames. An 1813 engraving shows Folly Ditch, the overflow, as an open drain, and a Bermondsey boy bathing in it. As grimly depicted in chapter 50 of Charles Dickens's novel *Oliver Twist*, it was 'the filthiest, the strangest, the most extraordinary of the many localities that are hidden in London, wholly unknown even by name to the great mass of its inhabitants.' Consisting of a maze of 'close, narrow and muddy streets' it thronged with the 'roughest and poorest waterside people, unemployed labourers of the lowest class, brazen women, ragged children and the raff and refuse of the river.' Everywhere the buildings were as decrepit and decayed as the people, and the nearer they were to the river the worse they got. There were

> Crazy wooden galleries common to the backs of half-a-dozen houses, with holes from which to look upon the slime beneath; windows, broken and patched, with poles thrust out, on which to dry the linen that is never there; rooms so small, so filthy, so confined, that the air would seem to be too tainted even for the dirt and squalor which they shelter; wooden chambers thrusting themselves out above the mud and threatening to fall into it – as some have done; dirt-besmeared walls and decaying foundations; every repulsive lineament of poverty, every loathsome indication of filth, rot, and garbage.

It was fitting that from the roof of one such derelict warehouse the murderer Bill Sykes met his end, dangling from a rope over Folly Ditch, in the mud of which his dog also perished. Three quarters of a century later Paterson himself would describe the same area in very similar terms.[9] So too would a boy who lived in a two-roomed house in Hickman's Folly, where he had to tip-toe around the upper room 'lest the vibrations displaced the cups from their nails in the room below'.

> Well, here we lived, in Bill Syke's land. Here I learned to utilize the holes in the flagstones for my games of "bung'ole," marbles, etc, and incidentally found one could do without boots with such a hard surface to tread on.[10]

9   *Oliver Twist* (1837–1839), ch.L; Paterson, p. 19. *Across the Bridges* provides the best description of life in Bermondsey in the early years of the twentieth century. Paterson had entered the doors and into the lives of many of his neighbours. His observations are detailed and perceptive. See *infra*.

10   F.B., 'The Autobiography of a Bermondsey Boy', in Gutman, pp. 303–320, at p. 305.

Charles Booth described turn-of-the-century Bermondsey as 'the greatest area of unbroken poverty in England'. He knew – and his knowledge was unparalleled – of 'no district of equal extent so depressing to the spirit as that which lies between Long Lane and Great Dover Street' and 'no set of people in London who look quite so poor as those who do their marketing in Bermondsey New Road on Sunday morning'.[11] This was in accord with Andrew Mearns's searing depiction of the same area, where he had discovered to his horror that in the locality of Long Lane there were 'some 650 families or 3,250 people living in 123 houses', and nearby had been 'found the bodies of nine infants which had been deposited at the foot of some stairs in an undertaker's shop'. In one court, eighteen yards long and nine yards wide, there were

> twelve houses of three rooms each, and containing altogether 36 families. The sanitary condition of the place is indescribable. A large dust-bin charged with all manner of filth and putrid matter stands at one end of the court, and four water-closets at the other. In this confined area all the washing of these 36 families is done, and the smell of the place is intolerable.[12]

Lack of work and lack of industrial clout were salient features. Hand-to-mouth existence was inimical to social advancement. The people were down-at-heel and so was the area they inhabited. In such conditions humanity was degraded and all vitality was sapped. A poem by F.C. Davis, a correspondence clerk in a local firm, captured the docile and depressed condition of so many of the residents:

11   Charles Booth, *Third Series: Religious Influences*, vol.4, *Inner South London*, pp. 101f. Booth, like Alec, was brought up as both a Unitarian and a Liberal. To refute a socialist's claim that a quarter of the population in London was destitute, in 1886 Booth had set out, at his own expense, to collect the data needed for an accurate assessment. It was an enormous undertaking, a survey encompassing four million people and a million households. His results were contained in seventeen hefty volumes which he published over the succeeding seventeen years. By 'the arithmetic of woe' he concluded that a quarter was in fact a gross underestimate. The poor and very poor (those living at or below the level of bare subsistence) constituted almost a third of Londoners. His strict methodology and herculean endeavours are related in Beatrice Webb's autobiography, *My Apprenticeship*, pp. 216–256. His analytical description of Bermondsey covers pp. 97–139 of volume 4. Barclay Baron studied it and in particular the 'poverty map' included therein (Snape, p. 267). It is likely Alec did so too. Booth's conclusion that deprivation damaged character would have resonated.

12   Andrew Mearns, *The Bitter Cry of Outcast London* (London, 1883), pp. 29f. This thirty-two-page pamphlet, published cheaply by a Congregationalist minister the year before Alec was born, caused a sensation throughout the country. It was not the first exposé of the appalling housing conditions in which so many lived, but it touched a nerve.

Herded, I saw them stand
Like tired oxen,
With filmed eyes.
And spattered legs,
And drooping mouths.
Waiting, waiting,
In the thin rain
Which fell aslant
Their bowed heads,
Their curved shoulders.[13]

The buildings in which the locals lived were always overcrowded and usually squalid, and 'even in the best the builder's ignorance has starved the life that he was meant to brighten and sustain'.[14] 'Gas lights, often muffled by fog, bathed the pavements in a dim yellow glow; horses labouring under heavy loads trudged through brickyard and alleyway, hooves clattering on cobbles. On it all 'a gentle shower of dirt' would 'fall and creep and cover and choke'. Dirt was not the only thing that fell and crept – the old houses were overrun with bugs and infested with mice and rats. 'The vapour of the slum', Paterson would record, 'is so indefinable as to be more of an atmosphere than a smell; it is a constant reminder of poverty and grinding life, of shut windows and small inadequate washing-basins, of last week's rain, of crowded homes and long working hours.' At best it was the cloying smell of strawberries emanating from the jam factory that permeated the air. In the earthy terms of one young resident, Bermondsey was 'but a pisse pot 'neath the arse of the City'.[15]

In conditions little improved since Dickens's time many of Bermondsey's 90,000 or so inhabitants lived hand-to-mouth on bread and beer. With little to do and less to enjoy, the men loafed around on street corners, gambled on the dogs and horses, or patronised the many pubs – there were four in a row in one Bermondsey street alone – which stayed open until past midnight serving 'fighting beer'. Many of the women joined them, or tried to extricate them, often dragging small children with them. Some children were neglected by absent parents or abused by drunken ones. Saturday nights were the noisiest and most violent;

13   'Cinema Queue', in Gutman, pp. 274f.
14   Paterson, p. 20. Ignorance on the part of the benefactors and their builders bedevilled philanthropy. In words as apposite to the 1960s well-intentioned but brutalist housing 'blitz' as to his own day, Paterson stressed that the builder 'needs know something of those for whom he builds, a knowledge of poor men, sympathy with their struggle and defeat, and yearning that they may climb to better days – these are the foundations on which houses and block dwellings may best be built.'
15   Paterson, p. 10; Tommy Steele, *Bermondsey Boy* (London, 2006), p. 1. Steele was a member of the Oxford and Bermondsey Club in the 1940s and 50s.

Sunday mornings the most desolate. They could also be the most desperate for offspring fearful of the consequences of a parental hangover, as one recalled:

> After a Saturday booze, Sunday morning would, of course, find [my step-father] with a terrible thirst. Then there was trouble if, overnight, a supply of drink had not been obtained, as the pubs did not open again till one o'clock. Often I was first in the queue, waiting for the doors to open.[16]

Heavy drinking by young and old was one way of coping with the grinding monotony of daily life, and a sure way of perpetuating it. Everywhere and every day the pawnbroker and 'loan-shark' prospered at the expense of the feckless or hapless or hopeless.[17]

In such surroundings infant mortality was high, life-expectancy low. Schooling began at the age of three and ended at fourteen. Yet the priority of most families was to get their surviving children to earn, not to learn. Childhood was short and burdens were imposed on the older children, from looking after their siblings to contributing to the family's income. They subsisted largely on bread and jam, charity and ingenuity. Fried fish was an occasional luxury, malnutrition commonplace. It is not surprising that most children were smaller than average for their age, with skin discoloured by pollution from the tanning factories. Many of the poorest, or most neglected of them, were 'weedy-looking, collarless and ragged, with boots so bad that to go barefoot would be better'. Some did. With little provision for their recreation and few open spaces, the dingy, rubbish-strewn streets were the sole playgrounds of the young, the dirty Thames their swimming pool. Of character-building adventure, exploration beyond the immediate area, stimulus to the imagination, there was no sign. For the lucky ones a holiday meant hop-picking in rural Kent. Long hours in the fields were followed by a sing-song and bed. Dead-tired they might have been, but the eerie silence of the countryside or the rustling sounds of who-knows-what creatures in the night kept many children awake or made sleep fitful. Yet for all the deprivations they endured, the young had not yet lapsed into the deadening routine of their parents nor into the torpor and apathy of the old. There was hope for them yet in the battle of life. They were the future and their future was not preordained to repeat the past.[18]

These were the hard facts of life that Stansfeld encountered when he first set foot in Bermondsey and which he was determined to ameliorate if not rectify. This was the human potential he wanted to cherish and nurture. He set

16 Paterson, p. 306.
17 *Ibid.*, p. 307; Booth, *op.cit.*, pp. 99, 117f.
18 Booth, *op.cit.*, pp. 119ff.

to work with the resources he had, and made an immediate if limited impact. There were urgent medical needs to be met, and they, along with saving souls, were his priority. He consulted the members of the local medical profession to ensure their co-operation and reassure them that he would not poach their patients. None complained, and one in particular, Alfred Salter, another devout Christian and a founder of the Bermondsey Independent Labour Party, would give much assistance.[19] Although secondary to his purpose, Stansfeld soon realised the necessity of a boys' club. This was established in a room above the dispensary. The innate vitality of some local children and youths had at last found a boisterous and benign outlet, but in 1901 it was still 'on a small scale'. That same year its evangelical credentials were burnished when Stansfeld became a Pastorate chaplain and Chavasse, by then Bishop of Liverpool, was appointed Visitor.

When help arrived in the shape of eager young Oxford men whose energy and enthusiasm could energise and enthuse others, 'the Doctor' could expand his outreach and incorporate more and more into his embrace. He looked for much bigger premises as his main centre, and began the process of setting up satellite or 'branch' boys' clubs to cater for the demand. 'We are all brothers' was a phrase he often reiterated, and '*Fratres*' was the motto he chose for his youth work and the name he gave to the club magazine.[20] Boys and men alike were all known by their Christian names or nicknames. There was a strong emphasis on self-reliance and on 'the lads making their own clubs'. And the clubs, it was hoped, would also make men. They exuded 'muscular Christianity', with boxing bouts sandwiched between Bible studies and prayers. They were very popular, much more so than those run by the more staid Methodists and Baptists or by the more conventional evangelicals of the London City Mission.[21]

Stansfeld was a hard taskmaster, but he tasked himself the most. Throughout his time in Bermondsey he kept his day job as a civil servant, donning a silk top hat in the morning when off to the City, and a white coat and stethoscope in the evening when he worked in the dispensary diagnosing ailments and lancing boils, or, once more donning his 'topper', visited the sick and dying in their homes. Work, study, prayer and play: all were crammed into each day until every minute was accounted for. In his 'spare time' he taught himself to play the violin. How much time and energy he had for his wife, Jane, and his own small children is hard to fathom.[22] He eventually burnt himself out, and in 1905 was compelled to take a prolonged rest on account of nervous exhaustion. He had to place

---

19   *The Lancet* (12th November 1898), pp. 1294ff.

20   Alec wrote 'Children and the Child' for *Fratres*, VII (December 1907), pp. 5–8.

21   Booth, *op.cit.*, pp. 109–114.

22   They married in 1902 when he was forty-six and she thirty-two. Their two children, Gordon and Phyllis, were born in 1903 and 1904 respectively. Jane died of the Spanish flu in October 1918.

his beloved Mission into the hands of another and chose Herbert Pelham, who from his undergraduate days had been a trusted stalwart, to keep things going in his absence. Thus Pelham became the first 'Warden' of the Mission.[23] Although he occupied this post for two years, his time in effective charge would be short. Within months, Stansfeld had returned to assume command and was back in role when another recruit was lured fresh from Oxford, one to whom he had been introduced by Pelham himself, Alexander Paterson.

Initially Alec lived with the other 'foot soldiers' on the top floor of the Mission itself, which by then had been re-housed in a disused corset factory at 134 Abbey Street. It had none of the grandeur and Oxford-air of Toynbee Hall or Oxford House. On the first floor was the boys' club, in the basement a dingy waiting area for patients, and on the ground floor the makeshift dispensary where all and sundry were treated day and night and where medicines were given away freely, while specks of whitewash, dislodged from the ceiling by the antics above, floated gently down upon them like snowflakes. Conditions were Spartan, the Doctor insisted on that. No curtains, no carpets, and sometimes no glass in the windows. Upon arrival the 'residents', as they were called, gave away all their own attire and donned cast-offs from the old-clothes cupboard. As Alec wryly observed, 'hair-shirts were too expensive, so ordinary ones were worn.'[24] The only reason the volunteers were not chilled to the bone was that they had no time to stand still or sit down, such was the pace of activity, whether assisting in the surgery, or with the boys' activities, or in the thousand other tasks that awaited their attention. They slept, when they could, in 'cheerful discomfort'.[25] A youthful, but amply proportioned, Archbishop of Canterbury-to-be recalled his travails:

> There was a tin bed, rather rickety, and I lay on it with some anxiety, for I have always carried weight in any assembly. There was a tin wash-basin and a chair with three legs, upon which I read Bosanquet's *Logic*.[26]

---

23   Herbert would publish *The Training of a Working Boy* in 1914. He came with the right pedigree, as his second cousin was Thomas Pelham, son of the Earl of Chichester, who had worked in ragged schools, institutes and clubs, helped to found the London Federation of Working-boys' Clubs, and was the author of the first *Handbook to Youths' Institutes and Working Boys' Clubs* which was published in 1889 (and of a later volume on *The Laws of Cricket*). He stressed that 'personal influence is one of the first conditions of success', a sentiment which chimed with Alec.

24   Having a civil service position, Alec, like the Doctor, retained a set of old but fine quality clothes, including the tweed coat and grey flannel trousers he had worn at Oxford (*Over the Walls*, p. 3).

25   Alexander Paterson, *The Doctor and the OBM* (London, 1910); Baron, *Once Upon a Time*, p. 11.

26   Baron, p. 31. Bernard Bosanquet published *Logic* in 1888.

How very Oxford! How very Bermondsey! It was very much a place for young men used to the rigours of public school and the collegiate life of university.[27]

Bread and treacle and kippers were the staple foods. Eating sweets or other indulgences were classed as 'pig life'. Alcohol was strictly forbidden – Stansfeld, unsurprisingly, was a staunch advocate of temperance. Smoking was frowned upon but illicitly undertaken by the Doctor's 'disciples'. Theirs was a quasi-monastic community under a strict rule, although very definitely not one of contemplative silence, and with 'monks' who acted like friars. Alec, although he would soon escape to the privacy of his own flat, applauded the self-sacrificial approach which marked out the Bermondsey Mission from all the other London settlements.

> The OMM was a stern ascetic brotherhood, deaf to the appeals of sisters and aunts ... The Doctor and his small band were laying strong foundations, and it is well that at the beginning the keynote of the Mission should have been clear and unmistakable. The utter abandonment of the self to work, the simple concentration on a spiritual aim and method were high ideals and gave birth to a stern tradition.[28]

In an earlier age they would have been Franciscans.[29]

Paterson and Stansfeld had a mutual and magnetic attraction. Different as they were – Alec would never be an evangelical, far less a Puritan – they complemented each other. They argued often but never quarrelled. The younger man, brimming with enthusiasm and ideas, remained utterly loyal to his mentor; the older man recognised in his acolyte a rare combination of dynamism and commitment allied with imagination and verve. Both were headstrong and both natural leaders, but they could work together in alliance rather than rivalry, and without rancour or jealousy.[30] Alec would shortly become Stansfeld's right-hand man, a position he assumed when Clifford Woodward, the local curate who had previously held that undefined post, left for Oxford in 1909.[31] Paterson modestly called himself the 'Junior Resident', but became in reality the 'vice-president' of the whole enterprise.

27   Attlee, *The Social Worker* (London, 1920), p. 198.
28   Alec Paterson, 'The Doctor and the OMM' (Oxford Medical Mission, London, 1910).
29   Walter Besant had drawn this analogy in his contribution to Reason's *University and Social Settlements* (p. 3). So too would Basil Henriques after he had begun visiting Bermondsey. He wrote in his diary, 'if I am to go among the lowest dregs of society, the down and outs, the prostitutes and criminals, and share my life with them, I know I must do so as their equal, their Brother' (L.L. Loewe, *Basil Henriques* [London, 1976], p. 15).
30   Baron, p. 162.
31   Born in 1878, Woodward was educated at Marlborough School and Jesus College, Oxford, obtaining a second-class degree in *Literae Humaniores* in 1901. After

As such he started a trend that, while ultimately leading to the end of the Oxford 'college community' life that had for so long been cherished, would create a greater identification with the Bermondsey people round about. While he jumped first, others followed. 'They lived among the people, with the people and for the people', all on a level.[32] This was unique. A temporary settlement of the kind found elsewhere would be replaced with permanent settlers, permanent at least until marriage and children drew them away, or catastrophe on the world stage scattered them. The impetus came when Alec moved out, first with two friends into a well-built flat in Abbey Buildings and then, on his own, into less salubrious accommodation in nearby Dockhead, the notorious and neglected area on the riverside fringe where Stansfeld had already set up the second of his clubs.[33]

The Dockhead Club as it was known was housed in a derelict building similar to (some said the same as) that from which Sykes had fallen to his death. It was bounded by Halfpenny Alley and Farthing Alley, next to The Ship Aground public house. Initially it was run by three senior boys from the Abbey Street Club – Jim Ford, Josh Jackson and Fred Gunning. They had been the first members Stansfeld had recruited and had shown leadership potential. Having been 'civilised' they were 'commissioned as junior officers' and sent out as 'missionaries'. Born in the back streets themselves, they did remarkably well, bringing in many new recruits, but were sometimes discouraged and often nervous, never knowing quite what to expect.[34] Despite their stunted growth, despite the malnutrition that often afflicted them, local children were streetwise, resilient and ready for a scrap. It was an area where fighting and vandalism were routine and policemen patrolled in

---

ordination he became one of the curates of St Mary Magdalene, Bermondsey's parish church. On his return to Oxford, he served as a lecturer at Wycliffe Hall, and chaplain of Wadham College, before becoming rector of St Saviour's (Southwark Cathedral) with St Peter's Southwark. He volunteered for the army chaplaincy in May 1916 and was posted with the rank of captain to the 22nd Battalion of the 47th Division, where he served alongside Alec. He was awarded the Military Cross for 'conspicuous gallantry and devotion to duty' during the battle of the Somme. He had tended to, and brought in, the wounded under very heavy shellfire, 'showing an utter disregard of danger, and giving confidence and relief to many'. He was consecrated Bishop of Bristol in 1933 and in 1946 was elevated to Gloucester. He died in 1959.

32 Henriques, p. 23.

33 The Decima Street and the Gordon Clubs (named after the Doctor's newly born son, who himself was named after Chinese Gordon) would follow, each pioneered by senior boys and with a membership of between eighty and a hundred. Donald Hankey, the future 'Student in Arms', would work five nights a week as assistant manager of the Decima Club under Will Clift, a local working-man.

34 Baron, *Once Upon a Time*, p. 3. Ford would become the owner of a paint works in Bermondsey; Jackson a farmer in Canada; and Gunning a hugely popular Anglican priest in Western Australia, in his early days living in a tent he called the 'wrectory'.

pairs. The Doctor would reassure his 'officers' that 'friction is a sign of life. Don't be afraid. Here are all these boys, and God is in every one of them.'[35] Dynamic oversight of their endeavours was required. Alec would provide it.

He rented a two-roomed flat in Wolseley Buildings, a noisy and dirty seven-storey housing block – or 'ugly barracks' as he called it – where casual dock labourers made their homes. It had been built the year before his birth and named in honour of 'the very model of a modern major general' who had been actively involved in setting up the Southwark Cadet Corps, Sir Garnet Wolseley.[36] It lay on the corner of Farthing Alley, a few yards away from the club and near to the Jacob's biscuit factory, which served the nation, and Holy Trinity Catholic church and its adjacent convent, which served the large Irish population in the vicinity. The 'monstrous black cliff' of the tenement block is long gone, and the whole area has been transformed, but The Ship Aground remains, as does Holy Trinity, although not in the form Paterson would have known.[37] With access via a steep concrete staircase, each landing held four two-roomed flats with one water-closet and one open sink to serve all four. Some flats held fourteen people, and in the one diagonally opposite Alec's lived a labourer, his wife and their nine children. Diseases such as typhoid fever transmitted by water contaminated with faeces, tuberculosis or 'consumption' as it was called, a terrible killer in those days, and diphtheria, which had 'a partiality for tenement blocks', were rife, and the mortality rate was twice the London average of the day.[38] While Paterson was resident there five of his neighbour's children succumbed to tuberculosis, and he watched their small coffins 'bumping down the narrow flight of stairs'.[39] It was supposed to be 'a model dwelling' compared

---

35   Quoted in Eagar, p. 233.

36   John Springhall, *Youth, Empire and Society* (London, 1977), p. 74. The Cadet Corps, having absorbed others and been renamed the 1st London Cadet Battalion, would provide many recruits for both the Boer War and the Great War.

37   As early as 1773 the Catholic Church had established a mission in Bermondsey, probably the earliest in the present Archdiocese of Southwark. The chapel built at that time was destroyed by the Gordon rioters in 1780. It was rebuilt, proved inadequate for the needs of the growing Catholic population, and was replaced in 1837–1838 by a new church by Sampson Kempthorne, in the Early English Gothic style, with a galleried interior. Adjoining it, a convent for the Sisters of Mercy was built in 1838 from designs by Augustus Pugin, his first convent commission. Kempthorne's church and Pugin's convent were destroyed by a V-bomb in March 1945. Christchurch on Parker's Row at the east end of Abbey Street was Dockhead's Anglican church until it was made redundant in 1956.

38   Booth, *op.cit.*, p. 138; Baron states that this particular statistic was established by a 'patient team of investigators at the Mission' (p. 48).

39   'Should the Criminologist be Encouraged?', *Transactions of the Medico-Legal Society*, 26/1 (1932), pp. 180–200, at p. 184; Ruck, p. 30.

with the older houses in the area; it was in fact a death-trap. For the elderly and infirm living above ground level it could also be a prison, as those with arthritic legs or congested lungs were unable to navigate the dark, fetid stairs. The new occupant from Oxford rapidly became the spokesman for his neighbours and as such called in the Borough medical officer, and together they confronted the rich owner, who 'shuffled his responsibility on to other shoulders', doing nothing to rectify things. The tenacious young tenant would become the unofficial lawyer for the residents, and, as Hankey once called him, their 'lay priest', as well as godfather to many of their children. One neighbour named her son Alec.[40]

His top-floor slum apartment – number 141 – was distinctive, during his tenancy, in that it boasted a bath – 'installed by Alec at his own expense in the face of lively opposition from the sanitary inspector' – and contained but one occupant.[41] No longer merely a settlement worker he had become a permanent resident. Alec made his home among the locals but tried to keep clean and maintain his privacy. A forlorn hope. The furnishings were basic but included a spare bed for the frequent visitors he anticipated coming to see Bermondsey and wanting to stay overnight or longer. Those who did were feasted upon by the hordes of bugs and fleas from which his flat was not immune. Some visitors wondered how their host endured living in such conditions.[42] His answer was that as others did, so would he. An unusual item for such a place was a bookcase and even more unusual were books. Nor was a writing desk a necessity for most of those living in this area. It was for Alec, who never ceased from putting pen to paper. The blue-washed walls of his small rooms were decorated with photographs of his many friends, among which he pinned up a list of the forty or so ragged schoolboys he had mentored, at the top of which he had written 'Of Such is the Kingdom of Heaven'.[43]

Boys' clubs were very much in vogue in the years before the great cataclysm. Doing something for the young was a mark of Victorian philanthropy. There were national resources such as the Ragged School Union, founded in 1844 to provide education for destitute children; Dr Barnardo's homes which from 1886 opened their doors to 'destitute waif children'; and the Boys' Brigade, started in Glasgow in 1883 by Alexander Smith to instil 'Obedience, Reverence, Discipline, Self-respect and all that tends towards a true Christian manliness', and which swept the land by the 1890s before spreading worldwide. At a more parochial level, boys' clubs of all sorts and sizes had sprouted everywhere, in city

40 Watson (1969), p. 62; Hubert Secretan, *London Below Bridges* (London, 1931), pp. 13f; Baron, p. 49; *Diary*, 20th August 1914.

41 Baron, 'Across the Bridges', *Four Men* (London, n.d.), pp. 30–40, at p. 30.

42 Henriques, p. 220.

43 Baron, 'Across the Bridges', *op.cit.*, p. 31.

and in town.[44] Many were started by university colleges or public schools which provided the money, the buildings, and the volunteers to run them. Others, less well-endowed, were housed in whatever facility could be commandeered for use, from a church or village hall to a shed behind a vicarage or a stable beneath the railway arches. The ideal clubhouse was one that was self-contained and reserved for club use alone. Other institutions' halls were less suitable than having your own space, however lowly. The premises of the Dockhead club were certainly lowly, consisting of 'a miserable, disused two-storied warehouse'.[45]

Yet Paterson once remarked that the best type of boys' club was 'the street corner with a roof on'.[46] His constant refrain was that buildings did not make clubs, people did, those who ran them and those who attended. Of the latter each paid a subscription and each subscribed to the rules. Gang-members became team-players. As one mother told Alec it was a good thing for her Bill 'to run wild in good company'.[47] They had become part of a company, the dignity and honour of which each had to maintain. There was nothing uniform about the clubs other than that they shared certain values and aspirations. They all wanted to instil a sense of fair play, to encourage sportsmanship along with sporting prowess, to afford distractions from temptation, and to nurture self-control. They were all 'clubbable', aiming to create a group loyalty and to provide a home for some and a family for all. They all aspired to be 'practice-grounds in the duties of citizenship', instilling 'the *esprit de corps* which is rarely planted in a boy at the ordinary elementary school, and arising out of this, the ideas of collective responsibility of all members not only to one another but to the outside public.' Above all the clubs 'should offer many chances for developing on right lines the powers of leadership which exist in a fair proportion of boys, and which, if undirected, may quickly result in far-reaching evil.' They realised potential, encouraged aspirations, and helped form strong, self-confident and well-educated working-class leaders.[48] Paterson described them in all their diversity and similarity thus:

> All clubs keep boys from the streets; all clubs imbue them with a corporate spirit; and they nearly all go a great deal further. In one the emphasis may be laid on discipline; in a second club, rather on friendliness. One club is

---

44 The history of the boys' clubs movement is recounted in *Making Men*. According to Eagar, the first in England 'recognisable as such by present-day standards and plainly so named' was the South London Cyprus Boys' Club established in 1872 by the Revd Daniel Elsdale, vicar of St John the Divine, Kennington (pp. 170ff.).

45 Henriques, p. 24.

46 Watson (1969), p. 136.

47 'How England Handles the Young Offender', *Proceedings of the Annual Congress of the American Prison Association* (1939), pp. 149–157, at p. 150.

48 Percy Ashley, 'University Settlements in Great Britain', *Harvard Theological Review*, 4/2 (April 1911), pp. 175–203, at pp. 185ff.

military, another is educational, a third athletic and gymnastic, a fourth social, with a strong religious basis. There are differences in payment, rules, government and tone ... In no single club can the strong points of all be found in one harmonious combination.[49]

Before the advent of the Welfare State voluntary organisations plugged many a gap. The further education of working-class boys was one. Clubs provided evening classes in such useful attainments as shorthand and typewriting, and in such esoteric ones as Latin and Greek. A high drop-out rate, fuelled by long working hours and erratic overtime, was inevitable and discouraging. Nonetheless the OMM's annual report for 1908 stated that during the preceding year 300 hours of private tuition had been given to 'the best boys'. Bermondsey may not yet have had a bookshop but it was not short of tutors.[50] In 1911 the new recruit Donald Hankey and the old retainer Barclay Baron formed a Shakespeare Club, as a result of which a singular production of *Julius Caesar* was performed in a rundown parish hall in Dockhead. It was the first of many.[51]

Exercising the body complemented expanding the mind. Sports and games of all sorts, with their disciplines and regulations and ethos, were seen as essential, not just to physical well-being, which since the revelations of the stunted growth of service recruits during the Boer War had become a national obsession and had led to the creation of the Boy Scout movement, but to character-formation, as well as providing an antidote to the all-too-prevalent gambling. Boxing and wrestling matches were commonplace in the clubs, as were games of billiards, draughts and dominoes, and, for a few, chess, all having 'some subtle influence on manners and morals, when played by strict rules in the atmosphere of the club, where fair play is valued above victory, and gambling is not needed as an accessory to the interest of the game.' Strenuous physical activities were much encouraged. There were long-distance runs through the city streets, and inter-club football and cricket matches in municipal parks.[52] Self-discipline was necessary for the first and sportsmanship for the second and third. The rules of

---

49   Paterson, p. 157.
50   The Bermondsey Bookshop, the first in that area, opened its doors in 1921. It was set up and run by Sidney and Ethel Gutman, and proved an immediate success. It even published a Quarterly Review of Life and Literature called *The Bermondsey Book* which contained stories, poems and articles penned by such literary luminaries as Vita Sackville-West and Siegfried Sassoon and by the less celebrated, such as 'F.B.', who contributed 'The Autobiography of the Bermondsey Boy'. For the bookshop's brief history see Gutman, pp.ix–xiv.
51   Baron, pp. 189f.
52   In the winter months the Bermondsey Boys' Club football team would get the tram to Greenwich, change at the terminus, and carry their goalposts up the hill to Blackheath to play for less than an hour before dark (Eagar, p. 103, n.1).

cricket were 'so framed as to be an almost exact parallel of the best moral code', and 'the spirit of football – help your side to score without fouling – [was] the spirit also of life.' It was this spirit that Alec embodied as he played for the Mission's cricket team every week. Many of the boys joined the Territorial Force, and the few evenings they devoted to it contributed 'to the[ir] appearance no less than the[ir] character'.[53]

All these activities could be provided on the streets and in the parks of London, but the environment was less than ideal. 'Below the bridges', even when 'the long, dark winter has drawn to a close and the sunlight filtering through the smoky atmosphere begins to feel warm', the green foliage of 'the plane trees in the Tower Bridge Road will all too soon be smudged with the city dirt' and 'nature struggles to break through the bonds that civilisation has imposed upon her.'[54] The ideal was to get the club members away from the grime and hurly-burly of city life and into the countryside for a week or more of fresh air, group-bonding and character-building. 'The Doctor' recognised this need and, at the turn of the century, impecunious as ever, nevertheless managed to scrape together the money to buy twenty-three acres of land at Horndon in Essex.

For children who had never seen the countryside, or had done so fleetingly on tiring day trips at most, or thought it was the preserve of gentlemen and ladies when they were not about town, this was to be a sylvan idyll. Not that it seemed so at first. The land was a 'rather bleak, clayey hilltop in Essex looking down on the mud flats around Tilbury' and the village of Mucking. To transform it into the rural paradise Stansfeld promised would take some doing. Trees, shrubs and flowers had to be planted. Wooden floorboards, doors, window frames and pews had to be transported by horse-cart from the site of a demolished chapel in the Old Kent Road to be resurrected in Horndon. The first structure was 'the castle', a crazy folly with battlements and ladders that delighted boys whose lives were devoid of 'romance'. Next to it was a more utilitarian hut named 'Wycliffe House' which was used for meals, storage and evening gatherings in wet weather. Years later one of the old boys, who had become an architect, concluded that 'this building only stands up by force of habit.' Nearby, a swimming pool was dug out of the clay. A four-acre wood was later added to the estate and yet another small piece of extra land was acquired

---

53   Paterson, pp. 160–166. 'Character' was a quintessentially Victorian and Edwardian concept. It entailed self-control, duty, courage and endurance. It was the foundation of citizenship. 'Character was about the mastery of self; good citizenship was about selflessness' (H.S. Jones, 'Civic Society in British Social Thought', in Lawrence Goldman [ed.], *Welfare and Social Policy in Britain since 1870* [Oxford, 2019], pp. 29–43, at p. 37).

54   Secretan, *op.cit.*, p. 149.

for allotments so that the boys, some of whom knew neither that timber came from trees nor that any flowers were 'wild', could be taught forestry conservation and kitchen-garden cultivation.[55]

Finally, the first camp took place with construction work continuing in the morning, football and other sports during the afternoon, and a campfire at night where the Oxford men, weary from their exertions, and the Bermondsey boys energised by theirs, sang the 'anthem' of the OMM, 'We're all pals together'. A Sunday service was led by 'the Doctor' who, in illustration of his sermon, knelt down and washed a number of the congregants' feet.[56]

Camps at a variety of locations would become a regular feature of the Bermondsey boys' clubs, and Corton on the Suffolk coast and Hopton on the Norfolk were very popular, especially with those who had never seen cliffs or the sea. Even more mind-expanding were the summer trips to camp at Équihen in the Pas-de-Calais, where Alec was a strict 'camp commandant'. Staff who offended, just like boys, were tasked with laboriously carrying buckets of water from the village well to the hilltop. Later, France would be out of bounds, but a permanent domestic retreat would be found in Kent to replace Horndon, which 'the Doctor' had donated to the diocese of Southwark.

Oxford remained the great annual treat, and an opportunity for reciprocity. It was organised largely by Paterson and Baron, both of whom had kept up their Oxford connections – indeed Alec maintained close contact with an admirer, Reginald Macan, Master of his old college.[57] The outing began with the excitement of the train journey there, followed by sightseeing and a lavish lunch, and culminated in escapades on or in the river, more food and a raucous medley processing down the High towards the station singing, unselfconsciously in those innocent days, 'let's be gay and hearty, don't break up the party.' Later, after Stansfeld had left the Mission, his son Gordon would organise an annual Oxford summer camp for the Bermondsey boys beside the Cherwell in the grounds of the Dragon School, of which he was then a pupil.[58]

For over two decades, apart from a four-year hiatus during the Great War, Bermondsey was to be home to Alec Paterson. It was 200 miles from Bowdon, and a world away. Even its best features, he wrote, 'have the sombreness of the second-rate'. On its 'mean' streets 'poverty has set its seal, and its many problems have sunk their tangled roots deep into the life of the people.' If 'goodness abounds' there is 'little greatness'.[59] The experience of this overcrowded, drab

55   Eagar, p. 103.
56   Baron, pp. 36–43.
57   Letter, 9th October 1911. Paterson went on this jaunt every year from 1903 to 1914 (*Letters*, 19th May 1915).
58   Baron, pp. 43f.
59   Paterson, p. 1.

Figure 11. Bermondsey in Oxford, 1907. Alec sits front centre
with William Temple to his right

and ignored underbelly of London would transform him. For all its poverty, for all the brutality and criminality, it had a vitality, gaiety, generosity and sense of community that, as he got to know the area and its people, beguiled him.

> Because streets are a bit narrow, or houses seem dark and untidy, the life within them is often conceived as one of perpetual strain and misery. Too little allowance is made for those many brave joys which even dirt and hunger cannot choke. The courts where Polly Crispin and Granny Smith live are its cobbled pathways, ill-lit at night and smelly in the summer-time. But when the children are out from school they are a far greater parade of happiness than any Casino in the South can show. They are the playground of unending and unnumbered games; and through a long evening of noise and disorder, there will be a dozen songs for every quarrel, a hundred shouts and chases for every tumble. The streets may be dark, but their very gutters brim with happiness. No colour breaks the close monotony of house and house,

but there is a vivacity of spirit and flush of life which neither art nor sanitation could create.[60]

He was describing the lives of those he called 'friends'. And he meant it. He deplored social segregation in itself, as well as the inequality and poverty that social segregation perpetuated. He echoed the concerns expressed by other resident professionals about the 'ignorance and apathy of landlords and employers as to the home conditions of their tenants or work-people; the selfish sluggishness of local administration [and] the powerlessness of paid officials to deal effectively with admitted evils.'[61] Apartheid led to indifference:

> Nowhere is the separation [of classes] so marked as in the city of London. The land of dividends is roughly in the West; beyond the Bank or across the bridges is a vast unknown land of wages. If only the houses of rich and poor lay side by side, and flats were also tenements, poverty would never have grown so baffling ... From this separation have arisen half the evils of poverty, and reform can only come through a union that is based on mutual sympathy and understanding.

Break down the barriers which had been largely erected by the industrial revolution and the growth of great cities and there was no need to take to the barricades. He thought that 'the greatest national danger was that we should cease to be a nation altogether, and become two nations.' Patriotism, for Alec and many like him, went arm in arm with social activism. Graduates going to inner-city settlements 'gained knowledge of the other nine-tenths of their fellow-countrymen', and 'made their own lives happier', because new avenues of thought and study, of observation and reflection, were opened up along with 'new channels of friendship and affection'. Legislators, before they framed policies, 'should live in an ordinary street among poorer neighbours than they have previously known, not as philanthropists, but as learners and sharers ... With a change of spirit and a widening of horizon will come a sense of trouble, and shame and responsibility, and then at last will come the knowledge that gives a broad basis for reform.'[62]

His years in Bermondsey demonstrated that genuine and enduring friendships between members of the different classes were possible. It also imbued him with the conviction that the lot of those amongst whom he lived could and should be ameliorated. There was such waste of human potential. So much promise was blighted at birth. When a boy left school at fourteen there was no

60   Introduction to *Halfpenny Alley* (London, 1913) by Marjory Hardcastle, a nurse who boarded at, and worked from, the OMM.

61   The views of Henry Lewis, rector of St Mary Magdalene from 1896 to 1914, as relayed by Booth, *op.cit.*, p. 102.

62   Paterson, pp. 268ff; speech delivered in Oxford, 4th November 1911.

knowing whether 'he was stepping out into a long life of unemployment to a life in prison or ... his foot was on the bottom rung of a ladder that should lead to a complete life. It was all chance.' It was a national scandal and a loss to the nation. The life chances of the young in particular could be transformed, were they just given some of the educational advantages of their middle-class peers, and a modicum of the self-confidence that a good education imbued. 'The primary object of a school', he contended, was 'not to convey knowledge or to teach a trade, but to make boys into men.' This task could be done only with much 'patience ... watching, wisdom and sympathy'.[63]

He would try his hand at the task himself, for a while working unpaid as a supernumerary teacher in the Riley Street elementary school. Before doing so he consulted with Augustine Birrell, the President of the Board of Education, who approved his project.[64] In order to do so he had to give up the civil service post which had earned him a meagre living since leaving Oxford, and rely on his savings and on money sent to him by his mother.

The council school itself was the usual 'three-decker', with classes of forty or more boys aged between five and thirteen. It was hard going at first for Alec until he had gained the confidence of the staff and the pupils. The former were won over by charm and tact; the latter by the interest he showed in them both in and out of school, visiting their homes and befriending their families. He noted the distinction that while in such schools there were teachers who commuted from the suburbs and served a limited and over-regulated function, there were masters in village secondary schools who lived nearby, or in public schools on site, with the 'power to mould and develop' their charges. The former were so often drudges with a grievance, the latter missionaries with a vocation. Yet the teaching staff he encountered were admirable, the women in particular being much involved in the lives of the children, making home visits and buying them food out of their own money.[65] Yet they laboured under many disadvantages that would make public-school masters 'pale before their task and sink beneath the handicap'. The size of the class and the daily choice between the Scylla of noise if the windows of the classroom were open and the Charybdis of smell if they were shut were but two of the factors militating against their best efforts. Books being scarce, there was a prodigious use of blackboard and slate. Discipline being hard to achieve, it was maintained by the ready application of the cane.

63   Paterson, pp. 82, 268ff.

64   *London Evening News*, 25th February 1911. Through his family's connections and from his own exertions, Alec always had useful contacts in high places.

65   Alec was also strongly in favour of women doctors but there was only 'one among a riverside population of a million in South London' (*Letters*, 7th April 1916).

The conditions in which the children lived added to the burden of their teachers. Many of the pupils, sharing meagre rations with equally famished siblings and sharing beds with them as well, came to school tired out, scantily clad and palpably hungry. These 'small and feeble folk' would sit 'limp and chill' on the school benches, unable to concentrate.[66] Even for the better-clad and better-fed long boring holidays, spent in idleness on the streets, would undo much of any progress made in class. Parents, alienated from the school which made no attempt to engage them, were easy to enrage, and would take umbrage over any criticism of their offspring, but would do nothing to enhance their educational prospects. To supplement an uncertain family income, or to compensate for its dissipation on alcohol, schoolchildren from the age of nine or so would be expected to get a weekend job delivering newspapers or helping at the greengrocers or coal merchants, or even an after-school job working in a shop until 10pm. Some of the more entrepreneurial set up their own businesses, buying watercress 'on tick' in 'half-pad' (as the market baskets were called) from a dealer, and selling it in bunches from a barrow pitched in the gutter outside the Old Dun Cow in the Old Kent Road.[67]

At fourteen children were adults; at fourteen they would leave school; at fourteen they would earn a full-time living for themselves and buttress the family income. A few precious years of disrupted schooling and so little achieved. And if achieved, so little retained thereafter:

> Boys who might have been classical scholars stick labels onto parcels for ten years; others who have literary gifts clear out a brewer's vat. Real thinkers work as porters in metal warehouses, and after shouldering iron fittings for eleven hours a day, find it difficult to set their minds in order ... With even the average boy there is a marked waste of mental capital between the ages of ten and thirty, and the aggregate loss to the country is heavy indeed.[68]

The waste!

Further, the curriculum in Riley Street and in other such schools was restricted, based on the 'three Rs' of reading, writing and arithmetic, ensuring proficiency in all three but, in Paterson's view, little else. These were merely the rudiments of a proper education, the foundation but not the structure. In overcrowded classes so much of geography and history was learnt by rote, and so much got mangled in the mind that 'all persons by the name of William' become 'one composite personality who conquers, has red hair, is silent, and has something to do with an orange'. He was averse to what we would call comprehensive education. All from the brightest to the dimmest had to follow the same

---

66   Booth, *First Series: Poverty*, vol. 3, part II: *London Children*, p. 207.
67   Gutman, pp. 308–311.
68   Paterson, pp. 259f.

syllabus, frustrating the former and baffling the latter. Such an approach trained clever boys to be clerks when they could aspire to a profession. 'The powers of voluntary thought and reason, of spontaneous inquiry and imagination' inculcated in well-to-do children by the public schools, 'have not been stirred'.[69]

So far as he could he sought to transform school life along club lines, by infusing it with camaraderie, enthusing pupils in their studies, instituting house colours to engage their innate sense of loyalty, and instilling the 'strict ethic' of sportsmanship by organising cricket and football matches. With greater self-discipline there was far less need of corporal punishment. One admiring observer concluded that by his efforts he had 'achieved among the boys a remarkable *esprit de corps* for what he called "Riley College"'.[70] His success in a Bermondsey school for local lads would inform his later approach to the development of the borstal system for delinquents.

During his long sojourn in South London, Alec accrued a formidable expertise in dealing with difficult and troubled youngsters in school and out, in all of whom he found a 'natural goodness'.[71] It was by consorting with many boys and young men who fell foul of the law that he had developed an interest in the criminal justice and prison systems. His endeavours soon came to the attention of another old acquaintance, Herbert Samuel, a radical Liberal MP and Under-Secretary of State at the Home Office, who around the same time employed Barkis as his private secretary.[72]

Samuel consulted Paterson over the provisions certainly of one and probably of two Bills which would be enacted in 1908 as the Children Act and the Prevention of Crime Act respectively. Paterson contributed over twenty amendments to the former, all of which were incorporated into the Act; his contribution to the latter is more difficult to assess.[73] The differentiation of juveniles from adult offenders was the key to both.

By instituting a national system of juvenile courts, abolishing the death penalty for young persons aged between fourteen and sixteen, extending the use of probation, ending imprisonment for children under fourteen and

69   Paterson, p. 65. Yet he was very much in favour of breaking down barriers in education, enabling those from different social classes but of similar abilities to learn in the same school classroom. Grammar schools, though he never mentioned them, fulfilled this task.

70   Baron, p. 163. *Esprit de corps* was a term much used by Paterson and many others at that time. He thought it hard to instil a sense of loyalty in schools named after streets. With 'an unimaginative sameness about the buildings', they were 'wonderfully and fearfully alike' with little to differentiate them. A school should be 'a world in itself, and more than a mere unit in a great uniform system' (Paterson, p. 94).

71   Paterson, p. 262.

72   Baron, *One Man's Pattern* (London, n.d.), p. 14.

73   Baron, 'Across the Bridges', p. 34; Bailey (1987), p. 9, n.9.

restricting it to young persons certified as being 'unruly or depraved', the Children Act transformed the criminal justice system's approach to the delinquent young. For these and the other protective measures it enacted it would soon become known as 'The Children's Charter'. The Prevention of Crime Act was just as significant, placing the innovative borstal system on a statutory basis, creating a new sentence of 'detention under penal discipline in a borstal institution', and authorising the Prison Commissioners to expand the scheme by acquiring land or buildings for that purpose. It was due to Samuel, perhaps acting on Alec's advice, that the institution for reforming young offenders 'of criminal habits or tendencies' was memorably named 'Borstal' and not the more cumbersome 'Juvenile-Adult Reformatory', but if Alec's sway had been greater the phrase 'under penal discipline' would have been omitted. Both Acts would reduce the number sent to prison. These were Paterson's first achievements in the arena of penal reform in which he would play so prolonged and influential a part.[74]

An earlier first-hand encounter with the prison system had enraged him. On a sunny day in early 1907,[75] attired in tweed coat and grey flannel trousers, he arrived at the gate of Brixton prison, where he was 'coldly surveyed' by the keeper. He had gone to visit a 'young friend', a nineteen-year-old club member called Jimmy Jones, who had been remanded there to await trial at the Old Bailey for murder. It was his first offence. Jimmy's father was a drunkard, his mother a prostitute. When his girl, Dolly, fell pregnant, Jimmy married her on Christmas Day 1906, and thereafter the newly-weds stayed with the young wife's widowed mother, Catherine. Despite Jimmy's efforts to find work, Catherine, who was often drunk, nagged and tormented him about being unemployed, and when he was hospitalised she pawned his boots and clothes. The baby was born in February 1907. Two months later Jimmy snapped and cut Dolly's throat with a bread-knife after she accused him of being 'a lazy bastard', threatened to leave him and hit him twice. Alec sat in the visiting box and conversed with the killer through three thicknesses of wire mesh. As they parted the young man asked, 'You'll see me out of this, won't you Pat, and I'm leaving the baby to you.' Alec agreed to arrange for his defence, and to adopt the three-month-old boy whom the lad's actions had effectively orphaned.[76]

---

74 Grew, p. 16; Baron, p. 164. Baron makes no mention of the latter Act and nor does Alec in his CV, but it would be surprising if he had not been similarly engaged.

75 In *Over the Walls* and elsewhere, Paterson erroneously gave the date as 1906. Other writers repeat his mistake.

76 *Over the Walls*, p. 3. As a single man, Paterson felt incompetent to raise the baby himself and so paid 'excellent foster-parents in the country' to give the child a home and bring him up properly. Twenty-five years later they were still in touch, the young man by then well-educated, in permanent employment and happily married (Ruck, p. 32).

In April Jimmy was tried at the Old Bailey. Convicted of manslaughter, he was sentenced to ten years' penal servitude. Dartmoor convict prison was to be his fate.[77]

Having visited him in Brixton Alec continued to do so in Dartmoor. In the summer he made the first of many monthly journeys there, cycling all the way by night since 'daylight and the cost of the fare from London were required for other causes'. It was an arduous journey: over 200 miles by road and uphill much of the way as the prison is 1,400 feet above sea level. On arrival, tired and bedraggled, and despite having come from the urban squalor of Bermondsey, he was appalled by what he saw in this grim 'iron and granite' edifice: hundreds of convicts in drab broad-arrow uniforms, with closely shaven heads and faces covered with a sort of dirty moss, reduced to utter servility, each one pressing his face to the wall as visitors passed. This was 'to avoid assault or familiarity, the two great offences in prison conduct, the relative gravity of which no one has ever assessed'.[78] It resulted in prisoners being ground down, losing all individuality, and sinking to such a 'depravity and degradation of life' it was impossible to exaggerate. They were the personification of hopelessness, but hopelessness was not a condition Alec could tolerate or countenance. He was an incurable optimist who believed in the redeemability of all, and especially of the young. He would never give up on them. The visits to Jimmy continued throughout the sentence, and on his early release on licence Alec would give him temporary accommodation, before helping him and his son emigrate to a new life overseas.[79]

'The frightened pup' was not the only beneficiary of such hospitality. Alec recalled that he had come 'to my tenement by the riverside to sleep in the spare bed which had been occupied only a short time previously by a young clergyman called William Temple'.[80] Temple was an old friend and frequent visitor both to the club – where he was just plain 'Bill' – and on its excursions

---

77   *Old Bailey Proceedings Online*, April 1907, Trial of James Albert Jones. Convict prisons, as opposed to local prisons, held the more serious criminals, those sentenced to terms of 'penal servitude' (imprisonment for three years or more).

78   *Over the Walls*, p. 7; Ruck, p. 11; W.G.V. Davis, *Gentlemen of the Broad Arrows* (London, 1939), p. 21. Benjamin Grew, on his arrival in 1926 as deputy-governor at this 'most feared and hated prison', shared Paterson's disquiet. He noted the 'pervading atmosphere of gloom and abandonment' and the 'silent and dejected [convicts] trudging along the road flanked by two officers carrying carbines' (Grew, pp. 39ff.).

79   Their photographs stood on his mantelpiece as long as he lived (Baron, p. 165). Jimmy was released before mid-1914 (*Diary*, 17th–20th August 1914).

80   Alexander Paterson, 'The Triple Alliance', *PJ*, April 1939, pp. 72–74, at p. 73. Previously Temple, who had first visited the club as far back as 1901, had stayed in the Mission itself. In a letter to his wife, written long afterwards, he reminisced: 'it is the only place where I have found bugs of the large brown variety in my bed and

to Essex. He was also another very remarkable individual. With a brilliant mind, photographic memory and oratorical flair, he was destined to become the most influential Anglican archbishop of the twentieth century. Yet he was, and remained, unpretentious, fat, funny and gregarious. With an infectious and unstoppable laugh, he was welcome in any society and had the ability to be at ease with, and to put at ease, anyone from any background that he encountered. He proved a great hit in Bermondsey clubs and on Bermondsey camps. He was greatly impressed and influenced by what he witnessed there, just as the boys were impressed and influenced by him.[81] In 1907, while still a don, he hosted the annual Whit Monday expedition to Oxford. He can be seen in a photograph sitting on Queen's College lawn with fifty Bermondsey boys around him, and Alec in the centre. The same year Temple took a place on the Mission's general committee, and retained an executive role throughout his many elevations. He acknowledged at the time to Randall Davidson, the then Archbishop of Canterbury, that his involvement with the South London Settlement had enlarged and deepened his faith. It was no surprise that he would become one of the leading proponents of a welfare state that would bind the people together in human amity, not entrench them in class enmity. Divided by differences of class, wealth and religion, society, he believed, needed to become a community grounded on common values, and with a common identity.[82] Although there was no common religion and perhaps there never had been, there had long been a common language and a common law. There also had to be a commonwealth, a 'New Jerusalem', built on justice in England's green and pleasant land. He first saw the stonemasons of such social integration at work in Bermondsey. Their begetter, 'The Doctor', was regarded by Temple as one of 'the greatest men and truest Christians' he had ever met.[83]

Bermondsey seemed to be irresistible to aspiring bishops and archbishops. Geoffrey Fisher, who would succeed Temple to the see of Canterbury in 1945, was one. He paid several 'casual' visits to Bermondsey, at first timorously when he was an undergraduate at Exeter College, Oxford, and then more boldly as an ordinand and young clergyman. Like so many others he volunteered to help supervise the Horndon summer camp. Few as these visits were they 'coloured

so I have what the Archbishop [Lang] calls "sacred memories"' (F.A. Iremonger, *William Temple* [Oxford, 1948], p. 41).

81   Iremonger, *op.cit.*, p. 43.
82   John Kent, *William Temple* (Cambridge, 1992), pp. 2f. See Figure 11.
83   Baron, p. 154. Temple would maintain his contacts with Bermondsey until his death.

and influenced [his] whole life'. Later, as headmaster of Repton, he would have Stansfeld's son, Gordon, in his own house.[84]

Eminent and influential as they would become these were but visitors to, or at most short-term residents in, South London, as were the many curates and Oxford dons who associated themselves with the Mission and went on, almost invariably, to high ecclesiastical preferment. Others would achieve recognition for their later work. One in particular stands out. Tubby Clayton, as irreverent as he was rotund, came under the sway of 'the Franciscan figure of Dr Stansfeld' when he had 'passed like the Pied Piper, through the "Varsity" and bidden us to the boys' clubs at Dockhead, Gordon, and Decima'. Responding, he attached himself 'to the tail of that most Christian comet which led far wiser men to Bermondsey'.[85] Between 1909 and 1910 Tubby, 'trailing a cloak of delicious whimsy', became an irregular Thursday night visitor, and thereafter, having become a curate in Portsea, he continued to pop in when he could. Short and intermittent as his involvement in Bermondsey was, it had a profound and lasting effect on him. He would go on to replicate the ethos of the place and the spirit of the people in his enduring creations, Talbot House and the Toc H. movement. He always acknowledged the great debt he owed to Barclay Baron and Alec Paterson in particular.[86]

But for Alec Bermondsey was no transit camp but a terminus. It became his home, as it did for Barkis who, in 1909, after his return from lengthy sojourns in Germany and Italy, finally moved into the Mission on a permanent basis.[87] So

---

84   Geoffrey Fisher's foreword to *The Doctor*. Paterson, Baron and Stansfeld were all present at the camp (p. 42, Plate III). This was in 1907, the same year as the first Scout camp at Brownsea Island, Poole.

85   P.B. Clayton, *Plain Tales from Flanders* (London, 1929), p. 106. The short and chunky Philip Clayton, who 'reversing Euclid had breadth and thickness but no length to speak of', was universally known as 'Tubby'. He was well-connected. He knew Bill Temple from his time at Colet Court Preparatory School, and Bernard Montgomery and Gilbert Chesterton from his days at St Paul's School. Indeed, some traits of Chesterton's famous sleuth, Father Brown, may have been modelled on Tubby. Another influential friend was Geoffrey Fisher, whom Tubby met when they were contemporaries at Exeter College. Although Tubby matriculated in 1905 there is no evidence that he knew Alec, who was then in his final year at Oxford.

86   Linda Parker, *A Fool for Thy Feast* (Solihull, 2015), p. 31; Baron, p. 207 and *The Birth of a Movement* (London, 1946), p. 3.

87   Alec was delighted, knowing Barclay was as tireless as he, and could do more than just devote his time exclusively to Bermondsey. Alec encouraged his friend to diversify, and would urge him to become the first editor of *The Challenge*, a new Anglican newspaper (or 'socialist rag') that he was helping to set up. Barclay took up the post in 1914 but the following year relinquished the editorship to William Temple (Baron, *One Man's Pattern*, p. 14; Iremonger, *op.cit.*, p. 183; Snape, pp. 266ff.).

FIGURE 12. Horndon, 1907. Alec sits first left on the second row.
Next to him is 'The Doctor', Barkis stands behind, holding a white hat

too would it become for Waldo Eagar, another Oxford contemporary, who after the Great War would take over the running of the OBM and write a history of the boys' club movement. With him at times Alec would have an uneasy relationship. They were both strong personalities, and in the small world of boys' clubs big egos could clash. That was never the case between Paterson and Attlee, perhaps because of the latter's temperament, or because his turf was elsewhere. During his ten-year sojourn in the East End, Clem would visit Alec frequently to discuss their similar experiences, but they were never in competition.

The same was true of others who came to work among the poor of Bermondsey. One particular ally was 'The Princess'[88], of the Dockhead Time and Talents Club for factory girls. Time and Talents was a nationwide and eventually international evangelical enterprise that sought to engage young women of the leisured classes in the service of those less fortunate than themselves. At the

---

88   Alec never identified 'The Princess', but stated that 'she married the junior curate of the parish church and went to be a bishop's lady in a palace.' This must be Grace Stewart (née Allen), a widow living at 187 Bermondsey Street who married Clifford Woodward in 1905.

request of Canon Henry Lewis, the local incumbent, a T&T settlement had been established in 1899 at 187 Bermondsey Street, next to St Mary's. The rather dilapidated premises comprised a club room and other spaces where classes on Christianity, health, cookery, reading, writing and painting were held. In 1903 an offshoot opened at 1 Halfpenny Alley, Dockhead, under the indomitable Violet Tritton and her principal assistant, Catherine Scott-Moncrieff. It remained there until 1910, when it relocated to bigger and better premises at 5 Jamaica Road. From its inception its staff worked closely with Stansfeld and his helpers.

'The Princess' stood out even among her remarkable co-workers, with 'every place she entered' being the 'sweeter and cleaner for her presence'. She knew 'the art of fanning good intentions into the flame of self-sacrificing actions'.[89] She also knew, was warmly accepted by, and closely identified with, the people of Bermondsey. For several years she and Alec 'shared and swapped human problems'. Their earliest encounter was in 1906 when she came to complain that a young man who had left Wandsworth prison a few months before had impregnated one of her club girls. She had just been round to see the girl and found her lying on the floor of a little back room in a dark court off the Tower Bridge Road, waiting for the baby to arrive, with no bedding, no baby clothes, and no preparations of any sort. She asked Alec to arrange for a wedding in the parish church as soon as possible. This was duly done for the following Saturday afternoon. As best man, Alec's duties began in earnest.

> The liberty outfit with which he had been presented at the gates of Wandsworth prison seemed a little grim and scanty for a bridegroom at the altar rails. We returned to my bachelor lodging, where I found the sub-fusc suit in which I had faced the examiners in Greats a bare fortnight before, and what had so recently clothed a budding philosopher adorned a blushing bridegroom. There was something missing, even when the bridegroom was suitably arrayed. 'What about a ring? Have you got one?' But the only ring he had known for many months had been a hand-cuff, and that hardly matches the spirit of the marriage service. So I repaired hurriedly to the largest pawnbroker in the Old Kent Road and was shown tray upon tray of rings, with every sort of flashy stone and graded in prices that would accommodate a bookmaker or a bookseller. The process, however, was not quite so simple as it seemed. The hopeful young assistant drew attention to the great variety of sizes and asked whether the lady in question had a large or small hand. When I stated with all the finality of truth that I could not be expected to know as I had never seen her, he was so startled that he nearly collapsed behind the counter. He could not be sure whether it was just courage or an old custom that was leading a man to take a chance.

---

89   Marjorie Daunt, *By Peaceful Means: The Story of Time and Talents 1887–1987* (London, 1989), pp. 4, 27ff., 32.

The marriage was duly solemnised, the baby born and baptized.[90]

On a later occasion 'the Princess' sent a girl called Charlotte round to see him. She was a club member who had married a young riverside thief called Alf, and was 'already laying the foundations of a large family on the somewhat uncertain base of casual labour, tuberculosis and a two-roomed tenement.' Charlotte was 'a nice-looking girl and even the juggernaut of the worst of private enterprise and laissez-faire had not removed all traces of the Madonna in her eyes and in her smile.' She was also 'one of the countless young heroines of the South London riverside, utterly devoted to her selfish husband and snuffling babies, and passionate in their protection and defence.' She told Alec that she had come to see him about her husband.

> You know all about him because last time he was up at Tower Bridge for pinching at the wharf, you put in a word for him. Perhaps that was why he only got six months when he'd expected twelve. His mates who were with him on the same charge all got six months too, so they're all coming out together on Monday morning. I've been to see my Alf in Wandsworth, and he's wrote me some beautiful letters all about what the chaplain said in chapel on Sunday.

She told Pat that Alf was 'not really a bad lot'. He didn't knock her about 'as some fellers do'. He was also kind to the children. When the third one died, he, impecunious as he was, bought a lovely wreath for the grave. But with his mates he had no mind of his own and was easily swayed. Although he had promised faithfully that this would be his last time in prison, she was worried that when he and his friends were released on the Monday morning, he would go with them to the nearest pub rather than going straight home. If the former it would not be long before he would be back in prison again. To entice him, she had promised to have his favourite breakfast on the table.

> He's very partial to haddock, is my Alf. But he likes it cooked in a special way, and I'm the only person who knows exactly how he likes it. And I'll have the kids all cleaned up and tidy for him, and a nice fire in the grate, and his Sunday paper, and he can put as much sugar in his tea as he likes, and pick out the best bits of the haddock and hand them to the kids. That's what he likes best, giving the kids just what they want.

But how could she be sure he would come straight home? Alec was the answer.

> What I want you to do, and the Princess says you're the man to do it, is to be outside them Wandsworth gates at 7am on Monday. You know Alf and he knows you. If you'll just go up to him – I don't mean tap him on the shoulder and say come along, like a copper – but just step up and put a hand and say 'Charlotte says she got a lovely haddock ready and all the kids are asking for

90 *Over the Walls*, p. 21. The young father would lead his section gallantly but fatally on the Somme.

you', I think that'll fetch him, and he'll leave his mates at the prison where they belong, and come straight home to me.

Alec took some convincing that this was the best course of action. Being rather proud of his culinary skills, and having cooked haddock for many years to his entire satisfaction, he was inclined to think she was miscasting the parts and that he might prove a better cook and she the better cajoler. He suggested that they reverse roles. He would 'come round early in the morning and prepare the sumptuous breakfast, so tempting after six months of prison porridge and margarine. She would attend at the prison gates and prevail upon Alf to come "straight home"'. She was unconvinced and Alec relented. The Monday morning came, and at 7am he reached the Wandsworth gates.

> A close rain and driving mist made the surroundings even more depressing than they were designed to be some hundred years or more ago. I joined a nondescript crowd of people presumably bound on an errand similar to my own. Events proceeded slowly in the next two hours. At intervals of ten or fifteen minutes the great gates swung very slowly open. They seemed unwilling to disgorge the flotsam and jetsam that the law had swept within their way, and which now must return to the seeding grounds of crime. Two or three would emerge, and one or two bystanders without the gates would drift forward and greet them. Then a pause and another batch. So the hours passed. The men being discharged stepped through the wicket gate with an attempt at jauntiness, then looked about them to see whether any one they knew or expected were there. They looked numb and dazed. Their faces were a bit pasty, as though they had been nursery gardeners in a hothouse. Their clothes were worn, faded and nondescript, such as the government in those days thought fitting for ex-prisoners and paupers. So far as shaving or hair cutting was concerned, they were ragged and unkempt. The suits they wore would be recognized by any well-informed police officer in London and fellow occupiers of a common lodging-house or casual ward, as being those of a man discharged from prison that morning. They said and shouted nothing. It was difficult to realise that men who had been long in exile were coming home at last. There was no sign or sound of jubilation or thanksgiving.

At last Alf emerged 'with his three or four mates grouped round him'. Alec told him about the haddock and he agreed to return to Charlotte as soon as he could. But first he had to bid farewell to his friends. With Alec in tow they adjourned to the Surrey Tavern for half pints to celebrate their release, 'and then Alf came along like a satisfied lamb to rejoin his Charlotte'. A job well done. Alf would not yet forego his errant ways and would pay the price in prison. Charlotte would produce yet more children and prepare yet more haddock for his release.[91]

---

91   *Over the Walls*, pp. 22–24.

In Alec's personal life there had been significant developments during this period: a death on the one hand and a new beginning on the other.

On Tuesday 19th May 1908 his father, while visiting the Uffizi gallery in Florence, suddenly dropped dead. His mother was devastated. When Churchill wrote a letter of condolence, she was so upset she burnt it.[92] The impact on Alec is not known. Since going down from Oxford he had scarcely spent more than a few weeks at home. Although there are no extant letters between them, we do know from Alec's later correspondence that he was devoted to his father and never forgot the anniversary of his death.[93] However hard the blow, Alec would let nothing interfere with his work,[94] and, because his siblings were still living at home with his widowed mother, he could justify his prolonged absence. Nor had he money to contribute to the familial coffers, but as his father had left over £4,000 in his will, and both his brothers were in well-remunerated employment, there was little need.

The following year Alec took the final step in a long pilgrimage from Dissent to Conformity. If Oxford had sown the seed, Stansfeld had nurtured the shoots and reaped the harvest. Alec had come to Bermondsey 'as a Unitarian, militant in this as in all the principles he held, but a short spell alongside the Doctor changed this deep-founded family tradition'. One night Alec told a friend: 'You simply cannot walk the streets of Bermondsey with him and not know that Jesus is divine.'[95] Example was all, not theological niceties. Stansfeld was an Anglican, so too would be his disciple. On 9th March 1909 Alec, while still living in Abbey Street, had been baptized into the Church of England by his friend, Leonard Compton. The sacrament itself took place at St Michael the Archangel's, Aldershot. Why that church was chosen over St Mary's Bermondsey is not clear.[96] Alec would remain a regular communicant of the Established Church for the rest of his life, and was both married and cremated according to Anglican rites.

92 Communication from Katharine Draper. A memorial service was held on 23rd May.

93 *Letters*, 19th May 1915.

94 At some stage during these years he was engaged to be married, but broke off the engagement when his prospective parents-in-law insisted, as a precondition of the union, that he relinquish his flat in Bermondsey and move somewhere more fitting (Katharine Draper).

95 Baron, p. 162.

96 *Baptismal Register*, Surrey History Centre. Compton graduated from Keble College, Oxford in 1889 and was curate in Bermondsey from 1908 to 1910, during which time he resided in the OMM. He left to become vicar of Kidderminster (*Crockford's Clerical Directory*).

Thus he was all the more equipped to take a leading role in the Bermondsey boys' clubs when in 1910 Stansfeld, who to the surprise of his staff had recently been ordained, was appointed vicar of the rather genteel St Anne's church, Bermondsey. Although nearby, it would absorb all his time and energy until two years later, for the sake of his daughter's health, he left the area permanently for St Ebbe's, a poor parish in Oxford with which Alec had been well-acquainted. Stansfeld's departure from Bermondsey was not an abandonment of his work there but an expression of confidence in its continuance, albeit along different lines and with no medical provision. He had founded clubs, created a tradition that would outlast him, and gathered around him a vigorous group of men who should be allowed to develop the work in their own way.[97] Thus he could leave his mission in safe hands, with Alec its guiding light and Barkis its warden. Both were 'willin'.

97   Eagar, p. 234.

Chapter 4

Bridging the Gap: 1910–1914

Ideally there should be two officers to each tent, one a trained club officer, the other fresh from school or college. Nowhere is the combination of qualities represented by the two so useful as in camp; nowhere can the shyness of the public school-boy be more quickly or naturally broken down and the way opened to real friendships. It is hard to remain conventional when sharing the task of washing up greasy plates, wearing the same simple camp kit and maintaining the tent's fortunes on the camp football field. Each type learns to appreciate the qualities which the other can contribute to the common stock.

Hubert Secretan

After the departure of 'the Doctor' and the end of its medical role, his foundation was renamed the Oxford and Bermondsey Mission, a telling duality stressing the mutuality of the association and the interconnectedness of those who had previously inhabited different worlds. The mission 'was no longer Oxford's effort to save Bermondsey, but a fraternal association of Oxford men with Bermondsey men and men-to-be, which had completely overcome barriers of class and education.' Indeed the novel idea of democratic self-governance in boys' clubs was initiated in Bermondsey by Paterson and his co-workers.[1] Going even further than the aspirations of Barnett and the practice of Stansfeld, Alec encouraged the members of the clubs to run their own shows, pay their own way, form their own management committees, and make and enforce their own rules. Bermondsey and Oxford were in it together. '*Liberté, Égalité, Fraternité*' could have been their motto, but they kept to the single word that encapsulated them all, *Fratres*. Alec composed a prayer for the future of this reconfigured venture:

O Thou that didst give us the Colleges at Oxford and the Clubs in Bermondsey, the love of friends and the shelter of home, teach us to honour and

1   Eagar, p. 236.

to use these gifts aright; and grant that, living in the presence of Christ and learning day by day the power of prayer, we may be strong in temptation, patient in trouble and faithful even unto death.[2]

Alec, the heir to the throne, had refused the succession, abdicating in favour of Barclay Baron. Indeed Alec would continue to support a series of wardens who came and went while he remained, digging himself ever more deeply into the life of Bermondsey. They would all readily admit that while he sometimes crossed them he more often led them. It was a pattern that would be repeated much later when he became the leading light in the Prison Commission for a quarter of a century but never its chairman. The role of a somewhat insubordinate *eminence grise* seemed to suit him.

Such dedication to his calling and accumulation of expertise did not go unnoticed, and was rewarded when, in 1910, at Churchill's bidding, the eager young optimist was recruited by Sir Evelyn Ruggles-Brise, chairman of the Prison Commission and Green devotee, as assistant director of his newly-created Central Association for the Aid of Discharged Convicts. This was very much an Idealist project aimed at unifying all individuals and agencies working with discharged convicts in order to provide more effective after-care for the most alienated.[3] The initial invitation came in a typically Churchillian manner. Alec had some forewarning of it, as he invited Barkis to dine with him at his club and to keep him company as he waited nervously for some news. Alec was called from the table to the telephone. It was Churchill himself, speaking from the House in the middle of a debate on civil service estimates to tell him that he had secured a small grant for a new venture upon which Alec was to start immediately.[4] He leapt at it. Churchill would ensure the formalities of his appointment were expedited and rubber-stamped by Ruggles-Brise.

Alec's duties involved interviewing in his office everyone discharged from the convict prisons. In addition he had to – or chose to – visit each convict prison at least once a month, some undertaking, but revelatory. Aylesbury held women convicts, while Dartmoor, Maidstone, Parkhurst, Portland and Wakefield held men. All were demoralising, but Dartmoor was the worst by far, meriting even more frequent visits than the rest. He grew to detest the place where 'an evil tradition hung like a fog about its walls and cells, a malicious sort of miasma seep[ing] like a Dartmoor mist through the bodies and souls of men,

---

2   Baron, p. 212.
3   Report (1911–1912), pp. 117–123. The Central Association began its work on 1st January 1911. It was chaired by Ruggles-Brise. Grant-Wilson was vice-chairman, and Basil Thompson, the Secretary of the Prison Commission, was its secretary. Thompson, that 'most humane of all prison governors in those times', when in charge of Dartmoor had authorised Alec's visiting Jimmy Jones.
4   Baron, 'Across the Bridges', *Four Men* (London, n.d.), pp. 30–40, at p. 37.

or like a Dartmoor bog suck[ing] their souls to the lowest depths, rusting and staining and weakening all it touched.'[5]

He went far and beyond the call of duty, as Stephen Hobhouse related. They had first encountered each other in 1907 when Hobhouse, the nephew of Sidney and Beatrice Webb, had been doing social work at Toynbee Hall. In January 1914 Hobhouse, who had been deeply moved by *Across the Bridges* [*infra.*], 'the greatest inspiration in [his] life', visited the author's Dockhead flat. There he discovered that Alec lived like any other in that squalid area and even opened up his home to those in need. Most significantly he made a practice of accommodating discharged convicts in their first precarious days of freedom. This unconventional welcome back to the world was crucial:

> If anything could set their feet upon the right road, a visit to this dedicated Christian and fine athletic personality, living in austere conditions comparable to those of prison and to the homes from which many of these criminals came, would do so.

Hobhouse was 'profoundly impressed' by the utter dedication to and identification with the underdog he had witnessed in South London. He had spent much time at Toynbee Hall and Oxford House but found them 'much too comfortable for [his] present purposes, an "oasis" of academic life, whose doors shut one off from the drab poverty of most of the homes around.' On Alec's advice he too, in his 'self-identification with the oppressed', opted to live at the top of a slum tenement flat in Hoxton. It was a transformative experience.[6]

Alec's exposure to the convict system entrenched his views that things had to change. There had to be a better way. He was not alone in his concerns. On several occasions John Galsworthy came to see him about a young man serving a sentence of penal servitude in Portland. Alec agreed to accompany the famous writer on a visit. Galsworthy was enraged by what he saw and wrote his denunciatory play, *Justice*, as a result.[7]

The Central Association was the entree into the prison world Paterson had been waiting for, and in addition it introduced him to that part of it to which he would devote more effort than any other – the borstal system. The reason for this was that it shared not just an office at 15 Buckingham Street with the Borstal Association, but also a director in Wemyss Grant-Wilson.

The Borstal Association had been set up in 1904 by Ruggles-Brise, as a necessary adjunct to his great creation, to help discharged 'borstalians'. Grant-Wilson put his stamp upon it and shaped its future. He was self-confident and outspoken, and so too would be his Association. He was kindly but authoritative, and

---

5   *Over the Walls*, p. 10.
6   Stephen Hobhouse, *Forty Years and an Epilogue* (London, 1951), pp. 133f., 174, 179.
7   *Over the Walls*, pp. 8–10; *Letters*, 4th August 1915.

kindly but authoritative mentoring was what he demanded of his volunteers. Supervision on release as well as gainful employment were thought to be vital factors in preventing re-offending, and providing the one and helping find the other were tasks these 'earnest and philanthropic gentlemen' could perform. The gentlemen were the social superiors of their charges, and could command respect and deference – or dismay. With patronage coming from the upper echelons of the State, the Church and the Law, the Borstal Association also had clout within respectable circles and influence with employers, not all of whom were eager to take on offenders.[8] Emigration for some and seafaring for many seemed ideal alternatives. Both would provide a fresh start, a milder version of transportation. Unfunded and independent, and with growing confidence and reputation, in time the Association would prove a Trojan horse, as its members – prodded by Paterson – were amongst the first to criticise the penal character of borstal and 'the inadequacy of the present system of training', and to question Ruggles-Brise's depiction of the inmates as 'young hooligans advanced in crime'.[9] At present they were content to testify to his creation's success, the low re-conviction rates published in its early annual reports providing a 'remarkable justification for the experiment'.[10]

Alec was eager not just to deal with the resettlement of 'old lags' but to become intimately involved with this radical and innovative approach to the treatment of young delinquents. He would go on to become a member of the Borstal Association's executive committee, its honorary agent for the supervision of borstal boys returning to Bermondsey, and by 1914 its Assistant Director. He would write articles on its behalf – including one putting the case for the appointment of a Prison Commissioner with a special interest in borstals[11] – and greatly influence the more progressive and critical stance that the organisation would take after the Great War. In the meantime he could at least have influence on the regime of the convict prisons. If these tasks were not enough, he became a volunteer probation officer at Tower Bridge Police

---

8   Moseley, p.xii. Jack Gordon bitterly contrasted the expectations raised by borstal training itself, and the rosy future promised, with the harsh reality of inadequate after-care, poor lodgings, lack of employment and the stigma attached to being a 'borstal boy' (pp. 210–217). The armed forces refused to accept ex-borstal boys, and even some boys' clubs rejected them (*The Magistrate*, September–October 1939, p. 245). Similarly, Cyril Joyce, in his autobiography, reproduced a lengthy appraisal sent to him by one of his former charges for whom the only negative was the lasting stain attached to the appellation 'borstal boy' (*By Courtesy of the Criminal* [London, 1955], pp. 120–134).

9   Radzinowicz, pp. 396f.

10   Shane Leslie, *Sir Evelyn Ruggles-Brise* (London, 1938), p. 142f; Hood, p. 204.

11   Neale, pp. 27–56, at p. 44; Hood, p. 172.

Court, a post he would hold for over three years. He was immersing himself in the criminal justice system.

Despite these new commitments he was still deeply involved with the youth of Bermondsey and would retain an active interest in the area for the rest of his life. The fate of the young was always on his mind. He wrote to *The Morning Post* appealing for support for a proposed scheme of child emigration to Newfoundland in preference to the then current practice of expatriating late adolescents to Canada. Alec had been particularly concerned about the fate of older boys who fell out of work at the age of eighteen only to trudge from factory to warehouse in the morning in the vain quest for a job, and loaf around the rest of the time, aimlessly frittering away their lives, scrounging cigarettes and food, until they were ripe for emigration. Many went woefully ill-equipped to accommodate themselves to the very different conditions of Canada, and soon returned to England to recommence their futile round. By contrast, younger children would, he believed, more readily adapt themselves to novel surroundings and adopt Canada as their homeland. He was particularly taken by the first farm school in Newfoundland where 'responsibility and reward are wisely mingled as the chief agents in producing character and knowledge'.[12]

But most would stay. Boys would become men. Something should be done for them, some social provision made. To help raise funds for the Stansfeld Memorial Fund, Alec wrote *The Doctor and the OMM*, a lively and attractive little pamphlet in an Oxford blue cover with silver lettering. Money poured in, the boys of the Abbey Street Club were moved out to other premises nearby to constitute the Canterbury Club[13], and the old headquarters had Stansfeld's name painted on its facade, announcing its new work. 'The Doctor' 'came himself to declare [the Stansfeld Club] open on Guy Fawkes' Day 1911'.[14] Alec, 'the true founder and leader' of this venture, had high hopes that it would meet a need and prove a resource, as well as eradicate a growing problem: the reluctance of boys who had grown into men to move on. Some were recruited as 'officers'; others had to be persuaded to leave in the interests of the new intake:

> In the first place it must be remembered that in each of the so-called boys' clubs at Abbey Street, Dockhead, Decima and Bermondsey Street, there had grown up a set of fellows who stuck so closely to their club that they were

12 'The Child Emigration Scheme', *Morning Post*, 24th May 1910. Twenty years later another Oxford man with experience of Bermondsey would reiterate these concerns. 'To transport boys from city alleys almost direct to prairie farm or sheep-run is to court disaster' (Hubert Secretan, *London Below Bridges* [London, 1931], pp. 151f.).

13 So called because of its close link with the King's School of that city.

14 Baron, pp. 166, 172.

in danger of suffocating it. The majority of them refused to be confirmed[15] and had abstained from officership, but they had absorbed more thoroughly than we can understand the tradition of their club. They were good fellows, keen and prominent. Their only fault was that they were fast becoming *the Club*. And a club should never be a little coagulated set of good fellows, but a stream of tumbling youngsters all on the way to life. It was hoped then that these old stand-bys, the rank and file in each club, who were as a rule forming both its character and its opinions, might be welded together into the Stansfeld Club where they could stay until marriage or death or emigration at last dissolved them. They would leave far greater scope for the youngsters between 14 and 18, left behind in the boys' clubs, giving them a world to populate with their own ideas and opinions, with their own heroes and exploits.[16]

The new venture did succeed in keeping 'a nucleus of the best boys, now men, in the family circle of the Mission'. Then the War came, and changed everything. Of the men and boys of 'the Mission who marched away, 120 did not live to return'.[17]

Alec had been commissioned by Edward Arnold, the publisher, to write a book about his experiences in Bermondsey. He had tried out the chapters when still in manuscript form on his long-suffering friend, Barkis, to whom he read them nightly after the clubs had closed, with the occasional bug dropping from the ceiling onto the coverlet of the bed on which they sat. It was a wonder, Baron observed, that any publisher could decipher the spidery handwriting that baffled even his oldest friends.[18] It was well that one did, as it would prove to be a publishing sensation. The result, in March 1911, was *Across the Bridges: or, Life by the South London River-side*, with an introduction by Edward Talbot, then Bishop of Southwark, and a dedication to Alec's mother, 'A Guardian of the Poor'.

For a first work it is remarkable. The style is terse, fresh and arresting, the wide-ranging observations considered and astute, and the author's empathetic engagement with his subject obvious. Although a heart-felt account of those living along the South London waterfront, depicting lives constrained and potential dissipated by unemployment, poverty and neglect, it is life-affirming, sprinkled with humour and affection. His approach was neither sensational and unconvincing nor statistical and uninspiring. His 'untechnical social survey', combining 'the sanity of a Blue Book with the fascination of a novel', stirred

15   He knew whereof he spoke. Alec, Barclay and Donald were commissioned by the Bishop of Southwark to prepare Mission candidates for confirmation.
16   Alec, quoted in Baron, p. 173.
17   Baron, p. 174.
18   Baron, 'Across the Bridges', *op.cit.*, p. 30.

'the layman without alienating the expert'.[19] It was an introduction to the so-cial crisis designed to appeal to the many who would never read a specialised textbook. It was an attempt to help them to understand and identify with the people among whom he lived. It was a call to philanthropic action.

He had no political axe to grind, and this for some on the left was a weak-ness. Indeed, what he advocated was an antidote to socialism. He declared that 'the only alternative to systematic socialism is a generation of good parents', the production of which required improving the life chances and living conditions of the children of the present. There was no mention of trade unions, nor of the incipient Independent Labour Party with which another doctor working among the poor of the area – Alfred Salter – had thrown in his lot.[20] Paterson laid more stress on personal service and the ability of boys' clubs, settlements and churches to elevate and energise the working class than on its self-regeneration by using its industrial clout and by investing in organised labour to improve its material lot. His approach could be, and was, criticised as being paternalistic rather than political.

This is unfair. He identified strongly with the people he described and with whom he lived. They were his friends, his family, but he saw himself as a sibling not a patriarch. The whole tenor of his work was fraternal rather than paternal. The whole thrust of it was to circumvent, by creating a 'motherland based on brotherhood', the danger of the nation splitting asunder. They were his compatriots, 'the men and women and children who make up' the coun-try. For Paterson patriotism had no meaning unless it implied fraternity, and the call of conscience and the claims of patriotism went hand in hand.[21] His aim was descriptive rather than prescriptive, to state the problem not to solve it, although he did suggest many ameliorations. Individual involvement and local initiatives were important. His own experience testified to that. Yet he recognised that charitable, philanthropic and religious bodies, while achiev-ing much, dealt only with some groups and sections of society and not with the community as a whole. Before the advent of the Welfare State, he stressed the nation's responsibility for social ills, and the role the municipal authorities

19 *Morning Leader*, 12th April; *Record*, 14th July; *Economic Journal* 2(84) (December 1911), p. 578.

20 When Eagar returned to Bermondsey after the Armistice, Salter jumped off his bi-cycle to welcome his return. '"Back again to the Club? Delighted so see you". Then he hesitated and added, with an enormous laugh: "But I don't know that I ought to be – you Oxford men have made the class-war impossible in Bermondsey"' (p. 185, n.1). He was right: comradeship between the classes was counter-revolution-ary. For his biography see Fenner Brockway's *Bermondsey Story: The Life of Alfred Salter* (new edition, Stroud, 1995).

21 *Liverpool Evening Post*, 8th January 1912.

should play in the provision of better housing and especially of better schools. He wanted legislative reform but wanted legislators first to know and understand the conditions and hardships under which millions lived, survived, and died. To be effective societal reform had to be grounded in reality. Even then, legislation on its own was no panacea. Nor did he, nor could he, offer one. He could, and did, offer a striking portrayal of that reality. He was painting a picture not tendering a tract.

After preliminary chapters on 'Streets and Homes', 'Family Life' and 'Customs and Habits', he traced the life of a working-class boy from birth, through schooling, to entering the workplace, getting married, and becoming inured to the daily grind, gradually the vitality seeping out of him to be replaced with spiritless resignation. 'At thirty a man has given up playing games, making love to his wife, reading books or building castles in the air.' The waste, the waste, the waste! At many times Alec seemed to seethe with suppressed anger at the waste. Yet even in this wasteland, flowers could bloom, and the most resilient was humanity. 'The greatest riches of the riverside lie in the natural goodness of its people ... [and] here, born of the struggle of life, unfold those lives of love and perseverance', is how he concluded his *cri de coeur*.[22]

Across the Bridges can still today be read with considerable profit as a vivid depiction of turn-of-the-century working-class life. In its own day it made an immediate impact and its author a celebrity. Alec was proud of what he had written and delighted with the public response. Not only did he keep copies of all the reviews it received – along with many congratulatory letters – in a large notebook, but he even indexed them alphabetically. They ranged from the *Aberdeen Free Press* to the *Yorkshire Observer*, and were, without exception, ecstatic. The first run of the book sold out within six months. It would be reprinted many times.[23] It was cited as an authority in the House of Commons during a debate on the employment of children.[24] It remains the definitive description of life in Bermondsey in the years preceding the Great War.

But it was more than a description of the life of the have-nots. Alec wanted the wider world to know about the microcosm that was Bermondsey and to enlist its active engagement with those who lived there. 'The real purpose of the book', he later wrote, 'was to invite, with such compelling force as I could

22   Paterson, p. 262.
23   A shilling edition was brought out in 1912, and in all there would be thirty impressions or reissues between 1911 and 2010.
24   HC Debates, 29th March 1912, col.77; *Manchester Guardian*, 30th March 1912. It was probably as a result of his celebrity status that Alec was invited to lunch with his 'ideal Englishman', Lord Kitchener of Khartoum, shortly before the great man returned to Egypt in September 1911. Kitchener may have been a family friend as Dorothy Paterson also knew him (*Letters*, 25th March 1915).

phrase, my friends from elsewhere to take that journey across the bridges, knowing well that, if they only stayed long enough to know them, they would wish to serve them. Many accepted that invitation, and I beg leave to doubt if any of them ever regretted his crossing the bridges.'[25] As an appeal to the hearts and minds of the haves, it struck its target. Or stung consciences, as 'it conveyed a vast reproach by depicting not only the essential decency but the greater goodness of the river-side poor, whose generosity, unselfishness and uncomplaining cheerfulness made all the more tragic the weary round of casual employment, ill-health and destitution, and the merciless crushing of youthful capacity and hopefulness.' Lionel Ford, the headmaster of Harrow, not only read *Across the Bridges* with his form, but invited Alec to the school to speak on 'the struggles of a London poor boy'. Ford's pupils were as 'enthralled' by the author as they had been 'thrilled' by his book. It became required reading for Etonians being prepared for confirmation. Undergraduates equally fell under its sway, as it 'had gone through Oxford like a flame'.[26]

One in particular, Basil Henriques, had gone up to Univ. in 1909 an uneasy young man. He had been brought up 'in luxury but not extravagantly' by parents who adhered to the claims of reform Judaism and Victorian philanthropy, and by a Christian nurse to whom he was devoted. Orthodoxy jarred and social conscience pricked. Claude Montefiore's *Outlines of Liberal Judaism* solved the first problem in its new interpretation of an ancient faith, revealing a religion 'which clearly showed man how to live, how to worship, how to serve both God and man alike'.[27] As regards the salving of his social conscience, another book was no less decisive. He acknowledged that while it was difficult to trace all the reasons behind his resolve to make social service his life's work, the one that stood out was Paterson's book, which he read in his second undergraduate year. It was, 'without doubt, the turning-point of my life'. It had left him 'spellbound'. It had impelled him, as it had so many others, to cross the bridge of class divide.[28]

25 *Over the Walls*, p. 1.
26 Eagar, pp. 382f; Letter from Ford to Galsworthy, 28th May 1912, in H.V. Marrot, *The Life and Letters of John Galsworthy* (London, 1935), p. 704; Leo Page, 'Sense and Sentimentalism' (1951). Page, when an Oxford undergraduate, forced his way into a packed meeting to hear Alec appeal for help in Bermondsey. He 'radiated unselfishness and inspired in others some shadow of his own passion to serve the poor and the unhappy'.
27 Montefiore had studied at Balliol and fallen under the influence of Jowett and Green.
28 Henriques, pp. 2–5, 20.

Shortly after Henriques had read the 'sacred text' he encountered the author himself during one of the latter's frequent 'missionary' visits to their *alma mater*.[29]

> I then met Alec. It would be foolish of me to try to describe his extraordinary, magnetic personality ... With great vision, with great humour, and with great originality, the man himself only emphasised what I had got from the book: 'There is a spot of work to be done in Bermondsey; you might as well come and do it.'[30]

The enchantment had not been dispelled by meeting Paterson in person but only deepened. The same occurred when he came face to face with 'The Doctor', who was then at St Ebbe's. The culminating event was attending a college gathering where he heard the new warden of the OBM, Barclay Baron no less, appealing for undergraduates to help. One or two volunteered on the spot. But it was all very Christian. At the end of the meeting a nervous Basil asked if it would be all right for a Jew to come amongst them. Baron laughed and invited him along.[31]

Nonetheless, when Henriques set out on his first visit he did so with a degree of trepidation. The place would smell. The people would smell. Worse, they would be alien beings. On Tower Bridge he hesitated. If once he stepped across to the South Bank would his fate be forever in the smelly and squalid slums? And would he, a social and religious outsider, ever be really accepted?[32] The answer to both questions was affirmative. Although he would eventually re-cross the bridges to

---

29   This may have been at a celebrated meeting to promote university settlements that was held on 27th October 1911 in the Oxford Examination Schools. It was sponsored by the Chancellor, the Archbishop of York and the Prime Minister. Paterson, on account of his 'classic' book, had been invited to take part, and shared the platform with Lord Selborne, a leading Liberal statesman and fellow member of Univ., and Sir John Simon, the Solicitor-General. Indeed by all accounts he outshone them both, delivering 'the speech of the evening', frequently eliciting laughter by his quips, such as when he commented on the incongruity of prisoners in Dartmoor chapel lustily singing 'brothers we are standing where the saints have trod', quoting from Galsworthy, and earnestly insisting that it was not merely a duty but a privilege and pleasure to take part in settlement work. He knew his audience. (*Oxford Magazine*, 26th October and 2nd November; *Oxford Times* and *The Spectator*, 4th November 1911, p. 19.)

30   Henriques, pp. 20f.

31   *Ibid.*, p. 22. In his later book, *Fratres* (London, 1951), pp.xivf., he gives a rather different account when it is Alec who reassures him that being Jewish was no barrier to taking part in an overtly Christian endeavour. Perhaps they both did.

32   Hankey's initial reaction to Bermondsey was similar: 'Once I loathed it. It chilled me. Its smells nauseated me. The aspect of its people sent my spirits down to zero ... It aroused all my aesthetic prejudices' ('Home', *OBM Annual Report*, 1915). In 1912, Alfred Ollivant wrote a 'slum novel' based on Bermondsey called *The Royal Road*, but subtitled *The Life, Death and Resurrection of Edward Hankey*. The choice of the

the North Bank, 'slums were to be his home for something like forty years'; and at the OBM he was accepted by all in the brotherhood and welcomed into full spiritual fellowship, with no one ever trying to convert him. Despite, or maybe because of, its lack of material resources, the OBM was rich in 'vigorous unselfishness' and 'sympathetic friendliness', and had a spirit he had never experienced before nor would experience again. He was amazed by the 'utter lack of pretence or side or class distinction', and by how completely naturally 'Oxford mingled with Bermondsey in a living brotherhood'. They were even on first-name terms.

> 'Fratres' was their motto, and as brothers they thought of, and acted towards, one another. There was no 'from above to below' about it. The undergraduate was called upon not so much to give as to receive, to learn even more than to teach. Love was the motive; love the binding force.[33]

So impressed was he by all this that Henriques encouraged one of his closest college friends to join him at the OBM. That person was the Old Etonian, William Llewellin. He too would fall under Alec's sway and work with him for years.

Henriques had found a home and made a home, even if it took some getting used to for this fastidious young man. Camping trips were the ultimate ordeal. Sharing tents with unwashed dock labourers initially revolted him. Nonetheless he quickly acclimatised and was completely won over by this way of doing things.[34] He would go on to revolutionise the provision for working-class Jewish boys by instilling a religious sensibility such as he had found and valued in Bermondsey, and by dissolving the hard and fast distinctions between managers and boys, making all involved one family.[35] In his founding of the Oxford and St George's Club with its magazine *Fratres*, Henriques would create in the East End, and for Jews, a mirror image of the OBM Mission.[36] One book by Alec Paterson had been a major factor in changing the course of his life.[37]

---

protagonist's name was no coincidence. While researching for his novel, Ollivant consulted both Hankey and Paterson.

33 Henriques, pp. 23f.

34 *Ibid.*, pp. 27, 30f. In contrast, when he took up residence in Toynbee Hall in October 1913, he 'never really got the hang of the place'. To him 'everyone seemed so fearfully "sociological"' (p. 38).

35 Baron, pp. 202ff.

36 The club was started in March 1914. Until they found their own land, the Jewish boys would make use of the camping-ground in the Weald, and thereafter a close connection with the OBM was maintained.

37 Henriques and his wife, who ran a club for girls, would go on to create the Bernard Baron Settlement, the largest in the country and named in honour of its major donor, no relation of Barclay. It was opened in 1930 by the Mayor of Stepney, Clem Attlee. Baron and Eagar attended. As a magistrate Henriques would emulate his mentor in devoting himself to the problem of juvenile delinquency. When

To understand the future course of Paterson's own life, and the ideas he put into execution, it is also essential to read this seminal work. Much of what he would later implement sprang from the insights he had gained south of the Thames. Most significantly, and long before he could influence its development, he applauded the borstal system, as a 'great and thoughtful plan to save the beginner from a career of crime', providing 'alternative methods of treatment ... for young offenders ... to distract them from the bad and to rebuild the good.'[38] He believed that 'while a rebuilding of character is the main object of reformative treatment, no method can be satisfactory which makes the process so easy and delightful as to rob it of a certain sting and struggle, which should be associated instinctively in the mind of every boy as a necessary consequence of guilt.' Penalties such as discipline and hard work must persist in order both to punish and deter. Heretically, he urged that punishments should fit the criminal rather than the crime. Presciently, he stated that 'the reformer that is needed must have something of the Spartan in him, and show both hope and penetration.' These were the attributes that would be required of anyone tasked to take control and bring to fruition this nascent scheme. These were attributes he associated with himself.[39]

While attending army officers' training in Bermondsey, Attlee stayed with Alec and other friends at the OBM. He recalled discussing *Across the Bridges* with its author, without betraying what was said.[40] Paterson remained true to his Liberal roots, and with his emphasis on encouraging self-reliance and self-improvement, he advocated sturdy independence, not dependence on state provision. If today's children could be nurtured into becoming 'a sound and industrious generation of parents that will not fall back upon the state', but 'by health and knowledge' support themselves and their families with 'old-fashioned independence', they would do all that was needed for the next generation and the State could 'once more confine itself to drains and bridges'.[41]

This was not how Attlee saw it. By this time he had changed considerably, or had been changed by his experience with working-class boys. They had taught him that their miserable lot and life opportunities could never be changed if it was left to what the Idealists saw as the mainspring of progress, their individual 'will', no matter how that 'will' was fashioned by the inspirational example of individuals such as Attlee himself or even Paterson. Clem was now convinced that

---

Paterson died, he mourned 'the greatest influence in my life' (L.L. Loewe, *Basil Henriques* [London, 1977], p. 14).

38   Paterson, p. 130.

39   *Ibid.*, pp. 188, 196.

40   Attlee, p. 24. Later he would use the phrase in the chapter on the settlement movement in his book, *The Social Worker*, without feeling any need to explain its meaning to his readers (p. 188).

41   Paterson, p. 29.

philanthropy in itself, no matter how large-scale, no matter how self-sacrificial, could not change the life circumstances of a whole class of people. Alleviating the worst aspects of poverty was not enough. It was necessary to eliminate its causes. Such social engineering would require a political solution, a solution only Socialism could bring.[42] Attlee had become a 'system-builder'; Paterson remained a 'character-builder'.[43] Attlee advocated a welfare state; Paterson a welfare society. Attlee had moved from Conservatism to Socialism; Paterson remained a Liberal. While their friendship and mutual regard never faded, their political paths were diverging. Paterson, perhaps a little too enamoured of his own charisma and too confident in his own abilities to change lives fundamentally, failed to grasp the over-arching political dimension that the less charismatic, less self-confident Attlee had been forced to recognise and embrace. This, however, was in 1911.[44] In the post-war world their ideological paths would begin to converge again, and Paterson's prison practice would more complement than counter Attlee's politics.

Attlee had become a dedicated social worker and would later write a book on the subject, although it was nowhere near as captivating as Paterson's earlier best-seller. Both in their own way had become experts on life in the East End or South London. Both would be recruited by the London School of Economics (LSE) as 'lecturers on special subjects' in the Department of Social Science and Public Administration which had been set up in 1912 by one of the great exponents of Idealism in universities, Professor Edward Urwick. Cheshire-born like Alec, Urwick was yet another Oxford graduate determined to tackle social problems. He had been sub-warden of Toynbee Hall from 1900 to 1903, and the following year had authored *Studies of Boy Life in Our Cities*.[45] At that time the still-fledgling LSE was utilising its links with individuals with special

---

42 Frank Field, *Attlee's Great Contemporaries* (London, 2009), p.xxiv. When a dock strike broke out in August 1911 Alec, along with the local vicar, and aided by club members, organised the feeding of nearly one thousand local children. In his appeal for charitable giving, he remained neutral about the merits of the walkout but welcomed its end (public letters, 17th and 29th August 1911).

43 Maurice Quinlan, *Victorian Prelude* (Columbia, 1941); Eagar, p. 68.

44 In November 1912 Paterson stood in the local council elections, but did so as an independent. Party politics were unsuited, he believed, to local issues and often led to paralysis. He pledged to badger the council into enforcing housing legislation, reducing business rates in order to protect jobs, paying 'a living wage' to its own employees, and ensuring contractors did the same (election leaflet, October 1912). As predicted by the party machines which had tried to enlist him, he was not elected.

45 The LSE had been founded by Sidney and Beatrice Webb in 1895 as a Fabian socialist teaching and research institute of practical economics or, as Beatrice put it, 'a school of administrative, political and economic science as a way of increasing national efficiency' (*The Diary of Beatrice Webb, ii, All the Good Things in Life*

knowledge and skills to supplement the work of the core teaching staff. From the new department's inception Attlee had been recruited by Sidney Webb as a lecturer, and he may have suggested that his old friend be invited to join him.[46] To his credit Attlee was never afraid of having an alternative point of view to his own being espoused in the same forum. He thought it healthy. Or Paterson's appointment may have been because of the impact of *Across the Bridges*. Or, most likely, friendship and reputation both played their part. Alec's academic career was to be short-lived, however, as it did not begin until the summer term of 1914. The syllabus of the department shows him contracted for two years to give six lectures on working-class life. If, as is very likely, he delivered those lectures in 1914, no record survives. He would not have been able to fulfil his 1915 commitment at all.[47] He would be otherwise engaged.[48]

Meanwhile another venture was afoot. In the winter of 1913, an estate agent notified the OBM of a property for sale called Halls Green in the Kent Weald. With Horndon no longer available, a search for a suitable alternative had been started some time before, and feelers put out. This sounded promising. Alec, Barclay and three others set out to investigate, trekking all the way from Sevenoaks. Eventually they found in the undergrowth a group of derelict buildings nestling in what could become an idyllic landscape. They were shown round by 'a half-witted old lady' whom Alec referred to as 'Barkis's aunt'. It had, in estate-agent argot, 'potential'. After much haggling, it was purchased, and in Easter 1914 the first camp took place.[49] But it was a camp with a difference,

---

1892–1905 [London, 1983], p. 239; Ralf Dahrendorf, *A History of the London School of Economics and Political Science 1895–1995* [Oxford, 1995], pp. 125ff.).

46   Attlee, p. 30. At the same time, Richard Tawney, an economic historian, was recruited to a part-time post. A graduate of Balliol, where he too had come under the influence of Green's philosophy, Tawney had spent three years at Toynbee Hall from 1903 to 1906, after which he had embarked on a career of university teaching. He was also a lifelong friend of William Temple, with whom he had been a direct contemporary both at Rugby and Balliol. Thus it is highly likely he knew Paterson, or a lot about him, before their paths crossed at the LSE.

47   LSE academic calendars and syllabi for 1914 and 1915 were printed a year in advance. The summer term ran from the end of April until the end of June. Franz Ferdinand was assassinated on 28th June 1914. Attlee also vacated his post, taking a commission in the 6th South Lancashire Regiment.

48   Oblivious to the fact that a war was on, in July 1915 Oxford would invite Alec to lecture that August, and Sheffield University that winter (*Letters*, 17th July 1915).

49   Baron, *Once Upon a Time*, p. 10. In *The Doctor*, he gives the date mistakenly as 1913 (p. 181).

consisting not of a multitude of boys but of a dozen Bermondsey managers and Oxford recruits. Work not play was the order of the day. There were trees to be cut down, bushes and bracken to be removed, drains to be dug, and buildings to be patched up. On Easter Sunday the staff and their helpers marched to the local church carrying a cross before them and singing hymns. One was 'Onward Christian Soldiers marching as to war'. It would take more than one weekend to transform the place, but transformed it was, providing a permanent and convenient 'retreat' for the club managers and the older boy helpers each Easter, and a campsite for the members from spring to autumn. Within a couple of years, and despite the unexpected depletion in the number of volunteers, a swimming pool would be carved out of one of the fields and the camp would be complete. For the rest of his life, and long after he had left Bermondsey for good, Alec would try each year to return to this rustic haven to relive something of his idyllic past, and in *Who's Who* he would record 'reading, digging and singing' as his recreations.

For the succeeding four years this was not possible as Alec had other things on his mind, and other duties to perform.[50] Beneath 'the actual visible world' there had been an underworld which had seemed 'utterly fantastic', but was leaping into reality, 'a world of monstrous shadows moving in convulsive combinations through vistas of fathomless catastrophe.'[51] The amorphous was becoming adamantine, water was turning to ice. The long 'Edwardian summer' was ending and a four-year winter was beginning. Although they would be carrying rifles rather than a cross, Alec and his Bermondsey boys saw themselves very much as Christian soldiers marching to war. The ideals of many would be challenged, and for some their faith destroyed. For others, and Alec was one of them, the camaraderie as well as the carnage of the trenches proved a catalyst that made them all the more determined to create a new society out of the wreckage of the old. What they had done in the Kent Weald they would try to do in the wider world.

---

50 Barclay, on leave and in uniform, managed to join the camp in 1916. From it he could hear 'the dull thudding of the guns on a French battlefield where so many of our *Fratres* keep Easter' (*Once Upon a Time*, p. 11). In *The Doctor* he gives the date as 1915, but as he did not leave for France until the summer of that year, this too is erroneous.

51 Winston Churchill, *The World Crisis, vol.1* (London, 1923), p. 13.

PART II

THE HAPPY WARRIOR: 1914–1922

CHAPTER 5

READING, DIGGING AND SINGING: 1914–1915

The Territorial is a soldier by choice, but not by taste. He does not like war, and the ways of the army are not to his fancy. But the Londoner finds an inconsequent happiness in the trifles and details of life, extorting comedy from a rissole and a farce from a little black hat, so that for the greater part of his day he forgets he is in the army.

Alexander Paterson

In the supreme moments of a shared experience, rare between men of any kind, in the ultimate, elemental affair of living and dying together, as in the Bermondsey Battalion in war-time for instance, the union [of the Oxford man and Bermondsey boy] reached its completion.

Barclay Baron

Despite the dark clouds gathering, there was one sunny interlude during the summer of 1914. Barkis got married. He had met his wife-to-be, Rachel Smith, two years earlier in Bermondsey when she was working at the Time and Talents Settlement. She came with a fine pedigree, being a descendant of the great Quaker prison reformer, Thomas Fowell Buxton, the brother-in-law of Elizabeth Fry. They announced their engagement in May 1914 and the wedding took place on 25th July in Southwark Cathedral. Stansfeld presided, and Alec was best man. A Saturday afternoon had been chosen 'to allow our Bermondsey friends to attend, which they did in surprisingly large numbers'. The guests provided a happy mixture of 'top-hat and cloth-cap coming together'. The cake disappeared 'under a wave of Bermondsey boys' before the 'West End' could get a look in.[1] There seemed not to be a cloud on the horizon, but the idyll of the newly-weds' Highland honeymoon would be truncated on the evening of the 4th of August when Great Britain declared war on Germany for violating the neutrality of Belgium. Barkis immediately returned to South London to enlist

---

1   Snape, pp. 268f.

with his friends. It was an opportunity for consummating his – and Alec's – ideal of Christian brotherhood between the classes. As their friend, Donald Hankey, put it during the war:

> To understand the working man one must know him through and through – live, work, drink, sleep with him. And the war gave us a unique opportunity of doing this. We knew that we could never become working men; but no power on earth could prevent us from enlisting if we were of sound mind and limb. And enlisting meant living on terms of absolute equality with the very men we wanted to understand. Filled anew with the glamour of our quest, we sought the nearest recruiting office.[2]

Thus it came as no surprise that on 13th August when Paterson volunteered for military service it was not in the University and Public School Brigade, the Old Boys' Corps, or the 'Sportsmen's Battalions', all unofficially reserved for the upper and middle classes, but in the Bermondsey Battalion. He did so not as an officer, a rank to which his background and education would have entitled him, but as an ordinary soldier. He was one of Kipling's 'gentlemen rankers'. So many of the Stansfeld Club members joined up with him at the drill hall of the 'terriers' that it became 'almost a Club Battalion'.[3] He was now Private Paterson, had the serial number 1876, and his pay would be one shilling a day. Having taken the king's shilling, for the next few days he and his companions were to be seen marching in fours through the streets in civilian clothes (uniforms took some time to be provided to Territorials), Alec looking very unsoldierly in an old suit and a straw boater that concealed his by now fast-receding hairline, 'his rifle at a dangerous slope, out of step as usual.'[4]

The day before he enlisted Alec had written to his mother telling her of his decision, and reassuring her that he would be away for months at most and that in any case there was little chance of raw recruits going to the Front. More likely they would be used to relieve regulars in Malta or Gibraltar.[5] He had also begun

---

2   Donald Hankey, *A Student in Arms* (London, 1916), p. 93. The second, posthumous series (1917) included a chapter unselfconsciously called 'Romance' in which he dilated upon the 'extraordinary affection of officers for their men' (pp. 101–114).

3   Eagar, p. 236. Samuel Bevington, the owner of the biggest firm of leather manufacturers in Bermondsey, commanded the 3rd Battalion of the Royal West Surrey Regiment which, as a result of the 1908 Haldane reforms, became the 22nd Battalion of the London Regiment. He built their drill hall at the corner of Old Jamaica Road and Abbey Street, adjacent to his factory, Neckinger Mills.

4   Baron, 'Across the Bridges', *Four Men* (London, n.d.), pp. 30–40, at p. 36.

5   *Letters*, 12th, 15th August 1914. He wrote to Willis in similar vein: 'we are going to have a good time ... we shall never go anywhere near the war ... we are too raw for that.' He apologised for leaving him 'the dull job of staying at home and looking after everything'.

keeping a record of events which he tellingly titled 'A Bit of a Diary showing a little hastily the Happiness of Private Paterson'.[6] It spans – with omissions – the period from 12th August 1914 to 16th February 1916, and is followed by two pages listing places he had stayed in for the rest of the war. It is an invaluable resource for reconstructing his career as a soldier and for much else.[7]

How he came to join up in the way he did is instructive. When war broke out he had been in Oxford visiting James Odgers. They had talked about the Germans they knew in England, 'more sorry for them than anyone'.[8] Erstwhile friends had become present foes. On his return to London Alec had been concerned to read in the newspapers that the only Territorial battalion still below strength was his local one. He worried that the Stansfeld Club members had become 'so pacific and non political' as to be unable to grasp the crucial issues of war. He tracked down a friend, Henry Charlewood Turner, who was recruiting for 'B' Company.[9] Captain Turner was keen to get 'decent people', and in particular 'a squad of club boys'. Paterson offered to help, but got a concession. Should the 'boys' be unwilling to enlist without him, the captain agreed to accept him as a private. Paterson thought it a 'poor game' to ask others to do what he was not prepared to do himself, and that if the OBM was to live up to its ideals and retain any relevance he had to accompany those going 'away for a year or two to live in strange places and face new troubles'. It was very much 'carry on camping'. War work was club work on a wider stage.[10] When they showed

---

6   He was not being ironic, his happiness being expressed many times in both diary and letters. While he may have wanted to reassure his mother and sister, it seems that he did remain sanguine throughout the war, finding in the 'rough comradeship' of the trenches a fulfilment of all he had tried to achieve in Bermondsey.

7   He wrote the diary in a hardback notebook which he sent to his mother for safekeeping. After his deployment to France, to evade the censors, he continued it in 'penny notebooks' for smuggling back to Bowdon. By August 1915 there were five, but the last three are missing, as are all subsequent ones. However, the diary does exist in typescript, to which are appended copies of letters to his mother and Dorothy, although most of his other correspondence – such as that with Macan, Master of Univ. (whose thirty-two-year-old son Robert was killed in June 1915) – is missing. Together they span the period from 12th August 1914 to 16th January 1919 and comprise 213 foolscap pages, bound in a single volume. The transcription was made after the author's death, by or on behalf of his sister, or wife. Some names are blacked out, others rendered by initials. Not all can be identified. There are no photographs.

8   *Letters*, 28th October 1917.

9   Henry's brother, George, would serve on the general staff of the 47th Division, become a public school headmaster, and sit on the executive committee of the Paterson Memorial Fund.

10 *Diary*, 12th August 1914. So thought Barkis, even though he failed in his attempt to join up with his friends. To his chagrin he was rejected for military service on

reluctance, Alec chivvied them into joining up, and 'quite fifty of these boys' did so, 'despite their mothers' protests'. They were loyal to the man they all called 'Pat'. He in turn felt personably responsible for their welfare and would later be aghast when they first went into battle without him.[11] He may have pushed from behind but he led from the front.

They enlisted in what they called the 'Bermondsey Terriers' or, to give it its full title, the 1/22nd (County of London) Battalion (The Queen's).[12] It was one component of the London Regiment, which, with eight City of London and eighteen County of London battalions, was the largest in the British Isles, big enough to form two divisions. It was also unique in that its battalions retained a measure of their original identity, each having a distinctive badge and uniform. With the outbreak of war, the 'Bermondsey Terriers', along with the 21st, 23rd and 24th Battalions, formed the 6th London Infantry Brigade of the 2nd London Division. This remained so until May 1915 when, to avoid confusion with the 2nd Division with which, as part of the First Army, it would soon be fighting on the Western Front, the 2nd London was redesignated the 47th Division, and the 6th became the 142nd Brigade.[13]

S ome questions need to be answered before we proceed. How had this come about? Why were Territorials part of a force fighting abroad? How was that force constituted? What was the command structure? A short excursus should explain.

In August 1914 the British Expeditionary Force consisted of 117,000 well-trained and experienced regulars in six infantry divisions and one of cavalry, the whole being divided into two corps constituting a single army. In addition, at home, there was a large number of Territorial divisions in which part-timers

---

medical grounds. He was left behind with a few other 'invalids' to run the Mission's junior clubs, with the consolation of seeing the birth of his first child in the spring of 1915. Persistence – and connections – would soon pay off, and in the summer of that year he was appointed to serve with the Young Men's Christian Association, the largest voluntary body working for the welfare of the troops, originally with the aim of establishing a club for army officers in Le Havre. He would find that the YMCA 'was just the OBM on a large scale' (Snape, pp. 273f.).

11   *Letters*, 28th May 1915.

12   In the last days of August 1914 it was decided that as soon as the original, pre-war Territorial battalion had mobilised and moved out to its war station, a duplicate, or second line, battalion would be formed. Henceforth the original battalion would have the prefix 1/ in front of its designation, and the second line battalion 2/.

13   *Official History of the Great War, Order of Battle of Divisions, Part 2A* (London, 1936), pp. 72f., n.20.

were trained to defend the homeland or relieve regulars for overseas service, their sole commitments unless they volunteered (as they were to do in droves) for duty abroad.[14]

By the end of 1914 the Regular Army had been tested to the point of destruction. The Territorials, despite being designated for home defence, initially made up the deficit. First line units such as the 1/22nd were made available for service overseas, while second line units formed a reserve and a pool from which frontline units could be replenished. To meet the exigencies of war, Kitchener raised a New Army, consisting wholly of volunteers until conscription was introduced in 1916. The initial uptake was staggering, young men enlisting individually or in large groups – whole football teams, those working in the same office, apprentices in the same trade, boys from the same borstal – who wanted to stay and fight together in what became known as the 'Pals' Battalions'.[15] So too was the problem of training and equipping these raw recruits. Given the paucity of Regular Army and Territorial divisions, there was an immediate shortage of commissioned and non-commissioned officers, and the high casualty rate among those existing further depleted their number. Few were available for training purposes. Retired officers were brought back into active service and frequently promoted to high rank, but the majority of subalterns (junior officers below the rank of captain), largely recruited from public schools and universities, were as untrained as, and were often younger than, the troops they commanded.

The structure of a British army was this. Of infantry units under the command of commissioned officers, the bottom rung was the platoon, consisting of some fifty men or more under a subaltern assisted by a sergeant and corporals in charge of sections of about a dozen men, and lance-corporals who led even smaller details. Four platoons constituted a company of up to 250 men under a major or, as losses mounted, a captain. Four companies (designated 'A', 'B', 'C' and 'D') made a battalion of about 1,000 soldiers under a lieutenant-colonel. The actual numbers in each battalion could vary (the 22nd, for example, having over 1,000 men), and would change throughout the war. A battalion was the basic tactical infantry unit, and for most 'rankers' their horizon went no further. Four battalions formed a brigade under a brigadier-general. A brigade was the smallest army formation, consisting, if up to establishment strength, of around 4,500 infantrymen. Three brigades constituted a division under a major-general. With the additional auxiliary personnel, each division numbered up to

14 Not without some cajoling. Alec deplored the 'press-gang measures' to which 'silly young pups of lieutenants' resorted, and noted that badgering and shaming dissenters only made them more obdurate in their refusal (*Diary*, 26th August 1914).

15 A thousand former borstal boys had enlisted by 1916. All were physically fit, and 90 per cent of them proved to be fine soldiers, including two who won the DCM. As many were promoted as proved unsatisfactory (Report [1916]).

20,000 when at full complement. Several divisions were allotted to a self-contained corps, averaging 40,000, under a lieutenant-general. Two to four corps made an army, varying in strength from 100,000 to 200,000 of all ranks, under a general. For instance, I Corps, commanded by Lieutenant-General Sir Douglas Haig, consisted of only two divisions. In late 1914 it joined with two other corps to become the First Army under the same commander, by then a full general. By July 1915 there were three British armies consisting of twenty-five infantry divisions on the Western Front. The commander-in-chief of the BEF, until December 1915 when Haig replaced him, was Field Marshal Sir John French.

Alec and his friends had enlisted not, they thought, into so gargantuan a force, but into their own intimate family of the 'Bermondsey Battalion', almost a regiment in itself under its comforting badge of the Paschal Lamb.[16] Little did they know it, but many of those rushing to the flag in the first flush of patriotic enthusiasm would become lambs to the slaughter.

But first there had to be proper training for these civilian soldiers. For that purpose, on 20th August, 'under a blazing sun', Alec's battalion entrained for the St Albans area, where it was to be stationed for over six months. Attired in full marching kit, Alec took with him a service rifle, 100 rounds of ammunition, and a box holding a knife and fork given to him by one of the boys who had been left behind.[17] To his satisfaction Alec, who when he joined up was just shy of thirty, the upper age limit for volunteers, was allocated along with his younger comrades to No. 4 Platoon of 'A' Company. He was described as 5' 9" tall, with a girth of 39", of normal vision, but of only average physical development. He would have some work to do to keep up with his 'pals'. Despite a series of ailments, he succeeded.

Billeting for so many recruits was a problem. Despite the willingness of locals to provide accommodation, there was not enough to go round, even with some men sleeping on the floor, and every school-house, parish-room and public building had to be requisitioned. Initially Alec and twenty-two of his confreres ended up in a classroom of a school where they slept amidst a chaos of equipment and with one blanket between two. At least they had a roof over their heads and glass in the windows. Others had to make do with barns and sheds which provided little protection from the wind and cold. Eventually many would be moved to the houses of local residents. Alec was one, and he soon endeared himself to his hosts, the Holt family.

16   A British infantry regiment, commanded by a full colonel, was not a tactical unit deployed on the battlefield but an administrative and recruiting organisation that produced operational battalions.

17   *Letters*, 17th August 1914.

The weather would not be kind for long. A very wet and prolonged winter lasting from November until March, along with problems in getting equipment, transport and even uniforms, added greatly to the discomfort of the troops and caused considerable delay in preparing them for war. Tedium was the order of the day. 'Spells of trench-digging in the neighbourhood of Braintree and Witham in Essex, at which each of the infantry brigades took a turn, made an almost welcome break in the monotony of life.'[18] Alec shared in these privations. His first months of service were spent in rigorous training, and they cannot have been entirely enjoyable given his inability to march in step, and the attentions of a bullying sergeant who constantly picked on him. George Neve, a fellow OBM 'rookie', was amazed by how Alec tolerated the abuse. When he and others wanted to take it up with a senior officer, 'Alec wouldn't hear of it'. That was not in his nature. Unsurprisingly, he proved 'a great inspiration to us during those very difficult days'.[19] His landlady, Mrs Holt, testified that 'he never grumbled, whatever they asked him to do he did so willingly'.[20] He insisted he was fit and healthy, never felt the cold and never caught a cold. He was well-adapted for the trenches.

Apart from singing while marching or digging, the main diversions from the deadening routine were parade services ('the worst of the Church's crimes'[21]), the YMCA canteen, swimming, boxing bouts, football matches, occasional games of whist and the not-so-occasional 'pub-crawls' – although these were curtailed by the 10 o'clock curfew. One useful thing he did learn was that grease could be removed from plates with cold water if the plates were rubbed with gravel first. Yet he was happy and well, and 'having a real holiday'. Even as a 'ranker' he soon made his mark. Barclay Baron, who visited him in September, related that he was 'working quiet wonders in his own Company and probably in the whole Battalion'. He kept an eye out for his 'own club boys who but for him would in some cases be in great difficulties'. And, of course, he had started up a 'sports club which fills up the spare time'. It was, Baron concluded, 'the old club work for him in a new place, without the ceaseless overwork of his life in London.'[22]

18 Maude, pp. 3–8.
19 Neale, p. 58. There is no mention of this in Alec's diary but as there was a break in it between October 1914 and March 1915 that may explain the absence. In contrast to this bully, the regimental sergeant-major, Charles Pannall, won Paterson's approbation. Not only would Pannall be promoted to the rank of major and be awarded the DSO and MC, Alec would recruit him to the Prison Service, where he would become governor of Dartmoor from 1932 to 1945 (*Over the Walls*, pp. 34f.).
20 *Letters*, 14th March 1915. Both she and her little daughter, Betty, would write the most affectionate letters to Alec when he was in the trenches, and Betty would run errands to earn money to buy cigarettes to send to him (*Letters*, 21st June 1915, and 18th March 1917).
21 *Diary*, 7th March 1915.
22 *Diary*, 26th August; *Letters*, 17th September 1914.

Insisting on surviving on army pay, at one point Alec found himself with so little money that he temporarily gave up smoking and drinking. Worse than this privation, in October he had his appendix removed. He spent convalescent leave in Bowdon and Llandudno, but was determined to be back with his platoon for Christmas. An unwanted yuletide gift was promotion. The reason for this is not stated. It could have been his age, social and educational background, or merely that he was balding. This is not as absurd as it may seem, since a second lieutenant of the 12th West Yorkshire Brigade, flummoxed on whom to appoint as corporals, simply allotted two stripes to all the men with moustaches.[23] In Paterson's case, however, it was his obvious leadership qualities that made him stand out. The commanding officer of his battalion, Lieutenant-Colonel Previté, had in fact offered him a commission with the added inducement of remaining with his platoon, but faced with Paterson's obduracy and a promise to reconsider if needs must, he compromised by bestowing on the reluctant private the lowest non-commissioned rank.[24] As a lance-corporal Paterson would be in charge of a small group of men. In them he would find the *esprit de corps* he had found, and helped instil, in the club boys. This was hardly surprising, for a man 'may join for the sake of "King and Country", but he goes over the top for the honour of his own platoon'.[25]

As ever food was a constant source of discontent among the 'Tommies': the quality, the quantity, but above all the lack of variety. 'Army bread and Pink's jam' was the staple.[26] Early in the new year it was discovered that army rations were being sold in the village shops. An investigation found that these goods had been sold by quartermasters and even officers, not out of cupidity but to provide a more varied diet for the men. They had been getting more jam than they could eat and too much cheese which they disliked. Much food was discarded or went off, so the surplus was sold by officers for what it would fetch and the money used to buy milk and other basics in short supply. Only Territorials would have had the temerity. The inquiry was truncated when, in March 1915, under the command of Major-General Charles St Leger Barter, the 47th Division was ordered to deploy to France.

---

23 Nigel Atter, *In the Shadow of Bois Hugo* (Solihull, 2017), p. 20.

24 *Letters*, 12th June 1915. He became lance-corporal on 28th December 1914.

25 Rudyard Kipling, *The Irish Guards in the Great War: The Second Battalion* (London, 1923), p. 15.

26 *Letters*, 19th May 1915. In his first months at St Albans Alec had repeatedly reassured his mother that the food was good and plentiful, and included stews and sirloin steaks. He did not want to worry her, but later told his sister that he had never been so hungry before or after. Likewise, he would minimise his injuries and exaggerate the comfort of dugouts when writing home.

Being pipped to the post by the North Midland Division, the 2nd London was not the first Territorial Force division to reach the Continent.[27] Its parts arrived piecemeal. After days of frustration, Alec's battalion left a tearful St Albans on 14th March, embarked at Southampton that evening, and landed at Le Havre the morning after. It was Monday the 15th, 'known to the elect as the Ides of March'.[28] To circumvent the prohibition on soldiers revealing their location in letters home, Alec devised a simple code. The first letter of each word in the opening sentence would give the name of the place. For example, 'Had a very rowdy evening' denoted Havre, 'Sunny times overhead – morning especially ripping' St Omer, while 'Big effort today – had usual noisy evening' indicated Béthune.[29] Keeping his mother informed of his whereabouts was more important than adhering to military regulations. It was also fun.

To Alec the British army seemed hopelessly disorganised. Incompetence had delayed their departure. On their arrival food was in short supply and rations, when they were available, consisted of tinned beef and dog biscuits. Silly restrictions – soon lifted – on the troops entering the nearby villages prevented this meagre diet being supplemented. And where were they to be deployed? Originally the Ypres Salient in Flanders was to have been their destination, but losses incurred at the battle of Neuve Chapelle meant that the 2nd London Division was diverted to the Béthune area of northern France, forty-five miles southeast of Calais and some seven miles from the front line. It was to form part of I Corps commanded by Lieutenant-General Sir Charles Monro, which in turn was part of Haig's First Army.

Finally, after much marching and grumbling, and despite the seeming chaos, the different elements converged on their destination. Divisional headquarters were established at Marles-les-Mines, and the troops billeted in nearby villages. On the march the men, as usual, had been singing ribald and irreverent songs of which the higher ranks were often the butt. One popular ballad went

> We've got a sergeant-major,
> Who's never seen a gun.
> He's mentioned in despatches
> For drinking privates' rum
> And when he sees old Jerry
> You should see the bugger run
> Miles and miles and miles behind the lines!

27 Territorials had been serving in France since the winter of 1914–1915, but as single battalions attached to Regular Army brigades.
28 *Diary*, p. 16.
29 *Letters*, 10th, 17th March 1915.

It was hardly surprising that Alec would take critical stock of No.4 Platoon. The subaltern in charge was 'fresh from school, full of keenness and healthy British ignorance'. The sergeant was good-hearted but 'woefully incompetent', derisively called 'Polly' by the men. One corporal was a bully, 'a slacker and a funk'; the other was weak and arrogant, 'a good boy spoilt'. Alec's most damning judgment was that 'none of these men would be made an officer in a club, or be on men's committees – they have not the power of character.' Thus 'the best of Bermondsey, the natural leaders in life', are destined 'as privates to serve under the second-rate'.

Similarly, Alec would muse on the quality of the officers in his 'funny Battalion'. The major was a greater coward than any of them; the captain, leading 200 men into action, was persistently drunk.[30] Officers 'are as a rule very cautious and set an excellent example to the men of self-preservation'. On one occasion, when he was talking to several of them at company headquarters, a 'whizzbang' came across, and he found at the end of the sentence he no longer had an audience as they had all fled to the dugouts. Others were too rash and unwilling to heed experience. Alec once warned a young officer, come to examine their post, that the corners were not safe. The novice ignored his warning, exposed himself far longer than was necessary, and just escaped a bullet through the head. Another, having a look out of curiosity, was wounded beneath the eye. Alec despaired of such foolhardiness.

For padres he had scant regard. Their presence 'did more to revive the old discredit and the contempt of the church than their absence'. Their position as officers divided them from the men whom 'they could not meet freely or with whom they could not gain any degree of intimacy'. He had never seen 'a chaplain in France doing anything except take services', whereas they should be 'moving in and out of the lines talking and smoking a pipe, taking [their turn] at the cricket net on the evenings, playing draughts in the YMCA at night'.

> Nothing sadder have I seen than the progress of an immaculate chaplain through a ward of wounded and gassed men in Boulogne. A pleasant swagger, more likely to affect women than men, a playful word for each nurse, talk with the sisters, a smile at several men, and he has to hurry home to be in time for mess.[31]

They were considered to have the softest job of all, and to be members of 'the idlest and slackest of all army services'. This was not an uncommon view – it was shared by Robert Graves, for instance[32] – but it has to be seen in context. His observations and criticisms, which would be revised as the war progressed,

30 *Diary*, 29th March, 28th April–1st May 1915.
31 *Diary*, 6th June 1915.
32 *Goodbye to All That* (Folio edn, 1981), pp. 166ff.

related to Anglican clergy in the early stages of the war when they were kept well back from the Front. Later in 1915, as a result of Neville Talbot brazenly ignoring the restrictive regulation, army policy would change and Church of England padres would be actively encouraged to go up to the line – and beyond – and identify themselves with their troops and their hardships.[33] There would be many fine exemplars among them of courage and pastoral care, of whom Studdert Kennedy ('Woodbine Willie') was perhaps the most famous if not the most decorated.[34] His vision of a 'Comrade God', sharing in the soldiers' suffering and embodied in their sacrifice, was very much shared by Alec.[35] There were some in his own division who would win his regard. One brave and assiduous chaplain, in the 22nd Battalion itself, was Clifford Woodward, his old friend from Bermondsey days. Another was David Railton, the son of George Railton, William Booth's 'first lieutenant'. He shared his father's dedication to duty and compassion for the needy. He was at Keble during Alec's first two years at Oxford, before serving his curacy in Liverpool during the episcopacy of Francis Chavasse. There he became close friends of the bishop's twin muscular-Christian sons, Christopher and Noel.[36] Given their similar backgrounds and beliefs, their overlap at Oxford and their mutual connections, with among others Tubby Clayton, Alec and David may well have known each other. Railton, who served with the 19th Londons in the 141st Brigade from March 1916 until April 1917, was an outstanding pastor, indefatigable in rescuing and consoling the wounded, and burying the dead in the field, often at great risk to himself. He too deplored the order to stay away from the Front, and unlike some of his colleagues would not desert his post. He thought it 'simply scandalous that all officers have to stick it for the duration of the war – and then a chaplain who

33   Melville Harcourt, *Tubby Clayton* (London, 1953), p. 56; *Diary*, 31st May–7th June 1915. Alec would have approved of Father Gwynne, the 'unusually beloved' Roman Catholic chaplain, who as a Catholic was not so restricted. His death during the battle of Loos was lamented by Kipling, (*op.cit.*, *The First Battalion*, pp. 121f.).

34   Three chaplains would win the Victoria Cross during the conflict, the first being Edward Mellish, who at the start of the war had been curate of St Paul's, Deptford. Around a hundred lost their lives. One was the popular padre, Basil Plumptree, a former curate of Bermondsey parish church, who joined the 47th Division. Having been awarded the MC, 'little Plumptree', aged thirty-four, was killed at the Front by a stray shell on 16th July 1917.

35   Stuart Bell, *Faith in Conflict: The Impact of the Great War on the Faith of the People of Britain* (Solihull, 2017), pp. 130–147.

36   Alec met the latter at a meeting of OBM in 1907. Along with Chris, Noel would run a Bermondsey-style boys' club in Merseyside. He would have the rare distinction of being awarded the VC twice, on both occasions for rescuing the wounded under fire. His bravery cost him his life. When asked why he had persevered when so badly injured, the dying man replied: 'Duty called, and Duty must be obeyed.'

has got to know the men well goes off as he has had enough of it – and as his year is up.' Both Woodward and he would win Military Crosses. While there is no evidence that Alec either knew or met Benedict Williamson, a Roman Catholic chaplain who joined the 47th Division in 1917 and was known as '"Happy Days" on account of his unquenchable optimism', he was another whom he would have respected. Similarly, Father John Lane-Fox with the London Irish Rifles in the 18th Battalion was considered to be 'the pluckiest man in Loos'.[37]

On Good Friday (2nd April) 1915, Alec reached the trenches, and in the early hours of the following morning got his baptism of fire: a heavy German bombardment. During it 'Sergeant C' was hit by shrapnel in both lungs. Paterson, rushing to his aid, found him 'in awful pain', but all he could do was administer two grains of morphia. The sergeant was 'in mortal anguish' and Paterson doubted he could be saved. He was determined to try, however, and did not want to leave him until it was dark when the stretcher-bearers would finally venture to his aid and take him to the medical officer at the dressing station. His diary records his efforts:

> Find there is a stretcher in our trench. S.A. and S.C.W. offer to come with me now and take him down to the M.O. Can't get him past corner in communication trench, so it means a mile across open country – but a sporting chance of getting there. Our new lieutenant agrees, if Welsh captain consents.[38] He won't. Says M.O. could do nothing, and we should only waste more life. Allows me to give another grain of morphia. C. sinks into a stupor and dies in sleep. Carry him out and fix him up in the open. Can't stay to cover him with earth as snipers sight us, and cover us with bullets.

That very evening Alec was in danger again when he was sent with a party of men on a ration fatigue to a railhead point two miles away. They got there safely but for five hours waited in vain for the transport which, sent to the wrong place, never arrived. They began the return journey at 1.30am. The way back was across open country, this time lit up by German searchlights. Tom Angliss, the tall, curly-haired Bermondsey lad who had been his boon companion since they first joined up together, led the way.

> At each flash we drop to the ground as one man, head down, flat on stomach – a perfect exhibition of drill. Thank heaven we are not carrying the big boxes of biscuits and cases of jam. All this in pouring rain, lying in puddles and thick mud. The bullets pass, 'pinging' over our heads. A flash comes – I see 6 ft. 1 inch like a poplar on the skyline. In the twist of a second he has dropped. Rush up to him. "Tom, are you all right?" And he turns up his face

37 Benedict Williamson, *"Happy Days" in France and Flanders* (London, 1921), pp.xif; Patrick MacGill, *The Great Push* (London, 1917), pp. 183f.
38 'A' Company had been attached to a Welsh regiment.

to me. "Get down you damned fool, what are you standing up for like that?"
So perfect a drill sergeant is our self-preservation.[39]

None of this was related in his letters home. In them he reassured his family
that he was eating well, sleeping comfortably, enjoying the good weather and
keeping fit. He was generally happy and healthy, as were his troop. Indeed 'everybody looks just like a boy after a fortnight's camp at Hopton.' Such action as
he had experienced was not as bad as he had expected or the newspapers reported. Although he had found himself in the trenches on Good Friday his platoon,
while having had 'adventures there', had suffered few casualties. He thanked his
mother for her never-ending supplies of tobacco, matches, home-made cakes,
chocolate and – at his specific request – hymn-sheets. He expressed particular
pleasure at getting a copy of his school magazine, *The Bowdonian*, a compensation for not being able to run in the old-boys' race on Easter Saturday. With the
spring had come nostalgia. Primroses, sent by Sid Ruck, had made him all the
more wistful for England 'now that April's there'.[40]

His diary broke off at Easter and was not resumed until 26th April. During
the intervening period Alec, despite accidentally shooting one of his own men in
the leg, was promoted to acting corporal, 'due to casualties among our N.C.O.s
rather than any merit on my part', he told his mother.[41] A long letter from 'Corporal Alec' was the last that she would ever receive. Again he counselled against
undue worry. While he was not one of those who thought that the war would
soon be over, 'the odds are greatly against any one man being killed, and in any
case you know I am not afraid of that, nor of pain, for I have some opium with
me.' This letter was read out to her two days before her death on Tuesday 20th
April. She had been his mainstay and confidante throughout his life. Almost all
his surviving letters up to this point had been to her. After his mother's death,
'dear old Dor', as he affectionately called his sister, filled the void, and she would
be the major recipient of the rest. In one he would confide that 'if it was not
for the absence of the daily letter I should hardly know Mother had died – she
seems as near to me as she was at Dudley House.'[42]

39 *Diary*, Good Friday 1915 (2nd April). The events spanned Easter Saturday and Sun-
    day as well.
40 *Letters*, 31st March–14th April 1915. Ruck would later edit and publish *Paterson on
    Prisons*, a compendium of his prison writings.
41 *War Diary*, 6th April, *Letters*, 8th April 1915. His promotion took place on 13th
    April.
42 *Letters*, 13th, 14th April, 6th May 1915. The executors of her will were Willis and
    Claude, and the estate of over £10,000 was to be divided equally among the siblings
    except for Claude, to whom his mother had given £1,000 in 1914. This amount was
    deducted from his share.

Alec was allowed five days leave to attend the funeral. On 27th April, twenty-four hours earlier than he needed to be, he was 'very glad to be back' in Béthune, only to be told that the 22nd were at the Front five miles east of there near the village of Cuinchy. They had suffered casualties. He was relieved to find that no one in his platoon was among them, but in others one of his friends was badly wounded, and 'Johnny Day, who always smiled', was dead. Alec was soon back in the trenches with all his comrades. There he was 'very comfortable and happy', despite the fact that their observation posts were only eighty yards from the Germans, two of his men were fortunate not to be shot for sleeping on duty, and the incessant rain transformed the pathway of the communication trench they had been laboriously digging into a quagmire, soon to be known as 'Paterson's folly'. Another trench was named 'Stansfeld Road'. Digging, digging, endless digging, in which task 'the club fellows justif[ied] their training in the mud of Horndon and Halls Green'. Nonetheless, he could read *David Copperfield*, there were practically no casualties, and the Germans, who boasted an impressive boy solo, entertained them with their singing. Over another lad, this time British, the doctor asked Paterson to read the burial service. He would have done the same had the youngster been German. Germans were the enemy, but they were still 'friends'.[43] Not for Alec the hatred of 'the Hun' that had engulfed England. Patriotism was enough; xenophobia too much.

The 47th Division was held in readiness to support the British attack on Aubers Ridge on 9th May, but such was the fiasco of that assault that it was soon aborted, without the division being engaged. At the same time Alec fell ill, stopped eating, and could barely walk. He had been feeling unwell ever since he arrived in France, but had concealed his condition, fearing he might be medically discharged. Finally, in mid-May, he succumbed.[44] He ended up behind the lines, laying on a stretcher alongside the wounded, in No.1 Casualty Clearing Station[45] at Chocques, three miles west of Béthune. Although one or two men died, it was not so much a mournful place for the dying as an expectant one for the surviving. He observed their attitude to the war, still in its early stages:

> The majority are in the highest spirits, counting very confidently on getting back to England, and vowing that they will never come out to the war again. That is the one anxiety of the oldest and bravest soldier – to get out of the

---

43 *Diary*, 1st–11th May; *Letters*, 1st–5th, 10th May, 7th July 1915.

44 *Letters*, 31st May 1915.

45 Casualty clearing stations were part of the evacuation chain, further back from the frontline than the regimental aid posts, and advanced and main dressing stations. Manned by troops of the Royal Army Medical Corps, their task was to treat the wounded sufficiently for their return to duty or, in most cases, to enable them to be evacuated to one of the base hospitals near the coast, at Étaples, Rouen, Le Havre and Boulogne for example.

war as soon as possible with as many limbs as fate allows. They all hope that the wound is bad enough for 'Blighty' but not so bad as to make them incapable for work. I have not met a single man who was enthusiastic for the righteous cause which the "Daily Mail" and our chaplains say is ours, or who was anxious to risk his life for it. They are all straining every nerve to get home by any means foul or fair, anxious for the war to end in any way, so long as it does end. And no man wants to stay in the Army and risk another Mons.[46]

There is no criticism of this attitude, but an understanding of it.

After a couple of days' rest and a diet of milk, Alec had recovered enough to be discharged. He was to be allocated to a 'convalescent company' and put on light duties for a week before being returned to the Front. There was no room for him in the convalescent camp, however, and he opted to rejoin his company straightaway. Not for long. He relapsed, and again ended up in hospital in Béthune, thus, to his great regret, missing taking part with his division in the battle of Festubert, which raged from 15th to 25th May and during which the 47th Division lost over 2,000 men killed, wounded or missing. One lucky survivor, Lance-Corporal Leonard Keyworth, became the division's first holder of the Victoria Cross.[47] The newly-named 142nd Brigade in particular suffered severe losses after an initial success exposed them to deadly enfilading fire from German artillery. Alec was marooned, worrying about the fate of his friends, and ever the more anxious to return to what was left of them.[48]

In hospital, Alec was finally diagnosed with jaundice, a condition that may have been caused by the stress occasioned by the death of his mother and the brutal reality of total war. For a couple of nights he had to endure sleeping on a dirty mattress, under 'blankets full of life', in a crowded and claustrophobic loft. Thereafter he was moved to various other hospitals to convalesce. He was enjoying himself by sitting in the sun reading *Martin Chuzzlewit*, and being invited out for lunch by visiting big-wigs, until 'one evil day' the inevitable happened as he knew it would. He received a letter from Lieutenant-Colonel Previté, informing him that as his company had lost all its lieutenants in the recent battle he was holding him to his 'promise to take a commission when it was absolutely necessary'. Loath as Corporal Alec was to become Second Lieutenant Paterson,

---

46 *Diary*, 14th May 1915. He would write in similar vein to his sister, whom he told 'every wounded man has to run the gauntlet of congratulations on his way to the dressing station for everybody wants to be out of it', while others 'growled' about not having 'the luck to get hit' (*Letters*, 7th September, 17th October 1915).

47 Maude, pp. 19f; Peter Batchelor and Christopher Matson, *VCs of the First World War, The Western Front 1915* (Stroud, 1997), pp. 121–124. In October Keyworth would be mortally wounded during the battle of Loos.

48 *Letters*, 28th May 1915.

and 'leave our picnic meals and general cheeriness for an officers' mess', duty dictated that he could no longer refuse promotion out of the ranks. He took the required medical examination and, as a Territorial officer, signed an undertaking to serve anywhere outside the United Kingdom. He got one concession from his colonel and that was that he should remain in his old company, and as double insurance that he would not be moved to another battalion he wrote to a friend of his in the War Office.[49] He would pull strings when necessary.

Although his commission would take time to come through, he was to return to his battalion as soon as possible. He needed no such order. Ever since hearing of the losses he had been impatient to get back. Doing so, however, was delayed. First he was moved to Rouen and from there to his division's base camp near Harfleur. He generally dodged parades and spent the days reading and writing in the YMCA. They needed more books. As a mere corporal Alec was not allowed to appeal to the readers of *The Times*, but he got round this embargo by writing to the novelist Alfred Ollivant, who incorporated the appeal 'from the author of *Across the Bridges*' in a letter of his own, headed 'Can you help?'[50] Readers could and did. At least while idling he was relieved to hear that 'by a happy miracle our club boys seem almost entirely to have escaped, and my special friends are all right.'[51]

It was not until 13th June that, feeling fighting fit, he arrived back in Béthune, and to more weeks of inactivity. Although the colonel assured him that he was making all the arrangements for his commission, Alec was once again back with his old section as corporal. As soon as 'the 22nd boys in the camp learn[ed]' that he was 'to exchange two stripes for a single star' they 'seemed strangely pleased'.[52] While they did not want to lose him to the officers' mess, they were delighted at his imminent elevation, having long appreciated his courage and daring, his good nature and sense of humour, and his unswerving leadership from the front in what must have been the grimmest circumstances.

Since the beginning of June, the 47th Division had been deployed to the erstwhile French sector opposite the coal-mining town of Loos, with its pitheads and slag-heaps. Alec settled into the routine of alternating between being in the trenches and behind the line. Initially enemy activity was desultory, the weather good, the billets comfortable. As summer reached its end, more and more were he and his men soaked and covered in mud. Since there was no point in grumbling about the weather, he encouraged them to 'make friends with the chilly trickle down your neck in the early hours and the squelchy hiccough of

49   TNA, WO374/52506; *Letters*, 3rd, 12th, 24th June 1915).
50   *The Times*, 28th June 1915.
51   *Letters*, 31st May–12th June 1915; letter from Barclay to his mother, 5th June 1915
     (Snape, p. 215).
52   *Diary*, 31st May–7th June.

your boots as you pull them from the mud.' Good humour got them through. He confessed to his brother Willis that such was his men's exposure to the elements, he had had to deploy the reading material he had sent as bedding, and what a difference it made:

> With *The Times* beneath (it wants sitting on sometimes), the *Bowdon & Manchester Guardian* on top, and with *Punch* (which is ever dry) for a pillow, you can spend a very tolerable night.[53]

There were diversions, of course, from cricket and football matches to hearing Annie Swan, the Scottish novelist on a morale-boosting tour, speaking at the YMCA. Night work was relieved by a 'wonderful amount of chocolate' and a prodigious number of cigarettes. Alec never ran short of the latter, as a friend of his sent over his 'special fags' every week. He even took the opportunity, when visiting an advanced trench, of picking flowers to send as a wedding gift. Once providence, or lethargy, saved him from a shell. On a Sunday evening he and his 'club fellows' had arranged to meet for a service at the corner of a field. As the devotional party were approaching the spot, a shell hit it. Alec joked of sending a fragment back to the OBM 'to show that unpunctuality has its merits'.[54]

He wanted to 'leave the ranks less each day that flies', having had one of his happiest years. He knew that neither 'heat, nor rain, not thirst, nor weight of pack can defeat the impetus that rough comradeship with many, and very close friendships with a few, give to daily life.' It was a sentiment many shared, and a compensation for all they endured. He had not yet experienced a major battle, nor seen many of his friends fall, yet he felt the poignancy of eating a slice of cake sent by the girl of one of the fatalities. It was to have been her beau's birthday cake which he would have shared with his 'pals', so she sent it to them to eat in his memory – 'a strange feast'.[55]

On 23rd June, to his 'infinite surprise', Alec was made a sergeant, and put in temporary charge of No.15 Platoon, which was without an officer. It was a trial run of being in command. It would also give him useful experience of all ranks before his promotion out of them, which his acting brigade commander, Lieutenant-Colonel W.G. Simpson, assured him was still highly likely to be approved.[56] His superior's suggestion that he go to another battalion he stoutly rejected, and, faced with such obduracy from a sergeant (and pleased by such loyalty to the 22nd), it was the colonel who backed down. Meanwhile, Alec thought being platoon sergeant was an ideal position considering that he had as much power and respect as a second lieutenant and, an 'incalculable gain, the

53   *Letters*, 18th August, 4th September 1915.
54   *Letters*, 7th July, 4th August 1915.
55   *Letters*, 15th June, 2nd, 7th, 18th, 30th July, 1st, 13th August 1915.
56   *Diary*, 14th–22nd July, 2nd–3rd August 1915.

company of the ranks instead of the company of the mess'. Although on one occasion he had to give 'an early and deep burial' to his sister's tin of shrimps which
had exuded noxious gases when opened, he much preferred 'jolly Bermondsey
picnics' to 'Bayswater dinners', and the disparity in food and comfort for officers and men he thought 'grotesque'. He was 'still with the men all day, and not
so Olympian [as to] miss the talk and current of life'. He did, however, have a
'merry evening in the sergeants' mess "wetting my stripes"', an alcohol-fuelled
celebration of his promotion.

He confessed to a certain anxiety about the responsibilities ahead:

> The strain on nerves is far greater for an officer than a man. If a man makes a
> mistake in a tight corner, with only a fraction of a second in which to make
> up his mind, it may cost him his own life, but an officer who decides wrongly
> will lose fifty good lives.[57]

Nor was he bothered about military etiquette.

> I am not enough of a soldier to care for the pipe-clay button-polish sort of
> parade life here. Everyone in step, all boots and uniforms spotless. In the
> trenches you would not know us for soldiers – anybody wears anything they
> like, and we are all as muddy and dirty as can be. When we do march, it is
> just a straggle of wandering pedlars with bits of luggage all over them. We do
> keep our rifles clean, but that's all.[58]

Thus he showed no resentment when at the end of August he was superseded
by a second lieutenant taking command. On his arrival, Henry Scott recalled,
his sergeant 'immediately began to talk about his men, what a great crowd they
were and all, like himself, Cockneys from Bermondsey'. The new officer was
amused by the very un-Cockney accent with which these words were enunciat-
ed, putting it down to 'the terriers' being 'a queer crowd where dukes and dust-
men rubbed shoulders'. Even more amusing was what Alec said next:

> There is one thing, Sir, which I think you ought to know. I had nothing to
> do with the Territorials before the war and just joined up like most of us in
> 1914, but I didn't want these stripes and I'm not a very good sergeant. What
> I have to admit to you, Sir, is that though I have tried very hard since I joined
> up, I just CANNOT march in step!

Scott 'very gradually began to realise' that there was more to this sergeant than
enthusiasm and incongruity, and recognise 'the power of his personality, not
only in the Platoon, but in the Battalion, a power which had nothing to do
with uniforms, stripes or stars or the army or king's regulations.' It made Scott

---

57   *Diary*, 22nd–29th July; *Letters*, 30th July, 6th and 18th August 1915.
58   *Letters*, 26th August 1915.

understand for the first time something which Alec had long grasped, 'that the only discipline which matters is self-discipline.'[59]

Self-discipline was an attribute Paterson possessed in spades. Self-discipline and self-composure. Just before midnight on Saturday 10th September two of his men – 'Price and Milky' – were buried alive and disinterred dead. On the Sunday afternoon Alec and seven others from the platoon took the bodies of their comrades to a ruined church a mile behind the line and dug a double grave. It was rough going as it was terribly hot and the ground was hard, but the group of friends were determined to do it themselves. Whatever the effort it would be worth it. 'In the moonlight we laid them gently side by side, the slow, sad words of the burial service giving us all a new glow of comradeship and hope.'[60]

On 23rd September Paterson was gazetted 'second lieutenant as of 11th inst.'.[61] Not that he was aware of his promotion. He and his platoon were in the trenches preparing for what was hoped to be 'the great advance', a combined effort by the French and British armies on a wide front to take pressure off the Russians and to cut into the German bulge between Arras and Rheims. The French would make a two-pronged attack in the Champagne region and in the area of Lens-Arras (including Vimy Ridge), while the British would strike across the Artois coalfields north of Lens. The battle of Loos took place largely in the three weeks between Saturday 25th September and Friday 15th October[62] over an area of open land that stretched from La Bassée Canal in the north to the village of Grenay in the south, a front of some seven miles. A four-day bombardment of very varying efficacy preceded it. Billed as 'the greatest battle in the history of the world', it constituted by far the biggest British attack so far, and the first mass engagement of Kitchener's 'New Army' units. Their baptism of fire soon would become an immersion in blood. The 47th, the only Territorial division involved in the first stage, had already experienced battle the previous May, and was well-acquainted with the Loos terrain, having been stationed in the area for months, entrenching and reconnoitring. Its seasoned men had considerably more success, and suffered far fewer casualties, than the raw recruits straight out of England.

---

59 Quoted, without date or attribution, in Neale (p. 59) and Baron (p. 166), the latter adding, 'Alec always made the pace, never followed it.' It is likely true since Scott assumed duties on 23rd August, and Alec, although not mentioning this encounter in either his diary or letters, around this time acknowledged that he was a 'slovenly sergeant' who 'could not keep in step to save his life' (*Letters*, 13th and 22nd August 1915).

60 *Diary*, 8th September; *Letters*, 17th September 1915.

61 *The London Gazette*, Supplement 29306, 23rd September 1915, p. 9417.

62 The official end date was 4th November when Haig informed the French that he could do no more, but by mid-October the battle was effectively over.

Making an assault on 'a jagged, scarred and mutilated sweep of mining villages, factories, quarries, slag-dumps, pit-heads, chalk-pits, and railway embankments – all the plant of an elaborate mechanical civilization connected above ground and below by every means that ingenuity and labour could devise to the uses of war', the British forces were at a marked disadvantage.[63] The dismal terrain was flat and exposed, festooned with industrial detritus which hindered movement, but provided little cover. The Germans, although initially far fewer in number, had built a strong second line and were well-entrenched on higher ground, their position secured by formidable redoubts, concrete-faced dugouts, observation posts, concealed batteries and machine gun nests, while their assailants lacked the firepower to eliminate these defences, cut the rapacious barbed wire, or destroy the enemy's morale. A 'reckless optimism' prevailed.

The 47th Division, by then part of IV Corps under Lieutenant-General Rawlinson, was deployed in the right-hand sector of the battlefield directly opposite the Double Crassier, two huge slag-heaps running parallel to each other, fortified and bristling with machine guns. Alec's battalion, along with the 21st, held the flank, the southern-most point of the entire British sector which stretched from the Ypres Salient to Lens. The French Tenth Army was to their right.

Before the battle began it had been raining for days, and the trenches in which Paterson and his men found themselves were filled with mud. 'The mud was so thick on my puttees', he recalled, 'that when I got them off after three days and nights live worms were in them.' Worms he could endure. But there was worse than worms. To his disgust chlorine gas, previously deployed by the Germans in the spring of 1915 at the second battle of Ypres, was to be used for the first time by the British. He considered it a 'tragedy that we are doing as a country just what all our finest spirits have fought against for centuries'. The British way was to continue to play fair when the other side played foul, 'and beat them all the same'.[64] Ironically, the sector where the gas attack would prove most effective was that of Alec's division.

At 4.55am on the 25th gas was to be let loose, but because of the mist and rain there was a delay of half an hour. Finally 'a cloud of vapour [went] out towards the German trench with a hissing noise.' The gas cloud, coupled with thick smoke from mortar shells, enabled the leading waves of the 140th and 141st Brigades to capture the first German positions before the enemy were aware of what was happening. British machine-gunners located in North Maroc caught enemy troops fleeing. German fire from the hamlet of Cité St Pierre caused losses, and some counter-attacks threatened the newly-taken positions. However,

---

63   Kipling, *op.cit.*, p. 113. John Kipling was killed during the battle, as was the poet Charles Sorley.

64   *Diary*, 8th–24th September; *Letters*, 29th September 1915. Despite Kitchener believing its use was against the rules of war, Haig went ahead.

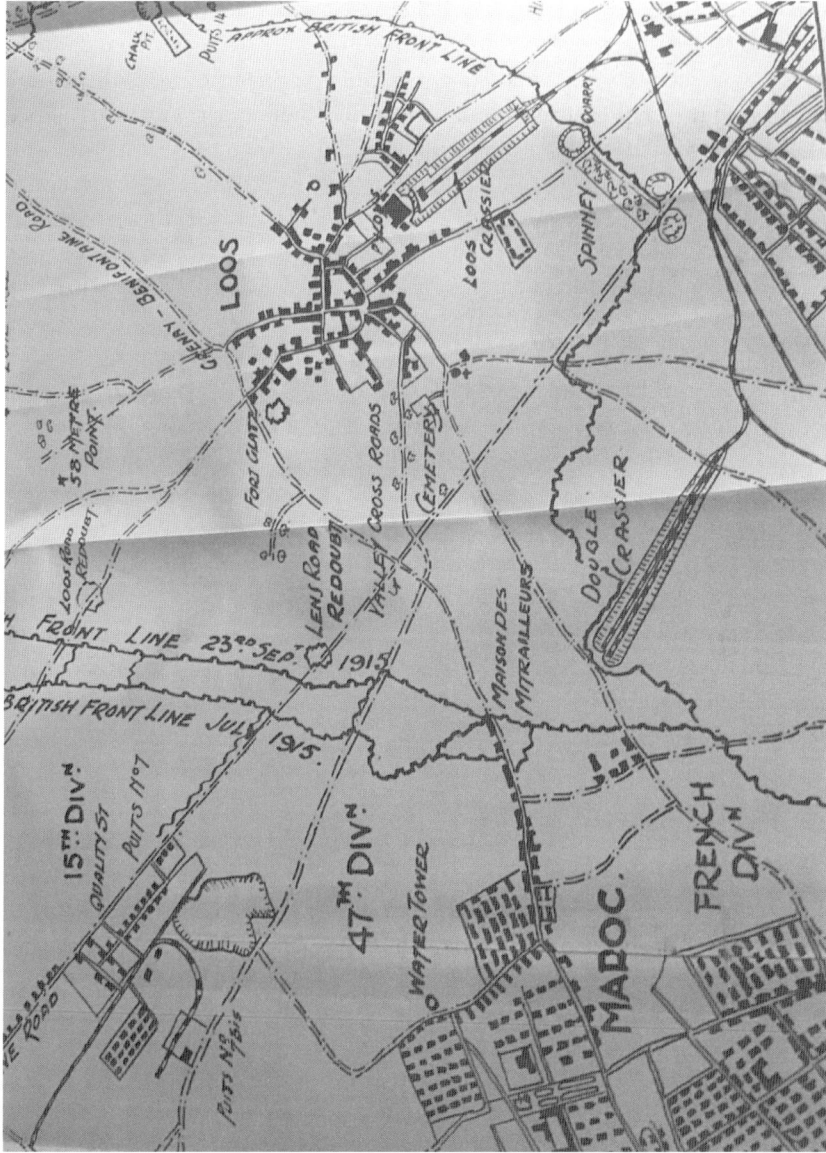

FIGURE 13.
The Battle of Loos, 1915
(the southern sector)

the 140th Brigade overran the German support trench that ran from the middle of the Double Crassier to the Lens-Béthune road, capturing 300 men and three field guns. The 141st Brigade had a harder time. While the 20th Londons captured the Chalk Pit, the 19th, the left-most battalion, suffered heavy casualties from machine guns, resulting in its colonel and most of its officers being hit. Although they took their objective, the pair of huge pit-head winding-towers Tommies called 'Tower Bridge', the companies were badly broken up by their advance through Loos, and the flank defence on another enormous dump called the Loos Crassier was not extended as planned. Nonetheless, the Londoners in their first major engagement, owing to a combination of factors – clear, limited aims, good planning, concentrated artillery fire, and favourable terrain – had achieved more than any other division and had formed a south-facing defensive flank between the Double and Loos Crassiers. In the afternoon and evening the division continued to consolidate the positions it had won, and was readied to meet any counter-attack that might be delivered from the southern flank, which a delayed French offensive had left exposed.

In addition, on their immediate left, the 15th (Scottish) Division had captured Loos itself. A hole had been punched in the enemy front line, although there was no reserve to exploit these gains and transform them into a breakthrough. Elsewhere things were very different: ineffective barrages, gas blown back upon the British themselves, uncut barbed wire, the strength of the German defences and the tenaciousness of their troops all taking a terrible toll. By the end of the first day 470 officers and 15,000 men had fallen. The 47th Division suffered the least but still had almost 400 fatalities, and many more wounded. Worse would follow.

Paterson and his men got off lightly. Their battalion and the 21st, although not in reserve with the rest of the brigade, were merely to hold the line from opposite the Double Crassier to the junction with the French, to give fire support, but not go 'over the top'. Apart from one early foray with Tom to pull up 'the dummy army' (mannequins designed to deflect enemy fire from real soldiers), Alec spent most of the day in a dugout.[65] The next morning he was summoned by Captain Turner, who had read in *The Times* that the sergeant had in fact been a second lieutenant for some days. Turner cheered up the disconsolate subaltern by telling him that he was to remain with 'A' Company and take charge of No.4 Platoon, the outfit in which he had served throughout his military career. Perfect! While 'making his bow to headquarters' the newly commissioned officer came through a hole in the wall and fell down some steps into a cellar.[66]

65   *Diary*, 28th September 1915.
66   *Diary*, 26th September; *Letters*, 29th September 1915.

Imperfect! At the same time, he learnt that Henry Scott was to be sent off to 'D' Company. 'A great loss to men and mess' was Paterson's assessment.[67]

Alec regretted most of all having to abandon his great pal, Tom Angliss. He soon realised, however, that now he was an officer he could have a batman, and who better than Tom? Tom was to remain by his friend's side throughout the war, and would remain so throughout his life. His admiration for the older man verged on hero-worship, as is clear from a letter he wrote to Dorothy in which he extolled her brother's qualities – although Alec had tried to put the censor's pencil through things that were 'absurd and untrue'.

> It is difficult to imagine, but Pat (we all call him that you know) thinks he is quite capable of looking after himself, in fact quite believes he looks after me … It is reckoned rather a joke in the Platoon, the officer and the servant, as we have always been such inseparables, but we really do have a rattling good time together. Your brother is the best fellow in the Battalion. If there are any wounded people about he is always with them, no matter how dangerous it is, and he always has a steadying effect on the men, and does a world of good.[68]

Since the first day of the battle the 47th Division had been ordered to hold its gains and maintain its position. Although not adventurous it was still danger-ous. On 28th September Alec witnessed the carnage on the road to Loos, where 'muddy corpses, men and horses, all in the stiffness of sudden death' were every-where. It was premonition of more to come. 'Pat's Platoon' was posted to a line of trenches on the Loos Crassier where they were heavily shelled and suffered many losses, reducing the fighting force to 'a sad little crowd' of ten men. Yet they stuck it out, and more of them would die. 'The whole day was one succes-sion of casualties – in pouring cold rain and inches of mud.' Paterson tried to get permission to withdraw, but none came. He had to stay and watch 'the club boys fall'. He found 'young Wal Dyke of Dockhead [lying], barely breathing, with a fearful wound to the back of his head'. He was stretchered out, but there was little hope for him. Young Wal would be but one of many 'little kids of seventeen and eighteen left under the muddy earth'. Paterson with a couple of others carried the body of 'little Bartell, a merry grig, on to the top, and amid a

---

67   After the war Alec ensured that Scott joined the Prison Service. He was very much in the Paterson mould. Stuart Wood thought Captain Scott the keenest reformer in the service. He made every effort to implement the reforms sanctioned by the Commissioners, and but for 'his practical idealism and utter devotion to the cause which lay very near his heart' they would have come to nought (*Shades of the Pris-on House* [London, 1932], p. 322). Scott would eventually become Director of the Borstal Association.

68   *Letters*, 15th October 1915. He would later promote 'our Pat' to 'the best fellow in the world' (4th June 1918).

tornado of shells, read together those grand words of hope and triumph, and lay the earth gently over him.' They did the same for 'poor Sammy Curtis, cheeriest of husbands, best of full-backs'.[69] They were 'sad at heart to lose so good a brother ... yet even so, in the dark, in the rain, in the mud, among the bristling shells, the burial service becomes a triumph song.'[70] Makeshift interments under heavy fire were not unusual, as his friend, Geoffrey Studdert Kennedy, knew only too well:

> And that night I'd been in the trenches
> Seeking out the sodden dead
> And just dropping them in shell holes
> with a service swiftly said.[71]

Despite the danger, Alec was determined that decencies be preserved.[72] After six hours of shelling in their 'little death trap', the half-dozen survivors got permission to move round the corner to a communication trench. Here they crouched on the stairs, out of the rain and secure from the shells, but short of rations. Paterson retrieved the packs and water bottles of the fallen to supply his men. Finally they managed to retire to Loos itself, which proved small respite as this 'museum of veiled death' was under heavy bombardment and strafed by machine-gun fire.[73] His 'plucky little lot' would be commended for their actions by French himself.

During the night of 30th September Alec was ordered to take half a company to a trench two-thirds of the way up Hill 70, south-east of Loos, in support of his brigade, which had replaced the 3rd Guards. The low hill with bare slopes on all sides was a 'rotten position', with 'nothing to hold the Huns in front, and snipers making a breeze behind'. One of his men went out to bring in some stragglers from the Welsh guards 'who have been happy in a dugout between the

---

69   The names of Privates J.H.B. Bartell, S. Curtis, W.R. Dyke and Sergeant A. Bates (*infra*) are inscribed along with many others on the battalion war memorial, erected in 1921 next to the drill hall. John Bartell was thirty, Walter Dyke twenty-two. Twenty-one-year-old Curtis had married in March 1915, as had Bates.

70   *Diary*, 28th and 29th September; *Letters*, 29th September, 3rd October 1915. So often did he inter the dead that Alec asked a friend to send out 'a little pocket copy of the burial service' since his own small prayer book did not contain it, and he was glad to say he did 'not know it off by heart yet' (*Letters*, 21st June 1915).

71   *Rough Rhymes.*

72   He would ensure the same for a gassed kitten he adopted. He asked his men 'to bury it decently, and next day found a little wooden cross, with white chalk stones neatly laid round the grave and an inscription: "SANDY" / Attached to the Recreation Officer's Division / Died of wounds – 22.6.18'.

73   Kipling, *op.cit.*, p. 113.

lines for some days, with some Germans similarly stranded supplying the grub'.[74]
Eventually what was left of his unit was relieved and pulled back. Paterson was
able to return to Béthune for a few days' leave. There he had a 'good hot bath
twice', wrote 'sad letters to parents and girls, breaking news', and laid flowers on
Wal Dyke's grave. He refused an offer of home-leave, at least until 'the show was
over'. It would be running away. During all this time he remained stoical, even
resigned. He had seen many boys he had known 'since they were nippers of ten
and twelve' die. It had been a bad week, 'but that is war'.[75]

Although by mid-October, after appalling losses, the bloody battle 'where
death and autumn held their reign'[76] was finally petering out, there was still
much for the survivors to do in consolidating such small gains as had been made
at the cost of some 50,000 men and 2,000 officers killed, wounded, missing or
captured. British losses included the deaths of three major-generals. German
casualties were around 20,000. Paterson was ordered to occupy a trench which
had recently been in enemy hands. There he mused that there were 'few things
sadder than a trench that has been hurriedly left by the Germans. All the letters
and postcards and little things they leave behind make them out to be so absurd-
ly like us.'[77] After a few days' respite, he was allocated a 'narrow and uncomfortable' frontline trench. There he and another subaltern were sent over the top
to examine the barbed wire laid by the Royal Engineers. They reported it was
very weak on the entire front and absent on both flanks. As a result, they were
deployed every night on wiring parties, at risk of both enemy and 'friendly' fire.
One major consolation was that Alec got permission from his captain to live
with his platoon in the trenches.[78]

And then the deluge. It rained for two days and three nights, everyone and
everything was drenched, mud was everywhere, hot food nowhere. Wet, cold,
shivering and hungry, 'the state of the men was pitiable.' Yet none in his platoon
'went sick', knowing that 'if they crept away into hospital' it 'would shorten the
numbers in the trench, and give longer hours on sentry to those left behind'.

74 *Diary*, 30th September 1915; Maude (p. 35) mentions a similar incident in which
Lieutenant Baswitz of the 22nd Battalion found six Grenadier Guardsmen and two
Germans 'in forced alliance' and brought them back to the British lines. This was
not an uncommon occurrence. The then Lieutenant Neil Weir of the Argyll and
Sutherland Highlanders recorded in his war diary that on the second day of the
battle of Loos he had 'discovered some wounded Boche officers in a dug-out guard-
ed by wounded Camerons' (Saul David [ed.], *Mud and Bodies: The War Diaries of
Captain N.A.C. Weir* [Barnsley, 2013], p. 37).

75 *Diary*, 6th–12th October; *Letters*, 3rd and 17th October 1915.

76 Patrick MacGill, 'In the Morning'.

77 George Coppard thought the same (*With a Machine Gun to Cambrai* [London,
1980], p. 90).

78 *Letters*, 15th; *War Diary*, 23rd; *Diary*, 25th–27th October 1915.

They were 'all sticking it'. Alec observed: 'That sort of thing makes you so happy that you don't care much about the rain. It is the triumph of spirit over flesh that in the long end shall win the war.' And then the sun shone, and there was 'a different world today with quite another race of men, all singing ragtime and shovelling for their lives as they sing'.[79]

But the 'worst day of [his] life' was approaching. On 6th November the battalion had been relieved, and moved back to Mazingarbe, two miles north-west of Loos. Four platoons remained to garrison some fortified outposts, Paterson's being assigned to the Lens Road redoubt. The next morning, a Sunday, began quietly enough, and by evening his men were to be withdrawn to safety well behind the trench-line. About 6.30pm Alec sent his 'old pal' and platoon sergeant, Alf Bates, across the road to give instructions to some other men. At that point heavy shelling started and Alec, hearing screams, raced onto the road, calling out 'Alf'. He dared not show a light as the firing was incessant. Finally he came across 'the bonny lad, stretched 6 feet 1 inch by the side of the wood, lying as if asleep'. He had no wounds and his eyes were closed. A shell had not killed him: the shock had. The Sunday before he had sung the solo of 'O Come All Ye Faithful', and that night at their service he was supposed to sing again. Now his lips were forever sealed. He was only twenty-one and recently married. As Alec was leaning over him another shell burst nearby, and he felt a sting behind his left shoulder and dampness spreading down his back.

He had been hit, but soldiered on, with a small dressing and a large brandy keeping him going. When he finally got to Mazingarbe in an ambulance he was inoculated against tetanus and sent to bed on a stretcher. A piece of shrapnel had entered his back and touched his lung. Despite having what others would proclaim was a 'Blighty'[80], he dismissed it as a 'flesh wound' as serious as if he had cut his hand 'opening a tin of bloater paste'. It was rather more serious than that. The following morning he was moved to No.18 Casualty Clearing Station in Lapugnoy, a small village five miles west of Béthune. There he noted the large number of 'Kitchener's officers', suffering from 'flu' or 'trench fever', making the most of a lengthy convalescence. He also noted that while five doctors tended to the wounded from Loos – 5,000 in four days – twelve more arrived after the battle was over. They had little to do other than tending to men with swollen feet, a condition that could have been prevented with grease and gumboots which, although they had been sent in good time, due to negligence had not reached the trenches. 'Some privates', he declaimed, 'will lose their feet because the staff lost their heads.'

79   *Letters*, 2nd and 3rd November 1915.
80   From the Hindustani, used by soldiers on foreign service for 'home'.

Small pieces of uniform as well as metal were extracted from his shoulder, and he seemed in his own mind to be on the mend. After nine days' 'rest-cure', he refused to go back to England, surreptitiously transferring a 'return home' sign from his bed to his neighbour's.[81] He insisted on returning to his battalion, which he did on 17th November. Three days later, still obviously nursing his wounds, he was finally persuaded to take long-delayed leave, incorporating a period as an outpatient in a hospital and for any other necessary medical interventions.[82]

Arriving in London on 22nd November, he met his sister, who had come down from Bowdon to see him. Thereafter he had a lot of sombre visiting to do. Returning to Bermondsey, he found it much quieter and darker. He saw many of the parents. Those whose boys were dead were beyond grief. Those whose boys were still alive 'found in their absence a loss that is unspeakably sad'. One mother could never stay in her house at 7pm when her son used to come home to his tea. 'That is the glimpse of the tragedy that must be common through the land just now', he concluded. If any blamed him for being the Pied Piper who lured their boys away, or if he felt any guilt over their sons' fate, he does not say. He took the temperature of the locals. Very few thought the war would be over in 1916 and nearly all recognised that 'no fighting will determine the issue but the length of our moneybags', the real struggle being 'in Wall Street and the Bourse'. While many of the women dressed in black and were vindictive against the Germans, the men for the most part were 'not filled with personal hate'.[83]

After a week as an outpatient, he was admitted into a surgical ward of a military hospital to be x-rayed and to have some remaining shrapnel removed. After the extraction, he did not see a doctor for several days, and when he did he was told that there was still some shrapnel in his back about which nothing more could be done. There was no reason for him not to return to the trenches, and, like many others, he was glad to do so. France, until hostilities ceased, was 'more home than England could be'. Waving him off at Waterloo station were his 'chief friend's' parents who, 'sensing a strong personality, made some comment about a spoilt son which went something like "look after him in France, Alec"'. Of course he would, and had. He and Tom had 'made an early pact to see the war through together'.[84]

Paterson returned to Béthune late on 10th December. He walked six miles to the village of Allouagne where the troops were undertaking training exercises, interspersed with football matches and a brigade boxing competition during

81   Scott, p. 68.
82   *War Diary*, 6th, 7th, 17th; *Diary*, 8th to 17th; *Letters*, 8th and 10th November 1915.
83   *Diary*, 22nd November–2nd December 1915.
84   Neale, p. 59; *Letters*, 29th May; *Diary*, 9th December 1915.

which the 22nd Battalion won every event they entered.[85] He had trained many of the young men and was delighted by their showing.

While on the march back to the trenches, Alec found his pack troublesome, and a sandbag falling on the wound caused such inflammation that he could hardly move and could not sleep. When the abscess on his back burst he was sent to Lapugnoy to have the remaining piece of shell removed. It proved elusive as it was small, jagged and had moved deep down between the ribs, so surgery kept being delayed. All the while Tom, who had accompanied him, remained by his side. Although officers customarily brought their servants along with them to hospital even when there was little need, Tom proved invaluable in washing, feeding and dressing the by then semi-invalid. Finally the operation was carried out at 10am on Christmas Day, and, at his wish, by the administration of cocaine, not chloroform, so that he could keep his promise to preach at the 11 o'clock church parade. The surgeon who had operated on him was in the front row, 'an odd inversion'. Although after the service the post-op patient was ordered to bed, he escaped with his trusty Tom to the house of the village barber, where they had arranged to have Christmas dinner for which, surreptitiously, they had bought a poulet. 'It was not bravado – it was merely maintaining an anniversary which he always regarded as of primary importance.' This was typical of the man who, although constantly in pain from an unresolved injury, carried on regardless and suffered silently.

Nonetheless he was kept in hospital, comfortable and well-fed, for another fortnight, such was the nature of the wound and the length of convalescence required. He remained as cheerful as ever, and was readily asking his sister to send out curry powder to flavour the stew, and top-boots that would cover his knees and reach higher than the ever-invasive mud.

Unbeknownst to him, things were not so cheerful for his battalion in that bleak mid-winter. Again it had been in fierce action. Its line in the north sector of the Loos salient came under sustained attack. In a single afternoon – 30th December – a hundred men were lost, mainly from Captain Woolley's 'B' Company which had been manning part of the trench-line known as 'the Hairpin' when it was blown up by mines. 'C' and 'D' Companies suffered heavily as well. On New Year's Eve men from the 22nd were coming into the casualty station 'thick and fast'. Alec and Tom, 'les bons camarades' as the locals called them, set to work going round the camp, administering cigarettes and consolation, and writing letters home on behalf of the wounded. Alec was called to the bedside of a dying boy who had wanted to say farewell. Later that day he and Tom buried the lad 'on the hill, in a little cemetery for English soldiers, full of flowers which the French peasants [brought] so regularly'. Subsequent days saw many more hospital admissions. In all the brigade's casualties totalled 116 men – twelve killed, sixty-eight wounded, and thirty-six missing. More would die: in four days Alec attended three funerals.

So far as he could gather, 'A' Company had escaped completely unscathed, as indeed it had. At least, with his wound 'healing with wonderful rapidity', he would soon be able to return to his rightful place among his men as they entered the year 1916. Alec was hopeful 'that it would be a far better one than 1915'.[86] In the event it would be far worse.

86   *Letters*, 14th–31st December 1915, 1st–3rd January 1916.

CHAPTER 6

WASTE OF MUSCLE, WASTE OF BRAIN: 1916–1919

War is a bad thing, and the sooner it ends the better. Was ever the world so sick of its folly and yet too proud to confess it? You would think that I am a sentimentalist, appalled at the sight of suffering, unacquainted with the duty of punishment. To the sight of blood and the sounds of pain I am alas accustomed. In the name of duty I have enforced the price, shooting a man in my own company. For the sake of discipline I did not on another occasion sway for a moment in sending the best of friends to his death.

Alexander Paterson[1]

Toc H. is flourishing, full to the brim, and a lot of the good wine of the keen boys' club being infused into the duller water of the casual passer-by.

Tubby Clayton

The doctors would not let their patient escape their clutches until mid-January. For a few days after his return to the platoon not much happened. Then on the 20th he and his men moved up to the front line by the chalk-pits at Loos, and for the next week had 'a very eventful time'. They were positioned at the extreme right of the battalion by a sunken road. A cellar was their only refuge. There was no trench yet, and it was their task to fortify their flank to prevent enemy infiltration into the village. Coming under heavy artillery and sniper fire, the platoon suffered many fatalities, reducing it to nine men, four of whom were wounded. These were the sole survivors of the sixty-two members who had left England in March 1915.[2]

Throughout this period Angliss considered Paterson to have been 'outstandingly brave', a man who 'never actually flinched to a closely bursting shell or

---

1   He makes no mention of these two incidents in his war letters or diary, perhaps unsurprisingly, so they cannot be clarified nor dated.

2   *Letters*, 21st January 1916.

grenade', and that he well deserved a Victoria Cross.³ When volunteers were needed to raid German trenches, 'Paterson would say to his men; "The colonel wants a party to go out tonight. I'm one. Who else is coming?". The response was pretty well unanimous.' Only once did he ever admit to 'some fear': when, before he could evacuate his men from an exposed sap, he had to wire it in, which he did, thirty-five yards from the German line. The only injury he suffered at this time was to his tunic 'when a gas shell burst in the dug-out where it was hanging and turned all the buttons into a beautiful green.'⁴

His lack of concern about his own well-being and attire was equalled by the extraordinary care he took of his men. He shared with them the good things that Dorothy regularly sent over from England, everything from cakes and cigarettes to books and 'vermin powder'. He arranged for food parcels to be sent to the POW camp where one of them was being held, and also to a young French prisoner of war called Raoul Cadet, whom he had first met during the Équihen summer camp in 1913.⁵ He asked a family friend in Bowdon to visit a girl in Manchester in order to break the news of her brother's death. He wrote regularly to a lad who was dying in a hospital in Ipswich, although the recipient struggled with his execrable handwriting. 'My officer is a shocking bad scribbler', he told a visitor, 'but there's no one, no one like him.'

That summed up Second Lieutenant Paterson as a soldier. He could not toe the line or even march in step; he could not keep his uniform clean or even on; he could not read maps or even use a compass; he could not ride a horse in military fashion or even in the right direction; he could not take himself 'very seriously as a company commander', and his company had 'like difficulty': but he was an inspirational officer and for his men there was 'no one like him'.⁶ He had similar high regard for them and especially for the club boys who had 'stood out among the rest'. He was proud of them, and convinced that his work with the Mission and 'many long hours of teaching' and training had borne the 'most unmistakable

3   Baron, p. 166. A number of writers repeat Barclay Baron's assertion that Alec was twice recommended for a VC, and Sanford Bates stated that he was awarded it. There is no evidence for such a recommendation in the War Office records or elsewhere and Alec never referred to it.
4   Scott, p. 68; *Diary*, 1st–5th; *Letters*, 11th February 1916.
5   Alec could speak French. Raoul Cadet was a teacher when they met, and Alec secured him a post in Tunbridge Wells for the following year. The outbreak of hostilities put paid to that. When Cadet was shot by the Germans, he was carrying a photograph of Alec in his tunic pocket. When he was returned home to Boulogne on account of his wounds, he showed Alec the blood-stained remnant (*Letters*, 22nd August 1917).
6   *Letters*, 29th January, 15th February, 9th April 1916.

fruit'.[7] It was a conviction he would carry into civilian life, and confirmation that character would be formed and reformed by didactic means and mentoring.

The 16th February 1916 marks the final entry in his extant diary. It refers to the court-martial of a soldier called Stevens who had fallen asleep at his post, a capital offence. Alec was appointed 'the prisoner's friend'.

The mechanism for rendering swift justice on active service was the field general court-martial, the procedure for which was laid down in the 1914 edition of *The Manual of Military Law*. It had 'the same power as a general court-martial, including the power of trying an officer, but is convened in an exceptional way (no warrant being required), and is subject to exceptional rules under which the procedure is of a more summary character than that of an ordinary court-martial.'[8] The tribunal had to consist of at least three officers, the senior of whom – normally an officer of field rank (a major or above) – presided. If three officers were not available then two would suffice, but the sentencing power of a tribunal thus truncated was restricted to the imposition of two years' imprisonment or three months' field punishment. Only a unanimous panel of three could pass a sentence of death. Unanimity could never be assured.[9]

A legally qualified judge-advocate could be appointed to assist the panel, although this happened intermittently. How independent or even fair-minded the members were is hard to assess as their deliberations were secret. Most knew no law. What they did know was that the court had been convened by a senior officer, often a general, who had stated in the authorising form that it appeared to him 'that the persons named ... have committed the offences'. Although this was merely stating that there was a *prima facie* case, it could easily be construed as being his settled view. To acquit would be to gainsay a superior.

In most cases, however, the facts spoke for themselves, and the real concern about courts-martial was not a propensity to miscarriages of justice but the severity of the sentences passed. From accounts by participants, it seems that many inexperienced officers stuck rigidly by 'the book', and passed death sentences too readily.[10] There were safeguards. The concurrence of all members was necessary, the procedure being that the most junior officer gave his opinion first to avoid his superiors exerting any undue influence, and any capital sentence imposed had to

---

7   *Letters*, 8th March 1915.
8   *Manual of Military Law*, 6th edn (HMSO, London, 1914), p. 39, paras 24ff; pp. 429f; Army (Annual) Act 1913, ss.49, 54.
9   The experience of one subaltern determined not to see injustice done is related in Henry Lawson, *Vignettes of the Western Front* (Oxford, 1979), pp. 72–75.
10 Guy Chapman, *A Passionate Prodigality* (Leatherhead, 1990), pp. 73f.

be subjected to the recommendations of a succession of senior officers, and confirmed by the commander-in-chief. French and Haig confirmed only 11 per cent. Throughout the war the British convened 238,000 courts-martial. These resulted in 3,080 death sentences being passed, of which 346 were carried out, the vast majority for desertion.[11] Those sentenced to be shot for 'sleeping at their post' were almost always reprieved. Out of 449 such cases only two resulted in execution.[12]

The prosecution was usually conducted by an adjutant of the accused's unit, while the accused was entitled to be defended by a junior officer, known as 'the prisoner's friend'. He would usually choose a popular or respected officer from his own platoon or company, irrespective of his forensic abilities. Such 'prisoner's friends' were often hopeless advocates, had no legal knowledge, and were easily overawed in the presence of superior officers.[13]

Paterson, by contrast, was a self-confident and experienced speaker, with considerable knowledge of the law and even more of human nature, and was on social terms with Churchill and Kitchener. Rank never impressed him; calibre did. He relished the task that others would rather relinquish. In his first court-martial, as was so often the case, there was no gainsaying the evidence, but his plea in mitigation met with success. Stevens had not wilfully shirked his duty but had fallen asleep out of sheer exhaustion. He was not put in front of a firing squad, but instead was sentenced to two years' penal servitude, suspended to allow him to return to his unit to prove himself by good or even meritorious conduct before the sentence was up for reconsideration a few months ahead.[14] 'Yawns in front of court' was the prisoner's final gesture, and Paterson's last entry in his diary.[15] This sudden cessation is not explained, and is all the odder since he continued writing it, albeit with less assiduity.[16]

---

11   Deterrence was the military rationale, and it, not justice, the priority. Brigadier-General Lowther adapted a Bloody Code dictum when he stated a man should be shot 'not to punish the man for having deserted, but in order that men may not desert' (TNA, WO71/405).

12   *Statistics of the Military Effort of the British Empire in the Great War 1914–1920* (HMSO, London, 1922); Cathryn Corns and John Hughes-Wilson, *Blindfold and Alone* (London, 2001), pp. 135, 180, 407.

13   *Ibid.*, pp. 91–104.

14   Under the Army (Suspension of Sentences) Act 1915.

15   *Diary*, 16th February 1916. Stevens was probably the same boy 'he had defended at a court-martial' who provided Alec with some shaving soap so that he could smarten up before attending a birthday tea with the colonel (*Letters*, 20th November 1916).

16   In April he told Dorothy that 'the diary has been laconic lately', and the following year, although he needed 'no diary refills at present', his writing of it continued in varying degrees 'from week to week'. The explanation for this portion's loss may lie in the fact that he sent those notebooks, not to his sister in Bowdon, but to his empty flat in Dockhead (*Letters*, 4th April 1916, 22nd February 1917).

As winter turned to spring Alec remained in good spirits, alternating between periods in the trenches and behind the lines. In mid-March the lines changed as his division was moved further south to take over the Carency and Souchez sectors (which included the west slope of the northern spur of Vimy Ridge) from the French Tenth Army, whose troops were needed to defend Verdun. For a while the 142nd Brigade was held in reserve. Seconded to look after the engineers on their working parties, Alec declined an offer to stay with them as he wanted to get back to his own battalion. At the beginning of April, he did. Fellow officers were promoted when he was not, but he had no desire to leave his 'boys of the 22nd' in order to undergo the training necessary for a higher rank. Being a subaltern suited him, and allowed him daily association with his comrades. Having been put in charge of digging parties and allowed to organise games and concerts, army life was, he wrote, 'much more of an endless Bermondsey camp to me, than a serious military affair.'[17]

Bermondsey camps, however, were not subjected to heavy bombardment by the Germans. The British lines were, constantly. Alec recounted an incident illustrative of the attitude of so many soldiers, now that what was supposed to be a short and glorious war had turned into an interminable slogging match. One of his boys thought he had been injured by a shell bursting nearby. There was shrapnel in his trousers, but no wound could be found when the cloth was cut away.

> So he will have to spend the afternoon sewing up his trousers, bitterly disappointed that he will not get back to England. We are really sometimes so tired of the war, that all wounds not actually serious are counted great bits of luck.[18]

There would be one such bit of luck for him. On 24th May, after 'a day or two of hell on earth' around Vimy Ridge, Alec and 'the two Toms' were 'very lucky' to be only slightly wounded. Alec was particularly fortunate as he had had to cross Zouave valley six times under heavy shellfire when reconnoitring.[19] After receiving 'the merest scratch', he was sent to the hospital in Estrée-Cauchy, a village eleven miles south of Béthune, for inoculation. He reassured his sister, telling her to remember that 'in the sort of scrap we have had, the man who gets slightly wounded and can walk out and miss the rest of the fight is the most fortunate of all.' Tom Angliss also informed Dorothy that Alec had been hit again

---

17   *Letters*, 9th April 1916.
18   *Letters*, 16th May 1916.
19   *War Diary*, 24th May 1916; *Letters*, 21st June 1916. The 47th Division, during the fighting at Vimy, lost 63 officers and 2,044 other ranks killed, wounded or missing. Zouave valley in particular was 'constantly visited with very searching shellfire' and 'during the heavy fighting could not even be crossed by runners' (Maude, pp. 56f.).

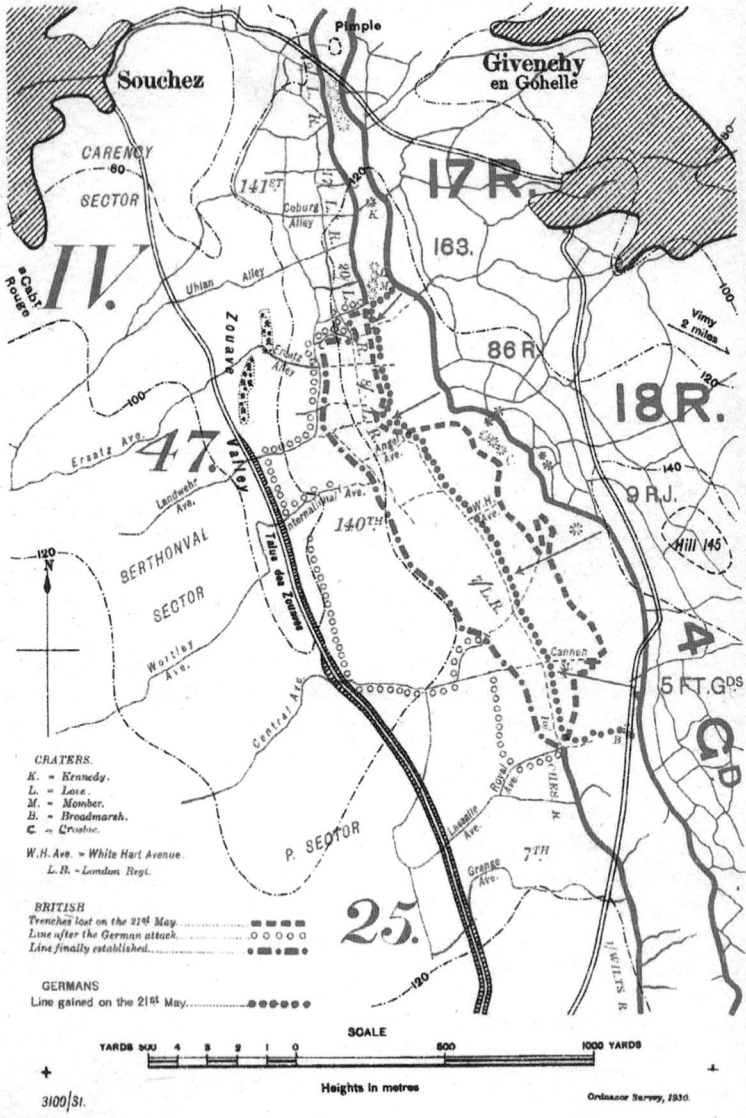

FIGURE 14. Vimy Ridge and Zouave Valley, 1916

by shrapnel, 'but as usual refused to have a decent rest, and would only stop in the hospital a couple of days.'

Having been informed by the surgeon that in his condition he should not return to the trenches, in June Alec was ordered to leave the battalion to take charge of the maintenance of a light railway for moving stores and equipment to the trenches.[20] He soon made his mark. On arrival he found his predecessor living 'in solitary glory 15 feet under the earth', eating his meals alone, while his men shared 'very damp picnics' in a leaky shed. Not for Alec this rigid demarcation between officer and underlings. He messed in with the others as he always had. He and his men constructed a 'summer-house' with communal dining facilities, which they called 'The Railway Hotel'. There they ate, lounged around, played games, read books, drank whisky, and, as before, shared out all parcels, all things in common. It was their little world, and a world apart. He described the new landscape and task to his sister:

Now we are out of it all, [we] can scarcely realise how complete our detachment is from the rest of the world. Somewhere in France, a bit to the right-hand corner of your map, as you face the enemy, is a vast wilderness of upland plain or prairie. Here and there a ruined farm, but not a building that has a roof for miles and miles. Across the rough untilled prairie must be carried every day food and water, ammunition of all sorts, and many stores like timber and wire and sand-bags, to the boys in the front line. For this purpose there is a light railway that climbs unevenly across and returns by a loop ... Half-way up the line in the deepest of dug-outs, live A.P. and T.B.A. and a corporal & 6 men of another battalion. We are responsible for the maintenance of the 'permanent way'. When the Germans are in a bad temper they break up the lines here and there, and we have to put in new rails.

It would be light and safe work, and a 'bit of a rest for Tom and me', but he hoped to return to his battalion 'some happy day'. Leaving it was as bad as leaving Bermondsey, but his new posting turned out to be a 'little Eden' where he was tempted to stay for the duration of the war, had he not felt homesick for the 22nd.[21] While enjoying his 'holiday', he learnt that he had been mentioned in despatches by Haig 'for gallant and distinguished conduct in the field'.[22] He also had time to read Hankey's recently published book, *A Student in Arms*, which

20 *War Diary*, 22nd September, 13th November 1917, 2nd February, 17th October 1918.
21 *Letters*, 3rd–7th June 1916.
22 *Gazette*, issue 29623, 13th June; *War Diary*, 15th June 1916. Consequently, his Victory Medal's ribbon displayed a bronze oak leaves emblem.

he found 'quite real' and recommended to Willis, who was by then in the Royal Garrison Artillery based in Portsmouth.[23]

He had neither time nor inclination to compile the daily statistics that headquarters expected. He did, however, reply to some queries in verse, which seemed to silence the inquisitors for a while. One from the orderly room was to ascertain the true age of a boy feared to be under fifteen. He was thirty miles away on a mining job. Paterson scrawled across the despatch:

Yes I think Pte Simpson 2571
Is certainly rather too young for the Hun.
But he's under the earth
So the date of his birth
Must wait till the tunnel is done.

His newly promoted commanding officer[24], 'one of the best in the world', mildly reprimanded him, telling him that if he was to reply in verse it would be better to write it on the reverse of the form, and put the prose version on the obverse. When Alec 'ventured to point out that no editor would accept it, if the paper was written on both sides', Lieutenant-Colonel Flower told him that '*Fratres* and A.P. and the OBM generally were more subversive of discipline in the 22nd than anything he had ever met.' However, he continued to ask for copies of the monthly magazine, and acknowledged that there was scarcely a club boy who had 'not been given stripes by now'.[25] Alec was vindicated in his belief that they 'were better soldiers for being club members'. On another occasion, after his 'Scotch cook' had been bitten by a mosquito, he sent off a 'casualty report' marked 'Urgent' with the lines

There was a little fly
Who didn't like the look
Of Anderson, the cook
So he bit him in the eye.

23   *Letters*, 21st, 29th June 1916. He asked Dorothy to render it into braille (which she learned as part of the war effort), or if that was too much effort, she could try *The Beloved Captain*, 'a collection of by far the best chapters' (*Letters*, 17th April 1917). In late 1914 Alec had read an earlier work by Hankey, *The Lord of all Good Life: A Study of the Greatness of Jesus and the Weakness of the Church*, and warmly praised it (*Letters of Donald Hankey* [London, 1919], p. 320).
24   Brevet-Major Flower DSO was promoted to lieutenant-colonel on 10th July, the rank being backdated to when he took over the battalion in December 1915 (*War Diary*, 10th July 1916). He was killed later in the war.
25   *Fratres*, the club magazine, continued during the war, helping keep families in touch, filled as it was with letters from servicemen overseas. 'The Doctor' added a subtitle in Greek meaning 'faithful unto death', which took on added meaning as the casualty list of members grew (Baron, p. 47).

He was informed that daily reports would not be required in future.[26]

His poignant 'casualty report', on the death of 'The Little Grey Mule', was published in the *Westminster Gazette*. One night Alec's train was machine-gunned as it reached the Front. Alec went to see if anyone was hurt 'and got the natural reply "it's all right, Sir, only a mule."'

> No one asked what he thought of war.
> How his conscience stood, or anything more
> But they took him to France, to stand his chance
> It's all right – only a mule
> He pulled his load to the top of the hill,
> A shot rang out, and he lay quite still.
> "Anyone hit?" "No, we're quite fit
> It's all right, only a mule".
> There is a field where the grass is long
> And God at the gate to right the wrong,
> You can hear him say, if you pass that way,
> "He's all right – little grey mule".[27]

Meanwhile, on 1st July 1916 the epic battle of the Somme had begun, but it was not until 1st August that the 47th Division began marching south to the battleground. Before being deployed to relieve the 1st Division in the High Wood sector, the troops underwent three weeks of training. In mid-September Basil Henriques, by then a tank officer, encountered two OBM boys, 'Smutty Smith and Tom Dean', and chatted about Bermondsey.[28] Within days they would enter 'a new world of war'.[29] Although successfully capturing that elusive prize, High Wood, and the trenches beyond, the 47th would fail in the daunting task of taking the German line, and suffer terribly: 'Battalions went in fit and strong, full of confidence to take their part in the great British offensive. They came out, a few days later, a handful of men, muddy and tired out.' Four days of fighting cost the division over 4,500 casualties. The 142nd Brigade, initially held in reserve, suffered the least. More would fall in the following three weeks, including many in the 22nd Battalion. The division's total loss at the Somme amounted to 296 officers and 7,475 other ranks killed, wounded or missing.[30]

Once again, Alec would neither be with 'his boys' nor involved in the battle. When he heard that they 'were going South to take their part in the fight' he

---

26 *Letters*, 11th July 1916.

27 *Letters*, 7th August 1916, 30th March 1917.

28 L.L. Loewe, *Basil Henriques* (London, 1976).

29 *The 23rd London Regiment 1798–1919 compiled from contributions by former officers of the Regiment* (London, 1936), p. 35.

30 Maude, pp. 61–73.

went to see Lieutenant-Colonel Flower and asked to be recalled to the battalion. Flower was reluctant to accede, but, with so many officers being fresh from England, he could hardly refuse. Alec was to be in charge of the leading company ('good old "A"') in the field. First he had to get the medical officer's approval. After an examination, this was not forthcoming. He would not be fit for front-line duties for another month or more. Marching and, in particular, carrying a pack were forbidden as they increased the risk of the wounds reopening, as they had twice in the past, and reopened wounds were much worse than the original. For a second time, on doctor's orders, he was denied the chance to die for his country. An officer in command of a leading company was almost certain to be shot by a sniper or machine-gunned in the assault. Someone, other than Tom, was looking out for him.[31]

Frustrating as he found it, Alec got on with his tranquil life. On the anniversary of the first day of the battle of Loos he cycled over to see his elder brother in the village of Balinghem, the site of the Field of the Cloth of Gold.[32] Claude was by then a second lieutenant in the 9th Battalion of the Royal Fusiliers and had been posted to France. One of his letters to Alec, giving his position, had been intercepted by the censor, as had one of Alec's letters to Dorothy. The siblings shared the same inability to be discreet. It was the last they would see of one another until after the war. In mid-October, having received news that Claude was listed as 'missing', Alec wrote to his brother's company commander (whom he had known at Oxford), to the colonel of his battalion, and to a friend in the casualty department, asking for any details. From what he heard he deduced that Claude had been taken prisoner on 7th October when his trench was overrun. Alec suggested to Dorothy that she get Uncle Arthur to make inquiries of the Red Cross.

At the same time he received further bad news: while leading his platoon during the battle of the Somme Donald Hankey had been killed on 12th October. He had been heard to tell his men as they went over the top, 'If wounded, "Blighty"; if killed, the Resurrection!'[33] Another much closer friend, C.W., who had spent every Tuesday night in Dockhead, was also dead. Alec rued the fact that there were 'very few of the old Oxford crowd that ran the OBM left now'. He was by then thoroughly war-weary, and anxious to get home early so that he could make arrangements in Bermondsey for his returning comrades. A club of

31 *Letters*, 1st and 20th August 1916.
32 A royal summit of lavish proportions that took place in June 1520 between Henry VIII and Francis I. There was an irony in that the Germans referred to the 1915 battle as 'The Field of the Corpses of Loos'.
33 *Letters*, 24th October 1916; Donald Hankey, *A Student in Arms, 2nd Series* (London, 1917), p. 38. Some sources erroneously give the date of his death as 26th October.

sorts, where they could meet and talk and drink together, would be essential, particularly in the disorientating first few weeks of demobilisation. But while the boys he had induced to join up were fighting and risking their lives, he was determined to stay with, or at least near, them.

Though nursing a 'beastly cold', Alec remained 'as usual, very cheery', as Tom, who did not know how he managed it, reported to Dorothy.[34] Soon he would be further buoyed by news that Claude was indeed a prisoner of the Germans after he had been wounded and captured.[35] He had no fear for him, as he believed that the enemy treated POWs very well.[36] So too did the British, although the absurdity of the war was apparent when his work party was supplemented by some 'cheerful' German POWs.

> They were lifting some heavy rails and one of our men called out to one of them, "mind-out, you'll pinch your fingers", and rushed to lift the rail – and a week ago they would have been throwing bombs at one another.[37]

Finally, as the offensive on the Somme was ending, and the 47th Division had relocated to the area west of Ypres, Alec returned to his battalion. Back in action he was eager to make up for lost time, and on 19th November he was recorded as having 'made a careful reconnaissance of the wire along our front'. Tom had been his sole companion in No Man's Land.[38] There was no point in them both dying. One sacrifice Alec would soon make was to get his friend a safe job as a clerk in the orderly room. They would have to survive the war without each other's company, but Tom, the only one of the 'old gang' left, at least would be out of danger.[39]

With leave approaching at the end of the year, Alec made plans for Dorothy and Willis to come down to London to meet him. On New Year's Day he would cross the Channel, they would dine in Romano's and, 'according to family tradition', visit the theatre to see on this occasion a performance of *London Pride*.[40]

34 *Letters*, 21st–31st October 1916.
35 Claude, having led an attack at Gueudecourt during the battle of the Somme, had been shot through his left forearm. His injury was severe and he underwent two operations during his captivity (TNA, WO339/47684).
36 Alec was right about this, at least until conditions deteriorated towards the end of the war. Claude was held at Crefeld Camp before being transferred to the *Offizier Gefangenenlager* at Schwarmstedt, Hanover in May 1917 (*Manchester Guardian*, July 1917). In September he became one of the first intake of the newly opened Holzminden prisoner-of-war camp.
37 *Letters*, 5th, 11th, 21st–25th September, 6th October 1916.
38 *War Diary*, 19th November 1916. 'Our front' was The Bluff Sector near Hill 60.
39 *Letters*, 2nd December 1916.
40 *Letters*, 18th December 2016. 'The Cockney War Play', *London Pride*, written by Albert Neil Lyons (1880–1940) in collaboration with the American playwright,

It seemed a fitting way to end one year and bring in the next, which could prove to be the long-anticipated last year of the war.

After ten days in London, Alec got back to the battalion on 12th January 1917. It was a cold and snowy start to the year. But cold and snow meant that the guns largely fell silent, and the main danger came from frostbite. As the weather improved his prospects of ever returning to front-line duties deteriorated. His wounds were to blame.

In February he was examined by Captain Wright. The doctor concluded that '2nd Lieutenant Paterson has kept himself going now for some months by force of will, but the time has now come when he is incapable of carrying on.' Lieutenant-Colonel Flower reluctantly concurred and, accordingly, sent a report to brigade headquarters. In it he stated that, while he was loath to lose that 'most valuable officer', Paterson was physically unfit for active service. In Flower's opinion the country was not making the best use of the services of an individual with 'remarkable mental gifts', and invaluable previous experience in civilian life, by keeping him in France. In other words, he should be returned to England.[41] With so few of 'the old crowd' left and most of those posted to jobs behind the lines, Alec was becoming reconciled to this fate. Nonetheless, leaving the battalion would be a wrench.

In the event it was not to be a desk-job at home that lay in store, but an instructor's job in Poperinghe, a small town and busy transfer station eight miles west of Ypres where troops fighting on the battlefields of Flanders were billeted and where the 47th Divisional School was situated. Although not a primary battlefield target, Poperinghe, crammed with troops, was a tempting one, and one near enough to the Front to be shelled or bombed frequently, the more often and the more savagely as the war progressed.[42] A sweetener for Alec was that the battalion depot where Tom was stationed was only a few miles distant and they would be able to see each other regularly. Indeed, on 5th March, Tom was posted to assist him, and on the 29th they celebrated his 21st birthday in the house of the Belgian couple, Réné and Alida Berat, with whom Alec was lodging.[43]

Gladys Unger (1884–1940), was first produced at the Wyndham's Theatre on 6th February 1916. The story is of a young costermonger who enlists in the London Regiment and is awarded a VC, instead of being shot for desertion.

41   A copy of this report and that of the medical officer is held by the family. Alec would suffer pain from his wounds for the rest of his life, though he never mentioned it.

42   Paul Chapman, *In the Shadow of Hell* (Barnsley, 2001), pp. 63–75.

43   In 1930 Alec would recommend to Barclay that the Berats be made the first stewards of Talbot House (*infra*). They would prove to be outstanding custodians, before being dispossessed by the Germans in 1941.

Alec's role in the school was less than taxing. He was to give a few lectures over three-week periods to subalterns and sergeants newly arrived from England, and instil in them some 'elementary ideas of manners and conduct' before they were sent to the Front.[44] He himself had never been so trained and was probably not trainable. Both his method and content were unorthodox, but he managed to be an engaging instructor and survived official scrutiny or initial disquiet. After his opening lecture on 'army discipline' before an audience of twenty-nine subalterns and fifty-six sergeants, the former Grenadier Guards colonel in charge of the school, H.V. Warrender, said that he had never heard anything so original, 'a tactful way of saying he was fearfully shocked.' What was so shocking was that this second lieutenant in the Territorials had defined effective discipline as being 'obedience based on consent and self-control'.[45] Officers should trust their men to do their duty. England expects, not England commands. These were novel concepts for a Regular Army colonel who had rather assumed that obedience to orders should be unthinking and unconditional. Alec wondered if he would be asked to repeat this performance. He was.[46] Indeed on several occasions he was invited to dine with the recently appointed divisional commander, Major-General Sir George Gorringe, whom he found 'wonderfully unstuffy'.[47]

Alec was, however, becoming ever more critical of the unending war and of the unbending military mind-set. Although he was still keeping a clandestine diary, he thought it would be of little interest since he could not bring himself to write much about the conflict itself.[48] Perhaps this was because he knew his views were out of kilter with those in positions of authority. His diary is lost, but his letters reveal his thinking. The war was not only 'breaking through all conventions', but after it 'a great movement would arise in favour of peace' and of 'a constructive system of international leagues'. Then there would be a need for 'the quiet, steady pacifist to restore the balance of the country', but at present he had to avoid 'the danger of being an extremist':

44 *Letters*, 13th February 1917.
45 Alec would concur with Frederick Shirley's definition of discipline as 'discipleship, following someone else, a thing from within, not imposed by authority' (David Edwards, *F.J. Shirley: An Extraordinary Headmaster* (London, 1969), p. 37.
46 *Letters*, 5th–8th, 27th March 1917.
47 Gorringe had replaced Barter on 28th September 1916 on the latter's dismissal following the division's heavy losses at the Somme, losses for which he was unjustly blamed.
48 *Letters*, 13th–22nd February 1917. He also doubted if his letters were at all illuminating and was sure they could not compare to those penned by Hankey. When *Letters of Donald Hankey* was published, it had the line 'In the OBM I believe. Through it I hope' on its frontispiece.

For once you are damned as a crank you lose the ear of all the men you want to listen. The fact is, I am not enough of a prophet to be out on my own in the wilderness, and the plains are so pleasant and the company so acceptable, that I am reluctant to jar on them too much. But when the war is over, or nearly so, there will be a natural revulsion from the military point of view, and then will be a better time to strike.[49]

Meanwhile he did what he could to make ameliorations where he was. The school occupied the austere precincts of a convent. He had a kitchen garden planted. He organised concerts for Easter Monday and May Day (for which he wrote a short play), whist drives, and cricket and football matches. He begged and borrowed books and games, and a fire and lights for the common room. He got his sister to send over tablecloths, lemonade powder, and magazines such as *Punch*. He wanted to make life as pleasant, and the place as homely, as possible. And he succeeded. Homely but not slovenly. Lieutenant-Colonel Warrender was so concerned about the way new officers promoted from the ranks ate cheese – putting the knives in their mouths – that he suggested that Alec write another sketch for a concert and 'bring it in'.[50]

Alec refers to reading H.G. Wells's recently published and much-acclaimed novel, *Mr Britling Sees It Through*, the principal themes of which are the initial national blindness to Prussian militarism, and the belated national resolve to confront it. The fulcrum of the plot is the death of the protagonist's son in October 1915 while serving at the Front, and that of a young German they had known before the war, to whose parents the grieving father writes a long letter of condolence. Mr Britling ultimately adopts an expansive, non-sectarian religious understanding of the personal and national tragedy. God alone could give meaning to it, and bring reconciliation thereafter. These sentiments chimed with Alec's experience, and were exemplified in something he found in Poperinghe.[51]

Being based there, Alec sought out an old friend from Bermondsey days, Tubby Clayton. In December 1915 Tubby and Neville Talbot, both 'the Doctor's men' in days past, and both army padres, had opened their unique and enduring creation in a wonderfully capacious but shell-damaged mansion in the Rue de l'Hôpital. Named Talbot House in honour of Neville's younger brother, Gilbert, who had been killed at Hooge in the Ypres Salient on 30th July 1915, it was to be an oasis of relaxation and tranquillity amidst the chaos of war. They envisaged an

49   *Letters*, 27th February, 30th October 1917, 29th July 1918.
50   *Letters*, 19th April–12th May 1917.
51   *Letters*, 21st May 1917.

FIGURE 15.
Talbot House,
Poperinghe by
permission of
Talbot House

'Emmaus Inn' or Christian 'Everyman's Club', a home-from-home where soldiers, regardless of rank or race or religious persuasion, could mingle freely and which sought to bring disparate sections of society together,[52] and a haven where fighting men could try to put out of their minds the dehumanising conflict, and reforge their own humanity. A notice in the conservatory invited visitors to 'Come into the garden and forget about the War.' Talk about it was not banned but was rare. 'The real thing was to get relief from it, relief comic, serio-comic, educational, spiritual', was how Tubby saw it.[53] Thousands would testify to his success.

52   On 10th November 1917 an amendment to a proposal that 'this house be opened to British soldiers only', inserting 'white' before 'British', was lost. Two West Indian sergeants made excellent speeches during a debate held in Talbot House on 'the Colour problem in the Empire' (Jan Louagie, *A Touch of Paradise in Hell* [Solihull, 2015], pp. 153, 253).

53   Paul Chapman, *A Haven in Hell* (Oxford, 2000), p. 34.

Tubby was put in charge as 'the innkeeper', and a merry inn he would keep for his clientele, filling it with his infectious laughter and bonhomie. With that clientele's enthusiastic co-operation, he put on parties – notably on St Nicholas' Day – for the local children, and organised debates and concerts, and, from the dark days of 1917, to let off steam and bolster morale, 'grousing circles' where men would vent their discontents and officers could try to do something about them.[54] The whole atmosphere of the place was a projection of the wit, good humour and friendliness of the man himself. Such were the vast numbers of itinerants that he attracted to Talbot House that a soldier could post a message on 'Friendship Corner' for a missing comrade who, if still alive, was likely to find it. But it was more than an inn; it was a refuge for all, or almost all. At the entrance visitors were greeted by a sign shaped as a hand pointing back to the street with the words 'To Pessimists, Way Out' embossed on it, an injunction that Alec, the eternal optimist, need never observe nor an exit he would ever take. This was to be a life-affirming place where you could relax. Tubby begged, borrowed and scrounged whatever he could to make it as comfortable and welcoming as possible. 'Give me the luxuries of life, and I care not who has the necessities' was Tubby's dictum for the house.

To lighten the spirit the walls were adorned with bright pictures, alongside the quirky, facetious and eagerly-awaited 'notices'.[55] There was overnight accommodation for twelve men, with carpet slippers provided for the guests. Officers alone had to fork out five francs for board and lodging, on 'the Robin Hood principle of taking from the rich to give to the poor'.[56] There was a sitting-room with armchairs, a music and recreation room with a piano, a library with an impressive and eclectic collection of books, a peaceful writing-room, a well-stocked canteen and café, a colourful and fragrant garden where 'Khaki Basking Lizards' could lounge on the lawn or doze on hammocks, and, above all, 'the Upper Room', a chapel constructed in the hop-loft, an attic spanning the entire building, the foundations of which 'were in the roof'. The chapel obtruded on no one but dominated everything. Large but intimate, with no communion rail or pulpit to put distance between priest and people, and with a well-used carpenter's bench for an altar, it proved ideal for communal religious services and private devotions. It contained nothing of any intrinsic value, but everything was of inestimable value. It was Anglican but available to all. In this sacred space

54 *Ibid.*, pp. 139ff. These were given sanction by the army staff who had recognised their beneficial effect.
55 Examples of the notices, such as 'IF YOU ARE IN THE HABIT OF SPITTING ON THE CARPET AT HOME PLEASE SPIT HERE', can be found in Clayton, *Tales of Talbot House* (London, 1919), pp. 125–139, and Chapman, *op.cit.*, pp. 29, 38, 46, 67, 75, 84f., 99–122.
56 *Ibid.*, p. 28.

FIGURE 16.
Tubby Clayton by
Walter Stoneman
© National Portrait
Gallery, London

equality reigned, as it did in Tubby's own 'Chaplain's Room', above the door of which he hung a rainbow sign bearing his own adaptation of Dante, 'ALL RANK ABANDON YE WHO ENTER HERE'. But equality could not be confined, and would spread throughout the house, the whole of which exuded comradeship and brotherhood, eschewed snobbery, and put no store on the temporary distinctions of rank. One staff officer, upon first entering this strange abode, had his cap removed and thrown under a bed. He was 'soon chatting with [a] corporal as if he was [his] best friend. Such was the magic of Tubby.'[57]

    Although shells obliterated a neighbouring house and restaurant, and landed in its garden, shattering windows, Talbot House survived the war virtually unscathed, even if its name did not. This was because Talbot House became abbreviated to 'Toc H', the army signallers' 'affectionate diminutive for it, "Toc" denoting the letter "T" in their spelling alphabet, and "H" for "House"'. (For

---

57   *Ibid.*, p. 87. Among the senior officers who made regular appearances were Tubby's second cousin and area corps commander Frederick Lambart, 10th Earl of Cavan, and the commander of the Second Army, Sir Herbert Plumer.

Tubby this welcome nickname came to signify something else: 'TO Conquer Hate').[58] During the war years all – of whatever denomination – who made their communion there were entitled to be 'Foundation members'. The battalions of the London Regiment provided more communicants than any other.[59]

One of them was Alec Paterson, 'the best of all men'.[60] But he did more than take communion. He gave lectures, took part in debates on social problems, and often led the weekly prayer meeting. In the last he was a favourite with the men. They would make written requests for intercessions and, as Tubby recalled, 'every clumsy sentence written down and humbly laid beside his kneeling figure would be transformed into a prayer, homely, direct and simple.' In the 'Toc H family', first encountered on the Western Front, Alec found 'an infectious atmosphere of faith and gaiety and deep purpose'. It reminded him of Bermondsey, and so it should since, as Tubby, for whom Bermondsey remained his 'first love', often acknowledged, it was modelled on 'the Doctor's' work, and mirrored his vision – if not his asceticism.[61]

At the beginning of June 1917, after the school had been closed, and just as his battalion was about to engage in the battle of Messines[62], Alec was posted temporarily to Advanced Corps Intelligence, where his brains would be deployed for the first time since he had enlisted. It involved the gathering, analysing and disseminating of military intelligence, and 'the hardship', during a sunny summer, of camping out in a field near Battalion HQ. Since Tom had been moved to another safe job as the battalion 'postman', Alec got 'an old friend, J.R.'

58 P.B. Clayton, *The Compass* (September 1937); John Durham, *Talbot House to Tower Hill*, p. 137; Tresham Lever, *Clayton of Toc H* (London, 1971), p. 52.
59 Five hundred members of the 1/5th London Regiment (London Rifle Brigade) received communion at Christmas 1915 (Clayton, *Tales of Talbot House*, pp. 29f.). With notable exceptions Talbot House appealed to 'civilian soldiers' and not to regulars, for many of whom the culture shock was too great.
60 Letter from Tubby to his mother, 14th January 1917, in Louagie, *op.cit.*, p. 108.
61 P.B. Clayton, *Plain Tales from Flanders* (London, 1929), pp. 7ff; Linda Parker, *A Fool For Thy Feast* (Solihull, 2015), p. 60; Durham, *op.cit.*, p. 99. Another regular communicant and constant visitor was Barclay Baron. Many of his watercolours of the House still adorn its walls and one of the rooms is named in his honour.
62 Maude, p. 98. The battle, a prelude to the third battle of Ypres, was carried out by Plumer's Second Army. It began on 7th June with a surprise attack after the detonation of nineteen huge mines. The battle raged for a week. Sergeant F.E. Collins of the 22nd Battalion, who got the Military Medal for his pains, recounted the battalion's success against little opposition (Malcolm Brown, *Imperial War Museum Book of the Western Front* [London, 1993], p. 172).

as his batman. However, within a fortnight, he had managed to wangle Tom's return to his side. They had been together for almost three years, and while Alec had wanted him well out of danger and had feared he would be returned to the trenches, their separation had been a considerable wrench.

During this time Alec engaged in lengthy correspondence with an unnamed recipient (probably Barkis), the extant part of which involved explaining what he meant by 'faint-hearted pugilists who shirked active service'.

> The passage was never intended to apply to ordinary people who for one reason or another do not take an active part in the fighting. No one wants the whole country in the trench. It was aimed at a very well known set of young boxers in Bermondsey, who cannot possibly claim any conscientious scruples about fighting. They still swagger about, idols of a footer crowd, boxing each other for hours at a time, for considerable sums of money. They prefer the safety of the boxing ring to real fighting at a bob a day. They box twenty rounds in a night – no light task – and then pretend to be unfit to join the army, when we have lads in the trench who have been three times wounded, and must still return to the old scene. No, when you see frank and unashamed cowardice, I think at a time like this it should be openly rebuked.[63]

Looking beyond the war, as he often did, he was equally outspoken on the matter of temperance:

> It is no good saying 'shut all the pubs', and then sitting down as if the matter was settled. It is not the attitude of one who sits among publicans and sinners. We have to take the streets and men of London as they are, and search for the best centre. We want the ordinary man. We don't want him to acquire the second-rate type of character that can only abstain from excess by total abstinence, but the higher type that can eat and drink of the fruits of the earth, but in moderation and decency. The best centre for meeting the average man and teaching him the lesson is a decent place where beer is sold in moderation. The old-fashioned temperance is dead. There is barely one man in 200 here who is an absolute teetotaller. It is because I am so afraid that this tremendous change in habit (for before the war most of our young fellows *were* teetotallers) may swing them in their return to excess, that I want to teach moderation. It may be a tragic failure. It may be a useful experiment.[64]

---

63   *Letters*, 7th June 1917. Conversely, Paterson was sympathetic to conscientious objectors. When in July 1917 Siegfried Sassoon denounced the continuation of the war in a letter published in *The Times*, Alec praised the bold action of this 'humble, sensitive spirit' (Preface to William Douglas-Home, *"Now Barabbas..."*).

64   *Letters*, 7th June 1917.

Towards the end of June, after the fighting had subsided, Alec was posted to another school, this time for regulars of X Corps. He and Tom were the only Territorials on the staff. The company was uncongenial, but he made amends, finding cool and isolated accommodation on top of a windmill, and getting permission to mess 'with a cheery crowd of eighty-four student officers' for whose behaviour he was responsible. He set about creating a football pitch and cricket ground, and trying to improve the programme and atmosphere.[65] During his time there he also had to go to Poperinghe on three occasions to act as defence counsel in courts-martial.[66]

Dismissive as he was of 'faint-hearted pugilists', Alec was more indulgent towards those who had joined up to serve but could no longer take the strain. Desertion was the one offence which usually resulted in the firing squad, and Alec was very concerned about the fate of a 'little boy' in his company who had run away the night before Messines. Once again, where many an officer tried to evade this duty, he was prepared to defend him at the court-martial held in Poperinghe in early July. He hoped to help the boy avoid the death penalty, although the odds were stacked against it. Nonetheless he put up 'a desperate fight' for the boy's life. Then, as was the rule when the decision was adverse, he and the lad had to wait several days for the verdict and sentence to be confirmed. When the inevitable guilty verdict came through, Paterson, although conceding that 'prison is no punishment' when compared to the trenches, was nonetheless jubilant since 'the small deserter with the big spectacles got off with ten years' penal servitude'. For Paterson at least, there was more good news, in that 'the serving of the sentence is postponed until after the war, and if he behaves himself in the meantime, will probably be washed out altogether.'[67] Most soldiers sentenced to penal servitude much preferred to serve their time in safe custody than to be returned to their battalion at the Front, and this young soldier was no different. Within a couple of weeks, he deserted again. Once more he was court-martialled, with Alec defending him. He had little doubt that he would be shot this time.[68] Although he does not give the result, it seems from the War Office records that once again the miscreant escaped execution.[69] Paterson was proving himself a most effective defence advocate, and was acquiring a reputation for forensic ability and tenacity.

65 *Letters*, 23rd June–23rd September 1917.
66 The cell where the condemned were held and the execution post can still be seen just off the main square.
67 Suspension of sentences became available in 1915 under an Act introduced to ensure that being sent to prison was not seen as an attractive alternative to fighting in the trenches.
68 *Letters*, 13th and 23rd June, 5th and 17th July, 4th August 1917.
69 Philip Brocklesby claimed that a man in his platoon had been sentenced to death three times for desertion, only for the sentence to be commuted or suspended on each occasion (Andrea Hetherington, *Deserters of the First World War* [Barnsley,

These were but short breaks from the army school, which absorbed most of his energies. It was not nearly as congenial as his previous posting. Badly run as it was, he did not have the clout to pull it into shape. Once again Alec was anxious to return to the battalion. Fortunately, he did not have to wait long. In mid-September he was recalled to Divisional HQ, and given the posting he had been hoping for, one which could have been made for him, as indeed it had. He was to be the 'Divisional Sports and Recreation Officer, charged with the duty of making things bright for the different battalions as they come out of the trenches.' He was responsible for football and boxing matches, and for catering and canteens, and was put in charge of 'The Bermondsey Butterflies', the battalion troupe of 'The Follies', the Divisional theatrical group.[70] He was also promoted to full lieutenant. After settling into his quarters in the front-line village of Roclincourt, and another period of leave in London (this time with Tom), by mid-October Alec was setting to work on his new job.

There was a brief interlude when, a few days later, the newly promoted officer was summoned to an emergency conference convened at St Omer by the deputy chaplain-general of the army, Bishop Llewellin Gwynne (whose appearance reminded Alec of an artichoke). It was concerned with the vital task of bolstering morale, which in 1917 had reached its nadir. There had been colossal casualties on the battlefield, a 'mutiny' at Étaples in September, and a peak in executions for desertion. There were fears that the revolutionary ideas that were infecting the Russians were taking hold in the British Army, undermining the war effort, eroding *élan*, and dissipating the will to win. As the perceptive Tubby Clayton put it, 'an evil spirit for the first time troubled both officers and men; and in the stagnation the phantom of failure, ridiculed before, walked grimly abroad, and was not always challenged.'[71] Religion was perceived as a patriotic antidote, and it was justifiably believed that padres played a major role in sustaining morale and maintaining a belief in the rightness of the cause. There were a number of chaplains in attendance, including Neville and Tubby, as well as one of Haig's

---

2021], p. 54). Throughout the war only three men in the London Regiment were shot: James Mayers, a private in the 13th Battalion, was executed on 16th June 1916 for desertion; Robert Barker on 4th November 1916 for cowardice; Frederick Slade on 14th December 1917 for disobedience. The latter two were riflemen in the 6th (Corns and Hughes-Wilson, *op.cit.*, pp. 132ff., 205f., 484, 498, 500).

70   For performances of 'The Bermondsey Butterflies' see *War Diary*, 25th–27th February, 13th and 16th March (at which 'Lt A. Paterson, Divisional recreation officer,' is named as being present), 23rd April, 13th May, 6th July, 16th September 1918, and 3rd January 1919. For photographs of 'The Follies' see Maude, pp. 208, 244. Rowland Fielding (*War Letters to Wife* [London, 1929]) observed that one of their jokes went down particularly well with 'a frontline audience': "What is a patriot?" Answer "A man who sheds *your* blood for *his* country."

71   Quoted in Chapman, *op.cit.*, p. 93.

staff officers acting as an observer. Alec was supposed to be there as a 'typical infantry officer', a description that Barclay Baron, who was representing the YMCA, thought utterly bizarre. He recorded what happened when each member was called upon to address the issue of political subversion in the ranks:

> When it came to Alec the DCG said, 'What about you, Paterson? Do you find signs of revolution in your Battalion?' 'I'm afraid not, sir', answered Alec, 'I've tried my best but the beggars just won't revolute.' A few of us laughed, the rest looked puzzled. I think most of us stole a glance at the observer whose face registered dismay and anger; he wrote more busily than ever in his notebook. Alec was never cashiered, but I wondered if some intelligence man would be told to keep an eye on him too.[72]

In fact, Alec knew a lot about morale and that his views on it were unconventional. Discipline, he acknowledged, was its backbone, but mechanical obedience induced by fear of punishment was quite unsuited to a citizen army. Volunteers were motivated by patriotism. They were not mercenaries fighting for lucre or conscripted criminals kept in order by the lash. Many, like Alec, were intelligent, or at least well-educated, and were quite capable of independent thought and responsible initiative. Discipline for such recruits should be 'secured by consent rather than constraint', and be based on a 'soldier-centred type of command, in which the authority of the officer was exalted by force of example, and through the cultivation of an *esprit de corps* and a high level of camaraderie' which united officers and men and did not make a demarcation between them. Officers and men should be fused not rigidly kept apart. He, a subaltern, wanted the army to be modelled on the OBM; his superiors did not. Field Marshal Haig, in particular, thought 'brutal, degrading and highly visible' field punishments and a resort to firing squads were essential to the maintenance of discipline.[73] No one was going to undermine the cherished views of the commander-in-chief. Such being the case, why should Alec take the conference seriously or contribute constructively?

His busy everyday life continued apace. Tom constituted the full complement of his staff. They were 'at it all day and half the night'. The work was multi-faceted. In addition to all his other duties, Alec lectured on the stage of a French theatre, footlights and all, on the subject of 'England after the War', and organised an 'A' Company dinner for 200 men. Amidst all this Alec never

---

72   Snape, pp. 168f. While Alec, in his letters home, mentions seeing Barkis on Thursday 18th October, he says nothing about the conference held on that date and the next.

73   D. Englander, 'Discipline and Morale in the British Army, 1917–1918', in J. Horne (ed.), *State, Society and Mobilization in Europe during the First World War* (Cambridge, 1997), pp. 131ff., 140. Haig was promoted to field marshal on 1st January 1917.

forgot his friends and their loved ones. He commiserated with the young widow of Dick W, and erected over his grave a beech cross he had commissioned.[74]

Then suddenly in mid-November he returned once more to Divisional HQ just west of Vimy, 'in a state of some unsettlement'. Although he does not give the reason, it was due to the preparations being made for a surprise attack on the Cambrai front after the muddy, bloody, and costly third battle of Ypres (Passchendaele) had been brought to an end. The assault began on 20th November. The 47th Division was to participate in the second stage. This entailed a march through the burnt villages and desolate landscape the Germans had left behind as they retired to their recently constructed Hindenburg Line. The weather was intensely cold, and the billets where units spent the night provided little succour from rain and sleet. Alec was put in charge of divisional details, organising football matches for tired but eager 'Tommies' on the march, and running canteens and soup kitchens 'a few hundred yards from the Germans', during the fighting. Although he was never in action, he was near enough the Front to come under artillery fire and to know something of what was happening on the battlefield. His division was rushed to Bourlon Wood on 28th November, in defence of which and withdrawal therefrom it suffered heavily.[75] Finally it went into winter quarters in villages behind Albert. Unscathed, Alec returned to his other duties.

Despite the tumultuous times, he was asked to represent three subalterns at their general court-martial.[76] It was the first time he had officers to defend, and he attributed his 'growing practice' to 'some lucky acquittals'. Acquittals were not unknown but were rare.[77] His success rate may have been helped by the introduction of specialist court-martial officers, who had been allocated to every corps in the BEF in early 1917, and who had been legal professionals before the war. To defend in what he called 'a long and anxious case' Alec had to leave the division for a couple of days, but it was worth it. In the end 'all three were acquitted to the great delight of all their friends, French and English.' He had burnished an already enviable record.[78]

In the run-up to Christmas 1917 Alec was exceptionally busy trying to ensure the very best in rest and relaxation for the battle-fatigued men. He himself relaxed by reading Stephen McKenna's latest novel, *Sonia Between Two Worlds*,

74   *Letters*, 9th and 19th November 1917.

75   Wilfred Miles, *Official History of the Great War: Military Operations: France and Belgium, 1917, The Battle of Cambrai* (London, 1948), pp. 167, 212ff., 221–230, 246, 251, 262–267.

76   Commissioned officers were often still tried by general, other ranks invariably by field general courts-martial.

77   The monthly conviction rate for the Fifth Army during 1917 was usually between 80 and 90 per cent (TNA, WO95/524–5).

78   *Letters*, 4th–28th November 1917.

which followed the political and social adventures of three young Oxford men from 1890 to 1917, and was praised for its depiction of the changes in the English ruling class brought on by the Great War. He also found time to write to his sister asking a favour. Would she write a letter in braille to a boy called 'K' who had been blinded some months before and was at St Dunstan's Hostel for Blinded Soldiers and Sailors, which had opened in Regent's Park in March 1915? She agreed, and thereafter Alec would send her his letters to 'K' for transcription. She also received a letter from Tom, telling her that Alec had been 'up to his neck in work' and had done 'wonders in helping the Div. for Xmas. It's the same old Alec always.'[79]

Surely this must be the last Christmas of the war? It proved so to be. Victory was at last in sight, or at least just over the horizon.

Not that, as 1918 began, anyone knew it. The end of the war had been anticipated so often and for so long that prognostications were given little credence. There was, in any case, much fierce fighting to come, and the final result still hung in the balance.

Already, however, thought was being given to the past and to posterity. Remembrance and setting the record straight were to the fore. In February memorial crosses for those of the 47th Division who had fallen at the battle of the Somme were erected in High Wood and at Eaucourt l'Abbaye. At the latter it was Major Boosey of the 22nd Battalion who was given the honour of reading the dedication.[80]

Not only should those who had given their lives be remembered, but the feats of all who had served in the division should be recorded. Thus, at the close of 1917, Alec had received an unusual commission from none other than the divisional commander, Major-General Gorringe, himself. His task was to compile material on the history of the 47th Division for an article that Sir Arthur Conan Doyle wanted to write for *The Strand Magazine*.[81] If that proved a success, Gorringe indicated that he might want Alec 'to start from the beginning and write the story of all our battles'. Although he had earlier turned down a suggestion by his publishers, Edward Arnold, to write a book about

---

79 *Letters*, 6th–29th December 1917, 2nd January 1918. *Sonia* was published in 1917 and ran into many editions.
80 Maude, pp. 144f.
81 *Letters*, 6th and 12th December 1917. Conan Doyle wrote many articles on the Great War which were published between 1916 and 1920 by Hodder and Stoughton in six volumes under the title *British Campaigns in France and Flanders 1914–1918*.

the war (on the ground that there would be too many such memoirs),[82] he acceded to his commanding officer's request to record the role of the division. He duly set to work, and by late January 1918 had completed a specimen chapter, 'describing our share in the last battle'. This was a reference to the division's sterling defence of Bourlon Wood against German counter-attacks during the battle of Cambrai, and the subsequent 'skilful withdrawal'.[83] He showed his draft to the Major-General with some trepidation, but he need not have worried as Gorringe 'approved of it, scratched nothing out, suggested a few additions, and asked me to carry on with its other chapters, saying it was just the thing he wanted ... not technical but readable.' From then on Alec would spend an hour or two a day on the divisional history, 'a rather pleasant change of occupation.' He took this task very seriously, and planned during his next leave to consult the records held at the War Office.[84] At the same time he was initiating a divisional magazine he intended to call *London Pride*, and would later be asked to contribute to a memoir of the barrister, John Whitworth, an old friend of Willis, and a major in the Manchester regiment, who had been killed in action. Indeed, against his better judgment, he agreed to write three other memoirs, but had not had time to begin. His mind was taken up 'with silly practical details like loading lorries'.[85]

82 *Letters*, 1st June 1915.
83 Maude, pp. 119–141. The narrative contains these poignant lines: 'One of the most pitiful sights of the war was to see the long queues of forty to sixty temporarily blinded men linked up, slowly wending their way through the wood guided by R.A.M.C. orderlies.' John Singer Sargent's 'Gassed' depicts such a scene.
84 *Letters*, 1st and 14th February, 14th March, 20th April, 27th May 1918. On 2nd August 1918 Gorringe wrote to the War Office requesting that Paterson be given access to the war diaries while he was in England, and a week later permission was granted (TNA, WO374/52506). In 1922 *The 47th (London) Division 1914–1919 by some who served with it in the Great War* was published. It was edited by Lieutenant-Colonel Alan Maude, but a major contributor was Paterson, who during the conflict had researched so extensively on it. How much he contributed is hard to say, but Maude named him among those who had written 'one or more chapters'. That on Bourlon Wood is so strikingly reminiscent of his style, abounding in phrases such as 'the cheerful pessimism of the other ranks', 'the field-kitchen, most fertile handmaid of rumour', or 'the devil's embroidery of barbed wire', that it can confidently be attributed to him, and many passages elsewhere bear his hallmark. Another contributor was one Lieutenant-Colonel Bernard Law Montgomery, who had been appointed divisional chief of staff in the summer of 1918.
85 *Letters*, 5th October 1918. Nor had he begun when the war ended. He may never have started.

Any hope of leave he may have had was dashed by the *Kaiserschlacht*, the German spring offensive during which the 47th Division, although again tenacious in defence, had to make a hasty and bloody retreat.[86] Amidst the chaos, and constantly on the move, 'old Alec' was hard at it, ensuring that convoys of food, cigarettes and ammunition were dispatched to the exhausted fighting troops, and supplies enough were ready for their return to base and the arrival of reinforcements from Britain. His own brigade had been heavily engaged and suffered severe losses, including Captain Saumarez, who was killed, 'Major W', who was wounded, Major Boosey, who was missing, and Brigadier-General Bailey and some of his staff, who were taken prisoner. Alec could find only eight members of his old company, and two of the five with whom he had messed were missing. 'A.G. and young M. had been killed.' At least 'S.S.', not a Bermondsey boy, but a 'small and cheerful' member of 'A' Company, of whose life he had despaired, seemed likely to pull through after all. Alec was able to write a letter to his mother with good news, a rare event, and one that would spare him the usual reply from grieving kin asking for more details of their boy's death, details too awful to reveal. In the event 'S.S.' did die of his wounds, but not before his parents had been able to visit him in hospital. In gratitude the grieving mother asked Alec if she could send him pads of writing paper.[87]

Alas, he had much use of them, as he had to reply to many anxious parents. One of the most bizarre was 'Mrs F', who had taken to communicating with her dead son 'A' in the spirit world. 'A' had told his mother that Alec was still alive and might be able to get some information about a friend of his who was reported missing. Accordingly, she had written to him in Beaucourt, giving the missing boy's name and battalion. As it happened, although the battalion was in a different division, it was based only half a mile way. Alec walked the few hundred yards only to discover that an old friend was the commanding officer and from him he got the required information.[88]

The war was dragging its weary way to the finishing line. Even so the inexorable wheel of military justice continued to turn. Acting Captain Paterson, as he had been since 12th April, was again asked to defend 'small boys who had deserted'. Although even the expedited procedure was 'slow and cumbersome', on the basis of his by then extensive experience, he did not think courts-martial unjust. On the contrary, accused soldiers got 'the benefit of every doubt and fared better than if they had been tried in civilian courts'.[89] On the comple-

86 *War Diary*, 21st March–5th April 1918; Maude, pp. 149–181. The *Kaiserschlacht* took place between 21st March and 18th July 1918.

87 *Letters*, 7th, 9th, 11th April, 23rd May, 24th July 1918.

88 *Letters*, 17th May.

89 *Letters*, 30th September 1918. He gives no further details of these cases, but as he called the assignment a waste of time, the hearings must have been postponed or

tion of this forensic task Alec had to organise the divisional sports day that was held at Canchy on 21st April, and yet another performance by 'The Bermondsey Butterflies' two days later.[90]

As the summer months slipped into autumn the tone of Alec's letters became ever more jubilant as the end to the fighting seemed assured, now that a major offensive was underway and the Americans were beginning to make their presence felt. The 22nd again distinguished itself, with one of its number, Private Jack Harvey, winning the 47th Division's second Victoria Cross.[91] The Division was active in the liberation of Lille, and on 28th October, with the 142nd Brigade leading the way, took part in a march-past in the town centre watched by Churchill, then Minister of Munitions. The fighting was almost over. Claude would soon be repatriated;[92] Willis would never be sent abroad; and Alec would eventually be demobilised.

The future loomed, and Alec harboured political ambitions. He told Dorothy that there was no question of his standing for Parliament in the forthcoming 'Khaki Election' as he would have to have sought his discharge in October to get back to London, which he had been unwilling to do. He did not mind, as he predicted that Lloyd George would 'fall with a bump' and the new parliament would not last long.[93] He would be proved wrong on both counts. Lloyd George's wartime coalition would triumph in the election held on 14th December 1918 and survive until October 1922.

Just after the armistice, Alec moved with the divisional train[94] from Lille to Lillers, a little town west of Béthune. Shortly thereafter he was 'sacked' from his job. He had failed abysmally in one crucial respect. The ninety-six officers' messes in the division relied on him to supply them with food and drink, but for a

abandoned or he must have lost. If the last, since no one from the 47th Division was executed during this period, their lives must have been spared.

90 *War Diary*, 21st and 23rd April 1918.

91 *War Diary*, 16th November 1918; Maude, p. 192. Harvey was born in Peckham in 1891 and was awarded his VC on 2nd September 1918. Although a company cook, he rushed German machine guns holding up his battalion's advance (Max Arthur, *Symbol of Courage: A Complete History of the Victoria Cross* [London, 2004], pp. 339, 648). He was not a Bermondsey boy but may well have attended one of the OBM's clubs.

92 He was on 18th December 1918.

93 *Letters*, 1st December 1918. He does not state for which party he might have stood, but given his comment, he would likely have been an Asquith Liberal or a Labour candidate. In the election, however, he felt obliged to vote for John Marriott, who was standing as the Conservative candidate for Oxford and who, like Alec, was born the son of a solicitor in Bowdon.

94 A unit of the Army Service Corps, whose function was to carry divisional baggage and to acquire and distribute supplies.

whole fortnight he omitted to provide the latter, as a result of which they spent the whole of Armistice Day 'in sober and rather moody silence'. When they reproached him for dereliction of duty Alec joked about it, so they petitioned for his removal. Major-General Gorringe did not want him to go, but Alec was delighted to get back to his battalion before demobilisation.[95]

In the new year Alec used his new position to introduce the Bermondsey style into the running of the battalion, as he described in his last letter:

> Things are very different now the war is over. I have started what the Bolshe-vists would call a Soldiers' Council, but which I call the Company Commit-tee. It consists of a private from each platoon with the quarter-bloke and one young sub. They arrange all the important things like games and sports, and make suggestions as to improvements in feeding and parades. The men are elected by their fellow-privates and are full of ideas. The theory will shock Claude as an ex-sergeant in a regular battalion but it works all right in these discontented days, and provides a useful ventilation for grievances.[96]

Once again he got into a spot of bother, an incident not mentioned in his let-ters. On 29th January he was billed to give a lecture on the 'Labour problems after the War', but it was postponed. The reason was revealed in the *War Diary*'s entry for the following day:

> The result of the Court of Enquiry held recently on the high prices at Christmas of the Divisional canteen, and the accusation of profiteering and inefficiency of the canteen resulted in the complete exoneration of Captain A. Paterson.

The 'complete exoneration of Captain A. Paterson' was hardly surprising, as a candidate less likely to be a war profiteer would be hard to find. As a result, the postponed lecture was given that very evening.[97]

But the time had come for him to return to civilian life. He had already ar-ranged for a job with the Ministry of Labour. Set up at the end of 1916 to co-or-dinate all labour and employment policies, it was to supervise the demobilisation and resettlement of ex-servicemen as well as being responsible for youth employ-ment. Barkis's father, Barclay Josiah Baron, by then a knight of the realm, held an important regional position in the ministry until his death in 1919, and he may have put Alec's name forward for the post of Principal Officer in charge of the Juvenile Branch. There were over two million children in Britain between the ages of fourteen and seventeen. These were 'juveniles available for employment'. It was a challenging role that he relished. He hoped that after the war the relations

95 *Letters*, 13th December 1918.
96 *Letters*, 16th January 1919.
97 *War Diary*, 29th and 30th January 1919.

between officers and men would be replicated by employers and employees. On 15th February, two weeks after Tom, Alec was 'disembodied' – demobilised – and got back to London in order to take up the position.

Not quite yet. Although on discharge he was 'A1 in terms of health', a week later, while at Tom's house in Bermondsey, he fell 'ill with a cold'. The doctors diagnosed pneumonia, probably a consequence of contracting the deadly 'Spanish Flu'.[98] His family got a telegram from the 3rd London General Hospital in Wandsworth telling them his condition was such that they should come at once. With only one fully working lung, his life hung in the balance, but he pulled through. He remained there for almost two months before being transferred to recuperate in the Red Cross Hospital at Cannes, from which he was discharged in mid-May.[99]

Meanwhile, on 28th March 1919, the 47th Division had ceased to exist. Major-General Gorringe issued a 'farewell order' in which he thanked the division as a whole, but particularised some for special mention. Among the named brigadier-generals, colonels and lieutenant-colonels (including Alan Maude), there was a single major and a solitary captain. The captain was Alexander Paterson, the lowest-ranking recipient of the general's written thanks.[100] He was also the only recipient who had no decoration after his name. That omission would shortly be rectified, and one final accolade would round off his military career. On 3rd June 1919 he was awarded the Military Cross – after the Victoria Cross and the Distinguished Service Order, the highest award for bravery.[101] Created in 1914 for warrant officers and commissioned officers up to the rank of captain, it was given for 'an act or acts of exemplary gallantry during active operations against the enemy on land'. The medal itself takes the form of a plain Greek cross with splayed ends to each arm, upon which are embossed the imperial crown, with the monarch's monogram in the centre. The recipient could put MC after his name, as Alec indeed did. Another piece of metal, but one he never mentioned, was the shrapnel still lodged in his body. It would cause him pain throughout his life, and he never recovered 'the full voice which had thrilled an

---

98 Influenza had hit his division in the summer of 1918, seriously depleting its fighting strength (Maude, p. 185).

99 TNA, WO374/52506; *Letters*, 15th February 1919. Alec erroneously states that the hospital was the 4th London. He was an inpatient in Wandsworth from 23rd February to 15th April 1919.

100 Paterson was still only an acting captain, holding that rank until 14th February 1919, the day before he was demobilised. After resigning his commission on 30th June 1920, he was granted the rank of captain (TNA, WO374/52506; *London Gazette*, 30th June 1920). He retained contact with his comrades and became a most popular if unconventional member of his Regimental Association, regularly attending its annual dinners (*The Times*, 7th October 1938).

101 *London Gazette*, Issue 31370, 3rd June 1919, p. 6382.

audience in the largest hall'.[102] No one was to know, and nor would they guess. An Alec slowed down or toned down was still faster and more sonorous than many others.

There was a coda to the division's demise. When an anonymous corpse was chosen by a blindfolded officer from four unidentified servicemen exhumed from different battlefields, and was taken back to London, one of the escort party was a private from the 21st Battalion of the London Regiment. With great solemnity, and amidst a national outpouring of grief, the embodiment of all hopes and tears was reverently interred in Westminster Abbey on Armistice Day 1920. The following year the 'Padre's Flag', the Union Jack which had been used as an altar-cloth and at the funerals of many of the men in the 47th, and had shrouded the coffin on its journey to the abbey, was dedicated and hung above the grave by representatives of the division. Alec would have heartily agreed with the originator of the idea, and owner of the flag, the Revd David Railton MC, that the tomb should have been 'inscribed as that of the "Unknown Comrade" – rather than "Unknown Warrior"'.[103]

Comradeship had been forged in the furnace of the War. Could it be reshaped on the anvil of the Peace, or would it too be interred in the mausoleum of remembrance, or left to rust 'in Flanders fields'? Could there be a 'living war memorial – something alive and eager and outgoing'?[104]

---

102 Baron, 'Across the Bridges', *Four Men* (London, n.d.), pp. 30–40, at p. 36.

103 Maude, p. 76; Ronald Blythe, *The Age of Illusion* (London, 1963), pp. 1–15; Michael Moynihan, *God on our Side: The British Padre in World War I* (London, 1983), pp. 46–79; Andrew Richards, *The Flag* (Oxford, 2017), pp. 195–199, 218f. In France Railton had come across a grave inscribed to 'an Unknown British Soldier'. He remembered how still it had been, 'even the guns seemed to be resting.' He pondered over the outcast's fate until 'quietly and gradually there came out of the mist of thought this answer, clear and strong. "Let this body – this symbol of him – be carried reverently over the sea to his native land".'

104 G.F. Macleod, 'What is Toc H?', in P.B. Clayton, *Earthquake Love* (London, 1932), p. 80.

CHAPTER 7

A LABOUR OF LOVE: 1919–1922

We have to go back to our beginnings to understand our growth and see our objective ... A boy in the War gains more by going to the Old House and imagining the refreshment of the tired soldier than by listening to many poor reminiscences ... [It] is more than a place of sentiment – it is a fact of history. I know fellows of straight and simple mind who have found the depths of Toc H in no crowded Guest Night, but in the strange simplicity of a Belgian house where it all began.

Alexander Paterson

Maurice Waller was determined to inaugurate a more liberal regime in English prison administration. With this end in view he took the unprecedented step of recommending the appointment of a Commissioner from outside the prison service and the Home Office – Alexander Paterson – and so introduced a creative force which was to affect within the next twenty-five years the transformation of the theory and practice of imprisonment, not only in England but throughout the world.

Harold Scott

W HEN Alec finally returned home, he took up residence in the old 'barrack block' before moving to 9 Grange Road, where he would stay with Tom Angliss and his parents for six years.[1] While working for the Ministry of Labour, he remained deeply involved in the local area and devoted his leisure time to his old interests. He found that Bermondsey, along with the rest of the post-war world, was much changed. For the first time the word 'Mission' had an old-fashioned Victorian ring, denoting an age of *noblesse oblige*. This would no longer do. Equality had always been integral to 'the Doctor's' dream and

---

1   Electoral Register.

could be better expressed by another slight change of name. The Oxford and Bermondsey Mission became the Oxford and Bermondsey Club.[2]

As the 'Bermondsey boys' were demobilised and came home there was a move for a new and enlarged club, composed of them but reinforced each autumn by drafts of eighteen-year-olds from junior clubs. Men and boys 'cemented together by memories of club-camps and campaigns abroad will grow up to make their mark in local history'; so it was expected, so it was hoped.[3] There might not yet be a country fit for heroes but there could be a club fit for them. It would also be a tribute to the fallen more fitting than any list of names on a war memorial. In any case the men's club had to move, as the tenancy for its old premises in Abbey Street had expired. The derelict Methodist Institute off Long Lane, with its many rooms and patch of grass, seemed ideal for the venture, and it was acquired as the new venue of the Stansfeld Club. The old name board was erected above the entrance, and the street leading to it was renamed 'Hankey Place', as a memorial to Donald, by the borough council. The Georgian building underwent a major transformation. The vault containing the bones of members of the congregation was sealed off, a boxing ring replaced the pews, and 'show nights' the services. An office, a library and a billiard room were installed, and cricket was played on the surrounding grass, under which lay more of the dead.

Alec, who had led so many of its members in the Bermondsey Battalion and had laid down an outline of the club's objectives while on active service, was acknowledged as its leader, and elected chairman of the management committee. In Paterson's view the club was to be a model of Christian self-government, and embody the wartime spirit and ethos of Talbot House. It was also to be a grown-up place, fit for men whose manhood had been forged in fire. He argued that the premises should be licensed.

> We fail in our function if we cannot provide men as they are facing life with some definite guidance on the more common occasions of stumbling. They do not require a mechanical rule of life, with a ready reckoner of benefits and a sliding scale of temptations, but rather the cultivation of a clear voice within them and the support of their brotherhood without. No two-foot rule can guide men to the narrow gate. We do not feel that we can wisely or honestly put before them a pledge of total abstinence as the normal and necessary way of life. If, however, we say cheerfully to all and sundry that there can be no possible harm in a glass of beer and leave the matter there, we are abjuring the negative system of morality and not doing our share in the cultivation of the

2   A title it retains to this day. The Stansfeld OBC and Youth Club both operate from 3 Webb Street, a few hundred yards from Grange Road.
3   'To Those Who Love Their Fellow-Men', a ten-page appeal published by the OBM Memorial Fund, undated and unattributed, but written by Alec in 1919 and reused as the preface to Hankey's *Letters*.

positive. For our only place of buying and drinking beer in Bermondsey is an overcrowded public house foul in atmosphere and association, brimming to the doors, whose only interest is the consumption of the maximum amount of beer in a minimum of time. We must, therefore, either say to our brothers of Oxford and Bermondsey that it is wrong to drink a single glass of beer, or we must provide some healthy place where it may be done. We have rejected the former alternative; the latter we hoped to try in the Stansfeld Club.[4]

His advocacy hit two rocks: the terms of sale of what had been Methodist premises, and the clear breach such a proposal, if adopted, would constitute to the precepts of John Stansfeld.

Another bone of contention arose when Waldo Eagar, who had also returned to South London after war service with the Royal Artillery, affiliated the Bermondsey clubs to the London Federation of Boys' Clubs and associated the OBC with other bodies with similar aims. While Stansfeld warmly approved of the OBC being brought 'into the mainstream of settlement and boys' club action and thought', Alec equally warmly did not, and would hold 'aloof from the subsequent formation of the National Association of Boys' Clubs' which took place at a meeting in Toynbee Hall in October 1925.[5] Why he was so opposed to this development is not clear. It may have been that he believed that the independent tradition of boys' clubs was sacrosanct, and that the uniqueness of the OBC would be compromised. It may have been a personality clash, or even jealous resentment. While Alec had been the dominant force in the pre-war period, his position had been usurped by Eagar, who was now very much in charge and had the gumption to overrule him, or the temerity to outrun him. As Alec once observed, 'South London always wounds those who serve her best.'[6]

Faced with such frustrations and usurpations, Alec withdrew from active involvement in Bermondsey and its boy's clubs, but never lost interest in them. He frequently visited his old turf, and for the rest of his life he would, whenever possible, attend the annual OBC summer camp in the Weald.[7]

---

4   Quoted in Baron, p. 177. Alec himself was partial to a drink, but it was red wine that he favoured.

5   Eagar, p. 236, n.1.

6   *Letters*, 23rd October 1918; Eagar (pp. 414f.) is enigmatic, referring to running into 'the primary resistance of minds at ease which shrink from statements of first principles.' It is hard to believe that Alec fitted this bill.

7   Clubs continued to thrive. In 1931 one was started in Downham, a new housing estate on the outskirts of London to which many Bermondsey families had been moved. Four years later Clem Attlee opened, in commemoration of Gordon Stansfeld, a new combined club for boys and 'old boys' which had been constructed in a converted leather factory in Grange Road. Alec was asked to preside over the

FIGURE 17. Alec at Willis's Wedding, 1920

Meanwhile he was active in creating another bastion of brotherhood: Toc H. When peace had broken out, the work of Talbot House had come to an end. Tubby Clayton was determined to resurrect it in some form, an idea he had been fermenting with Barkis and Alec as early as 1917.[8] Whereas Britain for four years had been turning citizens into good soldiers, the time had come to start turning soldiers into good citizens. At first, he 'dreamed of setting up a new Talbot House in Trafalgar Square … to inherit the spirit and the customers of the old.' He rallied in London the surviving 'foundation members', many of whom were finding adjusting to civilian life hard going, most of whom were lamenting the 'loss of spirit that had been so glorious in war and had strangely disappeared with the return of peace', and all of whom missed 'the reality of comradeship and the bond of common duty out of which it sprang'.[9] They wanted to regain the egalitarian ethos of Talbot House and perpetuate its sense of fellowship and purpose. They would reconstitute the Knights Hospitaller within their own

---

occasion, and both John Stansfeld and Alfred Salter attended (*The Times*, 19th January 1935).

8   Melville Harcourt, *Tubby Clayton* (London, 1953), p. 115.

9   Baron, *The Birth of a Movement* (London, 1946), pp. 71ff; G.F. Macleod, 'What is Toc H?', in P.B. Clayton, *Earthquake Love* (London, 1932), pp. 76f. George Macleod was padre of Toc H in Scotland until 1926, and in 1938 founded the Iona Community.

ranks, even if they had defended the Western democracies against the Germans rather than Christendom against the Muslims, and would establish hostels for the itinerant rather than hospitals for the infirm.

The birth of what would become an international movement took place in November 1919. At a meeting of 'intimate confederates', including Alec, Neville Talbot and Tubby's cousin, the celebrated vicar of St Martin-in-the-Fields, Dick Sheppard, it was resolved to go much further than originally envisaged. They would reanimate in the post-war world 'the brotherhood of the trenches' in a new venture to be called Toc H, 'a domesticated phoenix ... reborn from the ashes of Talbot House.'[10] Providing a club for old soldiers to reminisce and sing 'Auld Lang Syne' was not what they had in mind. Old soldiers would fade away and die, and with them so would any club. A 'living war memorial' was needed and new members were required to ensure its vitality. While retaining the fellowship and ethos of service engendered by the war, Toc H had to find its own wider purpose within a structure of core beliefs. United in their determination that this should be no mere revival of a relic, however sacred, the group formed an executive committee to give leadership and share the burden.

The venture needed a credo to attract and retain fresh blood, and so, the following summer, Alec and Tubby were invited to Dick's vicarage to discuss the matter. They resolved to draft a 'rule of life' for future members. Alec produced a document based on the 'Four Rules of Life' he had already devised for himself, which were that each day he would think for two minutes, read for twenty, 'treat every fellow-servant as a brother, not asking from what school he came or how his brother earned his daily bread'[11], and 'build a new and glorious future for my country, believing that the best is yet to come'. Tubby had his own list, which although different in wording, was similar in import. Then the three men whittled away at these ideas until they produced four short maxims, incorporating the meaning, but simpler in structure. Known as the 'Four Points of the Compass', they were:

Fellowship – to love widely;
Service – to build bravely;
Fairmindedness – to think fairly;
The Kingdom of God – to witness humbly.

Service and fellowship were conjoined twins. Fellowship and service were 'the whole gospel of Toc H'. Service was the purpose of the new organisation, and service was what its fellowship could engender. Individuals acting alone could do their bit, but acting in concert could do so much more. 'Active service' was 'the

---

10   Baron, *op.cit.*, pp. 12f. In jest, Alec had suggested another name, 'The League of 20th Century Ploughmen'. Sheppard had been a volunteer at Oxford House.
11   This was a riposte to the restrictive membership of the Cavendish Club.

essential spring and outcome of fellowship'.[12] Two years later these four points were embodied in a longer document, drafted in Alec's office at the Prison Commission, called the 'Main Resolution'. It was a manifesto proclaiming the aims and ambitions of Toc H. These were to preserve the traditions of active service begun in wartime; to encourage 'all kinds of social service as between and for the benefit of all ranks of society'; to promote among all people a wide interest in the well-being and needs of their fellows; and to mitigate the 'evils of class consciousness' in order to 'create a body of public opinion free of all social antagonisms'. 'Progress only comes', Alec would later write, 'when men of different experience understand one another and join together in a search for the truth, and in common service for the whole family of men.' 'Common service' was the watchword for Toc H, as it was for Alec.[13]

To put such egalitarian ideals into practice required premises to house young workers and students, anxious for cheap digs, who, it was hoped, would become 'infused with the traditional spirit of the old house' and perpetuate it.[14] After acquiring a property in Queen's Gate Gardens, Knightsbridge, Clayton opened the first Toc H centre named, in army fashion, Mark I. It had a chapel into which the old Poperinghe carpenter's bench was transposed, and replicated other aspects of Talbot House. It combined the functions of a hostel, clubhouse and headquarters. Once rooted, the plant propagated itself with rapidity. It helped that Toc H could engage the support of the good and the great. The Archbishop of Canterbury and Field Marshal Plumer became presidents, and Edward, Prince of Wales was an active patron, appearing at many annual festivals.[15] By 1921 there were three Marks in London and seventy branches in the United Kingdom. Within five years they were all over the world. This, despite the fact that new recruits had to demonstrate dedication. There were to be no 'shirkers' and no pessimists! An interested group was initially awarded a 'Rushlight', before being elevated to 'branch status', and consequently granted one of the trademark 'Lamps', which were introduced in 1922.

---

12   P.B. Clayton, 'Dick Sheppard, in Thanksgiving: A Sermon', *THJ* (December 1937); Baron, *The Birth of a Movement*, pp. 2ff.

13   Tresham Lever, *Clayton of Toc H* (London, 1971), pp. 127f; 'Give or Get', *THJ* (November 1924).

14   Tubby Clayton, 'The Situation Report', reprinted in Barclay Baron, *The Birth of a Movement* (London, 1946), p. 75.

15   The prince, a foundation member, had been introduced to Talbot House by Major-General Cavan, on whose staff he was. He left his name on the communicant's roll and donated a painting of Belgian peasants praying for the souls of the fallen (Jan Louagie, *A Touch of Paradise in Hell* [Solihull, 2015], p. 77, n.98).

The creation of this new enterprise suggested to Alec a consolidation of resources. While *The Challenge*, by then in a precarious state, provided temporary office space and, until its demise in 1922, extensive coverage for Toc H, a more or less moribund precursor was incorporated within the new, vibrant movement. The Cavendish Club had been set up in 1911 under the patronage of the Duke of Devonshire to promote the idea of social service among the 'old boys' of public schools and Oxbridge. It was housed in expensive premises in Piccadilly and operated just like any other private club. In 1913 some of its members set up a Cavendish Association to attract a wider clientele from all over the country who could dispense with a club but unite in service. In the post-war world such an organisation, based on class privilege and condescension, was an irrelevance and went into terminal decline. Alec Paterson and Dick Sheppard, the two 'revolutionary' members of its committee, set out to rescue its assets and transfer them to Toc H. In June 1921 Bob Shelston, the Cavendish clerk, and Barkis, its travelling secretary, moved the association's office furniture, pictures and books to the Toc H headquarters, and installed themselves there as staff. The new movement swallowed the old association, whose large membership and links with public schools and eminent benefactors were even more useful than its desks and typewriters.[16]

The Bermondsey influence was everywhere. Dr Stansfeld kept a constant eye on an organisation that embodied so much of what he stood for, eventually becoming a member of the Oxford branch, though without having to satisfy, by a period of probation, the requirements of demonstrating that he was a 'good mixer', had the instinct and desire to give service in his spare time, and was, at least, not hostile to the Christian basis of the movement. He saw Toc H, as did others, as the spiritual successor of the OBM. Tubby himself had remarked that 'Bermondsey was the true cradle of Toc H', and recognised how 'from the first days of its getting together leadership began to come to the new movement from "across the bridges".'[17] There was Alec, of course, and Neville Talbot on the committee, and there was Barclay Baron and Hubert Secretan, both of whom joined the staff, the former devoting many years of his life to Toc H's service, the latter becoming the second of its administrators, and vice-president. 'As for the word "family", which from early 1922 onwards is found in Toc H literature and on the lips of its members, it came direct from "the Doctor's" mouth and heart and was merely imported by one of his disciples at Toc H headquarters.'[18] That disciple was Barkis. Tubby, echoing Alec, portrayed Toc H as a bridge spanning the social gap.

16   Baron, *One Man's Pattern* (London, n.d.), p. 16; *The Birth of a Movement*, pp. 28ff, 115–118; *The Years Between* (Westminster, 1933), pp. 72, 75f.
17   Baron, p. 208.
18   Baron, *Birth of a Movement*, p. 4.

When it received its royal charter on 14th December 1922, Toc H became a corporation with legal rights and responsibilities. It was no longer 'Tubby's show', but a national institution with international ambitions. It was regarded by William Temple as 'one of the two good things to come out of the war', and would long outlast the other: the League of Nations.[19] Alec became the first chairman of its Central Executive Committee. As such, on the following day he was included among the distinguished company which gathered to witness Tubby's induction as vicar of All Hallows-by-the-Tower, 'the guild church' of the movement. That evening, seven years after the opening of Talbot House, a 'Birthday Festival' was held in the Guildhall in the presence of the Prince of Wales, the Lord Mayor, the burgomasters of Poperinghe and Ypres, and Bishop Talbot. The bronze lamp, the recently devised symbol of Toc H, having been lit for the first time by Prince Edward, the rubric for the Ceremony of Light proceeded with a representative of each branch receiving an identical lamp and answering four questions:

> What is this? – *The Lamp of Maintenance*
> What first lit it? – *Unselfish sacrifice*
> What alone will maintain it? – *Unselfish service*
> What is service? – *The rent we pay for our room on earth*

With the lamps alight and the Guildhall's chandeliers extinguished, a voice rang out: '*In lumine tuo videbimus lumen*' – 'In Thy light shall we see light'.

Alec delivered the final address, a rousing exhortation, before the audience of 2,000. After referring to Tubby as one 'who never sleeps in the same parish as his pyjamas', he went on to define the essence and soaring aspirations of the movement. Comradeship was its core; service its mission. Comradeship across the class divide; comradeship across the racial divide; comradeship across the religious divide. Service in all lands, service to all in need, and service in all areas of life.

> What is Toc H? I can only say that it is just a gathering of young men who seek to rebuild a broken world with the mortar of comradeship and the bricks, the solid bricks, of personal service. There is bequeathed to us a country where men are divided by education, by industry … and, alas, very often by religion. Englishmen of the same spirit and the same instincts are by the futility of our educational system afforded such different experiences in the first twenty years of their life that when they come to meet each other they do so in shyness and constraint. We hope to see springing up

19   *Manchester Guardian*, 5th February 1924, p. 11. Toc H still exists, although in a much-truncated form, while Talbot House, bought for Tubby in 1930 by Lord Wakefield, thrives to this day, incarnating the wartime spirit of the place, providing bed and breakfast accommodation, and boasting a fine new museum.

in the name of Toc H non-class clubs in every great city ... where the sons of the west and the sons of the east shall meet on equal terms. That is the first thing, that Toc H shall provide places where we can learn comradeship. Having learned that, then there shall enter those places the spirit of personal service, which is the negation of selfishness and boredom, and the only sure road to happiness and knowledge. That spirit of service shall ... rebuild a disordered world that every child born into it shall be born into a home and not, as at present, into a mere lodgment against the rain. It shall face fearlessly and without partisanship the great economic problems of the day, and help to solve the riddles of labour, industry and commerce. Toc H shall go far across the seas. It shall, by comradeship and service, bring peace to those places where there is still bitterness, and light to those places where there is still darkness.

My fellow members, ours is a task that knows no limits. It is not an easy task, but it is not one beyond our endurance. There is no true comradeship without surrender, no true service without sacrifice. We hope to carry on a holy and ceaseless war against pride and snobbery wherever we meet them ... In the spirit of Jesus Christ we are joined together, and we shall go forward, setting our course not by the waves but by the stars.[20]

Such was his vaulting ambition for this new venture. Fired in the furnace of war, it would transform the world. It never did that, but it did transform many lives in many places.

Although three years later pressure of work would force him to relinquish the chair, Alec would maintain close association with Toc H throughout his career. On his travels abroad he never missed an opportunity to visit existing branches or even found new ones, such as that in Gambia. For Alec Toc H would always form a bridge not just between nations but between generations. At its twenty-first birthday reception he said that 'if it were but an echo of the war it would have died as men's memories grew dim.' Its members 'had Flanders at their back [but] their faces to the future, offering that same spirit of service and comradeship for the solution of urgent problems, whether social, imperial or international.'[21] More immediately he would find within its extensive membership a resource on which to draw when he wanted recruits for the prison service of which he had recently become a Commissioner.[22]

20 Baron, p. 209; *The Birth of a Movement*, pp. 58–61; *The Years Between*, p. 99.
21 *The Times*, 24th June 1936.
22 Baron, p. 208. Mark XXII in Putney was named after the Bermondsey Battalion and 'will remain his monument in Toc H', *THJ* (July 1947), p. 167.

The Prison Commission had been established in 1878 by statute to oversee the newly nationalised local prisons. In tandem with the Directorate of Convict Prisons, the Commission thus became responsible for all prisons in England and Wales. It was a body corporate of usually three and not more than five members and was empowered to hold property for the purposes of the 1877 Prison Act. Its duties included the maintenance and inspection of prisons, and the appointment of prison staff. It was empowered to formulate and apply policy subject to submission to the Secretary of State of any issues which could arouse public concern or lead to political embarrassment. It was also required to submit annual reports to Parliament, together with other returns. Although the Commissioners would have considerable autonomy and be free from the vagaries of party politics, they were housed in the Home Office, their functions were subject to a general supervision in matters of policy by the Home Secretary, and he retained the power of appointing the chairman.

The first to hold this august office was Edmund Du Cane, who also chaired the Directorate of Convict Prisons. One man held the reins of two horses. Du Cane was no penal philosopher and no prison innovator, but he was paramount in giving effect to government policy. He got to work on a task of 'prodigious magnitude', ending 800 years of local control and creating a modern prison system and a crushing uniformity of regime. On 1st April 1878 he took over all 113 local gaols, all of which would become Her Majesty's Prisons. By the end of May thirty-eight prisons had been closed, with others to follow, bringing the number down to fifty-nine by 1885. The convict and local services, while retaining their distinctions in uniform, pay and purpose, became two parts of a single state entity of which Du Cane was the lynchpin. Without his energy and expertise, it would have been all but impossible. The regime he ran, however, was notoriously punitive with 'hard labour, hard fare and hard bed', and during his autocratic tenure the Commission became little more than a cypher.

In 1895, as a result of the Gladstone Committee's inquiry into prisons, Du Cane was replaced by Evelyn Ruggles-Brise, who would introduce major reforms, initiating sixty years of penal optimism. The most inspiring of them was the opening of the first institution for 'juvenile-adults' on the site of Borstal, an old convict prison near Rochester, an experiment that would in time grow into the borstal system.[23] In addition, under the Prisons Act 1898, the Commissioners and Directors became one and the same. For the first time England and Wales had a unified prison system under central control. Ruggles-Brise's last year in office coincided with the falling of the 'Geddes Axe'. Geddes had been appointed by the Prime Minister to find economies, and the prison system was a prime target. Budgetary constraints would bedevil all efforts at penal reform,

23   On the Du Cane era, penal reform thereafter, and the development of borstals see Harry Potter, *Shades of the Prison House* (Woodbridge, 2019), pp. 272–281, 325–357.

and to proceed future Commissioners would have 'to exercise all their ingenuity in the fine art of adaptation'.[24] Fortunately, Alec proved adept at making bricks without straw.

In August 1921 Ruggles-Brise was succeeded by Maurice Waller. A civil servant at the Home Office, latterly serving as private secretary to the reforming Home Secretary, Herbert Gladstone, Waller had been one of the Prison Commissioners since 1910, and most significantly had been particularly responsible for the nascent borstal system which Alec had praised in *Across the Bridges* and had experienced at first-hand with his work for the Borstal Association. As a result of Major Briscoe's retirement from the Commission a vacancy had arisen and Waller recommended an outsider to fill it.

Alec's appointment was an unusual and even daring one, as he had never held a position within the prison service itself, nor been a civil servant in the Home Office. He had visited prisoners in the capacity of a friend, and prisons in his work in after-care. He had been a probation officer, given evidence before the departmental committee on their training, appointment and payment,[25] and had been involved with discharged borstal boys. His experience stood him in good stead, as did his celebrity as a writer about young people and their families in Bermondsey. He had also been a great success in his job at the Labour Ministry. The permanent secretary there, Sir James Masterman-Smith, made sure to put on record his appreciation. In a letter to Downing Street he expressed

> genuine admiration for the manner in which Paterson has carried out his duties, and my great regard for him as a man of exceptional capacity and character. As an official he has all the merits that a good Class I officer is expected to possess. He is industrious, he writes excellent memoranda and letters, and has a peculiarly attractive and lucid exposition of his subject whether on a platform or in the office. Beyond all this he has an attractive personality and had a fine war record.[26]

But there was another reason why he would stand out as the ideal choice.

In 1919 Alec had been invited to collaborate in a Labour Party Research Department inquiry into the prison system. His prior history with the inquiry secretary, Stephen Hobhouse, as well as his involvement with both the LSE and the Borstal Association, may explain the invitation. A committee had been set up under the chairmanship of the Fabian socialist Sir Sydney Olivier.[27] Its members included the Webbs, George Bernard Shaw, Margery Fry of the Howard

---

24   Watson (1939), p. 83.
25   'The Baird Committee' was appointed in 1919 and reported in 1922.
26   TNA, HO45/21687/446037/1: 19th October 1921.
27   Olivier had worked at Toynbee Hall, living in the Whitechapel slums and teaching Latin at the Working Men's College.

League, the stipendiary magistrate Sir William Clarke-Hall (Hobhouse's brother-in-law), and Paterson himself, who by then, it seems, had migrated from radical liberalism to ethical socialism. Their extensive report, *English Prisons Today*, 'the Bible of penal reformers', would be published in 1922. Its main contention, and one dear to Alec's heart, was that reform should be the main objective of the prison system, not, as heretofore, deterrence. It expressed the hope that 'every offender would be given an opportunity to turn back from the path of crime and again become a good and useful citizen'.

From its style, content and the endnote attributing recent reforms to his accession to the Commission, it is highly likely that he had not just contributed material and ideas, as Hobhouse attested, but had written much of chapter XXVI, the section on borstals, himself.[28] In it can be found the blueprint for the reform of borstals that he would ultimately realise. The penal, disciplinary and military element was still too dominant. There should be 'the separation of violent and mentally-abnormal offenders from other inmates' so that, once the misfits had been segregated, the authorities 'would be able to deal with the remainder on educational and much less penal lines'. Education, general and vocational, should be paramount. All this would take time, but so long as borstals retained their penal character it would be unjust to keep boys for the requisite period. It also stressed the importance of *esprit de corps* and the personal influence of staff, quoting with approval Ruggles-Brise's observations on the subject. Tutors represented a hopeful innovation, but the retention of uniformed warders was regressive. 'It is self-discipline that the borstal boy needs most, and the army (and prison) system of mechanical obedience fails to engender it.' The worst example of a 'boys' prison' was Portland borstal where, within three months of its opening, a suicide, an attempted suicide, eight attempted escapes, and allegations of staff brutality had garnered much bad publicity.[29] A separate section on 'borstal treatment of girl offenders' was more encouraging, although the number of punishments in Aylesbury, at that time the only girls' borstal, had risen along with the reconviction rate. Nonetheless, great advances were being 'made on ordinary prison methods in the treatment of girls at this institution', the greatest of which was the rapidity with which rules were changed, an innovation 'marked by that fact that there [was] a consciousness of experiment about it'. The most positive innovation was the Borstal Association, founded by Ruggles-Brise to supervise and assist 'lads on release'. It represented 'one half of the Borstal System'.

28   Stephen Hobhouse and Fenner Brockway (eds), *English Prisons Today* (London, 1922), pp. 410–439; Bailey (1987), pp. 195f.
29   *HJ*, 1/1 (October 1921), pp. 45f; *The Spectator*, 29th October 1921, pp. 8f; *The Manchester Guardian* (16th February 1922) believed that the recent scandal surrounding Portland was a factor behind Paterson's 'welcome appointment'. In his time Portland was reconfigured in keeping with its new role.

For the whole to be salvaged, transformed and expanded, the report seemed to be saying, someone with expertise in working with working-class youths, an informed interest in borstals, a gift for getting things done, and a talent for public persuasion was needed. Alec fitted the bill. He was expert on juvenile criminals, had a reputation for dynamism, and was seen as a fecund source of new ideas with the oratorical ability to put them across. In *English Prisons Today* he had even written his own job description.

In 1921 Sir Evelyn Ruggles-Brise retired as chairman of the Prison Commission after a tenure of more than a quarter of a century. What had been radical in the twilight of the Victorian age seemed conservative in the post-war era. While the regime over which he had ruled was much criticised, the appointment of Waller to act in his stead was explicitly welcomed by *English Prisons Today*. Its authors hoped that his elevation to the chairmanship would initiate the transformation in prison conditions they advocated. In addition, the Borstal Association wrote to the new appointee, accusing the Commissioners of not taking their responsibilities seriously enough.

> They have not provided in borstal institutions something sufficiently different from prisons to render justifiable long sentences to borstal treatment which are given as an alternative to short sentences of imprisonment.[30]

Waller agreed. He would live up to and surpass the association's expectations. In contrast to Ruggles-Brise, who had refused to co-operate with the Prison Service Inquiry, he studied its findings. He was determined to hasten the rate of change, and eager to transform the whole prison system from one which degraded and debased to one which elevated and improved. He needed allies and also wanted someone to replace him in overseeing the borstal system, 'someone here in the Prison Commission who is more or less of a specialist in borstal work, that is to say, someone who has been successful in dealing with bodies of boys of the class we have in borstal institutions', someone who shared his views. Yet, he told Thomas McNamara, the Minister of Labour, it was 'not altogether easy to find the right man'.[31] Odd! Had he not heard of the OBC? Had he not read *Across the Bridges*? Was he not aware of Paterson's work with the Borstal Association, and of the resolution he had submitted to the executive committee deploring 'the inadequacy of the present system of training', and proposing the appointment of 'a special Borstal Commissioner'? Or, more likely, had Waller mentioned his dilemma *because* he was aware that Paterson fitted the bill precisely and was currently working in McNamara's department? The chairman was fishing, not poaching. The minister took the bait, and while loath to lose his highly-regarded official, was prepared to make the sacrifice. McNamara, in turn,

30 *Borstal Association Minutes*, 8th April 1921.
31 TNA, HO45/21687: Letter from Waller to McNamara, 25th January 1922.

approached Edward Shortt, the Home Secretary, with the recommendation, one that Shortt approved.[32] The appointment was initially sanctioned for one year only, but Alec would remain a Commissioner, one could say *the* Commissioner, for twenty-five years.[33]

And so it was that on 3rd March 1922 *The London Gazette* recorded that 'The King is pleased by warrant under His Majesty's royal sign manual to appoint Alexander Paterson to be one of the Commissioners under the Prison Act 1877.'[34] This was the first commission Alec was keen to accept.[35] It would give him the power and authority to put into practice the ideas he had been formulating over many years.[36] His salary was set at £1,000 per annum. Each Commissioner was allotted a third of the thirty-five establishments in the prison estate, and each had a speciality, such as security, staffing levels or education. The Commission's complement included four Assistant Commissioners, one of whom acted as secretary. At that time the headquarters were in the Home Office building in Whitehall. Although, perforce, he would have to spend much time there, Alec could not be kept desk-bound for long. During his long career he would be constantly on the move, visiting prisons at home and in many countries within the Empire and beyond. He became known as 'the chief prison wallah'. The dignity of the office required him to adopt a smart and formal appearance, and he was usually attired in a well-fitting three-piece suit, a shirt with a wing-collar and a cravat or bow tie.[37]

Alec was one of three 'Administrative Commissioners', the number set by the Home Secretary for reasons of economy from the more generous pre-war quota. He joined the two serving members, Waller and the former medical inspector, Sidney Dyer. Their names appear together in the *Report of the Commissioners of Prisons and the Directors of Convict Prisons for the year ended 31st*

32   *Ibid.*: letters, 30th January, 7th February 1922.

33   On 6th February 1922 the Under-Secretary of State at the Home Office indicated that the Treasury sanctioned filling the vacancy for a period of one year only in the first instance. In January 1923 his appointment was made permanent and backdated to 7th February 1922 (TNA, HO45/21687).

34   Issue 32631, p. 1949.

35   In a letter of 15th February 1957, Walter Eagar, albeit an unreliable source, told Barclay that Alec was so anxious to become a Commissioner that he asked Lloyd George to intervene on his behalf (Bailey [1987], pp. 194f). I have found no connection between Paterson and Lloyd George. If he approached anyone it would have been Churchill.

36   In his letter of resignation from the Borstal Association Alec assured his former colleagues that he would do his best to fulfil their common aim and if he succeeded it would be because he had already discussed so many of his ideas with them (*BA Minutes*, 19th April 1922, cited in Bailey [1987], p. 196).

37   *Over the Walls*, p. 1.

March 1922. Waller and Paterson had not wasted time. 'Gusts of fresh air began to blow through the pages.' Alec had already begun to influence the system over which he was presiding, his input being detectable in the immediate and bold expansion of the prison visitors' scheme by the introduction of male visitors to men's prisons. They were 'an essential feature of any system which has for its object the rehabilitation of a social failure, and his re-establishment as a sound citizen'.[38] That he wrote the section on this subject is clear from both style and content and the force with which the expansion is defended.

> One misconception ... is that prisoners are being 'pampered'. Those who will pause to consider mental and spiritual values will not make this mistake. Pampering is not the object, nor is it the result. It is our duty, as custodians of those who are for a time forcibly separated from life in the civic community, to restore them to it at least as fit as when we received them. To this end we should feed and exercise their minds as well as their bodies; else we shall return them to the stern competition outside torpid in mind and nerve, and quite unfit to take their part.[39]

The impact he would eventually have would be profound. Perhaps no other could have injected such energy and optimism into the penal system of his day. As a reformer who was also a Commissioner, he could put into practice what he preached. He did so with the help of others, which was just as well since he had one major deficiency: a 'fundamental lack of interest in civil service methods and administrative detail'. This 'most unorthodox of civil servants' had no use for red tape and little respect for regulations. Fortunately, he 'had the unusual ability of admitting his own limitations' and the good fortune always to have colleagues who could make up for his defects and translate his seminal ideas into the orders and regulations that would give them effect. Throughout his time in office his fellow Commissioners, rather than resenting a whirlwind in their ranks, blew in the same direction. This was vital as, however charismatic Paterson undoubtedly was, he could never have succeeded alone and in opposition to his colleagues. The backing of successive chairmen was especially important. In particular he owed a lot to Waller, under whose leadership he had

38 Report (1922), p. 14; Watson (1939), pp. 97–109. Prison visitors were lay volunteers approved to visit prisoners on a regular basis. Elizabeth Fry had initiated such a scheme, but it had fizzled out. Since the 1890s women visitors had been active, and from 1924 they began to visit boys. The same year the National Association of Prison Visitors was formed with the Home Secretary as its president. The venture blossomed and proved to be one of Paterson's most enduring achievements.
39 Report (1922), p. 15.

learned his craft and most of his major steps had been taken or projected, and to Harold Scott, who defended him from critics and supported his initiatives.[40]

The whole approach to youth justice that he would advocate rested on the twin assumptions that most adult criminals had been juvenile delinquents, and that delinquent acts were warning signals of trouble to come and the product of social and environmental factors over which offenders had little control. But they could regain control and the grim progression from 'young hoodlum' to 'old lag' could be stemmed. They should be helped to succeed, not just punished for their failures. Borstal was the answer. It was also the avenue through which similar changes could be introduced into prisons.

He was aware of those aspects of European Positivism which attributed criminality more to breeding than birth, thought bad behaviour could be eradicated more effectively by internal than external restraints, and emphasised individualisation of treatment alongside indeterminate sentences and release as a result of assessments made by experts. He was happy to find support for his beliefs in Positivism but did not derive those beliefs from that source. Moreover, he never denied free will nor moral responsibility nor culpability, and never subscribed to the determinist theory propounded by Cesare Lombroso, the Italian criminal anthropologist, that some people were born criminals or had physiological and phrenological traits that disposed them to crime. After all, his Christian faith, emphasising the intrinsic worth of every individual, held that *all* were born in sin, *all* sinned of their own volition, and *all* could be redeemed. There was no such thing as 'criminal man', only fallible humans, but all with a 'divine spark'. This belief was reinforced by the Idealist non-deterministic view of human nature, and its assertions that crime as a freely-willed act was deservedly punished, and that the reformation of criminals could only be achieved by impressing on them the antisocial nature of their acts. Real change could come only as a result of a conscious personal decision and not of any external pressures to conform. The dignity of individuals who had erred was preserved by treating them as agents, not as patients.[41]

He also had no truck with the more outlandish aspects of Positivism, and was buttressed in his scepticism by the findings of Charles Goring, Parkhurst's medical officer, who had been commissioned by Ruggles-Brise to examine the evidence for this alien theory. In 1913, after exhaustive research which compared convicts with soldiers, undergraduates and schoolboys, Goring published *The English Convict*. He had found that there was no evidence 'confirming the existence of a physical criminal type', and concluded that 'this

40   Gordon Hawkins, *Alec Paterson: An Appreciation* (privately printed, n.d.), pp. 16, 25; Scott, p. 78.

41   For the influence of Idealism and Positivism on Ruggles-Brise and his similarly eclectic response to the latter, see Bailey (2019), pp. 40ff.

anthropological monster has no existence in fact'. English empiricism had exposed and demolished a fashionable foreign fallacy. Goring did, however, advocate compulsory sterilisation for certain categories of prisoner, very much a eugenicist proposition. Eugenics, at least, was British![42] Paterson differed fiercely from this and from Goring's other conclusions that criminals, through deficiencies in intellect and physique, were hereditarily prone to crime, that crime was 'only to a trifling extent (if to any) the product of social inequalities, of adverse environment, or of other manifestations of ... the force of circumstances', and that prisons did no damage.

In short, while Paterson's views coincided in some respects with the tenets of Positivism, they diverged far more often. He is unlikely to have been influenced by its practitioners, and more likely reached some similar conclusions by his own devices. He had seen 'the prisoner' type, created by years 'in the half-light of prison', but not the born criminal.[43] From his close acquaintance with many actual or potential criminals he knew they were no different – except by breaking the law or by getting caught – from their law-abiding neighbours. From his experience of the slums, material and emotional poverty, poor parenting, idleness, lack of stimulation and excitement, lack of education and opportunities for employment, lack of self-control and want of guiding principles were at the root of the malaise. These factors deprived children of value and worth in their lives. These were what led the young into crime. These were what must be countered. And if they could not be eradicated at source at least they could be compensated for by inculcating in wayward youths a sense of self-worth and achievement, the habits of hard work and industry, and the benefits of discipline and team-working. They could be made to feel part of society and not remain rebels against it. Boys' clubs were instrumental in achieving this through the personal influence of charismatic volunteers. So too were elementary schools where dedicated teachers, despite labouring against huge disadvantages, could try to give their charges a second chance. Alec grasped the truth that 'a school is a teacher with a building around him, not a building with a teacher inside.' It was the quality of staff that mattered not the physical infrastructure.[44] This was an insight he would take with him into the prison service, where those who fell through these meagre safety-nets would end up. They should not be outcast and abandoned or further harmed by imprisonment. Never give up.

---

42 Charles Goring, *The English Convict: A Statistical Study* (London, 1913), pp. 173, 370f; Radzinowicz, pp. 21–27.

43 'Should the Criminologist be Encouraged?', *Transactions of the Medico-Legal Society*, 26/1 (1932), pp. 180–200, at p. 183. He had also seen 'a monastic type and a scholastic type'.

44 Paterson, pp. 57ff; *EPBS*, p. 87.

He never would. Alec would prove to be the right person at the right time, and that time was upon him. He had found his life's work, and for the rest of it he would devote himself to reforming the prison system in general and transforming the borstal system in particular. On both he would leave an indelible mark.

PART III

PRISON COMMISSIONER: 1922–1945

CHAPTER 8

PATERSON'S LIGHT HORSE: 1922–1934

A prison system can be no better than the men and women who direct it. It is not enough to recruit officers who are looking for a secure job, and can be trusted to carry out the rules with fairness and fidelity. Men and women must be found with a burning zeal for the work, an understanding of the frailty of human nature, and a belief that there is in all men a divine spark which, if it can be quickened, will lead even the worst into new life. It was precisely this kind whom Paterson attracted into the service, and who set out, inspired by his enthusiasm, to test the new ideas and make them work. He could judge the right man for the job, and infuse him with some of his own ardour.

Harold Scott

The best to the worst, the strongest to the weakest ... Give the best chance to those who need it most.

Alexander Paterson

The appointment of this young, inexperienced 'missionary', as Alec called himself, was met with reservations by the *Prison Officer's Magazine*, an organ that well reflected the views of its increasingly dissident grass-roots membership.[1] Nor did it meet with the unqualified approval of governors, all of whom were older than the new Commissioner, and most were former military men of higher rank than he, loyal to Ruggles-Brise and his methods of disciplined compassion. Some resented a 'novice' being put over them; others feared that they would not have the requisite skills to fulfil the new role expected of them.

---

1   On the other hand, it had welcomed Waller's appointment, and affirmed Paterson's view that 'the sure path to reform is through the influence of good men and women, and through a well-paid, efficient and spiritually-minded prison staff' (*Prison Officers' Magazine, 1922*, p. 226).

A dedication to 'social service' was displacing 'sterling worth' as the criterion for advancement and high hopes were trouncing hard facts.[2]

Captain Gerold Clayton was one ambivalent governor. 'Old One Lug', as he was called, had joined the service in 1920 when one system was coming to an end and another was about to begin.[3] His father had been Ruggles-Brise's lieutenant, and the son valued much of what they had done. He thought Paterson 'a remarkable man', but, defensive of his father and his legacy, bearing a grudge for being twice passed over for the inspectorate in favour of his juniors and, in his opinion, being unjustifiably reprimanded for some of his actions, he could be scathing about his commander. Clayton's gripes related especially to Paterson's attitude to staff and their pay, the lack of consultation, his disinclination to take advice from more experienced men, some of the senior appointments he made, and the haste with which he acted. Yet at the end of his career Clayton acknowledged that, with all his reservations, it had still been 'a great experience' to have served under 'the greatest prison reformer of the century and perhaps of all time'. He had always admired the way Paterson 'culled the honey which the bees had collected in various bonnets and added to it his own theories'.

> If ever a man poured new wine into old bottles, Mr Paterson did. There was a sound of straining, not a little groaning, and a great deal more improvisation. But the prison service began to adapt itself to a new decree ... [so] that before he died [he] saw his pattern of prisons and scheme of social reform of outcasts leaving the drawing-board, as it were, and become practice – in spite of the difficulties.[4]

Colonel Charles Rich was less ambivalent about, and more antagonistic to, someone he considered to be an inexperienced amateur. Although nowhere in his autobiography does he name Paterson, it is quite obvious of whom he scathingly writes.[5] Rich was very much a scion of the 'old school', and a colonel to boot. In addition, as an officer in the Regular Army, taking orders from a younger man of inferior rank in the Territorials must have galled. He was, in fact, to prove a most successful borstal governor and a more variegated one than Paterson gave him credit for. In January 1920 Rich had taken charge of Rochester, with its four hundred lads. It was some task. Post-war disillusionment and lack of opportunity had had a demoralising effect. Absconding was a problem, and the place was porous, but there was worse. Shortly before Rich arrived the officer in charge of the punishment block had been killed by one of his many

2   Watson (1939), p. 75. Paterson, by his own avowal, was a member of 'the school of high hopes', but he never ignored hard facts (Ruck, p. 83).
3   Macartney, p. 57. Clayton had lost an ear in the Great War.
4   Clayton, pp. 21f, 19ff, 66, 81, 160–166, 179ff.
5   Rich, p. 279.

charges. Ruggles-Brise urged the new governor to take a firm hand and restore staff confidence and inmate compliance.

This he did by reorganising the institution 'in such a way as to bring up the standard of discipline and to create ... a better sort of "school spirit"'. This involved imposing military discipline, and an insistence on 'politeness' and deference to those in authority. 'I impressed upon them that when addressing an officer it was their duty to stand to attention, salute and call him "sir"'. He considered that 'one wholesome thing ... was the uniformed officer', the uniform constantly reminding the 'lad that he was in a penal establishment, and not merely in "a home"'.[6] He was upholding the stated aims of Ruggles-Brise of punishing, deterring and reforming, and was doing so by combining 'the strictest discipline' with 'a humane inculcation of hard work, obedience, respect, and good manners'. To the outside world Rich 'conveyed the impression ... that he was a military martinet and a perfect terror to those under him who in any way transgressed the rules'. Thus he tranquillised opposition while in reality his regime became ever more benign and the environment of the 'sinister prison' was transformed.[7]

Rich attributed his success to a combination of laying down strict routine and clear boundaries and encouraging industry and application. It was a classic case of instilling order and then relaxing restraints. He had told the lads to see him as a friend and as governor but never to forget he was both. He received many appreciative letters from his former charges, not all of whom he thought should have been there. He deprecated the tendency of the courts to bend the legislation and send ever more minor offenders to Rochester 'for their own good'. He did not think that those who pilfered apples or played football in the street should be associating with criminals or building up resentment at disproportionate punishment. Probation would be better suited for the likes of these.[8]

He was not opposed to experimentation, so long as it was controlled. Acting on his old chief's instructions, he had instituted the innovatory 'House System', whereby boys were allocated to 'Houses' to which they would develop a loyalty and in which they could be closely monitored and counselled by 'housemasters' who knew them well.[9] When the newly appointed Commissioner suggested that Rich take some of the better-behaved boys to Deal on a summer camp, he was willing to comply, sixty 'Special Grade' lads benefiting as a result. There was, however, a clash of cultures, exemplified by one young university man whom Paterson had sent along to help. He 'habitually walked about in a rather tight and

6   Rich, pp. 214–220. Feltham officers disagreed, considering uniforms a barrier to 'winning the unfortunate borstal lad from the border-line of crime' (Report [1922–1923], p. 71).
7   Grew, p. 17.
8   Report (1921), p. 51.
9   Grew, p. 22.

scanty bathing-suit ... was far too familiar with the lads' and hated them calling him 'sir'. Rich commented acerbically that 'the gentleman in question was later appointed as a housemaster', his views coinciding with those of 'the high official who was by this time more or less running the prison service.' That 'high official' was not yet running the camp, which was conducted 'on strict military lines', much to the approbation of the locals. Rich observed that 'strict discipline does not of necessity imply the absence of an affectionate relationship.'[10] Ruggles-Brise would have agreed.

But Ruggles-Brise had gone and a new era had dawned, the Paterson era, and there was no place for the likes of Colonel Rich in a borstal system that was about to be transformed. At the end of 1923 he was posted, against his will, to Liverpool prison. Despite his success at Rochester, and although he firmly believed in the borstal ideal, his stern disciplinarian reputation, his increasing conviction that his chief's retirement marked the beginning of the rot, and his concerns about Paterson's increasing dominance, put him in opposition to the prevailing *zeitgeist*. For him the revolution brought about by 'the new influence' had 'done nothing except harm'. 'Dangerous idealism' had run riot, sacrificing good order and discipline 'on the altar of ideals that can never be realised'. When he retired from the prison service he rushed into vitriolic print, an act of insubordination which could have led to prosecution.[11]

Rich's successor at Rochester, his erstwhile senior medical officer, Dr John Methven, was very much of the modern stamp, so much so that in 1930 he would become an Assistant Commissioner (as inspectors were renamed that year) and a full Commissioner in 1938. Meanwhile he was to initiate and establish the new training principles that Paterson advocated. Methven recruited by direct entry like-minded individuals to the key post of housemaster, in which they were to provide inspiring leadership and set an example of gentlemanly conduct. They were young men with little or no prior prison experience, poorly paid, overworked and utterly committed, two of whom, Gilbert Hair and Frank Ransley, were destined to become governors of Wormwood Scrubs and Wandsworth respectively.[12]

---

10   Report (1922–1923), pp. 30f; Rich, pp. 82–86, 91, 100f, 111f, 122.

11   Rich, pp. 96f, 128f, 277. Ex-borstal boy Jack Gordon took this 'military man' to task in *Borstalians*, published in 1932, the same year as Rich's *Recollections* came out. Rich was not without allies. He got support from Lieutenant-Colonel H.M.A. Hales, a widely respected former governor of Parkhurst, who in a letter to *The Times* (6th August 1932) denounced 'the protagonists of so-called prison reform' for destroying the deterrent power of imprisonment.

12   Grew, p. 21. Housemasters began as Grade II Assistant Governors. For some prison officers it was with the introduction of amateurs from outside the service, enthusiasts for the relaxation of all restraints, that the rot set in. And the rot would spread as they were promoted to full governor grade, and brought their borstal ideas into the prison system (Cronin, pp. 72f).

The disaffected governors' distrust of Paterson was mirrored by his distrust of them. The longer they had served under the *ancien regime* the more likely they were to be always 'looking back, comparing present with past, and generally inclining to the instinctive opinion that things were at their best when [they] were in [their] prime.'[13] Alec was ever on the look-out for a new breed whom he could inspire and upon whom he could rely. The quality of staff was crucial to Paterson's contention that even if 'we do not have the best prison system ... we have the best prison service in the world.' Service was what mattered, not system. He made great demands on those who served under him, not through inconsideration but because 'such was his fanaticism about the job in hand, to the exclusion of nearly everything else, that he expected others to share his devotion.' He did not want to attract 'young men who are concerned about their pay, or their careers, or their prospects of marriage', but only those who were 'so keen about this job that nothing else matters'. He was after disciples and evangelists, and he found them in profusion. Those still at school or university when they first encountered him spoke of the experience 'with the awe appropriate to a religious conversion'. While for some the demands and the sacrifices proved too great, stalwarts remained and in time many of the borstal housemasters would become the finest prison governors.[14]

Major Benjamin Grew was an early but not uncritical protégé. He described a chance meeting with Alec at the Oxford and Cambridge Club in 1922:

> The man I shook hands with was of medium build. He had a kindly face and a most disarming smile. His hair was receding, giving great depth to his already high forehead. His shrewd and penetrating eyes were the eyes of a man of compassion, a man to whom one could appeal and not in vain ... I found him as good a listener as he was a talker.

Paterson told him a great deal about life in the slums, and of how he had visited friends in prison and been appalled at what he had witnessed there. He blamed the conditions on the complacency of officialdom and that 'complacency was as bad as neglect and a great deal harder to shift'. Most of all Grew could tell 'he was concerned about boys ... who had got into serious trouble and had no one to help them, boys whose weaknesses led to crime, and crime to despair, misery and ruin.' Yet, Paterson insisted, all bad boys had an element of goodness in them, 'if we could but find it and if we searched hard enough.' They could be redeemed and turned into useful citizens 'if men strong enough in character and patient enough in their ways would be their "schoolmasters" and help them

---

13   Alexander Paterson, *A Report of Visits to some Belgian and Dutch Prisons and Reformatories in the Autumn of 1924* (Maidstone Prison, 1924), p. 18.

14   Watson (1969), p. 70; Rupert Cross, *Punishment, Prison and the Public* (London, 1971), pp. 32f.

along the way.' Such a vision was springing up under the borstal system 'which, as he put it, "sought to teach wayward lads to be self-contained men".'

Inspired by this serendipitous encounter, but unaware that his 'engaging companion' was a Prison Commissioner, the following year Grew applied to join the prison service. Paterson was one of his interviewers and, after interrogating the applicant about his military career – he was an East-End lad who had risen from the ranks – his attitude to his men, and his service on the Western Front, recommended his recruitment. He was appointed deputy-governor of Rochester, where he remained after Rich's removal. Thus Grew embarked on what he believed was pioneering work in 'a great penal adventure', taking to heart 'the precept that we were no longer trying to make the punishment fit the crime but attempting to make the offender fit into society.' To 'the liberalism and far-sightedness of Paterson' he attributed the welcome replacement of 'the surviving characteristics of discipline by repression' with the discipline of 'wise, kind but firm leadership'.[15]

Despite the well-publicised fact that six boys had absconded from the Feltham camp the previous year, in 1924 Grew, recognising that such ventures were a risk worth taking and a test of trust worth setting, led a summer camp on the Isle of Sheppey where boys nearing release lived alongside staff in disused army huts. At Alec's instigation, the first Labour Home Secretary, Arthur Henderson, visited the camp and had his picture taken sitting on the grass with the lads. So successful had this expedition been that the following year Grew got approval from the Commissioners to go one step further and, without discipline officers, take a group of trainees on a week's walking tour during which they would be allowed to associate with boys of their own age from the nearby towns and villages. By bringing his charges into direct contact with the outside world he wanted to dispel myths that had accrued about borstals, and better inform the public of the aims and methods of these institutions. It was an unalloyed success, and the Commissioners congratulated him warmly.[16]

They also promoted him. In 1925 he was made deputy-governor of Dartmoor, and three years later governor of Shrewsbury. Being a small local prison predominantly holding short-sentence men, the discharge rate was high and the need for after-care paramount. Grew organised a concert to raise money for the Salop-Montgomeryshire Discharged Prisoners' Aid Society. Supportive as ever of such initiatives, Alec travelled from London for the occasion, and during the interval gave 'a most effective talk' urging his audience to repay their interest in crime 'by reinvesting in the criminal'. His appeal had its effect. Money poured in.[17]

15   Grew, pp. 13ff, 17, 24, 38.
16   Grew, pp. 24, 35–38. He and many other writers following him state that this was in 1923, but as Henderson was in office only in 1924 it must have been that year.
17   Alexander Paterson, 'The American Court', *The Spectator*, 12th September 1947, pp. 9f; Grew, pp. 76f.

In 1930, in an attempt to apply some of the techniques successfully deployed on young offenders in borstal to adults in custody, Grew was sent to Maidstone, a convict prison that was being re-forged into a 'training prison' for 'star-class' prisoners (first offenders), including many of the best-behaved: reprieved killers, sex offenders and homosexuals.[18] Grew proved just the man for the job. The pace of reform would quicken and the prison get a make-over. Grew had to improvise. He transformed the environment at virtually no cost to the public purse by using prisoners to clear derelict ground and turn it into an Italian garden, putting on evening classes and lectures, and holding sports days, musical appreciation groups and even a motor-show with a Rolls Royce being exhibited. *The Daily Mirror* lampooned this particular enterprise and, although he had official backing for his endeavours, it was not repeated.

Significantly his bold initiatives were supported, and not disowned, by Commissioners who applauded innovation and had the confidence to stand up to the press. One controversial initiative was of their own devising. They came up with 'a bold and somewhat daring plan which aroused the protests of many cynics who mistook any attempt at reform as "pampering". This was their decision to send a small party of long-term prisoners from Maidstone to Rochester for a month each year to work in the open on government land and buildings. It would let them do a worthwhile job in a healthy environment, and demonstrate they could be trusted. This venture was attacked as 'a holiday for murderers', whose escape could endanger law-abiding citizens. 'Fortunately', Grew observed, 'the authorities were neither afraid of their critics nor of their own reforming zeal and the scheme went ahead', without anything untoward transpiring.[19]

The Commissioners refused to panic. Once, when Major Wallace Blake, the governor of Pentonville, telephoned Paterson to report an escape, the cool response was 'Dear, dear, what a pity!'[20] On another occasion Alec, pragmatically, covered up a mistake at Manchester prison when the wrong man was subjected to invasive medical intervention. An anxious governor and medical officer informed Alec of the mix-up and asked him what they should do. Having consulted the unfortunate's record and discovered that he had never been in prison before, Alec told them to do nothing, assuming that 'the luckless victim ... would think that all prisoners on reception were treated in this savage fashion', and not sue. There was no repercussion.[21]

The prison service is usually risk averse, but in Paterson's time prison staff knew that they would be supported if they went out on a limb to secure some great good. When in doubt governors would 'ring up A.P.' to ask his advice or seek his

---

18   *Ibid.*, pp. 47f, 83ff.
19   Grew, pp. 88–95.
20   Clayton, p. 61. Blake fails to mention this incident in his autobiography.
21   *Over the Walls*, p. 26.

approval. He encouraged them to do so. He adopted the novel proposition that prisons and borstals should be judged not by their failures but by their successes. 'The prison record that shows no escapes and no assaults is too often counted a record of success', Alec wrote, but 'it is the record of many receptions and few returns that is the triumph of a good prison administration.'[22] It was a giddy time.

With a premium put on experimentation and initiative, the service increasingly proved attractive to high-calibre candidates. And sometimes the wrong calibre: those who thought they could pull strings or pull rank to wheedle their way in. They could not, however, pull the wool over Alec's eyes. To make plain that only quality of character counted, not connections, he appended to the application form an unequivocal warning:

> Attempts to influence the Prison Commissioners' selection through Members of Parliament or other persons, unless they are in a position from personal knowledge to testify to character or qualifications, will be regarded as indicating that the applicant himself does not consider his character or qualifications as sufficiently good to justify his appointment on his own merits, and may prejudice his chances of success.[23]

Nor would he take otherwise suitable candidates before they were ready. When a young man straight from university applied for a job, Alec told him that as he had less experience of the world than some of the lads with whom he would have to deal, he should go away for two years and gain experience. 'Ship as a sailor before the mast – see life', was his advice. The young man took him at his word, signed on a merchant ship bound for Japan, and told his father that he would be away for eighteen months. Confronted by the irate parent demanding to know what he had told his son, Alec displayed great skill and charm in converting him to the view that it was a good thing after all. Eighteen months later, on his return from the sea 'with his extra stock of experience', the young man was appointed a housemaster in North Sea Camp.[24]

One who needed neither connections nor further grounding was also one of his most endearing 'catches'. When Cyril 'Jack' Joyce met Paterson in 1922 he was immediately captivated by this man 'of infinite vision and extraordinary ability'. His 'unquenchable faith in the fact that if you trust people they do not, in the main, let you down' was what impressed Joyce most. Inspired by 'the great man', he joined the prison service as the first assistant housemaster Paterson had appointed. At that time no one was very sure of the role of such an appointee. Alec tried to explain: 'You may wonder what your place in the hierarchy of this

22 Ruck, p. 29.

23 William Healy and Benedict Alper, *Criminal Youth and the Borstal System* (New York, 1941), p. 99.

24 Scott, p. 78.

Service is? Well, the subordinate officers give salutes, and the superior ones receive them, but you will do neither.'[25]

Joyce's first postings were to Portland borstal, and Wakefield, Durham and Wormwood Scrubs prisons, in the last of which he was in charge of the boys' prison. In 1931 he was chosen to create a new borstal out of Camp Hill, the former preventive detention prison on the Isle of Wight.[26] There he would remain until 1938, when he was made first governor of the open borstal at Hollesley Bay. Alec had chosen well for what would be the ultimate expression of his hopes.[27] Joyce decided to take seventeen of his older boys with him to act as seniors for the fresh intake. As such he wanted them to commit to six months or so while the new boys were arriving. For some this meant having to give up the chance of early release. Only 'Harry' demurred, and he later approached the Commissioner to tell him that he would like to go with Joyce after all. When Alec asked him why he had changed his mind, Harry replied: 'Well, sir, I couldn't refuse the honour.' The venture, under the direction of 'the old man', or 'the squire', as he was affectionately known, went from strength to strength. Its most celebrated 'colonist', Brendan Behan, would testify to that. Joyce wrote two autobiographical volumes, both of which give a vivid and highly personal account of life as a borstal governor, of his affection for his boys and their high regard for him.[28]

John Vidler was another enthusiastic recruit. An 'explosive extrovert', he had worked in boys' clubs during his undergraduate days, both at St Ebbe's in Oxford and at the OBM in Bermondsey, and had come under the spell of Stansfeld. After a period in Ceylon during which he married Dorothea, Macan's second daughter, he returned to England after the war. Initially he and his family lived in the Master's Lodge at Univ. and then in the matrimonial home in Boar's Hill. Alec, who had remained devoted to Macan and his family, was a frequent visitor at both addresses. This 'broad-shouldered, dynamic personality' enlivened their evenings with conversation 'that showed a depth of feeling

25   R.H. Ward, *The Hidden Boy* (London, 1962), p. 3. 'Superior Officers' were appointed by the Home Secretary and comprised governors, chaplains and medical officers. All other staff were 'subordinate officers' and were appointed by the Commissioners.

26   Preventive detention, introduced in 1908, was a sentence of extended custody that could be passed on habitual criminals.

27   Sir Samuel Hoare, the then Home Secretary, proclaimed in Parliament that any penal aspect and terminology had been expunged. There would be no walls, the boys would be called 'colonists', and the whole concern would run more on the lines of a public school. One newspaper referred to it as the 'Borstal university' (*Daily Herald*, 2nd March 1938).

28   Brendan Behan, *Borstal Boy* (London, 1958); Harry Potter, *Shades of the Prison House* (Woodbridge, 2019), ch.31; Cyril Joyce, *By Courtesy of the Criminal* (London, 1955), pp. 19–26; *Thoughts of a Lifetime* (London, 1971), pp. 25–61.

and a fund of creative ideas'.[29] Vidler proved a receptive audience, and when Paterson asked him to become a borstal governor, he jumped at the chance, believing that trying to help wayward youths back to a normal life would give meaning to his own.

In 1932 Vidler was appointed deputy-governor of Feltham, arriving there a complete novice. He rapidly acclimatised to the Patersonian ethos as exemplified in the governor, another recruit from the Territorials, Captain James Holt. Holt was a man who never gave up on the high proportion of 'dull and backward lads ... born invertebrates, instinctively taking the path of least resistance' that he was sent. Like so many, he found the 'process of vertebration a slow and painful one', and considered that two years was too short a time to train such unpromising material.[30] His methods were unconventional. On one occasion when Vidler asked to put an abusive runaway in a canvas restraint jacket, Holt refused outright and told his deputy to kit the boy out in oversize shorts and slippers so that he would have to waddle around hitching his trousers up. Immobilising him and making him look ridiculous rather than putting him in restraint was the Feltham way. Even the boy could see the funny side.[31] Vidler himself put in ninety hours a week, and testified to the equal dedication of the staff. His time there coincided with the introduction of Christmas home leave for twenty-seven selected lads. All returned punctually except one, who was handed over to the police by his parents. On only one matter did he disagree with Paterson – 'bad apples'. If one boy or man was adversely affecting others Vidler's answer was to get rid of him. He told the Commissioner that he did not 'want the really evil types polluting an atmosphere' that might benefit the

---

29 Vidler, pp. 8f.

30 Report (1934), p. 63. Richard Maxwell testified to Feltham's transformation under 'the gentleman governor'. When the boy arrived there in 1934, he was astonished by his reception and the plentiful meal that welcomed him, with real cutlery, china soup bowls, salt and pepper, and large helpings, much better fare than he would enjoy at home. During his stay Maxwell escaped, and got into more trouble, yet Holt had him back. He thought that 'if there were more like Captain H in those responsible positions then one of the country's most pressing problems would be viewed with a more humane understanding, and there would be far fewer habitual criminals.' Yet on his release Maxwell reverted to a life of crime. Looking back, he thought most boys were given a fresh start, but for a minority of which he was one it was just temporary respite from a life of crime. Borstal carried a stigma and it required determination to make good. The easier course was to relapse (*Borstal and Better* [London, 1956], pp. 109–119, 148f).

31 Vidler, pp. 13f. It had not always been thus. In the 1920s escapees were stripped of their borstal clothes, put in the penal class and, like Victorians undergoing hard labour, had to smash stones during the day and in the evening pick coir – coconut fibre – for mattresses (Gordon, p. 171).

remainder. At this Paterson interjected: 'Really evil types? Surely not. You can never tell.' Vidler thought you could and that Paterson was 'simply unrealistic'.[32] Yet he continued to be devoted to his mentor and, despite many disappointments, never lost faith in the rehabilitative endeavour. In 1964 he would dedicate his prison memoir 'to AP in grateful and affectionate memory'.

Moving to Portland in January 1934, Vidler succeeded by trial and error in putting his mark on the place. As Alec had encouraged him to make his own furrow in his own way, he encouraged his own subordinates to do likewise. Initiative and independence were traits to be cherished. There was no one way of doing things. There was no *modus operandi* imposed from above. There should be no mould into which to put a creative maverick. The individuality of the staff at all levels was as important as the individuality of the trainees. Let them get on with it.

Vidler himself employed 'training by paradox', paradoxically with considerable success. On one occasion he reversed roles, putting a recalcitrant boy in the governor's chair and letting him award punishment to the governor who was standing before him. When the positions were reversed the real accused took his punishment without a murmur. While this charade was going on Paterson walked into the office unannounced. Even he, 'the most understanding and imaginative of men', was nonplussed. Another example involved a truculent youth of Italian extraction. Every sanction having failed, Vidler, aware that he was dealing with a staunch Catholic, informed him that the only punishment he received in future must be self-imposed in the form of penance. The lad promptly gave himself fifteen days on bread and water, never caused any more trouble and went on to become a successful businessman. Another tearaway, R.J. Gowdey, testified to the success of Vidler's methods in a lengthy article published in *The Spectator*.[33] For many of the boys the 'grey fortress' had become 'the jam factory', and fun was in favour. The governor rather admired the survival instinct of one quick-witted lad who had been allowed out on a day's boating trip. When asked what HMBI on his lifebelt stood for, he replied 'Harry Mason's Boxing Institute, of course.' Surviving, standing on their own two feet, was what the training was all about. Vidler set up a discharge house in which the boys looked after themselves. This was later turned into an open camp at Bovington, albeit short-lived, as it was closed with the outbreak of war.

---

32   Vidler, p. 16; *The Magistrate*, May–June 1935, p. 1018.

33   'Borstal Methods' (3rd September 1937), pp. 8f; Vidler, pp. 45–49. Vidler never gave up on Gowdey, whose 'worst actions seemed to strengthen' the governor's faith in him. In time the boy realised he 'was not beyond redemption', and in place of gambling became addicted to Beethoven and Bach. When they had to say farewell Gowdey broke down in tears. They remained in touch for years until Gowdey emigrated.

It was at Portland that Alec first met a frequent visitor to the borstal who would become an influential ally. One Friday evening John Watson drove up from London in his recently purchased vintage motor car, an open two-seater Hillman, to dine with the governor and spend the weekend there. He arrived late and, after making his apologies to his host, was introduced to Alec Paterson, who put him at instant ease by quipping that he thought 'the Hillmen were a barbarian tribe that you travelled with'. The young volunteer fell under the older man's spell and when a vacancy occurred he applied, but failed, to become an assistant borstal housemaster. Instead he would end up as a prominent juvenile court justice. The two remained in close touch and became good friends. When Alec gave Watson a copy of *Across the Bridges*, the inscription on the flyleaf read: 'To John Watson from Alec Paterson, in memory of Portland camps and lonely men in small cells who deserve and shall receive a better chance.'[34]

---

34 Watson (1969), pp. 67–73. Alec would advise Watson on his first book, *Meet the Prisoner*, and recommended he become a magistrate.

CHAPTER 9

SOLVITUR PERAMBULANDO: 1922–1924

> Look on my works ye mighty, and despair!
>
> *Percy Bysshe Shelley*

When first appointed to the Prison Commission, Alexander Paterson had strong opinions on penology, considerable experience of the workings of the English prison system, but little knowledge of any other. What he also had was a determination to rectify this deficiency. He was insatiably curious, firmly believed in the value of comparative study, and harboured an ambition to become *the* expert on penal matters. He knew full well that if his project of transforming the prison and borstal systems, as yet in its infancy and amorphous, was to succeed against inevitable opposition he would have to travel far and wide to acquire a detailed understanding of other systems. Thus he would be able to marshal a formidable factual arsenal which he could deploy in both offensive and defensive capacities to progress and protect his great reformatory aim.

His motto was *solvitur perambulando* (by travelling problems are solved). Like Howard and Fry, he was prepared to learn from other countries and to use their methods and results to challenge or reinforce his own ideas. Like them he had to see 'with his own eyes how others have faced the same problems and tried to solve them'.[1] During his prison career, in peace and in war, he would travel extensively in Europe, in North America, and throughout the British Empire, sometimes on official business, sometimes on holiday and at his own expense. He wasted no time. In his first three years as a Commissioner he was constantly on the move.

In August 1922 Paterson visited Germany, the first time a Commissioner had done so since Ruggles-Brise in 1905. It was also the first time that Alec had visited the country he had been fighting just four years before. Taking Barkis

---

1   Ruck, p. 155.

with him to act as an interpreter, Alec would be a John Howard *redivivus*, his endeavours greatly eased by the co-operation of the German authorities. Over a period of two months, he saw a large number of prisons and reformatories from Munich in the south to Berlin in the north, and from Munster in the west to Breslau in the east. On each establishment he kept copious notes which he incorporated into his thorough if idiosyncratic report. His whimsical style was very unlike bureaucratic Mandarinese. To give but one instance, at the Burg Reformatory School near Magdeburg, 'the lads looked as shifty as some of the staff.' His report was as readable as it was informative.[2]

Unsurprisingly, in the wake of the war, he found the German penal estate in disarray. Overcrowding was omnipresent. There was no paint and little coal. Clothing was in short supply for prisoners and staff alike. Governors could not afford new suits and so wore their old army uniforms. They were also bewildered and indecisive in face of the political uncertainty and lack of stability. There was no clarity or unanimity about the purpose of imprisonment, and he doubted 'whether Germany ha[d] yet assigned a place to the prison system in her philosophy of crime'.[3]

He found no evidence of brutality, or 'that order was maintained by fear', yet was dismayed to discover that the 'silent system' was very much in operation during the initial stage of a lengthy confinement. Such a system of prison discipline had been tried out in England, only to be abandoned as inhumane and ineffective.[4] It all seemed so outmoded, a regression to early Victorian times. '"Pentonville" [was] the only English word familiar to all prison staff, and "*panoptische*" was in common use.' Under the German system inmates over eighteen would 'ordinarily spend three years in isolation more complete than any known in the whole history of English prisons'. Even in chapel, as had been the case in Pentonville when it was 'the Model Prison', they would be strictly separated in cubicles.

Thereafter they were not only put to work together but had to share cells or dormitories. Strict immuration was superseded by promiscuous association. Nor was there any attempt at classification, the separation of prisoners into different

2   He also composed a parable about Count von Catchem, a prison inspector who knew and enforced each and every regulation, however irksome, and discovered each and every fault, however trivial, in his search for 'the perfect prison'. When he found it, he finally asked the only question that mattered: 'what was really happening behind this wonderful facade of order? What was happening within the minds and hearts of the prisoners?' What he had come across was not a model prison but 'a very excellent machine, the exact purpose of which is hard to discern, and the effect of which it is by no means easy to assess' ('Prison: The Great Illusion or the *Tertium Quid*' [unpublished, 1947]).

3   *German Prisons 1922* (Maidstone prison, 1923). The next few pages are based on this report.

4   Harry Potter, *Shades of the Prison House* (Woodbridge, 2019), pp. 204–244.

groups 'according either to age or degree of turpitude' that would prevent 'that most accursed feature of prison life', contamination (the corruption of the young by the old or neophytes by recidivists), and facilitate effective training.[5]

There were a number of prisoners serving life imprisonment, which, for most, meant death in prison. Perhaps more merciful was the guillotine, which was still in use in local prisons such as Butzbach in Hesse. Oddly, the governor there was one of the few who could give a good account of penological theory and practice. He followed the principle that prison was a place of punishment and reform, and reiterated that 'no-one is hopeless'.[6] Paterson felt that 'from this basis he will continue to build, and will pursue his philosophy more fearlessly, and will in his province leave behind a prison administration more humane and more far-sighted than the one which he found in operation.'

One thing that won Paterson's approval was the use of 'kinder' prisoners to be nurses and companions of the sick. Another was the variety of prison industries, unencumbered by any restraints put upon them by trade unions fearful of competition. Being Germans, the prisoners worked hard and rarely broke the rules. Food was better prepared and tastier than in England, but the servings were smaller. There was a clear recognition that education was a necessity 'for any kind of training and reclamation'.

Alec was particularly interested in the treatment of the young. Plotzensee, a local prison three miles from Berlin, housed both men and boys. The governor believed that the primary purpose of imprisonment was to punish but in such a way as to reform. He had been to England before the war and had gone to Rochester, where he had been 'revolted by the barbarity of compulsory physical jerks', although he implemented games of football as a result of his visit. He was an advocate of individualism, and insisted that every officer knew each child in his section. Fresh flowers were in every cell and 'each lad had a small patch of garden to cultivate.' The Wabern Reformatory for boys near Cassel was a former hunting lodge of the Elector of Hesse. The director was 'kindly and intelligent and would seem to understand boys and rate them more highly than cabbages.' He stressed individual treatment and personally spoke to every boy at least once a month. There was no corporal punishment, there was a degree of self-government, but the officers wore uniforms and the boys had their heads shaved. Alec had misgivings and became convinced that 'this was not a place where boys would develop. The tradition of prison life seems still to hang over the school. The doors are everywhere locked ... as in every other prison. There seems to be a common assumption that unless every precaution is taken, the boys will do something wicked.'

5   This second rationale, a Patersonian innovation, would be incorporated into the 1933 Prison Rules (L.W. Fox, *The Modern English Prison* (London, 1934), p. 76.

6   *Over the Walls*, p. 5.

Nonetheless, given Germany's recent disastrous history and its long-standing reputation for brutality, the prison system which survived amidst economic and social turmoil could have been much worse. Paterson 'came away with the sense of hope, qualified by a measure of bewilderment.' There were many local initiatives but no coherent policy behind them.

The following year he was off to spend 'many happy and arduous days' investigating the Italian prison system.[7] While there was nothing in the buildings or equipment worth imitating, their work and wages scheme, unfettered by the objections of trade unions, was impressive, encouraging prisoners to become more skilled, and enabling the convict prisons to become largely self-sustaining. The government had succeeded in proving 'that such a system was not only possible, but so far succeeds in stimulating the industry of prisoners as to reduce materially the cost of prisons, and to train men more effectively for industrial life on discharge.' To supplement the meagre food ration or to buy luxuries such as wine or tobacco, the prisoner had to work.[8] Alec was impressed by the Castiadas penal colony in Sardinia, where men engaged in agricultural work, and by a scheme for adolescents where they were allowed to attend college in the evening to acquire the technical knowledge of the trades they were pursuing. This was something he would try out in Rochester. He was not impressed when he wandered through the convict camps that Mussolini had ordered to be set up where criminals and political opponents could be sent to drain the malarial swamps on the island. Alec found it impossible to distinguish between murderers and rapists and 'those who had gone so far as to oppose the Fascist regime'.[9] It was a taste of worse to come.

While in Rome he wrote 'Give or Get', an article that would be published the following year in the *Toc H Journal*. Inspired by the 'beastliness' of the Colosseum and the aspiration of St Peter's, he began in characteristic voice, appealing for mutual understanding between social and racial groups since 'truth is not painted black, or white or yellow', and 'progress only comes when men of very different experience understand one another, and join together in common service for the whole family of men.'

> You may divide Gaul into three parts, and the compass into four; the seas into five oceans, you may cut all the earth into five continents; but there

7   'Should the Criminologist be Encouraged?', *Transactions of the Medico-Legal Society*, 26/1 (1932), pp. 180–200, at p. 187.

8   Ruck, pp. 109–113, excerpt from *Italian Prisons*, a report I have been unable to locate.

9   'Transport the Gunman?', *The Spectator*, 22nd May 1947, pp. 11f.

are only two sorts of men – the givers and the getters. The issue that divides them is far deeper than time or space, language or colour: for the motives of service and acquisition are directly contrary to one another, and are at the root of conduct.[10]

Even on the banks of the Tiber, 'service' and altruism were never out of mind.

In 1924 Alec went on a similar mission to the Low Countries. He began his report lyrically, discoursing on the character of Belgium and its people, before turning to its penal policy. Despite the deep misgivings of 'its thinking citizens', Belgium still adhered to a punitive prison regime of hard work and prolonged solitary confinement, in serious cases ten years of solitude in 'the grim convict prison' of Louvain serving as a preliminary to a lengthy period of silent association in Ghent. Such 'repression and monotony [had] secured ... clean, industrious and peaceful' prisons but, he thought, 'souls must wither in the process'.[11] The Belgians had replaced physical violence in prisons by 'a mechanical repression which saps the blood instead of shedding it. If indeed this system of repression is a slow form of death, then we kill more cruelly than did our forebears with their bloodstained hands.' With most prisoners incarcerated in individual cells, the lot of prison warders was an easy one, but as life in association became more prevalent the strain on the officers would increase and their 'power to command bodies of men [would be] more severely tested'.

Paterson, the evangelist hoping to bring the enlightenment of his thinking to this benighted land, and as ever with an eye to his compatriots, espoused his penal creed in a series of interrogatories and comments:

> What is the object of your prison, for the object must decide the method? Once assured that your object is sound, you may fearlessly pursue any method that best promises to achieve it. But what is your object ...? Merely to deter and repress, to punish and detain? If so, bravo, you have succeeded in punishing if not in deterring, in detention if not in complete repression. Yet there is in every quarter an under-current of doubt whether this is the right policy. It repels, it does not satisfy in theory; it does not even in fact succeed. There is manifest in Belgium as elsewhere a strong desire to turn away from it to some other theory of treatment. But to what else may a country turn? Will not any other theory make prison so pleasant that it will cease to deter from crime?

10   'Give or Get', *THJ* (November 1924).
11   *A Report of Visits to some Belgian and Dutch Prisons and Reformatories in the Autumn of 1924* (Maidstone Prison, 1925), p. 24. The following pages are based on this report.

He hoped that those discontented with a negative policy of repression 'may in time discover some positive policy of training each individual delinquent to be fit for social freedom', and in the application of that policy find that the prison regime it demands is neither easy nor pleasant, but 'more exacting than one founded on purely negative principles of restraint'. It was the old refrain. Reform and deterrence, far from being irreconcilable enemies, were in fact mutually compatible. The obdurate criminal would still be deterred by the rigours of prolonged detention; the rehabilitated delinquent would need no external deterrence.

He concluded the first part of his report with a comparison between the contrasting prison systems of England and Belgium. In the former was 'association and much idleness', in the latter 'separation and industry'. There had been 'much to study and much to learn', even if more could be learnt from mistakes than successes.

Alec then expatiated on his favourite theme: the treatment of young offenders. The contending advocates of repression and reform could both appeal to the statistics of recidivism to confirm the success of their respective methods. Perhaps fearing that they did not help his cause, he marginalised them as a useful guide and stimulation to inquiry.

> The real criterion between the different systems of training the young offender in habits of honest industry will be found in a study of causes rather than results. Choosing a system that appears to work well is operating a weapon without understanding, but adopting a system in the belief that it touches first causes and is in accordance with first principles, enables statistics to be viewed as a useful servant rather than a compelling master.

This was disingenuous. When facts supported Paterson's contentions, they were a useful buttress; when they cast doubt they could be circumvented.

Naturally he made a point of visiting the provision for juveniles. Ghent boys' prison was far removed from the English borstal with which it was often compared. Silence reigned and 'all the negative gods are duly worshipped'. There was no contamination, no dirt, no disorder, no broken windows, no assaults, but there was nothing positive. Moll reformatory for boys under eighteen with its house system was more promising, yet lacked coherence. It was 'a strange place, full of old ideas, with new ones bursting through in all sorts of places.' Differences between one house and another were inevitable and desirable, but not, he thought, 'a difference of centuries'. The place that best seemed to reflect what Paterson was initiating in England was Merxplas boys' prison. Its purpose was wholly reformative, 'the element of deterrence having become negligible'. The training regime was educative, not punitive. Its deputy-director, 'a man of great enthusiasm, desperately keen to help his lads, exploring every possibility to improve his system, eager to learn, wholly devoted to his task,' was key to its success. If Merxplas mirrored a borstal, the deputy-director was a mirror-image of Alexander Paterson.[12] Half a mile away was the 'Observation House' where boys spent a few months being assessed and classified. Paterson found this 'experiment full of initiative and original ideas ... An accurate diagnosis of a lad's failing in the early teens, with means of providing the right treatment indicated by that diagnosis, are the weapons that will one day close many convict prisons, and convert liabilities into assets.'[13] This was an innovation he hoped to initiate in England.

Turning to the Dutch he noticed 'a stirring, as in other countries, a sense of wonder and inquiry.' Some questioned the efficacy of solitary confinement, which was still the norm. Some, doubting the value of outward conformity induced by isolation, were beginning to look for a more constructive alternative. Alec predicted that there would come a time when the people of Holland abandoned much of their present system and tried to 'fashion their cellular prisons into places of communal training'. They would then experience the same problems he was confronting in trying to carry out a new programme in old buildings built to 'enshrine the contrary ideas of a previous century'.

As with Belgium, Alec visited many and varied carceral institutions. In Nijmegen House of Correction, he discovered a novel way to deal with a suicidal boy who had made many attempts on his own life. Thrash him. It worked! Amersfoort Reformatory School for boys was housed in a fine building and had a staff of forty for an intake of 130. Fifteen boys were placed in each of six houses. It was an expensive proposition, costing around £250 for each boy per year. When rescuing young lives, it was foolish to question whether it was worth it, but it was legitimate to ask if the work could be as well done at less expense. Future policy, he urged, should be to spend less on buildings and more on equipment, and to employ fewer but better-paid staff. He was, however, adamant that 'the total amount required for the most expensive experiment in this field of service is not very great, and the human issues involved are beyond computation.'

One prison stood out from the rest. This was Veenhuizen, a colony for petty recidivists – mainly 'tramps' – and an association prison for men. Both were run in stark contrast to the cellular prisons. Their success was attributed by the Dutch authorities to the personality and character of the deputy-governor, and not to the system he championed. Alec conceded that may have been part of it, but thought it would be quite possible to find many other able governors to continue and spread this novel regime. 'It is to the credit of a system that

12   Alec invited him to visit a borstal.
13   *Over the Walls*, p. 5.

it should demand such gifts for its administration. A system that calls neither for character nor personality in its administration cannot efficiently deal with human lives.'

In accordance with his didactic intent, Paterson added a six-page addendum on the rival claims of solitary confinement or association to be the more effective means of reformation. He dismissed the usual contention that the former was a barbarous form of mental torture and that it drove those subjected to it mad. These fears were grossly exaggerated. He acknowledged that it was safer, easier and cheaper to isolate and immure inmates, free from contamination and subject only to the benign attentions of chaplains and teachers. So what could be said for association? Paterson asserted that 'virtue in seclusion is no achievement' since it was effervescent. 'Moral asepsis' weakened 'moral fibre', rendering 'law-breakers' less fit to re-enter society, not more. As sailors could not be fully trained on land, or pilots upon the sea, nor could criminals confined to cages. To equip them to re-enter society, they had to have the opportunity in prison of confronting the normal temptations, problems and frustrations of social interaction. There also had to be opportunities for moral and intellectual improvement through classes, lectures and debates; an environment that elevated; and, above all, there had to be staff whose character invited emulation and who encouraged their charges to 'rule themselves by their better instincts'.

By his foreign travels Alec had gained useful insights into how others were tackling the problems he faced, and a growing conviction that his 'principled approach' was the right one.

CHAPTER 10

THE 'PATERSON ERA': 1922–1939

The object of modern changes in prison treatment has been to remove or modify the features which conduced to deterioration of mind or character and to make imprisonment, so far as possible, a period of training. This aim is not inconsistent with the deterrent function of imprisonment. In addition to deterrence resulting from loss of liberty, training – if the system is efficient – is a deterrent experience. It should demand from the prisoner a higher standard of effort in work and behaviour and self-discipline than is demanded by a purely punitive system.

Report of the Departmental Committee on Persistent Offenders

To some no doubt progress has seemed inordinately slow; others have expressed fears that it was too rapid and, that in pursuit of new ideals, discipline – the necessary basis of prison treatment – has been lost sight of. Such a view is not shared by Visiting Justices, experienced prison officers and others well acquainted with the facts. Discipline continues to be maintained in HM Prisons – of a different kind from that of the past, but not less effective on that account.

Report of the Prison Commissioners, 1934

The words in both the above reports could have been written by Alexander Paterson, and perhaps were – he had given evidence before the departmental committee, and co-authored the Commissioners' reports. He at least inspired them, since they encapsulated his philosophy.

Its origins lay in the fact that Alec was part of the liberal, middle-class Christian activism, so strong in the inter-war years, that believed in close personal ties between the classes and not in class war, and wanted to reshape society but not destroy it. This was reformation, not revolution. It was an alternative and antidote to the fashionable totalitarianisms of Fascism or Communism, or even to 'systematic socialism'. Those from privileged backgrounds had a duty to get to know, understand, assist, encourage and rescue the less fortunate, and especially the young from a life of grinding poverty and crime. Thus, in his chosen arena of penal reform, he embodied a more imaginative and constructive approach to the treatment of all offenders than had hitherto been countenanced. 'No man is a criminal and nothing else' was the principle that ruled much of his thinking.[1] And he meant it. No one was beyond redemption.

Imprisonment was more of a curse than a cure. He doubted if anyone who had been incarcerated for ten years could leave prison undamaged, and the longer the term the more damage done. He believed that imprisonment should be avoided wherever possible as 'it is ... a clumsy piece of social surgery, tearing a man away from the social fabric of home and work and club ... causing distress to others, and rendering his replacement in social and industrial life a matter of grave difficulty.' Courts should not 'weigh out a dose of punishment' but diagnose and 'prescribe the right form of training or treatment for the condition.'[2] More alternatives to custody should be found, and more recourse to those alternatives made. He wanted the name 'prison' abolished, and the Prison Commission renamed the Board of Welfare, responsible for all aspects of criminal disposal, from imprisonment to non-custodial disposals.

This may have been a fancy too far, but it was not far-fetched. 'Welfare' was a word much in vogue. The ethos of the embryonic 'welfare state', inaugurated by Lloyd George, was spreading. It was Alec's friend William Temple who coined the term. The young as well as the elderly were prime concerns. The Liberal government, which had introduced juvenile courts and probation, had consolidated the earlier provisions of child welfare, notably school meals and medical attention. This whole process would culminate in the 1933 Children and Young Persons Act, which, like its 1908 counterpart, was designed to protect them from abuse, exploitation or harm. In it the duty of courts to have regard to the welfare of the child would be enshrined in law. Concern that neglected or deprived children were more likely to offend took effect in a provision blurring the distinction between industrial schools and reformatories by terming them all 'approved schools'. Paterson would welcome all this legislation, but wanted much more. For him the welfare of young offenders and older prisoners should no more be neglected than that of pensioners. In 1922, a proposed Royal Commission on Prison and Borstals had been abandoned for lack of public interest. Paterson would not only tirelessly devote himself to making the public interested, but would engage their support and utilise their talents. In his breadth of vision and ability to convey it to others, he was to be 'the "Beveridge" of the penal system.'[3]

---

1   Vidler, p. 9. The dictum originated from William Temple. Paterson quotes it in his report *On the Treatment of the Offender in the Maltese Islands* (1944), p.ii.
2   Evidence before the Persistent Offenders Committee, 3.669.
3   Bailey (1987), pp. 2ff.

He was undoubtedly very idealistic, perhaps over-optimistic, but certainly not ignorant or ill-informed. During his tenure he educated himself about the problems of the prison system and visited a wide variety of penal institutions in England and abroad. In-depth knowledge as much as inexhaustible compassion would inform his actions. He brought to the Commission his great understanding of human nature, gained in the slums of South London and in the trenches. He was able to see through the Uriah Heeps of this world, whose outward conformity, submissiveness and overt penitence were designed to please, and deceive, the authorities. But he knew that Uriah Heeps were made by the prisons in which they lodged, where all self-reliance and initiative was lost, to be replaced with a cloying sycophancy cloaking 'dishonesty with the paint and plaster of a well-behaved inmate of an institution'.[4]

Hypocrisy created by, and displayed within, the institution was bad enough; enduring resentment engendered by its dehumanising ethos was even worse. 'The Christian conception of the value of the individual soul' had to be introduced into the fabric of prisons. This moral imperative was closely allied to a civic duty. It was the duty of the prison administration to protect the public. To release prisoners, unchanged or changed for the worse, back into society meant that there was but a temporary respite for the period of incarceration. Long-term safety required a change for the better. Caging wild beasts, starving and goading them, reducing them to outward submissiveness while impotent and at your mercy, and then setting them free, was fraught with danger. Keeping them under humane restraint, while taming and training and encouraging them, was the only way to ensure safety on release. Discharged prisoners should be made fit for freedom and not made into the implacable enemies of society. Pragmatism was the consort of morality. Doing unto others as you would have others do unto you was not only right, but sensible.

His stance, repeated in every annual report, was summed up in the classic maxim: 'men are sent to prison as a punishment not *for* punishment.' Deterrence and retribution were already achieved by the disgrace of appearing in court, the loss of liberty, and the restrictions thereby imposed on choice. The prisoner could not leave the prison at will, and while he might have books and cigarettes, he could never have prostitutes or alcohol. That was the punishment. How individuals were otherwise treated within prison had nothing to do with punishment but all to do with rehabilitation. The real purpose of prison was 'to protect society' by making law-breakers 'fit once again for social freedom'. The function of the regime under which they were detained was to educate, train

4   Paterson, p. 62.

and reform. It was Paterson's great achievement that this maxim became the norm, 'our guiding principle' as Grew put it.[5]

Although he was an outsider, and although he would never be chairman of the Prison Commission, Paterson would be the dominant figure within it, and his influence all-pervasive. While chairmen came and went, it remained constant.[6] It was first evident in the 1923 report, which Margery Fry lauded as 'a *Howard Journal* in itself'.[7] His tenure was lengthy, his connections excellent, and his personality galvanising and disarming. Harold Scott, his third chairman, referred to Paterson as having a reputation for being 'difficult', but he never found him so nor had they ever had a serious disagreement, since Alec was 'always open to argument and could quickly recognise another man's point of view'.[8] He was stimulating company with 'a quick grasp of what was possible' and 'never let the best be the enemy of the good'.[9]

Above all he was the great motivator. He would motivate his staff and they in turn would motivate their charges. Or so he hoped and believed. 'The choice of a staff suited to the needs of the establishment' was for Paterson 'the foremost task of a prison administration'. While he demanded loyalty to his ideals from them, he was utterly loyal to them. On one occasion he asked John Watson, by then the secretary of the newly established National Association of Prison Visitors, to write in defence of prison officers who had been libelled 'in a rather scurrilous book by some ex-convict'. This was Wilfred Macartney's *Walls Have Mouths*, which, although vitiated by its many errors of fact and the author's deplorable blindness to the true nature of Soviet prisons, was widely and appreciatively read when it was published in 1936 and caused a great deal of controversy.[10] As members of the civil service were debarred from defending

5   Ruck, pp. 13, 23ff, 79. Thomas Mott Osborne, whom Paterson may have met when he was touring England in 1922 and certainly much admired, had expressed similar views in *Society and Prisons* (New Haven, 1916), p. 74; Grew, p. 97.

6   He served under five chairmen: Maurice Waller (1922–1928); Alexander Maxwell (1928–1932); Harold Scott (1932–1939); C.D. Carew Robinson (1939–1942); and Lionel Fox (1942–1960).

7   Enid Jones, *Margery Fry* (Oxford, 1966), p. 121. Similarly, Cicely Craven, secretary of the Howard League, called the yearly publication 'an excellent textbook of penal reform' ('The Prison Commissioners' Reports, 1930 and 1931', *HJ*, 3/4 [July 1933], pp. 59–64, at p. 59).

8   Scott, p. 78.

9   Bailey (1987), p. 195.

10   H.W. Wicks, *The Prisoner Speaks* (London, 1938), pp. 99–112. Macartney, a drunkard and liar, was a communist traitor who was sentenced to ten years for espionage. Wicks, based on his experience of Wormwood Scrubs, while agreeing with some of Macartney's observations, particularly over 'the mental and moral stagnation appertaining to life in a prison', disagreed with many others. Even 'sea-pie', if served

themselves in public, Alec thought an objective assessment by volunteers, who worked beside them day by day, would carry weight. Watson not only wrote to *The Times* but published a book in which he defended the staff against aspersions made by former prisoners and 'certain well-known writers'.[11]

Yet some staff posed problems, particularly in prisons. Many of the old guard remained in place, and a more punitive culture prevailed. Thus his idealised view of what prison officers could be was often belied by the actions and words of those in day-to-day charge. When Giles Playfair, at Paterson's suggestion, visited Wormwood Scrubs in 1934, he was required to keep his hat on because if he took it off 'prisoners would interpret the act as a sign of respect to which they were not entitled'.[12] Not all staff were or remained true believers. It was the old clash between idealism and experience. As one veteran officer put it, 'it is the shameless and incorrigible ... beastliness of the average jailbird that gives the prison officer, who has opportunities to see this type in the raw, a very different view of the potentialities of prison reform to that held by those who believe all such jailbirds need is "understanding"'.[13] The writer was another erstwhile acolyte, Harley Cronin.

Discharged from the army in 1926, Cronin was living with his mother, the matron of Feltham borstal, when he met Paterson, a 'big, bluff man, whose charm, wit and affability reflected a career in which he had mixed with "all sorts and conditions of men"'. The Commissioner encouraged and inspired him to become a prison officer. After a short spell as a temporary officer at Feltham, Cronin was sent for training to Wormwood Scrubs which, having been set aside to hold mostly first offenders, was then 'more or less a laboratory for Paterson's reforms'. His first posting would be to a very different institution: Horfield gaol in Bristol, where 'the governing principle was still retribution'. There he heard 'one of the older officers mutter to a companion, "Ha! another of Paterson's Light Horse!"' Despite the initial hostility towards him as one of 'the disciples', and his revulsion at the practice of 'slopping-out', which survived all efforts at reform, Cronin would remain in the service until 1963, for the last twenty-five years of which he would be general secretary of the Prison Officers' Association, a quasi-trade union which he helped found in 1938. While always having a high regard for his mentor, who, although an 'outsider', was 'a different and superior kettle of fish', Cronin wanted 'to call a halt to appeasement'. First offenders in

---

with mustard, 'could be quite appetising'. Similarly, James Leigh repeatedly exonerated the Prison Commissioners and the governors for the deficiencies or failings of the reforms (*My Prison House* [London, 1941], pp. 30, 54, 99, 114f).

11   *The Times*, 18th September 1936; Watson (1939), pp. 75f.

12   Giles Playfair, *The Punitive Obsession* (London, 1971), p. 185.

13   Cronin, p. 55. His views were shared by other uniformed staff, as articles in the *Prison Officers' Magazine* showed (XXVII/11 [November 1939], pp. 341f, 348ff).

Wormwood Scrubs deserved a chance and had the potential to be rehabilitated. So too adolescents. He approved of one of Paterson's 'most noteworthy' measures: the appointment of 'Leaders' and 'Red Bands'. The former wore armbands of gold and silver, had limited supervisory duties, and acted as spokesmen; the latter had no such duties but were allowed to move around the prison and work on their own. The trust was rarely abused. Then there were the 'habituals', so immersed in crime as to be beyond trust – or hope. He was particularly nauseated by the 'appeasement' that went on in Parkhurst (where he was stationed during the war). The most sought-after jobs were given not to the most trustworthy but to the worst troublemakers. As his career had progressed, his worries had grown with his gripes. He had concerns that Paterson 'was inclined at times to give too little thought to the impact of his reforms on those who had the closest and most continuous contact with men under sentence'. He had reservations about some of his radical ideas, and became ever more cynical about the 'treatment' model, which had gone too far in encompassing 'savage and persistent thugs'. Paterson seemed unwilling, or unable, to distinguish between 'incorrigibles' and 'redeemables', 'old lags' and 'one-off' offenders.[14]

Not all officers shared these reservations. Many welcomed the new approach and their new role. In 1936 Henry Wicks referred to 'the general kindness of the officers at Wormwood Scrubs' who bore 'little, if any relation, to the old idea of brutal warders'.[15] Some of the most successful housemasters were recruited from the disciplinary staff, and some of those went on to become governors, the first being John Taft, who was put in charge of Feltham in 1925. When asked what was the greatest change he had seen, one old convict officer replied, 'We don't turn 'em out so bloody-minded as we used.' Another veteran of 'one of the best jobs a man can have' told researchers that most of his 'young colts' had 'never had a kind word' and 'you have to alternate between giving them their head and then pulling in easy'. However 'hard-boiled' they appeared, each one had 'a spot through which he can be reached'.[16] Even in the borstal system with its array of housemasters and matrons there was a rehabilitative role for disciplinary officers and civilian instructors. All the more so in the prison system, which lacked them.

---

14   *Ibid.*, pp. 13–17, 45–110, 136.
15   Wicks, *op.cit.*, p. 18. He also devoted an appreciative chapter to prison staff of all grades (pp. 144–156). Wicks, a conspiracy theorist, was imprisoned for a year for criminal libel. In 1946, for assisting the Nazis, he was sentenced to four years' penal servitude. Odd, since he had made friends with many Jews during an earlier sentence (pp. 196–206).
16   *The Times*, 1st July 1925; Watson (1939), p. 96; William Healy and Benedict Alper, *Criminal Youth and the Borstal System* (New York, 1941), p. 101.

Backed by his fellow Commissioners, and in particular by a succession of forceful and reform-minded chairmen starting with the remarkable Waller, Paterson was the driving force behind the major changes of the 1920s and 30s when England became the epicentre of prison reform. His approach and that of his colleagues was revolutionary. It implied 'not an aggregate of certain individual innovations, however significant and vital, effected in the domain of the prison system, but rather the basic and radical reconstruction of that system', even its ultimate dissolution.[17] Prisons over time would become like borstals. The great aim was to restore humanity to those from whom it had been taken, and to instil humanity into a system hitherto largely devoid of it. This was simple to say but hard to put into execution. It was alien to existing staff, and the antiquated prison estate was not designed for it.

But no one and nothing would stand in Paterson's way or frustrate his ambition to convert criminals into good citizens. They were always individuals and never just prisoners. The prison estate could be reordered; the staff regenerated or replaced. If, in the lyrical sentiments of a future Commissioner, Du Cane had built a system in 'the powerful and perdurable Norman' style, and Ruggles-Brise in his 'Transitional style' had modified the structural features while retaining the ambience of the old, Paterson had opted for 'Early English ... releasing the true spirit of the structure in a "first fine, careless rapture" of seminal ideas'.[18] Du Cane's anchored-to-earth Durham Cathedral was being replaced with soaring-spired Salisbury. That was the grandiloquence shading the harsher reality that prisoners were still housed not in Gothic cathedrals but in decaying Gothic-style Victorian citadels, under the control of staff not all of whom were enraptured by this brave new world of penal practice. Paterson aimed at the complete demolition of the antique structure, both figuratively and physically, yet economic reality, and the persistence of the principle of 'less eligibility' whereby no prisoner should be better off than any law-abiding citizen, put severe restraints on how much could be spent and how much done.[19] One of the Commissioners' greatest achievements throughout the inter-war period was how much they accomplished with so few resources, and how imaginative they were in utilising and adapting the resources they had.

Even simple changes that cost little or nothing could have beneficial effects, bidding good riddance to one era and heralding a new. Waller, who had already rung in some changes, rang in more with Paterson by his side. Separate confinement and the rule of strict silence began to disappear. Instead, 'recreation in

---

17   Leon Radzinowicz, 'The Evolution of the Modern Prison System', *Modern Law Review* (October 1939), pp. 121–135.

18   *EPBS*, p. 66; Alyson Brown, *Inter-War Penal Policy and Crime in England* (Basingstoke, 2013), p. 40.

19   Hermann Mannheim, *The Dilemma of Penal Reform* (London, 1939), pp. 56–59.

association' and 'conversational exercise' were permitted, leading to a healthier atmosphere and markedly better behaviour.[20] Banished was the broad arrow. Provision was made for such basic necessities as shaving. Better cell furniture was provided. The raised daises in chapels for invigilating officers were removed in 1922, and compulsory chapel attendance was suspended in most prisons in 1924. The previous year a seven-hour working day was implemented, and in October 1929, at the urging of Margery Fry of the Howard League, an earnings scheme – the payment of pocket-money wages – was introduced into Wakefield. In correspondence with the League, Paterson had agreed that if outside sources funded the experiment for a year it would be trialled. The Howard League raised £250 and the trial began. As a result, output increased markedly, and the scheme was expanded until it covered all prisons and borstals.[21]

Early in his tenure Alec became chairman of the Prisoners' Education Committee, the purpose of which was to administer and co-ordinate adult education within prisons. Previously it had been restricted to little more than basic literacy. The impetus was for much more, and necessity was the mother of invention. Convicts were encouraged to attend educational classes, some of which were taken by well-educated prisoners such as the disgraced MP Horatio Bottomley until the Home Secretary, Joynson-Hicks ('Jix'), put a stop to it.[22] The reading of books beyond the Bible and religious tracts was actively encouraged. Rudyard Kipling, who had been given a tour of Dartmoor in December 1929, donated a large number of books written by famous authors, including himself.[23] Wireless broadcasts were allowed, as were films, amateur dramatics, concerts, lectures and debates, although the last three had been a feature for a number of years. With no adequate funding for full-time qualified teachers, the Prison Commissioners harnessed the enthusiasm of volunteers for the task. They would, in addition, bring with them into the stale atmosphere of prison life a breath of fresh air. High culture as much as remedial learning should be on offer.

20 Rupert Cross, *Punishment, Prison and the Public* (London, 1971), p. 31; Lionel Fox, *The Modern English Prison* (London, 1934), pp. 41f; Grew, pp. 103, 126; Merrow-Smith, p. 23.

21 The Commissioners' report of 1934 summarised these and other improvements that had been made over the previous twenty-five years (pp. 5–16).

22 Joynson-Hicks's successor, John Clynes, was persuaded to reinstate the practice after hearing of illiterate gypsies taught to read and write by other prisoners at Wakefield before the ban, and the current lack of volunteer teachers at Maidstone (HO45/24800).

23 Clayton, p. 139; Thomas Pinney (ed.), *Letters of Rudyard Kipling, Volume 5, 1920–1930* (Iowa, 2004), p. 518.

From late 1922 Wormwood Scrubs, at that time a local prison for adult men, was to be the scene of an educational experiment run by Charles Douie, another war veteran. Having visited Alec at the Home Office, he was invited to promote 'a scheme of liberal adult education in the widest sense'. With his connections in the London theatrical world, Douie decided to introduce the prisoners to Shakespeare. It was reasonable to suppose, he said, that the audience in the Globe theatre in Shakespeare's day would not have been very different from the ill-assorted inhabitants of a modern prison. Copies of the plays were requisitioned from the supply the army acquired during the war. The Scrubs allowed volunteers to put on play readings with prisoners as the cast. The director observed that in a performance of *As You Like It* 'a youth with the most acute cockney accent had acquired the part of Orlando, an Indian of ferocious appearance the part of Rosalind, and a guttural gentleman who had lived on the wrong side of the barbed wire during the war was now Jacques.'[24] Thereafter eminent performers were welcomed into the prison on Sunday evenings to read plays before a captive audience.

One person of some literary eminence was a prisoner at the time, and yet makes no mention of these endeavours. This was Lord Alfred Douglas, the 'Bosie' of Oscar Wilde notoriety. In 1923 Bosie had been imprisoned for six months, having been convicted of criminal libel. On absolutely no evidence he had implicated Churchill in a Jewish conspiracy that involved the murder of Kitchener and treasonable communications with Germany during the battle of Jutland. Incarcerated for the first time, like others Douglas found that the worst part of the experience was the food. Unlike others he was 'pampered', being asked by Father Musgrave, the Catholic chaplain, to play the harmonium during Mass, and being allowed to spend most of his time in the hospital wing. One odd thing about his imprisonment stands out since it seems at variance with the reforms already afoot. He had been allowed writing materials and set about, 'with the assistance of Saints Anthony of Padua and Thomas Aquinas', composing a series of seventeen sonnets which he called *In Excelsis*. Before his discharge the Commissioners, presumably on the instructions of the Home Secretary, confiscated his notebook. This was all the stranger, given that twenty-five years earlier, when Ruggles-Brise had been in charge, Wilde had been allowed to take the manuscript of *De Profundis* with him when he left Reading gaol.[25]

Music was not neglected either in Wormwood Scrubs or elsewhere. Prison orchestras and bands were created for the gratification of their members and the edification and entertainment of their fellows. Their efforts were supplemented by illustrious outsiders. In February 1922 the band of the 1st Life Guards

---

24 Watson (1939), pp. 128–145.
25 Montgomery Hyde, *Lord Alfred Douglas* (London, 1984), p. 266. Bosie, however, had memorised the sonnets and had them published.

performed in Pentonville and 'a little later Stainer's Crucifixion was sung there by a well-known choir'. Despite stiff opposition from the staff, Clayton later introduced concerts into Parkhurst. In the 1940s a Huddersfield choir sang Handel's *Messiah* in Wakefield prison.[26] Wormwood Scrubs could even boast its own matinee idol. As a result of a four-week sentence imposed on him in 1944 for fuel rationing offences, Ivor Novello, the actor, playwright, and composer of 'Keep the Home Fires Burning', ended up there. The chaplain took this effete celebrity under his wing, and put him in charge of the choir, a 'cushy number' indeed. In gratitude Novello donated a piano to the chapel (where it is still in use) and arranged occasional concerts by performers from West End shows to bring some light relief from the drab tedium of prison life which he had found so irksome.[27]

Nor was the body ignored. Gymnasia were constructed in male prisons, and all prisoners were encouraged to improve their physiques and to participate in sport. They were also latterly encouraged to smoke. Until 1922 so strict was the prohibition on tobacco that a prisoner would have to get himself sentenced to death to satisfy his craving. Thereafter those serving sentences of four years or more were granted the privilege of smoking, and finally, in 1936, it was extended to all, and permitted even in cells.

The effect of these minor reforms was marked, as literate prisoners (Macartney and James Phelan for instance) and some prison officers acknowledged.[28] Merrow-Smith, a Parkhurst officer and another enthusiast for Paterson's initiatives, observed that 'where we had seen men sullen, resentful of discipline, indifferent to their personal appearance, we now saw them coming on parade like soldiers – hair neatly brushed, ties adjusted in well-tied knots, and boots polished.' Henry Triston, at Dartmoor, considered that the reforms had not gone nearly far or fast enough. Much more needed to be done. Above all Dartmoor should be closed.[29]

---

26   Clayton, p. 62; Macartney, pp. 354ff; Merrow-Smith, p. 119.

27   Paul Webb, *Ivor Novello: Portrait of a Star*, revised edn (London, 2005), pp. 166–169.

28   Phelan was an IRA murderer who served thirteen years in English prisons between 1924 and 1937. After his release he wrote *Jail Journey*, a measured and fair account of his time inside. He railed at some of the restrictions and regulations, but praised staff of all ranks. The governors and deputy-governors he encountered did him 'a myriad of small kindnesses': Clayton at Maidstone and later at Parkhurst; Morgan and Grew at Dartmoor; Hales and Pannall and Henry Scott at Parkhurst. Kember and Battiscombe, the chaplains of Dartmoor and Parkhurst respectively, a few doctors and many 'screws' won his respect. It was the calibre of the staff that were being attracted into prison work that made all the difference.

29   Report (1921), p. 21; (1922), pp. 13f; Merrow-Smith, p. 25; H.U. Triston, *Men in Cages* (London, 1938), pp. 233–254.

The Commissioners sympathised, but there were severe constraints on how much they could achieve, not least the existing infrastructure that militated against their best efforts. Although they could not rid themselves of Victorian prisons, they could use them for distinct and different purposes, replacing classification *within* prisons with classification *by* prisons. Although his plans for a complete reorganisation of the prison estate would never come to fruition, Paterson set to work on what he could do, albeit piecemeal.

Wakefield, one of the most unprepossessing Victorian gaols, was to be the great 'experimental' prison where his 'new deal' began. From 1923, under the leadership of his protégé, N.R. Hilton, a successful training regime was established for long-term 'star-class' prisoners from the North and the Midlands. The men were addressed by their name, not number. They were allocated to 'crews'. They lived in blocks renamed 'Houses'. There were flowers in their 'rooms', framed pictures on the corridor walls, and garden allotments where they grew vegetables. Good industrial work was available, honour parties worked without supervision, association was allowed at meal-times and in the evening, and educational classes were provided. At night 'it seemed rather like a busy evening school'. It was the prime example of the 'borstalization' of prisons, the 'triumph of man over unsuitable buildings', as one early enthusiast put it.[30] Other inexpensive attempts at classification were tried out elsewhere. Thus in 1925 Wormwood Scrubs was set aside for first-timers from the London area, and in 1931 Chelmsford was opened as a training centre for men between the ages of twenty-one and thirty who had previous convictions and were serving sentences of a year or more or a first term of penal servitude. It had a rocky start with inadequate staffing, a governor who banned concerts and curtailed evening classes, and prisoners expecting a reformative regime and not getting it. Discontent culminated in a 'mutiny' during which an unpopular officer was badly beaten. Over time matters improved to such an extent that by 1936 Colonel Turner, one of the Assistant Commissioners, could declare that the scheme 'was unique in the world in bringing together a lot of combustible material, inveterate young criminals, in order to pull them up before they start on a career which will probably end up with a life sentence at Dartmoor'.[31]

In May 1936 a 'prison without walls' was established, as an adjunct to Wakefield, at New Hall in Yorkshire. The acorn had been planted by Paterson when he told a governors' conference about 'minimum-security camps for non-criminal

30   Fletcher Allen, 'The Wakefield Scheme', *The Humanist* (February–March 1925), pp. 3–8.
31   Benney, pp. 320–324; Scott, p. 87; *The Magistrate,* July–August 1936, p. 1044.

first offenders'.[32] It soon took root and grew, as his dictum that 'you cannot train men for freedom in a condition of captivity' gained wider currency. Captain Williams, Wakefield's governor, another avid innovator, was the first to find a suitable site. Alec, determined to be hands-on with this venture, joined twenty prisoners and two officers working in a forest clearing and sleeping in huts seven miles from the nearest town. There they erected the first prison camp in England, and the first addition to the prison estate since Camp Hill a quarter of a century before. The aim of this open-air venture was to prevent prisoners becoming inured to carceral life and enable them better to return to society. Symbolically, the first building put up was 'a curious little cabin built of the discarded doors of prison cells'.[33] In July 1937, at the request of the prisoners, Paterson laid the foundation stone of the bridge they were building, another structure as symbolic as practical. Despite press criticism of 'prisoners in Sylvan Solitudes', so successful was the initial stage it was decided that a few 'specials' (those under the age of twenty-five with previous convictions) could be mixed in with the 'stars' in the belief the majority would influence them for the good. Later, a number of murderers who had served ten years or more were sent to New Hall, an 'action that would have seemed unthinkable only a few years before, so quickly was the attitude to penal reform changing both in and out of Whitehall. The result was beyond all expectations.' After a few weeks these 'listless, hopeless men became alert and cheerful'. It was 'like watching a dead flower in water and watching it revive', one officer observed. The long-term results were equally impressive as few absconded and the recidivism rate remained low. After the Home Secretary, Sir John Simon, visited the project and gave it his blessing it was recognised as an acceptable method of dealing with first offenders, no longer a temporary experiment but a foretaste of the future. Cicely Craven declared it to be 'an outstanding example of the skill with which Mr Paterson, once he makes up his mind to carry through a really drastic change, puts it through with gradualness which eludes the eye and therefore the criticism of the more nervous section of the public.'[34]

Success would lead to expansion, although the next camp, Leyhill, would not be established until 1946. It was hoped that well-ordered camps, rather than generate fear, would dispel hostility, build up a rapport with the locals and even

32   Alexander Paterson, 'The American Court', *The Spectator,* 12th September 1947, pp. 9f. Alec acknowledged his debt to his American colleagues in a letter of 27th May 1936, reproduced in Sanford Bates, 'Anglo-American Progress in Penitentiary Affairs', in Manuel Lopez-Rey and Charles Germain (eds), *Studies in Penology* (The Hague, 1964), pp. 30–41, at p. 39.

33   *EPBS,* p. 101.

34   Scott, pp. 88f; *HJ,* 4/4 (July 1937), p. 400; 'The Wakefield Prison Camp', *The Magistrate,* November–December 1938, pp. 143f; (1939), p. 105.

FIGURE 18. Alec in the foreground laying the foundations of New Hall Camp, 28th July 1937

help revive rural life. One would go so far as to provide players to fill gaps in their village's football team, 'a practice which the Commissioners with some regret felt bound to frown on when it came to notice.' The frown was tempered with a smile.[35]

Paterson wanted to go further if adequate funding had been available from the Treasury, and approval gained from the Home Office. Prisons, he believed, should exalt and not degrade, but the current estate was not conducive to exaltation. Although economy favoured a small number of large panopticon-style prisons, holding more inmates and needing fewer staff, Paterson feared that classification and training could not long endure within such institutions. The partition walls were 'so thin that a myopic bat could see through them'.[36] Existing prisons should be torn down and no more like them should be built. A larger number of smaller 'Training Centres' and 'Places of Detention', which would allow for classification by establishment, and in which the staff could get to know their charges, were a far preferable, albeit a more expensive, option. The maintenance of proper staffing levels was vital but also costly. Reformation of

35   Lopez-Rey, *op.cit.*, p. 39; *EPBS*, p. 231.
36   TNA, HO45/19453/507631/1.

character did not come cheap since adjusting 'the perspective of the individual is a costlier task than [reducing] a crowd to uniformity'. To get solid future returns in the form of fewer crimes and lower recidivism, initial investment had to be substantial. But the country was deep in depression, there were many other priorities, and lack of money would curtail Paterson's ambitions in terms of both personnel and buildings. Staff reductions took place in 1931, and as a result the hours of associated labour were curtailed. New recruitment did not begin for three years. As for the infrastructure, the most that could be done in the 1930s was an upgrade: an extensive programme of electrification, the installation of central heating, and the provision of clear glass and sliding panels in some 18,000 cell windows. Hard economic facts trumped high utopian hopes. Paterson expressed his frustration:

> It would [be] comparatively easy to wipe the slate and start afresh. At every turn however, economy has barred the way, or buildings that were on the right spot have been thought unsuitable for the purpose desired, and on consideration have been dismissed as incapable of alteration. The castles, therefore, that were built in the air have altered their shape considerably in coming down to earth. Great, indeed, are our hopes and high our ideals, but because they must fit within stern walls not easily re-sited, the problem has been a jig-saw puzzle, with many more pieces than spaces, and in the end we present the compromise exacted by unalterable facts.[37]

Throughout his career Paterson's plans were bedevilled by lack of money and resources for this Cinderella of social services.[38]

Nonetheless, Paterson believed, and he thought the country as a whole was coming to believe, that the 'hoary old dilemma' between punishment debasing humanity, and reformative measures undermining deterrence, was no dilemma at all, and that 'the contraposition of reform and punishment is just a bogey that has deceived both the reactionary and the sentimentalist.' The two methods of preventing inmates returning to prison – deterrence and reform – were not contrary but complementary.

37 'A Scheme for the Redistribution of Prisoners among the prisons of England and Wales submitted to his colleagues by a Commissioner at Sea' (unpublished, November 1925), p. 6.
38 Paterson, pp. 53, 68; Report (1934), p. 14. Alec did his best to secure private donations, persuading William Morris, the motor manufacturer, to fund parental visits to borstals to the tune of £10,000 (Forsythe, p. 195). For Hobhouse Paterson was 'the guiding and most beneficent spirit of [the Prison Commission] bringing hope and healing to many thousands of offenders.' But for financial constraints imposed by the Treasury he would have achieved even more (*Forty Years and an Epilogue* [London, 1951], p. 178f).

The changing of habits and the growth of self-control is an arduous and thorny process for any man or woman, boy or girl, and any species of training that will effect these things is necessarily both long and painful. The young nun in the convent, the recruit on the barrack-square, the dipsomaniac in the home, the tuberculous in the sanatorium will all testify to the unpleasantness of their training. The very length of its duration, and its domination over the minutest detail of personal life are sufficient to make it unpopular. There is no real dilemma between a reformatory and punitive basis for prison treatment, for any training that is truly reformatory is also truly punitive. This is already illustrated in England by the preference of the lad for three months in prison, where he is punished, to three years in a borstal institution, where he may be trained.[39]

The diminution in prisoner numbers, and the apparent impact of borstals in cutting off recidivism at its source, created an expectation that the number of prisons would soon be halved, and indeed between 1914 and 1930 fifteen of the twenty-six local prisons were closed, mainly due to budgetary constraints. Nonetheless, the Commissioners were praised for having produced a system which heralded an epoch in the treatment of juvenile crime. They had found the elusive Holy Grail of penal success. They had drained the cess-pit, and in straitened times, by closing prisons and substituting borstals, they had saved money. Borstals would proliferate throughout the British Isles, and spread throughout the Empire.

Several factors were in Paterson's favour. Public opinion was increasingly sympathetic to measures of penal reform, its changing attitude illustrated by debates in Parliament and by articles, editorials and letters in the press. Legislation was being passed which facilitated reform and removed barriers to it. The courts were more and more amenable to passing sentences of probation or borstal training. The perception was growing that while serious crime was decreasing, petty crimes were mainly committed by the young. But for the purpose of effecting major and enduring reforms the most important factor was the decline in the numbers on remand or sentenced to imprisonment, demographics helping in this as, until the mid-1930s, the proportion of young men – the most crime-prone group – was lower than at any period in the century, so many having been killed or crippled during the war, and couples thereafter preferring 'a baby Austin to one in the perambulator'.[40] In time the apparent and startling success of the borstal system – lauded as the first

39   Alexander Paterson, *German Prisons 1922* (Maidstone prison, 1923), p. 3. 'English Prisons', *The Annals of the American Academy of Political and Social Science* (September 1931), vol.157, pp. 164–173, at p. 171.

40   Terence Morris, 'British Criminology: 1935–48', *BJC*, 28/2 (Spring 1988), pp. 20–34, at p. 21.

'organically conceived system for the reformation of prisoners' – would give momentum to penal reform and encourage further innovation.[41]

Paterson knew that ultimate success depended on securing a dedicated work-force. Some uniformed staff resented aloof governors whose social standing marked them out as members of an officer-class, as indeed many had been, but whose civilian garb belied it. They also looked askance at the amount lavished on borstals, swimming pools and sports fields when their own quarters were in urgent need of refurbishment. Many shared the view that lionising prisoners meant demonising prison officers.[42] It did not. Paterson recognised their vital importance to his project, for upon them fell 'the task of putting into practice the principles and ideals of the administration'. He endeavoured to inculcate in them the idea that their duty was more than that of mere custody, and that they were integral to 'a national work of training and reformation'. He was often to be found in borstals encouraging disciplinary officers and housemasters to work together within the house set-up. He wanted them to be one united body, 'intolerant of division by caste or income'.

Just as he had approved of 'rankers' in the army becoming commissioned officers, he firmly believed in promoting prison officers to governor rank, even if they should be leavened by direct entry accessions from outside the service. He thought 'the ideal combination in a penal system would be to place half its establishment under the direction of men who have acquired their experi-ence of service in the lower ranks, and the other half under the direction of men formerly in other professions, who bring to their new career new ideas, a fresh inspiration and different viewpoints.'[43] Cross-fertilization was what he had in mind, or mix-and-match. The Commissioner's high level of commitment proved infectious and infection led to emulation. As Harold Scott noted, 'no one could be with him and not catch the fire of his enthusiasm.' Soon house-masters and uniformed staff alike were broaching new ideas and suggesting im-provements, which were well-received by Alec.[44] The obverse of this was that he had no truck with brutality. In 1935, for instance, he dismissed four officers who had assaulted two escapees from Wandsworth and reprimanded the governor for not at once reporting all the circumstances to the Commissioners.[45] Bad apples should be discarded; good ones polished.

41 Leon Radzinowicz, 'The Evolution of the Modern Prison System', *Modern Law Review* (October 1939), pp. 121–135, at p. 134.
42 Clayton, p. 64.
43 Quoted in Gordon Hawkins, *Alex Paterson: An Appreciation* (privately printed, n.d.), pp. 26f.
44 *The Magistrate*, 9, 1951, p. 151; TNA, PCOM7/542; Bailey (1987), p. 201.
45 Clayton, pp. 164f. In 1929 Alec had carried out an inquiry into the unusually high rate of assaults on officers in Wandsworth. He refuted the suggestion that this was

An important innovation, intended to counter the ethos of the past and imbue raw recruits with reforming zeal as well as professional pride, was the creation in 1925 of an officer training school at Wakefield, with the deputy-governor, Gilbert Hair, in charge. Applicants, who numbered about 10,000 a year, were shortlisted by Paterson himself and the thousand or so remaining were interviewed by him, whenever possible, or otherwise by one of his colleagues. After careful vetting in which character and temperament were assessed, the 200 selected spent nine weeks at Wakefield, learning the new methods of prisoner management.[46] Under the old regime warders had been employed as turnkeys and enforcers of rigid discipline. Under the new their role as officers would be more demanding as well as more rewarding.

> If prisoners were to be trained and not merely restrained, to be helped and not merely held, it would be essential to employ mentors rather than warders, and educators rather than mere invigilators. So a new race of men has joined the ranks of the government service, ... recruited from every walk of life, the main qualifications being character, personality and leadership.[47]

Macartney, who was in Parkhurst when Clayton was governor, encapsulated the change by observing that, whereas in 1928 it had been difficult for a 'jailer' who wanted to retain his 'roof and job to be a decent fellow', by 1935 it was easy.[48]

---

due 'to the slackening of discipline in recent years'. He found that a few longer-serving officers in particular were subjected to them, and concluded that in part it was their old-fashioned attitudes and behaviour that had provoked the attacks (Report [1929], TNA, HO45/24535). He was probably justified in so concluding.

46   Report (1934), pp. 14f; Clarence Peterson, 'Prison Officers' Training Schools', *JCLC*, 22/6 (1932), pp. 895–898; Joseph Schlarman, *Why Prisons?* (Illinois, 1937), p. 7.

47   'Salute the Prison Officer' (unpublished typescript, 1947).

48   Macartney, pp. 107f. Clayton, governor of Parkhurst from 1930 to 1935, had a partiality for the 'underdog', and proved to be the most reasonable governor with whom Macartney 'ever did "stir"'. Assaults and floggings almost ceased during his tenure, and men embittered by harsh handling left prison markedly better adjusted. In short, he turned the harshest prison in the system, where talking was absolutely prohibited, men were reported for the 'slightest thing', and a 'reign of terror existed', into one of the most relaxed, allowing the better natures of well-disposed officers to flourish (pp. 58, 148–155, 162). Phelan, who was at Parkhurst during the same period, 'never knew another governor like him. He might have done a life-lagging, so well did he know and understand and sympathize with the convict mind.' When some of the Dartmoor 'mutineers' arrived in Parkhurst, Clayton did not put them into the segregation block but into the Autolycan Chess Club. 'He preferred people to solve chess problems instead of sawing their window-bars.' Yet he remained 'a realist not a dreamer' (pp. 358–362).

Paterson took great interest in the new school, devising the curriculum, compiling a reading list, and lecturing. New recruits were instructed in prison routine, but in addition they had to study the principles that underlay the policy of penal administration, and learn about the different methods employed elsewhere in the world. They were also 'encouraged to read, to think, to argue and to criticise'. As 'officers', they were required to lead. Alec told the story of an artist commissioned to paint a picture for the chapel of a large metropolitan prison. To find models for a thief, beggar, harlot and murderer among the mixed inmate population was easy, but he was initially baffled as to who would make a suitable candidate for the central figure. Finally, he alighted on a junior prison officer 'who had the face and bearing of a leader among men'.[49] This should be their aspiration. Alec would assure them that they were going to do great work, to help in the vital task of reclaiming the lost from a life of crime and training them for citizenship. This would be their calling, if they were chosen.

It was for Alec to do the choosing. He would read all the instructor's reports and examine the freshly trained recruits, with a view to accepting them or not. Even in this weighty task, and despite his eminence, Alec never lost his sense of humour:

> As each presented himself for his *viva voce* examination, he held in his hand a large buff-coloured notebook in which he had entered laboriously the fruits of his instruction. He would hand the book to me and I should rustle through the pages and stop occasionally to ask him some question on a vital or irrelevant detail. So doing one day, I descried the notes of a lecture designated 'the duties of a gatekeeper at a prison', and among the other *obiter dicta* of an experienced gatekeeper, was delighted to see the salutary warning to a young recruit 'never give your keys whatsoever to the Commissioner'.

'So their time at the training school was not altogether wasted', he concluded.[50]

A further Paterson-inspired if Scott-initiated innovation began in March 1935 with the introduction of a course for the selection and training of younger officers for higher posts. 'All ranks', he had long contended, 'should be assured that if they acquit themselves worthily they have ... the prospect of promotion.'[51] Promotion depended on passing examinations. So successful was it that both the Scottish Prison Department and the Colonial Office wanted access for their staff. This was an opportunity to spread 'the new methods and ideals of the

---

49 'Salute the Prison Officer', *op.cit.*

50 *Over the Walls*, p. 39. Usually, a quarter of those passing through the school were rejected. The successful then spent ten months on probation.

51 Report (1934), pp. 15, 43f; *PPA*, p. 146.

English service over a wider field'. Consequently, in 1937 Sir John Simon, the Home Secretary, laid the foundation stone of a completely new building which would open two years later as the Imperial Training School for Prison Officers.[52]

Criticism has been levelled at Paterson that, with his emphasis on prison work as a 'vocation', he expected senior staff to forego adequate pay or decent accommodation, and could ride rough-shod over their sensitivities. Once, he asked the well-born wife of a borstal housemaster how she liked the change in her conditions. When she replied that she was thinking of writing a book and calling it *From Castle to Slum*, Alec brushed the remark aside as snobbery or self-ishness, since he would have opted for the latter. When he went to Pentonville to attend an entertainment put on in the new staff club, he arrived late after din-ing with Major Blake, ignored all the senior officials present, and spent the eve-ning speaking to a staff representative about the discontent of ordinary officers with their pay and conditions, a discontent he shared.[53] As ever, the Commis-sioner was on the job, seizing an opportunity to enhance his rapport with junior staff and show he took their concerns seriously, somewhat more important than enjoying a jamboree, or flattering the egos of senior management.

Whatever sacrifice he expected of his own sort, Alec was determined to el-evate the status of ordinary officers, and hoped to equalise their pay with that of the police. He agreed with them that 'if the prisoner is to be reformed' it could 'only be done through a good, well-paid and contented staff.' In response to the refusal of the Stanhope Committee, set up in 1923 to look into pay and conditions, to recommend parity on the grounds that the responsibilities of the police were greater, Paterson countered that prison officers were even more vital in the fight against crime. The function of the police was to turn bad citizens into prisoners, that of prison officers to turn captives into good citizens, to turn liabilities into assets.[54] It was not the case that disciplinary officers were ignored or sidelined by the Commissioners, least of all by Alec. He took personal inter-est and pride in his staff, just as he did in prisoners and borstal boys and girls. It was said that 'in his prime he knew personally every officer in the service and most of their wives and children too.'[55] Whenever and wherever he found talent he wanted to keep it and promote it. He also wanted to keep staff 'onside'.

52   Scott, pp. 79f.
53   Clayton, pp. 65f. The lateness of his arrival was not his fault, however, but his host's, and Clayton's accusation of rudeness looks like pique. Later, undergoing a nervous breakdown, he acknowledged the solicitude Paterson had shown him (pp. 166f).
54   'Salute the Prison Officer', *op.cit*. In August 1947 Alec was asked by the Home Of-fice not to publish this article as it could be seen as supporting the Prison Officers' Association's claim for parity with the police, then under negotiation.
55   Unidentified newspaper obituary.

Alec was also a proponent of involving outside experts in his remedial work, but recognised their limitations. He encouraged the work of psychiatrists, psychologists and psychotherapists in treating, assessing and classifying inmates in prisons such as Wormwood Scrubs and trainees in borstals generally. They had a role to play, but not a determinative one.[56] These disciplines were in their infancy and their adherents often exhibited an unwarranted self-assurance. Worst was the prison officer with a smattering of knowledge, since there was 'no more dangerous individual than the superficial psychologist who thinks himself infallible.'

Housemasters were a different matter. They were usually well-educated, and not easily beguiled by the allure of untested ideas. They could be trusted with a little knowledge. Yet they should all have acquired practical experience before deploying theoretical insights gained from study. John Weldon was unusual. Having worked in London slums while still at school, he read psychology at Oxford, before becoming a housemaster in 1924 at the age of twenty-one.[57] Those without such a degree were encouraged to acquire some psychological expertise. From the mid-1930s each borstal was to second one established housemaster for on-the-job training at the National Institute of Industrial Psychology which, at Alec's request, had undertaken a review of vocational guidance.[58] Common sense, empirical understanding and theoretical knowledge could combine in a healthy partnership.

Alec's reservations about the unsubstantiated claims of the 'scientific approach to the treatment of inmates' were shared by many governors and by his equally cautious colleague, Dr Norwood East. Yet both valued criminology. The Medical Commissioner received Alec's support, advice and help in his research on borstal boys for the book he published in 1942, *The Adolescent Criminal.*[59] Alec was also gratefully acknowledged by Hermann Mannheim for the assistance he provided in permitting access to borstal records when the eminent criminologist was carrying out research for his seminal work, *Social Aspects of Crime in England Between the Wars.*[60] Alec, while recognising the merits of criminological study, considered the anthropological approach of Lombroso misguided. British criminology

56   TNA, PCOM9/21; Report (1936), p. 26; Ruck, pp. 104f; C.T. Cape, 'Learning a Trade: A Borstal Experiment in View', *HJ*, 4/4 (July 1937), pp. 406–409; Ruck, pp. 129–132.
57   Schlarman, *op.cit.*, p. 34.
58   Mark Benney, 'Borstal as it might be', *The Spectator,* 5th March 1937, pp. 10f.
59   Preface, p.vii, p. 2.
60   (London, 1940), pp. 7, 250, 298, 324. Mannheim examined the records of 606 boys and 411 girls. Only one sixth of the boys had been members of a club at any time, and few of these had taken it seriously. There were no figures available for the girls. Few middle-class children were borstal inmates. An extract of his findings was published in the Commissioners' 1937 Report, pp. 38–42.

should adopt a legal, psychological and sociological framework rather than pursue the 'criminal type', falsified by Goring's research. Alec wanted criminology to have greater academic clout, and in an address given in June 1932 urged that a chair in the subject should be endowed at Oxford.[61]

This muted enthusiasm for the medical and social sciences was not a reversion to pure social Positivism. Classical and Christian beliefs about moral culpability and the possibility of redemption remained the bedrock of the prison system, with the insights of these nascent disciplines being 'additional extras grafted on'. To put it another way, at its core the reformatory project was 'one in which the latest teachings of science might be called into the service of [older] beliefs about reformation, moral example, appeal to the sensitivities, and the overcoming of evil by good.'[62]

Expertise should not be the sole preserve of these groups but should be gained by day-to-day experience in custodial work. Paterson pioneered what is now called 'sentence planning'. This was related to the individualisation of treatment by which he laid such store. Senior and subordinate officers all had a part to play in assessing and assisting criminals to become productive citizens again. In theory suitable employment, evening classes and prison visitors should be assigned. This was firmly linked to after-care, 'one of the key-stones of the modern prison system', enabling each prisoner on release to 'pick up the threads', to regain employments and to reintegrate into the community. To aid success the maintenance of family links was vital, but for many years penal policy had frustrated this, especially in denying a wife the chance of visiting her spouse during the first stage of the sentence. Alec recalled how this policy began to change after Salter Davies, in his capacity of chairman of the voluntary visitors and teachers at Maidstone prison, came to see him 'to point out how foolish, and how destructive of our purpose was this privation'. Davies recounted the case of a penal servitude prisoner who was devoted to his wife, and she to him. Their future happiness and that of their children was jeopardised by this policy. He pleaded, 'with real imaginative common sense that was unanswerable, that this privilege of seeing his wife and writing to her should be allowed from the start of a man's life in prison.'[63] The appeal had its effect, and early visits were encouraged. Subsequently England adopted the American practice of giving all privileges on reception, but 'making it clear that any slackening of effort in conduct and industry must lead inevitably to their forfeiture and a swift return

61   'Should the Criminologist be Encouraged?', *Transactions of the Medico-Legal Society*, 26/1 (1932), pp. 180–200, at p. 191. In fact, Cambridge beat her sibling to it when Radzinowicz established a Department of Criminal Science in 1938.

62   William Forsythe, 'The Garland Thesis and the Origins of Modern English Prison Discipline: 1835–1939', *HJ*, 34/3 (August 1995), pp. 259–273.

63   Salter Davies also protested against the ban on prisoner-teachers.

to the *status quo ante* of featureless captivity'. For Alec this was self-evidently a more logical procedure, since he thought it absurd that if 'concerts, lectures and classes, all integral to training, were regarded merely as privileges, they could be withheld for weeks or months.'

The whole prison system should be an integrated whole, geared to return prisoners to freedom better adjusted to it than when they first were incarcerated. They were citizens before they became criminals, and they always must be treated as individuals. For Alec 'the first axiom in the knowledge of crime and criminals [was] to disassociate the crime from the criminal'.

> Anyone who has dealt with criminals and prisoners for any length of time has long discovered the fallacy of associating the criminal with the crime. He knows from long and varied and perhaps painful experience that the crime for which a man is held in prison, far from being typical affords little or no indication, as a rule, of his character and temperament ... He who has earned his experience neither from the Sunday papers nor from lectures in criminology has long ago learned that the criminal must be so completely disassociated from his crime that he can be studied anew as a human being, and the student is well-advised to take little or no interest in the nature of the offences which has made a free citizen into a prisoner.

Alec readily followed his own advice, but whether this was being far-sighted or blinkered is open to question. While 'the crime may not define the man it may illuminate him'.[64] What was less controversial was his insistence that no one was beyond redemption, and the most redeemable and the most important were the young. Reforming them would be Alec's priority.

---

64 *Over the Walls*, pp. 40f.

PRISON WALLAH: 1925–1926

To keep a wide horizon, a balance and perspective, read your daily *Times*. It will save you from becoming a 'jungle-wallah', a man with a desert mind. You will still be a man of the world.

Alexander Paterson

In 1925 Alec was travelling again, but this time not within Europe but to Asia, and not on official Prison Commission business but in response to an appeal by the colonial administration of Burma for his expert advice.[1] To make the trip he had to take unpaid leave. He was not merely sacrificing his salary; he was jeopardising his pension.

On his way to Burma Paterson arranged to stop off in Ceylon to see for himself the fruits of an encounter in 1922 with that colony's Inspector-General of Police, and Toc H member, Herbert Dowbiggin. Dowbiggin had heard of Stansfeld's work and thought that therein might lie the solution to the problem of boys living on the streets in Colombo. While on leave he had called on Paterson at the Prison Commission, and on a number of occasions had been taken by him to the OBC, where he was soon convinced his intuition was right. When he had returned to his post, Dowbiggin had set up a police-run street boys' club with seventy members ranging in age from seven to seventeen. Some lived there permanently. Sports, instruction and the promotion of self-respect took place. To counter the prevalence of knife crime, he promoted boxing, 'maintaining that a boy who could use his fists would never use a knife again'. The Pettah Boys' Club, as it was called, was affiliated from the beginning to the OBC, and the Singhalese motto chosen for it – 'on the turf and under the turf we are all the same' – was of the same import as *Fratres*. Alec was duly impressed. In the visitors' book he wrote that it was 'delightful to enter so many miles away, a club

---

1 Alexander Paterson, *Report on the Prevention of Crime and the Treatment of the Criminal in the Province of Burma* (Rangoon, 1927), p. 1. The following is largely based on this report.

that reminds me so much of our Oxford and Bermondsey Club at home. The lads with no homes and not very regular jobs face life with a smile. They box keenly and ... are too good for me at Ping Pong!'[2]

Back aboard ship he got back to work, finishing a twenty-eight page 'Scheme for the Re-distribution of Prisoners among the Prisons of England and Wales submitted to his Colleagues by a Commissioner at Sea', the nearest thing to a manifesto for a complete overhaul of the prison system that he would produce.[3] At sea, but not at rest. He had always enjoyed sailing in boats as 'the most perfect way of doing nothing and feeling the better for it', but being on an ocean liner was a different matter.[4] It provided an ideal opportunity for reflection and writing. At the end of November, he arrived in Rangoon for a four-month sojourn in Burma.

The British had seized half of the lower part of the country after the Anglo-Burmese War of 1852 and the rest after that of 1885. With its absorption into the Empire, it became a province of British India. Rangoon was transformed into a commercial and political hub, and was made the capital. With its spacious parks and lakes and mix of modern buildings and traditional wooden architecture, colonial Rangoon was known as 'the garden city of the East'. With its hospitals and a university, by the early twentieth century it had public services and infrastructure on a par with London. With dynamic commercial expansion, Rangoon's population – a mix of Burmese, Indians, Chinese and British – exploded, leading to the growth of select residential suburbs to the north of the Royal and Inya Lakes. It also led to the growth of the prison population.

Soul-searching about the purpose of prisons was becoming commonplace throughout the Empire, and a new emphasis on reform and rehabilitation was coming to the fore. For reasons that are still unclear, Burma's incarceration rate was very high, the highest *per capita* of any Indian province. There was a view that for a variety of social and economic reasons the Burmese were more criminally active than most and, whether or not that was true, violent crime did seem to be on the rise. With large numbers incarcerated, and poor provision made, the effectiveness of Burma's prison system to do more than contain criminals

---

2   'The Apprentice to Crime', *Police Journal* (1st January 1928), pp. 139–148, at pp. 146f; 'Privileges' (undated typescript); Baron, pp. 197f. In September 1932 Dowbiggin would visit Lowdham Grange and spend two nights there.

3   TNA, HO45/19453/507631/1. His classification scheme, while warmly welcomed by his colleagues and prison governors, was much criticised by Home Office officials, and was never adopted. For a detailed analysis see Bailey (2019), pp. 133–140. Alec anticipated failure, but thought his proposals and the ensuing debate would 'at any rate clear our minds and suggest some programme that is founded upon a policy' based on clarity of purpose, not *ad hoc* expediency. He wanted 'a coherent programme for the future', even if this one was still-born.

4   *Letters*, 16th June 1916.

was coming into question. On release they would be worse, but if circumstances had made them criminals, a change of circumstances could remake them as citizens. In a number of annual reports on Burmese prison administration the argument for a regime of reformative treatment was put forward.

The Inspector-General of Prisons, Major H.H.G. Knapp, was a prominent contributor. He was also a staunch advocate of a radical change in direction. He reiterated the old caveat that it was hard to see how prisoners could be reformed and 'made fit for freedom ... within the walls of a gaol', given the lack of categorisation, the inevitability of contamination, and the tendency to adaptation resulting in many 'good prisoners leav[ing] gaol thoroughly bad citizens'. He urged the necessity of exploring every alternative to prison, and even of closing rather than constructing 'these costly institutions'.[5]

Knapp retired in 1924, to be replaced by an Indian officer of similar ilk, Major P.K. Tarapore. He too sought alternatives to imprisonment, recommending the introduction of borstals and a probation service. While on leave in England he not only examined its prison administration but met the leading exponent of penal reform and font of penological innovation, Alexander Paterson. So too did his predecessor when attending the International Prison Congress in London in the summer of 1925. It was probably as a result of these encounters that the idea of inviting the Commissioner to Burma was conceived. Both inspectors shared Paterson's views, and may well have wanted to engage his support for their radical designs. Whatever the origin of the invitation, ultimately it was up to the local government of Burma to make the formal request that the Commissioner come to the province to 'advise generally on jail conditions in Burma, as well as on the possibility of introducing a modified form of borstal system'.[6] In doing so he had to join temporarily the Burmese prison service and take leave of the English one. Always one to master his brief, Paterson read extensively during the voyage. The book at the top of the list was *The Soul of a People* by Harold Fielding Hall, which spoke sympathetically of Burma, its Buddhist faith and its attitude to crime and punishment.[7]

During his stay, Paterson inspected prisons, walked the streets in the company of a police officer well-versed in the night-life of the capital, gave public lectures in Rangoon, and explored possible sites for a training establishment for juveniles.[8] Faced with some scepticism on this last point, he needed to prove its viability.

5   *Reports on the Prison Administration of Burma*, 1921, p. 6; 1922, pp. 14ff. These reports are cited in Ian Brown, 'A Commissioner Calls: Alexander Paterson and Colonial Burma's Prisons', *Journal of Southeast Asian Studies*, 38(2) (June 2007), pp. 293–308.
6   Brown, *op.cit.*, pp. 296, 302.
7   Published in London in 1898.
8   'The Apprentice to Crime', *op.cit.*, pp. 144f. Paterson specifically thanked Tarapore and his staff for 'the whole-hearted way they stepped aside and let me see all that I asked to see. Without their co-operation, the four months would have been a

FIGURE 19. Alec with young colleague in Burma, 1925–6

To the consternation of his hosts, he insisted on taking a party of sixteen teen-age murderers, rapists and *dacoits* (armed-robber gang members) from the juvenile gaol at Meiktila, a hundred miles north of Rangoon, to an open camp by a lake in the jungle. So risky was this expedition that 'the betting in the clubs of Rangoon was 10-1 against his returning alive'. Implored to take a weapon with him, Alec went to the bazaar and bought a half-rupee whistle.[9] He was accompanied by four other unarmed adults, including Professor Pe Maung Tin of Rangoon University and C.L. Atkinson of the Borstal Association. For a while the little platoon marched in silence, the boys unaccustomed to their new-found freedom, self-conscious in their khaki shorts and striped jerseys, and bemused as to what would befall them. But 'their chief jailer ... had exhorted them to repay trust with good sense and they were determined to do their best.' After a week of

---

waste of time' (*Report*, para. 214). One perceptive commentator who witnessed late colonial government and its criminal justice policy in action was Eric Blair, later known as George Orwell. He was in the Burmese police from 1922 to 1927. Given their overlap in time and interests, it is likely that he and Paterson would have met in Burma either professionally or socially, but neither mentions the other.

9   Ruck, p. 13, n.1; 'How England Handles the Young Offender', *Proceedings of the Annual Congress of the American Prison Association* (1939), pp. 149–157, at p. 157.

hard manual work, team-building exercises, communal games, lessons in Burmese history from the professor and in Buddhism from a local *hpongyi* (monk), and of course 'singing and digging', the party arrived back in Rangoon safe and sound. The boys asked two things; that they might keep the shorts as an alternative to prison uniform and that Alec stay and live with them always. He granted their first request but had to decline the second.[10] The 'smiling lads returned to the gaol to face some years of imprisonment' without him. They had confounded the doomsayers and proved that they could be 'trusted in the open [and] controlled effectively without walls or wire'. A whistle had sufficed. Many eager punters lost money as a result. Alec drew a moral from this successful experiment:

> It is essential for the proper training of a lad that his vitality should not be suppressed but should find a healthy outlet. The freedom of life in camp with its noise and rivalry and laughter, offered this outlet, but in no way interfered with control and discipline. In a word it was found worthwhile to appeal to the better nature of the lad rather than to dwell gloomily upon those weaknesses of character and temper, from which none of us is altogether free.[11]

At the request of the Indian government, he also made an excursion to the Andaman Islands, where many Indian political prisoners were held in the most inclement conditions, and where the most malignant of malarial mosquitoes were to be found. The British officer who accompanied him was infected shortly after his arrival at Port Blair, and was dead before he could be evacuated to Rangoon. Most of those doomed to be marooned suffered a similar fate, and those who survived to be released were 'racked and riddled with every symptom and stigma of malaria, so weak and wizened they could scarcely stand, ... so dazed as to be almost bereft of speech, without hope or health or heart.' In contrast the Burmese seemed to survive nature's ravages unscathed, although they harboured grievances about the way they were treated, deprived of any opportunity to practise Buddhism, bullied by Indian prisoners and staff, and ignored by British officers. Alec told the Indian government that 'you cannot colonise with convicts'.[12] Despite this, in his eyes, the place had potential, and he recommended to the Burmese authorities that 'murderers and dacoits' be deported there, providing conditions improved and those sent were volunteers. This suggestion was not adopted.

---

10 Sir William Hamilton Fyfe, 'Retribution or Reform' (transcript of a radio talk, 8th January 1952), p. 5. Paterson typified these delinquents as 'friends', relating that 'one young adventurous friend of mine in Burma always stole buffalo, sometimes in pairs, on occasion in a herd' (*Over the Walls*, p. 45).

11 Alexander Paterson, 'A Borstal Camp in Burma', *Rangoon Gazette*, 8th March 1926, reprinted in Ruck, pp. 179–182.

12 'Transport the Gunman?', *The Spectator*, 22nd May 1947, pp. 11f.

FIGURE 20. The Burmese Experiment, 1926

FIGURE 21. Digging in Burma, 1926

Paterson produced his report in May 1926.[13] It put forward a comprehensive blueprint for the transformation of the prison system of Burma and of its criminal justice system. In short, there should be a major reduction in the use of penal custody. This should be so for all, but especially for the young. Probation should be deployed extensively. Preventative, reformatory and training schools should be established, and after-care should be provided. In three appendices he even included a draft Prevention of Crime Bill and draft regulations that incorporated his recommendations for juveniles. He meant business.

The report, far from being a stuffy civil service tome that would either be read and discarded or not read at all, sparkled, its moral earnestness sweetened with a lightness of touch. Officials would read it with pleasure. William Brander, the chief secretary to the Burmese government, expressed gratitude to Paterson not only for 'the insight, labour and industry that he has displayed in preparing this report but also for the spirit of humanity and enthusiasm which he has infused into it.' Others were equally vociferous in their praise. A reviewer for the *Rangoon Gazette* stated that the author was 'a man with his head in the stars and his feet on solid ground', combining 'hard practicality with near-utopian vision.'[14]

Praise was one thing, implementation was another matter. Many of his proposals were too radical and expensive for the provincial government to undertake. The response, however laudatory, was in effect lukewarm, perhaps complacent, and those suggestions that were adopted were a mere tinkering rather than the complete overhaul he had advocated.[15] It was, however, an improvement and a start.

13 It was published in Rangoon the following year.
14 13th December 1926, quoted in Brown, *op.cit.*, p. 301, n.36.
15 One of his more bizarre recommendations, that the cat-o'-nine-tails be deployed in lieu of the cane in the administration of corporal punishment on the grounds that it was more painful without leaving permanent marks, was rejected forthwith.

One recommendation that was adopted was the establishment of a training school, a borstal in all but name, for offenders between the ages of fourteen and eighteen. Borstal officers, sent from England to supervise the early stages of this venture, had to be enthusiasts for 'the pleasures of camp life'. Paterson had scouted out potential sites at Shwebo Barracks, Meiktila Barracks and Myindair, and concluded that only the last was suitable. Near Kalaw, fifty or so miles southeast of Meiktila, it was a virgin site, ripe with potential, having a good water supply, lots of cultivable land, and easy access to timber from its extensive pine forests. Constructing a road, erecting buildings for the staff and huts for themselves, and growing potatoes, coffee, strawberries and cabbages, would keep the trainees busy, healthy and hard at work. Once again he was adamant that a borstal should be disassociated from anything penal. This struck a chord with the local authorities, and in January 1934 Colonel Findlay, the director-general of Burmese prisons, would attend the seventh course on prison administration put on by Alec annually for overseas officers, and visit Lowdham Grange to see an English open borstal in operation.[16] Road camps would also be created but, as a result of complaints from the police about finding recently-sentenced dacoits at liberty, were soon abandoned.[17] Another institution that would still be thriving in the late 1950s was a Rangoon boys' home 'marvellously organised and imbued with life and love' by the Burmese woman who ran it. The inspiration behind it was a brief encounter with Alec Paterson.[18]

Having imparted his wisdom and experience, Alec set sail for England. The long sea-journey again gave him time to think and write, and he did both on the voyage home. He drafted another document called 'Borstal Regulations by a Commissioner at Sea'. It was 'a curious hybrid, a hotch-potch of regulations, standing orders and sections of the Prevention of Crime Act'. When Harold Scott, a meticulous civil servant at the Home Office, received it on his desk he 'fell on it and cut it to pieces', and sent the 'severely mangled' paper back to its author. A few days later he was confronted in his office by 'a stocky, cherub-faced, quick-speaking enthusiast' who had bounded up the stairs three steps at a time 'to find out who had handled his work so roughly'. When the pen-pusher had to concede he had not actually seen a borstal institution, Paterson rectified that omission and took him on a tour of all four. Scott was enraptured with this 'strange world' so different from what he had expected, and 'caught from the young governors and their deputies something of the crusading ardour with which they had been fired by that pioneer of prison reform'. He could see for

16   LLGJ, 24th January 1934.
17   TNA, CO323/1344/7: letter, 31st October 1934.
18   Alec Dickson, 'Technical Assistance and Idealism: Misgivings and Mistakings', *British Association reprint from the "Advancement of Science"*, 55 (December 1957), pp. 177–185, at p. 180.

himself 'the effect of [borstal] life on the inmates, and the burning faith in their work of those in charge'. He openly acknowledged that Paterson, one of the most remarkable men he ever met, had 'wholly converted him to his ideas'. Just as well, since in 1932 Scott would become chairman of the Prison Commission, and would give his subordinate full backing in the face of influential detractors and 'a good deal of misrepresentation in the popular press'. 'Pressure for sterner measures, and accusations of "pampering" criminals are well-known accompaniments of the life of any prison administrator', he observed, and should not be taken too seriously.[19]

19 Scott, pp. 65ff. Scott credited his appointment as chairman to Paterson (p. 71). Alec had the knack of picking the right superiors as well as the right subordinates.

Chapter 12

Expert Witness: 1925–1933

> Imprisonment leaves no visible scar to shock the eye, but it may well have done damage to a human character that nothing can repair. There are cases where it is kinder to break a man's neck in a second than to spend twenty years breaking his heart.
>
> *Alexander Paterson*

Energised by his foreign travels, Alec was all the more active at home. He was already recognised as an expert, perhaps *the* expert in his field, and his expertise would be repeatedly called upon.[1] Alec's reputation was growing apace, as was that of England as being 'in the van of prison administration'. His rehabilitative approach was rapidly gaining ground at home and found resonance abroad, and he made every effort to ensure his message was heard. His was not a voice crying in the wilderness.

In August 1925 he attended the IXth International Prison Congress, which was being held at the Imperial Institute in London, presided over by a stalwart of such occasions, Sir Evelyn Ruggles-Brise.[2] Throughout, Alec played 'a splendid

---

1   As early as February 1923 the Home Secretary, William Bridgeman, appointed Alec to the Advisory Committee on Probation. It met until 1926 (TNA, HO45/16204).

2   Under American auspices the first Congress took place in 1872 in London. Its purpose was to engage reform-minded participants from around the world in the comparative study of different methods of dealing with criminals and to encourage a greater humanity in their treatment. From its success sprang its governing body, the International Prison Commission. It consisted of one or two representatives from each member nation, and usually met biennially to transact necessary administrative business and to discuss issues of current importance. A small executive committee met more often. Thereafter, large quinquennial Congresses were held in various world capitals. It was only in 1895 that Asquith, then Home Secretary, acknowledging that this country could learn from others, decided that England should adhere. Ruggles-Brise attended the Paris Congress in 1895 as the first British representative, and did so on subsequent occasions. He became president in 1910.

part as guide, orator and chorister'. Many of the issues that engaged him were on the agenda, including the individualisation of punishment, classification (on which he submitted a paper), employment, alternatives to imprisonment, indeterminate sentences and preventive measures to save the young from a life of crime. The Congress had no powers of compulsion, but its resolutions had moral suasion and Britain in particular had implemented many previous ones.[3]

Encouraged by the 'common desire to introduce into the punishment and prevention of crime more reason, more justice and more reform', Ruggles-Brise concluded the conference on a note of optimism. On 6th September he wrote to express his gratitude for the decisive contribution his younger colleague had made to the success of the whole undertaking, and to inform him that he intended to bring this to the notice of the Secretary of State, Sir William Joynson-Hicks.[4] The latter had spoken at the Congress and had shown himself to be an unlikely recruit to the new mode of thinking. He had told the assembly that

> In arresting a human being, and depriving him of his liberty for a period of time, which is often prolonged, the executive government has undertaken a new responsibility of the very gravest kind, namely, that of the treatment and training of the offender during the period of incarceration. A man does not lose his rights as a human being because he has broken the laws of his

---

Because of the war no Congress was held in 1915 or 1920, but at a meeting of the Commission in Berne in 1922 it was decided to start the movement afresh and hold the next Congress three years later. This 'jubilee' event lasting from 4th to 10th August was prestigious, and was addressed by several dignitaries, including the Lord Chief Justice, the Lord Chancellor and the Earl of Oxford, as Asquith by then was. In 1929, to reflect the reality that its mission had expanded to encompass penal policy, the International Prison Commission would change its name to the International Penal and Penitentiary Commission which would convene the identically renamed Congresses (Evelyn Ruggles-Brise, *Prison Reform at Home and Abroad* [London, 1924], pp. 1ff).

3   Britain would play an increasingly prominent role. In the first meeting of the IPC after the Congress, Waller's suggestion that a set of minimum rules for the treatment of prisoners be drawn up was accepted. Waller asked Paterson and Lord Polwarth, chairman of the Scottish Prison Commission, to assist. They circulated a code to other member states in 1927 stipulating that any country falling short of such standards should forfeit its right to be considered civilised. As a result, a sub-committee was appointed which drafted a somewhat watered-down version which the IPC adopted in 1929 and, at Polwarth and Alec's bidding, submitted to the League of Nations for its imprimatur (TNA, HO45/20458). It was adopted by the League of Nations in 1934 and approved in 1955 at the first United Nations Congress on Crime Prevention and the Treatment of Offenders.

4   Letter in the family archives.

country. The State will not have done its duty if it releases him, after his period of imprisonment is over, and in consequence of such imprisonment, in such condition of mind and body, that he is no longer fit to take his part in society as a citizen.[5]

It could have been Alec speaking. It was certainly his influence talking.

Such a glowing appraisal from so eminent a source as Ruggles-Brise was all the more useful as he would have to work with – and on – this particular Home Secretary for the following four years, and was already involved in one of his initiatives. On 6th January 1925 a Departmental Committee on the Treatment of Young Offenders had been set up 'to inquire into young people who, owing to bad association or surroundings, require protection and training, and to report what changes, if any, are desirable in the present law or its administration'. So wide was this rubric that it would take over two years to report.[6]

Encouraged by the wording of the committee's instructions stipulating that the young required 'protection and training' rather than punishment, almost a hundred witnesses gave evidence. Those on behalf of the Prison and Borstal Services included Lilian Barker (Aylesbury), Dr Methven (Rochester), T. Paterson Owens (Portland), Elizabeth Cronin (Holloway)[7], J. Landers (Wandsworth), Major FitzClarence (Manchester), the medical inspector, Dr East, and the Commissioner, Alexander Paterson. Margery Fry of the Howard League, Cyril Burt, the psychologist, and representatives from the probation service and Prison Visitors' Association, also testified.

Two of the last were Alec's friends: Basil Henriques and Lilian Le Mesurier, a relative by marriage of Tubby Clayton and a well-travelled economist. In the autumn of 1922 Alec had asked her to become the first woman visitor at Wandsworth boys' prison, which he was in the process of transforming. Before then, male remands aged between sixteen and twenty-one had been sent to Brixton, where little was done to separate them from older prisoners. To prevent contamination and facilitate the preparation of reports for the courts, Alec put forward the idea of using the boys' prison (which held London youths serving less than three months) as a collecting centre for those on remand as well as a reception class for those sentenced to borstal. The other Commissioners supported the proposal, so in December 1923 Dr Landers was appointed governor and medical

5   'The International Prison Congress, August 1925', *HJ*, 2/1 (1st July 1926), pp. 7–12; *The Times*, 5th August 1925.
6   *Report of the Departmental Committee on the Treatment of Young Offenders* (London, 1927).
7   Harley's aunt.

officer for the revamped boys' prison. Remand cases were closely investigated by the medical staff of the prison, their work supplemented by enquiries made into home circumstances by voluntary workers recruited by Le Mesurier. Those destined for borstal were assessed and allocated. This improvisation was better than nothing but was far from ideal, especially for remands. Although the boys' section was detached from the main prison building, it was impossible to prevent all contact with adult prisoners and the unconvicted young would inevitably get a taste of prison life even if prison would not be their ultimate fate. This would not do. '"Prison" and "boy" must come to be regarded as unrelated terms.' In his evidence, backed by that of Landers and Henriques, Alec advocated moving the remands out of penal surroundings and into secure homes.[8]

He held a meeting at the Home Office with Henriques and Le Mesurier to discuss this issue and others relating to young offenders, during which he expressed the hope that the Departmental Committee – which included Waller and Grant-Wilson – would agree with him that all offenders under eighteen should come under the children's court, and that for those under twenty-one either probation or borstal should be the only two possible sentences except in the case of murder.[9] In its origins, borstal had been conceived as an alternative to fairly long sentences of imprisonment that would have been passed on young offenders 'advanced in crime'. Paterson's view that it should be an alternative to short sentences for those who might benefit from training was based on his assumption that one short sentence would inevitably lead to another. Better three years in training than a succession of short periods in prison. Borstal could nip reoffending in the bud, while prison would perpetuate a vicious circle.

In the event he was too sanguine, although the resultant report, published in 1927, went much of his way, recommending the abolition (with some qualifications) of imprisonment for those aged between sixteen and seventeen, the replacement of imprisonment by probation and borstal, 'as far as is possible', for those between seventeen and twenty-one, and that all under seventeen, except those charged with murder, should be dealt with

8   Bailey (1987), pp. 175f, 182. Le Mesurier continued her work when the boys' prison was transferred to Wormwood Scrubs. A medical officer noted: 'it was typical of Alexander Paterson that he was the first to employ women as volunteer counsellors to boys ... awaiting their borstal sentence (Guy Richmond, *Prison Doctor* [British Columbia, 1975], p. 12).

9   L. Loewe, *Basil Henriques* (London, 1976), pp. 72, 80. In successive annual reports the Commissioners stated that for many of the youths imprisoned borstal would have been a far more appropriate disposal. From 1936 committals to borstal increased sharply after the raising of the age limit from twenty-one to twenty-three (Report [1936], p. 23).

in the juvenile court. Young remands should be allocated to a central re-mand home or 'observation centre'. Problems with the after-care of those discharged from borstal should be rectified.

Alec's most important impact on the report can be seen in its conclusions and in particular in the lengthy section dealing specifically with borstals. In addition to his input the committee had heard compelling evidence from Barker about the turnaround at Aylesbury and from Methven about the beneficial effects of letting his lads work outside the walls and attend evening classes at the local college. As a result, the report not only proclaimed the borstal system a success, it recommended a considerable expansion 'to give more young offenders the advantage of this form of training in place of imprisonment'. Echoing Alec's criticism of Portland's prison setting as hindering the development of training, despite the ingenuity of the staff, it stated that borstal training had been 'handicapped by being started in old prison or institutional buildings', and recommended that 'special buildings be erected for future borstal institutions'. It also agreed with him that in all cases the length of sentence should be three years and that the statutory definition of suitability should be altered so that the need for training rather than established criminal propensity should have greater prominence, and that 'commitment for training in a borstal institution' should be substituted for 'sentenced to detention under penal discipline'.[10] Finally, it recommended that magistrates be given the power to commit directly to borstal, obviating the need for a period of prison remand pending committal by quarter sessions or assize judges.

Important as the committee had been, its recommendations, so many in accord with what Paterson wanted, did not lead to immediate legislative action.[11] The Home Office could not make provision for such an increase in the borstal population as envisaged. There was no money for further borstals, not even for a fourth to relieve current congestion. Nor was there funding for 'observation centres'. All that could be done was, in 1931, to move the boys' prison to Wormwood Scrubs where 'stars' were housed, and the risk of contamination would be reduced. In a circular the Home Secretary urged courts to avoid imprisoning young offenders if an alternative could be found, but exhortation was not legislation.[12] Given that the only custodial alternative to short-term imprisonment

10 Cicely Craven denounced the new designation as camouflaging borstal's penal character (*HJ*, 2/2 (May 1927), p. 105.
11 Some were enacted in the 1933 Children and Young Persons Act, others, including those relating to borstal, in the 1948 Criminal Justice Act. In March 1928 the Home Secretary did, however, reconstitute the Advisory Committee on Probation under Sir Vivian Henderson to consider after-care as well as probation. Alec was one of the six former members reappointed (TNA, HO45/16204).
12 TNA, HO45/20947.

was three years in borstal, worries were expressed that such lengthy detention was too drastic for minor offences. While adolescents continued to be sent to prison, the committee's report did, however, give the borstal system a considerable boost, and as judges increasingly imposed borstal detention the call for more institutions was eventually heeded.

Also in 1927, Alec appointed Basil to membership of the visiting committee for Feltham borstal. While at Wandsworth, Henriques, finding that Jews went unclassified, had put the problem to the Commissioner, who 'of course did his best to help'. And help he did. Jewish cases were soon graded, as a result of which some were sent to Camp Hill, some to Rochester, but most to Feltham. Henriques was to take charge of those visiting there. Alec conveyed the Commissioners' gratitude 'for the patient and methodical way' in which he and his colleagues had dealt with the Jewish boys. He only wished 'that for every 65 boys of the Christian faith there was another B.L.Q. Henriques to attend to their needs'.[13]

Three years later, on 22nd July 1930, Alec was called to give evidence before the House of Commons Select Committee on Capital Punishment which, after lobbying by such redoubtable worthies as Margery Fry, had been set up by Ramsay MacDonald's minority government. The chairman was the Presbyterian minister and Labour MP, the Revd James Barr. That a clergyman should chair a Commons committee and that a weighty part of a Commons report should be on 'scriptural considerations' is indicative of the central role religion played in the history of hanging.[14] Indeed one prominent witness was Alec's old friend, William Temple, by then Archbishop of York and a vocal opponent of the death penalty. The report's theological sections were drafted by Barr and underpinned by his biblical and patristic expertise.

Alec had been asked to testify because of his wide experience of those who were sentenced to death or life imprisonment, and his extensive knowledge of how other countries dealt with murderers. He had witnessed the infliction of both capital and corporal punishment.[15] As a leading exponent of the rehabilitative ideal he might have been expected to oppose a punishment redolent of vengeance and devoid of all such potential. It hung like a pall over the entire prison estate, casting a shadow over all reformatory efforts to such an extent that 'the possibility of having to deal with an execution' discouraged 'the type of men and women

13   Loewe, *op.cit.*, pp. 81f.
14   See Harry Potter, *Hanging in Judgment: Religion and the Death Penalty from the Bloody Code to Abolition* (London, 1993).
15   *Over the Walls*, p. 2.

whom we want to see in the prison service from entering it', and meant that some recruits refused promotion to avoid having to participate in something they abhorred. The Howard League made precisely this point to the select committee, asserting that it was 'difficult to reconcile the existence in a prison of the execution shed and reformative systems of training for citizenship'. For them the very pinnacle of penal reform was cutting the rope.[16] It was corrosive of any rehabilitative purpose. Yet Paterson, while having reservations about capital punishment, 'on humanitarian grounds', did not support abolition. His reasoning was unusual, a result of his own knowledge of the effects of lengthy imprisonment.

In a written submission, and in answers to questions, he argued for retention, mainly because the alternative was worse.[17] He gave a brief nod to deterrence, the usual rationale. While the death penalty did have a deterrent effect on professional criminals who killed to avoid detection, it had none on what he called 'incidental'[18] or 'first-offence' murderers whose ire was directed at a specific individual but who were not in other respects criminals. For those reprieved a worse fate awaited: fifteen to twenty years in a convict prison, a 'monastery for men who have not chosen to be monks'. There, murderers, with little to lose and much to gain by escaping, must be constantly watched and subjected to such surveillance and other constraints as to 'cramp free movement and make life small'. Despite 'the ameliorative conditions which have of recent years been introduced into our English prisons', he had seen 'a definite deterioration among men serving a long sentence of imprisonment', and doubted 'whether an average man can serve more than ten continuous years in prison' without deteriorating. 'Whatever means of education, stimulation and recreation may be employed', only 'a superman' could 'survive twenty years of imprisonment with character and soul intact'. On purely humanitarian grounds he concluded that 'confinement in the twilight of prison life' for such a time was 'worse than death itself'.[19]

He rejected the simplistic resort to the experience of other countries since 'there is no ideal prison system that will fit the temperament of every race – nor are the same forms of punishment applicable to all people.' Some countries imposed shorter sentences but prolonged periods of solitary confinement; others

16   Potter, *op.cit.*, pp. 182f; Bailey (2019), pp. 11f.
17   *Evidence taken before the Select Committee on Capital Punishment*, pp. 484–495.
18   In parts of the transcript a typographical error rendered this as 'accidental murderer', an even more bizarre term.
19   John Stuart Mill had said the same and to similar effect during a Commons debate on capital punishment in April 1868 (PD [Commons] 3rd series, vol.cxci, cols.1047–1055). Phelan, a reprieved murderer, sympathised with Alec's view, but was glad to be alive, having survived his thirteen-year incarceration relatively unscathed (p. 162). Another who served twenty years with 'character and soul' improved, at least in Alec's opinion, was Harold Jones (*infra.*).

resorted to exile on some 'devil's island'. England should never follow suit. He alluded to his experience of the penal colony on the Andamans where prisoners could take their wives with them, or get married, while they were serving their sentences. The Boy Scouts troop on the islands consisted entirely of the children of criminals. This was a possible solution, but he acknowledged that there were insuperable difficulties in implementing it in England.

In short, unless and until satisfactory alternatives could be provided or no life sentences of more than ten years be imposed, then the death penalty for murderers was preferable to prolonged imprisonment. It was 'a far more humane thing to allow [a murderer] to take that part of him which was good and pure into the next world than to keep him for twenty or thirty years and kill that good in him'. Discordantly, he put forward two 'constructive suggestions': that the number of 'first-offence murderers' respited be greatly increased; and a period of abeyance be essayed. How he reconciled these proposals, which would lead to an increase in the prison population serving very lengthy sentences, with his earlier argument that such sentences were inhumane is unclear.

Like their leader, most members of the prison service called to give evidence – doctors, chaplains, governors – supported retention, particularly to deter those tempted to use firearms, but with modifications or gradations. Alec's contribution was generally recognised as being the most influential of all and was a blow to the abolitionists. In the event, although a majority report recommending a five-year suspension of the death penalty was published, it came to nothing when the Labour government fell.

Young offenders were one end of the spectrum of concern for the Commissioners. At the opposite end were 'habitual criminals'. The 1908 Prevention of Crime Act had introduced two new sentences relating to these non-identical twins: borstal detention for young delinquents and preventive detention for 'old lags'. In 1931 the focus was turning on those in the middle: persistent offenders between the ages of twenty-one and thirty, and those over thirty whom it was undesirable or impracticable to indict as 'habitual criminals'. How to deal with them?

Given his expertise and facility at exposition, it was hardly surprising that Alec was called to give evidence before the Departmental Committee on Persistent Offenders. This was set up in April 1931 under the chairmanship of Sir John Dove-Wilson, and both the other Prison Commissioners, Maxwell and East, were members. The counterpart of the Committee on Young Offenders held a few years earlier, it was concerned with that minority of relatively youthful repeat offenders whose criminal propensities had not been checked by incarceration. The worry was that the current custodial regime caused 'progressive deterioration by habituating offenders to prison conditions, which weaken rather than strengthen their characters'. If after release they re-offended then all the expenditure and effort exerted in catching, trying and imprisoning them had been wasted. After holding thirty-nine meetings, examining sixty-six witnesses and visiting convict and local prisons, a borstal, and Camp Hill, the preventive detention prison, it produced its report thirteen months after being appointed.[20]

For Alec the committee provided yet another stage upon which he could declaim his well-rehearsed lines and reiterate some of the arguments he had used when writing his 1925 'Scheme'. He would not divorce the subject at hand from the overarching framework of penal policy. In short, prisons should be replaced with 'Training Centres' and 'Places of Detention', probation expanded, and restitution orders and attendance centres introduced.

He reassured the members that the problem of recidivism was 'small, diminishing, and not incapable of resolution'. In 1909 there had been a daily average of 2,500 recidivists in the convict prisons, while in 1929 there were only 1,200. In the local prisons the decrease was even more dramatic, falling from 111,000 to 27,000 in the same period. Probation, industrial and reformatory schools and, of course, borstals, by draining the swamp, had contributed to this decline. The provision of decent homes, an education that was a proper preparation for life, and regular employment would lead to further reduction. Such persistent offenders as remained, he went on, could be divided roughly into three categories.

Firstly, there were those who chose a life of crime, many of whom were young and might be amenable to reformative treatment. Secondly, there were the weaker characters who drifted into crime because they could not cope with the difficulties of life. Thirdly, there were the pathological for whom medical and psychiatric treatment might be efficacious. In relation to the first group, many youths between sixteen and twenty-one whose previous convictions indicated that they had criminal tendencies were sent to prison for short periods from which they were likely to emerge with their chances of becoming persistent offenders enhanced, instead of to borstals for more prolonged periods of training where those chances would greatly diminish. Appropriate after-care was another factor in rehabilitation since, for many offenders of all ages, punishment began not when they entered prison but when they left. Unless on release they could find employment and be restored to some social status, the chances of relapsing into crime were increased. More contentious were his views on the fate of those in both latter groups who evaded all efforts at reform, remained a menace to society, and were unfit for freedom. For them, he said, only a completely indeterminate sentence was appropriate. If length of detention should be determined by the response to it, then for the unresponsive there could be no other disposal. The recidivist should be 'treated on the merits and demerits

20   For an account of the committee's work, see Bailey (2019), pp. 170–179.

not of the specific offence but of his career and prospect as a whole', a proposal anathema to the judiciary, who condemned it as being grossly disproportionate to the criminality.

The report's conclusions endorsed many of Paterson's submissions. It began, as he hoped, by attaching 'great importance' to the proper use of probation and borstal training for young offenders. For persistent adult offenders, the present system provided neither adequate protection for society nor the sort of treatment required for reform. Of the offenders sentenced repeatedly to short terms of imprisonment, there were some who, if subjected to a substantial term of training, might well respond positively. The judicial authorities should have their powers enhanced to enable them in suitable cases, and subject to proper safeguards, not merely to order a term of imprisonment of such length as was warranted by the offence, 'but instead to order detention of such character and length as seems requisite either for the training of the offender or for the protection of society.' For some – particularly those in the twenty-one to thirty bracket – the object of detention should be reformative training. For others, the main object should be to incapacitate the offender and protect the public. 'But in all cases the objects of detention should be remedial and custodial rather than penal.' The borstal model of a lengthy period of training, and with officers performing similar functions to those of housemasters, was one that should be emulated. Different 'detention establishments' along the lines of the Chelmsford regime, less repressive than prisons, should be provided for each of these two groups. Paterson's desire to abolish all prisons and replace them with 'Places of Detention' and 'Training Centres' proved too radical, but new entities should be constructed for 'training' purposes.[21] What should be abolished was the term 'penal servitude', since there was precious little distinction between it and imprisonment, and there should be only two designations, 'Imprisonment' and 'Detention'. 'Imprisonment' would cover all ordinary sentences up to life sentences; 'Detention' all sentences 'of a tutelary character of either reformative training or public protection'. For none of the few women who might receive such sentences were 'fortresses' required, and converted country houses might be more appropriate. To Alec's satisfaction, the committee had been particularly impressed by the arrangements at Lowdham Grange, where borstal boys had been living in huts while building the new institution. It recommended that public work camps for suitably compliant adults, like those Alec had seen in the United States, should be set up to provide productive

---

21   This was not 'gerrymandering with words' as Rupert Cross would allege (*Punishment, Prison and the Public* [London, 1971], pp. 163ff), but reflected Paterson's desire to take as many as possible out of prisons and train them, admittedly under coercion, in distinctly different institutions. A more valid criticism is that the adoption of the training model led to longer periods of detention than justice warranted.

employment with minimum security. The problem of persistent petty offenders, as intractable as ever, was left unresolved, the proposal that they, along with young adult offenders, should be sentenced to between two and four years detention being unconscionable to the judiciary and the public.

Although some recommendations were implemented in whole or in part, such as young recidivists being put into a 'Special' class in all local prisons, the development of open prisons, and in 1934 the engagement of the psychotherapist, Dr William Hubert, to treat appropriate cases in Alec's third category (mainly sex offenders, homosexuals and arsonists) in Wormwood Scrubs, others were not, or at least not yet.[22] The whole tenor of this 'landmark in English penological thought', however, was an emphatic endorsement of the methods of reformative treatment so long espoused by the Prison Commissioners, and of which Alec was the leading proponent.[23]

A lec had long been concerned about the problem of work for prisoners. In 1923, as a member of the Prisoners' Employment Committee within the department, he had asked an old contact at the Ministry of Labour for advice about the best way of getting prison-made products onto the market. He advised diversification. Slow, if any, progress was made over the next decade. Old prisons were unsuitable for expansion much beyond mailbag-sewing. The unions took umbrage at 'unfair' competition, even at the manufacturing of goods for government departments or the construction, maintenance or repair of prison buildings. Then, with the Depression and cuts in staff numbers, the hours of associated labour were reduced. The problem was acute. If constructive employment was lacking, why would judges inflate sentences for the purposes of non-existent training? In 1932 Sir John Gilmour, the Home Secretary, set up a Departmental Committee on the Employment of Prisoners, known, after its chairman, as the Salmon Committee. Maxwell and Scott were members, and Alec was asked to give evidence. Unsurprisingly, the resultant report largely complied with their concerns.

D uring this period there was hardly any aspect of penal affairs for which Alec's expertise was not mined or upon which his opinion was not sought, at home and abroad. There had also been major changes in Paterson's personal

---

22 Many were incorporated into the 1938 Criminal Justice Bill, and enacted in the 1948 Criminal Justice Act.
23 *EPBS*, p. 302.

FIGURE 22. 3 Christchurch Terrace

life: one subtraction and three additions. On 28th September 1926 his aunt Nellie died while visiting friends in Sussex. Then on Saturday the 23rd of April 1927 Alec, to the astonishment of many of his friends who thought him a confirmed bachelor, married a thirty-year-old secretary, Frances Margaret Baker, the daughter of an Oxford tutor. How they met is not recorded, but it may have been on one of Alec's many sojourns to his *alma mater*. Frank, as she was called, was living with her parents in St Giles. She had a lively manner, and they soon became devoted to each other. They would remain so throughout their married life.[24] The wedding ceremony was performed by H.B. Reiss, the vicar of St James's, Forest Gate, London, but it took place at the university church of St Mary the Virgin. James Baker gave his daughter away and signed the register, along with Alec's siblings, Willis and Dorothy. On the same day Alec made a will leaving everything to his spouse. She was sole executrix, and the will was attested by Willis and Reiss.

The newly-weds initially lived with the Angliss household in Bermondsey, but, wishing to start a family, within a year they bought 3 Christchurch Terrace, a small house in Chelsea. The ground floor held the dining room, with a round table by the window upon which their large marmalade cat would disport himself. Alec's study was at the back. On the first floor was a spacious sitting room and bathroom, and the two bedrooms were on the upper floor. A few yards from their front door was the parish church and just across the road was *The Surprise* public house. Both were well frequented by the Patersons. Nearby in Oakley Gardens lived Sidney Ruck, a friend and colleague. Ruck was director of the Central Association for the Aid of Discharged Convicts and assistant director of the Borstal Association and, at Alec's invitation, would present papers at the International Penal and Penitentiary Congresses held in Prague in 1930 and Berlin in 1935.[25]

Their daughter, Margaret, was born in Chelsea on 29th October 1928. Shortly after the birth Alec confided in John Watson that 'whatever his rank in the Prison Service he had been demoted in his own establishment: "Before I was

24   It is sometimes asserted that Alec Paterson, with his dedication to boys, was homosexual. In all my researches, I have found nothing to substantiate this, and his long and happy marriage would seem to negate it. He was if anything inordinately uxorious. No one claims that Stansfeld, Attlee or Henriques were homosexual, but they too devoted many years to running boys' clubs. Men of that era and class, educated at single-sex boarding schools and Oxbridge colleges, usually felt more at ease with members of their own gender. Men of that era and class, suffused with a desire, and often a Christian compulsion, to serve, found the obvious outlet in working with and mentoring working-class boys and young men. The friendships they forged were undoubtedly deep and lasting, but platonic. That was particularly so, as Alec noted, in the intensity of the trenches when 'pairs of pals always together' were commonplace. He and Tom were known as '*les bons camarades*'. No one at the time thought anything untoward about such associations or expressions of passionate same-sex friendship or love, even when they broke the class barrier.

25   Ruck became secretary of the *New Survey of London Life and Labour* which had been established in 1928 by Beveridge and the governors of the LSE to replicate Booth's great survey and to enable comparisons to be made (Paul Knepper, 'Falling crime rates: What happened last time', *Theoretical Criminology* [2014], pp. 1–18, at p. 5; H. Llewellyn-Smith, 'The New Survey of London Life and Labour', *Journal of the Royal Statistical Society*, 92/4 [1929], pp. 530–558). By 1935 Ruck was the Inspector of Public Assistance Institutions on the London County Council.

FIGURE 23. Alec, Frank and Baby

FIGURE 24. Frank returning home from *The Surprise*

married I was governor. Then I became deputy-governor. Now I am merely a temporary night-patrol.'"[26] The occasion of her baptism in Bermondsey parish church became a double event: Alec was finally confirmed.

Then there was a second birth. When the Prison Commissioners had warned that due to overcrowding a fourth borstal institution would be required, and proposed to build an innovative open borstal where self-discipline would be promoted, Joynson-Hicks had concurred, providing the money was available. In July 1927 he had urged the House of Commons to finance the project, estimated to cost £150,000 over a number of years. It demurred and he had appealed, again unsuccessfully, to public-spirited individuals to provide the money needed. Finally, in 1929, Churchill, by then Chancellor of the Exchequer, despite his doubts about the 'tendency to impose unduly long sentences in the belief that it is so bracing', stepped in with the revised figure of £13,000 required for the first year.[27] Joynson-Hicks, who had lobbied Churchill, told the Prison Commission to 'get on with it at once'. After a search for a suitable location in the East Midlands, an ideal site was located in Nottinghamshire. This was Lowdham Grange and its 340-acre estate. Its price was £15,000. The long-serving Surveyor of Prisons, Lieutenant-Colonel Rogers, drove a hard bargain and persuaded the owners to part with their property for £11,300. On 30th April 1930 the sale was completed.[28] The progress of borstals seemed assured.

26   Watson (1969), p. 72.
27   TNA, HO45/16224/512613/7; Bailey (1987), pp. 228f.
28   Jeremy Lodge, *Lowdham Grange. Borstal!* (Nottingham, 2016), p. 49. On 27th June 1935 Henry Rogers, after a tenure of twenty-eight years, retired.

CHAPTER 13

THE TRANSFORMATION OF BORSTALS: 1922–1930

Bars and bones and bricks and brain
Build the home of tears and pain.
Jim Phelan

If the institution is to train lads for freedom, it cannot train them in an
atmosphere of captivity and repression.
Alexander Paterson

Paterson exaggerated when he told a friend that he had found borstal 'little more than a boys' prison' and re-founded it on educational lines. In truth he would build on his predecessor's work. Evolution, not revolution, even though the evolution was rapid and the transformation considerable. As borstal boys after the Great War were no longer being released directly into the armed forces, the institutions could be thoroughly 'civilianized', the emphasis being on individualised treatment, education and industrial training. It was the means to achieve the end that differed between the borstal system devised by Ruggles-Brise and that developed by Paterson, not so much the end itself, which for both men largely converged: to turn wayward youths into conforming members of industrious working-class society. In Alec's case, however, there was a further aspiration: some working-class boys could become not only working-class leaders but commanders over the 'better-born'. Alec knew that there were 'natural leaders' in every section of society. There should be no social barrier to success or elevation. Merit was what counted or what should count, as he had observed on the Western Front.[1]

---

1   Alec had come to this conclusion in Bermondsey, and was confirmed in it by his wartime experiences. He was 'class-unconscious', evidenced by his promotion of staff from the ranks and in his lifelong friendships with men from very different backgrounds. Tom Angliss, to whom he was devoted, was the son of a coppersmith but would become a chartered surveyor, earning considerably more than

Character-building measures aimed at instilling 'stern and exact discipline' through external controls were replaced by methods aimed at changing attitudes through personal example and developing self-respect and self-discipline.[2] Alec Paterson was Elizabeth Fry reincarnate.[3] Rather than re-founding the system as he boasted, he re-animated it and re-dedicated it to the rehabilitative ideal, taking away the military and disciplinary element and distancing the whole borstal system from the penal. The system as he developed it was 'a reflection, in many ways, of his personality, his experience, and his faith'.[4]

Alec learnt a lesson from the most recent acquisition to the borstal estate: Portland in Dorset. In August 1921, the same month as Ruggles-Brise's resignation, the old convict prison had reopened as the third borstal for boys, although Edward Shortt, the Home Secretary, admitted that had money been no object he would have preferred a custom-built establishment on a different site to this 'great grey stone fortress', frowning 'from its rocky eminence over the English Channel'.[5] Although its convicts had been moved to Dartmoor, phantoms of its past haunted the deserted prison. Sentry-boxes lined its grim walls and 'it was not difficult to imagine that the ghosts of old warders with carbines still kept an alert eye open for escapes.'[6] Apart from a few officers transferred from

---

his mentor. Ruggles-Brise was an aristocrat, Paterson a meritocrat. Thus I disagree with those who think their ends were identical in every respect. Hood (pp. 107–111), for instance, states that 'the idea of "service" *from* the working class was firmly entrenched in the minds of the *bourgeoisie*' and links this with Paterson's injunction to borstal boys to become masters of themselves that they 'may be fit to be the servants *of* others'. But 'service *of*' is not the same as 'service *from*'. For Paterson the service of others was the purpose of life, 'the rent paid for our habitation on earth.' The mastery of self liberated the impulse to serve. Nor was it just the working class who should serve others. All should. All were brothers. Alec did not concur with the class-based sentiments of Colonel Rich. He had him replaced.

2   Evelyn Ruggles-Brise, *The English Prison System* (London, 1921), p. 99; Hood, p. 94. All these principles can be found in *Across the Bridges*, pp. 41–68.

3   There are striking resemblances. Both thought no one irredeemable, both exuded compassion, both exhibited empathetic charisma, both abhorred degradation and neglect, both deprecated contamination and lack of categorisation, both stressed the vital importance of education, employment and after-care, both considered the quality of staff more important than that of buildings, both encouraged volunteer involvement, both travelled extensively to gain insights from others, both yearned for alternatives to imprisonment for children, both considered the Gospel in action the prime means of redemption.

4   H&B, p. 440; J.E. Thomas, 'Policy and Administration', in Louis Blom-Cooper (ed.), *Progress in Penal Reform* (Oxford, 1974), pp. 54–67, at pp. 56f.

5   Watson (1969), p. 65.

6   Benney, pp. 217f.

Rochester, most of the staff were hangovers from the old convict service. Many of the boys sent there were rejects from Rochester or Feltham. Discipline suffered, and corporal punishment and close confinement were both deployed on the unruly. On his first visit as Commissioner Alec found 'ninety lads during their hour of recreation with no less than sixteen officers, all in uniforms, all with truncheons'. Discipline relied 'on force and fear'.[7] The buildings with their iron-barred cells, however well they served their old purpose frustrated their new until the interiors were transformed by the labour and ingenuity of borstal boys.[8] After one boy killed himself and several escaped, public concern was roused by allegations of staff brutality. There were demands for an inquiry. The Home Secretary himself paid a visit. So did Sir Arthur Conan Doyle. Both luminaries were reassured.

The public and the press were not, and their fears went unassuaged until a well-known popular journalist and erstwhile critic, Sydney Moseley, who had been given unfettered access to Portland and the other borstals, published his reassuring vindication of them, *The Truth About Borstal*, in 1926. Many of the evils reported in the press had either been exaggerated or had been ameliorated. 'New methods and new men' had transformed the old system into something staggeringly different. Many of the criticisms and suggestions he did make – such as closing down the borstal allocation wing at Wandsworth and bringing in more outsiders as housemasters – had already been made by Alec himself. A convert's case for a more reformatory borstal system unshackled from its penal past was even more convincing than a Commissioner's cleverly crafted articles on 'Borstal Lads' in *The Times*.[9] Welcome in the sceptics, make converts of them and use their condemnations and recommendations to force the pace of change and confirm its direction: that was Alec's way, and it worked. Moseley even reproduced the Commissioner's exhortatory Christmas letter (published in Feltham's magazine, *The Weathercock*, and signed 'Yours till the trains stop, A. Paterson') 'as an illustration of the altered official attitude which, if properly applied, should go far to change borstal from place of punishment to an arena of reform'.[10] Quite! Under Paterson's nurturing the prestige of borstals was growing.

7   'How England Handles the Young Offender', *Proceedings of the Annual Congress of the American Prison Association* (1939), pp. 149–157, at p. 156.
8   Clayton, pp. 55f. Clayton was deputy-governor as the transformation took place. He thought Portland 'a perfect example of how things should not be done.' He had personal experience of borstal failures when he was assaulted by a youth serving a life-sentence for murdering an officer in Rochester. Clayton refused to report this incident, saving the lad a flogging (pp. 122f.).
9   4th, 5th, 6th August 1925.
10   Moseley, pp. 50, 67, 77f, 164.

Even Portland's atmosphere improved if its effectiveness remained in doubt. Sixteen-year-old Mark Benney, who was there in 1926, wrote that, despite its prison-like appearance and his first impression that 'the far-famed borstal system was no more than a re-organized prison system', the atmosphere of Portland was different. 'The oppressive sense of social disapprobation was several degrees removed. In prison one is always intensely aware of the world beyond the walls and therefore aware of one's criminality. In borstal you could frequently forget both.' On the other hand, while reviving his 'schoolboy values of fairplay and team-spirit' and eradicating 'resentment from [his] criminal attitude', borstal did nothing to dispel his attraction to crime. Indeed, it equipped him for it by building up his physique and giving him the opportunity to study engineering and chemistry, thereby enhancing his skills as a safe-blower.[11] John Fletcher, who went there in 1933 when Henry Scott was governor, found it far less harsh than Durham, and noted that 'the staff were picked for the job, they were youngish or out of the army and specially trained.' Despite living 'a military life', gangs proliferated, and, he concluded, 'everyone gets out of borstal worse.'[12] One who did not, because he could not, was Billy Hill, who, by the age of sixteen when he was sentenced to borstal, was untameable, let alone untrainable. In 1927, after three months breaking stones at Wandsworth reception centre, he was allocated to Portland. Put to work carrying baskets of stones up a steep quarry face, or harnessed to a truck which he then had to pull along each night, to prevent infection iodine was applied to the cuts and sores on his back. After an escape during which he committed an aggravated burglary, he was sent back to borstal to be whipped and subjected to nine months' hard labour. The Home Office dispatched a birch – three-and-a-half feet of twigs tied together into a bundle into which a handle of similar length was fitted – for the punishment. It was first soaked in brine to make it more pliable and then applied to the bare backside of the boy. His wounds dressed, he was sent back to pounding stones or, worse, evil-smelling bones into powder, all the while confined in a cramped cage-like structure. He would later give his professional opinion of this Fagan's kitchen. There could be no better academy for breeding hardened criminals. If a boy was lacking in essential criminality on arrival that deficiency would soon be made up; if he had a 'spark of honesty' it would be snuffed out; 'if there was a remote hope that he might degenerate into an ordinary dull citizen' it would be 'killed stone dead'.[13]

---

11   Benney, pp. 217f, 236–239.

12   John Fletcher, *A Menace to Society* (London, 1972), pp. 45f.

13   Billy Hill, *Boss of Britain's Underworld* (King's Lynn, 2008), pp. 20–25. Hill was moved to Rochester where, despite having lost all remission, the governor wanted to give him a fresh start which he took, excelling in sports and being top boy in his house. It was to no avail. Had they given him 'six, short, hard months of glasshouse

Paterson had sensed that all was not well, and knew that the Portland model was not one to be emulated. The whole sorry saga merely confirmed his conviction that borstals were not boys' prisons and should not be created in existing or former prisons. He was determined to distance his conception of a completely reformatory system from any penal associations. Within months of his appointment he had done away with the term 'modified borstal' – a prison wing dedicated to borstal-style training to instil 'duty, obedience and self-control' into those serving short sentences – which to him was more like 'modified prison', and replaced it with the more accurate 'Young Prisoners' Classes'.[14] In the longer term he would try to remove all links between borstals and prisons, verbal and physical, and encourage the growth of new establishments 'on modern lines'.

Whereas early borstals represented a quasi-military model of discipline and authority, Paterson has often been accused of remodelling them on 'public-school' lines with their 'muscular Christianity' and 'house' affiliations, and inculcating the middle-class virtues of honesty, integrity, thrift, loyalty, self-reliance, honour and duty.[15] Both the remodelling and the analogy can be pushed too far. Under Ruggles-Brise the House system had already been introduced, and both Waller and Paterson 'were alive to the differences' between public schools and borstals where there was continual supervision, no holidays, and little contact with the outside world, for instance, while insisting that the values inculcated were not middle-class but universal. *Esprit de corps* was not the preserve of the elite, as Paterson had found it in working-class boys' clubs and among the ranks in the army. Borstals were not to be replica public schools, but all that was best in terms of character-building that those schools provided should be incorporated in them for the benefit of the less-privileged youths sent there. Public-school pupils, through team spirit and camaraderie, through loyalty to individuals and houses, through self-discipline and sense of duty, acquired the self-confidence, ingenuity and determination to run an empire. Give such an opportunity to wayward

---

treatment' he might have tried to go straight, or so he said. But that was what he claimed he had had at Portland. It did not work, nor did the more positive approach of Rochester. Before becoming a borstal boy, he was already beyond hope, and yet blamed the institutions for making an animal out of him. Hill was as guilty of self-deceit as he was of self-glamorisation. His account is questionable.

14   Report (1922), p. 10.
15   Bailey (1987), p. 199. Melanie Tebbutt, in 'Questioning the Rhetoric of British Borstal Reform in the 1930s', *Historical Journal*, 63/3 (June 2020), pp. 710–731, goes further, but her whole approach is based on the gripes of one chaplain in one borstal at one period, and is vitiated by her stereotypical assertions about the ethos of both public schools and borstals, her misunderstanding of Paterson's background and beliefs, and her lazy reliance on questionable 'scholarship'.

working-class youths, build up their moral sense along with their physique, imbue them with self-worth and ambition, and they too could go on to higher things. Similarly, there should be no 'caste system' in education, and all should be 'subjected slowly to the unconscious discipline which should be the chief instrument of every educational establishment'. Education in life and literature would go side by side. Borstal boys should be weaned off 'drivel that once enslaved' them, and be introduced to a higher culture of which they had been deprived. They were to be encouraged to explore and discover for themselves, and find the level appropriate to their varying abilities: 'the intelligentsia play chess and the proletariat argue about the Arsenal.'[16] Cultural diversity and civic responsibility, rather than class identity, were inculcated.

Borstal training has been damned as patronising and worse, an attempt to 'prise working-class boys from their indigenous values', but this latter criticism is excessive since 'a concerted assault on proletarian values would hardly have countenanced pigeon-fancying!'[17] Was it paternalistic? To an extent, but good parenting was what so many lads lacked. Paterson viewed his attitude more as fraternal, the big brother helping his younger siblings along life's treacherous way, and helping them stand on their own two feet. He genuinely wanted to bring out the best in the least-privileged, but at the same time he knew what the best should be. It was the same attitude that could be found in officers for their men in the army, or among schoolboys or undergraduates who devoted their holidays to running youth clubs for urban working-class youngsters or soup kitchens for the homeless, just as Paterson had done. In a pamphlet issued by the Prison Commissioners in 1932, following on from his 1925 articles in *The Times*, he asserted that the principles of the borstal system were 'based on the double assumption that there is individual good in each, and among nearly all an innate corporate spirit, which will respond to the appeal made to the British of every sort, to play the game, to follow the flag, to stand by the old ship.' The language is of its time, but fair play, patriotism, loyalty and duty are timeless, if sometimes neglected, virtues.[18] As one working-class youth put it, 'critics of the public school may contend that a better objective could have

16 See the comments by Alec and others on the expansion of the borstal system generated by a memorandum circulated by Waller in 1925 (TNA, PCOM7/540); Paterson, p. 61; *Principles of the Borstal System* (Prison Commission, 1932), pp. 11, 54; Erica Stratta, *The Education of Borstal Boys* (London, 1970), p. 9.

17 Bailey (1987), p. 203.

18 *Principles, op.cit.*, pp. 8f. The armchair jurist, Rupert Cross, found this statement nauseous, 'one of the most pernicious manifestations of the disease of "PLU" (people like us)' (*Punishment, Prison and the Public* [London, 1971], pp. 131f). The dyspeptic Cross was as much a man of the 60s and 70s as Paterson was of the 20s and 30s.

been found; but it cannot be denied that, for all social purposes, its spirit is an immeasurable improvement on the spirit of the panopticon.'[19]

Lads brought up in 'the school of hard knocks' were re-schooled in borstal. They wore shorts and flannel shirts, the games kit of the schoolboy, but were allowed to wear a brown and grey jacket with lapels instead of the more institutional high-collared jacket. They lived in buildings which were designated as 'houses', presided over by 'housemasters', many of whom were scions of public schools and Oxbridge. As 'adjutants' or 'auxiliary officers' housemasters had 'house-captains', chosen by them or sometimes elected by the inmates themselves. On his appointment to the privileged and powerful post Mark Benney 'felt as Hitler must have felt when he became Führer'. The bully may have been brought out in some, but, despite his anachronistic analogy, not in Benney, or so he said. But 'if the object of this distinction was to induce a sense of responsibility, the experiment was singularly unsuccessful', he concluded. According to his account, he carried out his prefectorial duties with sufficient application to retain his post but with insufficient rigour to alienate his peers.[20]

Hard work and strenuous outdoor activities were encouraged so that borstal boys would go to bed healthily tired out after a long day's exertions. Cross-country rambles and camping trips began in 1922. Team games in particular were emphasised, as was inter-house rivalry, culminating in an annual sports day with a cup presented to the winning house. Paterson was to the fore in encouraging this and he himself arranged and refereed matches with outside clubs, including his beloved Bermondsey Boys.[21] Borstal teams would play home and away matches against public schools, while individual athletes would compete against public-school pupils. The captain of a cricket team from Eton told the opposing Feltham side that he envied them for being allowed to smoke, whereas if he were caught smoking he would be thrashed or even expelled. Expulsion would break his parents' hearts whereas their early discharge would delight their parents. Another, 'much annoyed at this display of freedom was overheard to remark "I say what cads!"'.[22] One poignant cricket match was played between the boys in Rochester and those from Howard House in Maidstone prison, where Clayton was by then governor. The latter were either reprieved murderers[23] or those whose offences were so grave that they had been given long sentences of

19   Benney, p. 218.
20   *Ibid.*, pp. 240–243. Benney was made house-captain in 1927 but wrote his account in 1936.
21   Gordon recalled the excitement when Paterson refereed a match at Feltham, and of how he was cheered at tea. He was very popular and 'in Borstal language, "one of the boys"' (pp. 134f, 190f).
22   Vidler, p. 63; Richard Maxwell, *Borstal and Better* (London, 1956), pp. 147f.
23   Harold Jones, a proficient sportsman, was likely one (*infra.*).

penal servitude. With Paterson's warm approval Clayton took eleven of them in a coach to play the Rochester boys. They won. It was confidently predicted that such an ethos was growing among the trainees that the time would soon come when the 'traditions of Borstal would be at least equal to those of Eton and Harrow', and the Borstal 'Blue' engender as much pride as a Varsity Blue.[24]

This too has been depicted as the inculcation of middle-class values and attitudes on working-class boys, but for Paterson those values and attitudes were not class-based but universal: honesty, integrity, self-reliance and self-worth. Working-class youths were as capable and deserving of them as their middle-class peers. These were what he held dear and wanted to impart to others. He did not want derivative clones but self-sustaining individuals. He did not want to bring out the best in them but to enable them to bring out the best in themselves.

At the heart of the system was the recognition of the individuality of all those sent there. Where the prison system in the past had been expected to crush individuality and had prohibited social interaction between the keepers and the kept, Paterson's vision was the reverse: the task was 'not to break or knead [the lads] into shape, but to stimulate some power within to regulate conduct aright, to insinuate a preference for the good and the clean', to make them want to use their lives well 'so that they themselves and not others will save them from waste'.

> [They] are not raw recruits of a conscript army to be arranged neatly in rows according to their physical stature, to be swung rhythmically in a mass across the parade ground to the beat of a drum. Each is a different and difficult problem. It is because they must be handled individually with sympathy, firmness and discernment that those who handle them must be rare individuals. The strength or weakness of the borstal system lies in the strength and weakness of the borstal staff.[25]

Paternalistic or not, for a while, under inspiring leadership and the spirit of eternal optimism, at least for many it gave a fresh start, and cut down recidivism. In a quintessentially English way borstal was a beacon of hope, of which there has been a sad lack in the history of imprisonment.

Paterson knew, however, that he had to reassure the fickle public, whose concern over brutality was matched by its disapproval of 'molly-coddling', that borstals were not Scout camps, and the expense lavished on juvenile delinquents

24   Clayton, pp. 101f; Hood, p. 54. 'Blue boys' were the best behaved of the borstalians and were in their second year, having spent their first in brown clothes, and having passed through all four stages or 'grades'. With the colour came perks, such as having a pipe or going on summer camps. They were frequently given 'staff' jobs in their house and reputedly lived up to the responsibility (Report [1934], p. 61).
25   *Principles, op.cit.*, pp. 12ff.

was justified. For this audience his refrain was that punishment and reform were not antagonistic. Borstal was 'at once more deterrent and more reformative than prison'.[26] It was certainly the latter, but given the many 'graduates' who looked back on their time in borstal with gratitude, it is not obvious that it was the former. To Paterson it did not matter, for it was a distinction without a difference, as the effect of internal reform was the same as external deterrence. Reformed individuals had no desire to re-offend and so no need to be deterred. He was also adept at using the press to advertise success. When prefects from Feltham organised a march-past of the Dover Patrol War Memorial and all the boys gave the 'eyes-right' as they paraded, he made sure that the newspapers were informed and the gesture reported.[27]

To succeed in his endeavours to reduce further the prison population by utilising alternatives, Alec had to win over not just the public and politicians, but the magistrates and judges who imposed the sentences. They seemed to prefer a short, sharp dose of imprisonment for the errant adolescent to a more prolonged period in borstal. For many judges, probation was too soft, and two or three years in borstal for a minor offence meriting two or three months in prison was unjust. Paterson thought otherwise. Probation should be the norm for petty or first offenders; borstal a resort for those likely to become recidivists. Prison and borstal sentences were not comparable. Borstals were not prisons. Borstal training was an opportunity that should not be thrown away. All training took time, and the time it took depended on the individual. Thus, borstal detention should be for a minimum period as punishment and have a maximum extent for training. The sentence should be tailored to the offender and when the offender was fit to return to the community he should be released. Thus, the period in detention need not be justified by the gravity of the offence, although it should never be out of all proportion to that offence.[28]

He assiduously cultivated the magistracy by attending and addressing their meetings, and urging them to divert the young from custody since at present they were doing their best to create more habitual prisoners. He expressed his frustration that they were more difficult to train than borstal boys.[29] He was ever willing, in print or person, to engage the judiciary, whose influence could be decisive, and whose criticisms of borstal had often been scathing. Two instances involving the

26 Cross, *op.cit.*, pp. 36, 130.
27 Forsythe, pp. 181f.
28 Paterson, pp. 63f. He thought minima and maxima should also apply to prison sentences, and that 'incorrigibles' should be detained indefinitely. Jack Gordon thought that borstal sentences were too short to be effective and that the period should be extended to five years (p. 239).
29 However, in the report on the conference of 26th November 1935 (HO45/20084) I can find no reference to Paterson shouting at the assembly as Forsythe asserts (p. 198).

same judge demonstrate his ability to impress potential critics and turn them into staunch allies. The second also illuminates his attitude to corporal punishment.

In the early 1920s Sir Alexander Roche, a High Court judge sitting on the northern circuit, wanted to consult a member of the Prison Commission about a young man of respectable birth and public-school education who had committed a number of burglaries. Despite the fact that he had previously served a prison sentence, the recommendation was for borstal training. It was Alexander Paterson who turned up at the judge's lodgings. They discussed the matter for a considerable time as Roche took some persuading, but at last he was convinced to give the boy a chance. Alec kept him informed of the miscreant's progress. He had behaved well in borstal and had emigrated to one of the Dominions thereafter. 'What immigration restrictions were by-passed', Roche did not know, 'or whether the Prison Commissioner had any knowledge of it', but he was 'not sorry that it happened'.[30]

In 1931 Roche encountered Paterson again, this time in the south. The judge had to sentence a boy under sixteen who had been convicted of a brutal rape of an underage girl. The judge felt that borstal was quite inadequate and that the boy should be whipped. Again, he wanted to consult a Prison Commissioner, and Alec again arrived. He offered to speak to the lad, and when he had done so asked Roche if he was sure of the boy's guilt. When the judge had reassured him on that point, Paterson agreed that the boy must be whipped – not by the birch but by the cat-o'-nine-tails! Under section four of the Criminal Law Amendment Act 1885, the 'cat' could be ordered by an assize court for 'carnal knowledge' of a girl under thirteen by a boy under sixteen. The 'cat' consisted of a short, stout handle to which were attached nine thirty-three-inch cords tipped with lead. It was applied to the bare back. Paterson told Roche that when the boy had been taken down from the triangle to which he had been strapped for the lashing to be administered, he had murmured 'well, I will never do this sort of thing again.'[31]

Efficacious or not, it is hard now to understand why a humanitarian, such as Paterson professed to be, could countenance so barbarous a punishment. Paterson's views on this were at variance with his adherence to reformatory as opposed to retributive measures. Did he really adopt the biblical adage 'thou shalt beat the child with the rod and so deliver his soul from hell', or the secular one 'spare

---

30   HL debates, 28th April 1948, vol.155, cols 504–508. In the case of a man who had reverted to crime only after he lost his job and his wife needed medical treatment, Alec persuaded the judge to reduce a prison sentence of three years to six months and to direct probation to assist him upon release (Leo Page, *The Young Lag* [London, 1950], p. 299).

31   HL debates, 29th April 1948, vol.155, cols 509f; 2nd June 1948, vol.156, col.196. In this Paterson agreed with Joynson-Hicks, who in 1927 had minuted that 'nothing could be better for a lad, if convicted of rape, than whipping' (TNA, HO13403/510865/12).

the rod and spoil the child'? He clearly believed, as did his colleagues, that the occasional use of corporal punishment in prisons for assaults on staff was justified as a deterrent and to prevent unofficial reprisals. It should be retained as a last resort and a diminishing recourse. He also believed that birching, being an ineffective way of dealing with adults generally and young offenders usually, should be largely abolished in prison, but that the courts should retain the power to impose the 'cat' as a sentence in rare instances, the case of the teenage rapist being one.[32] That 'moderate chastisement' was in lieu of custody for young boys may well have influenced him in its favour as the lesser evil. At the time such a stance was in keeping with the views of many of the public, most of the judiciary, the police, prison governors and staff, and even some progressives. Charles Russell thought that flogging for such offences as cruelty to animals was 'a much kinder and more effectual corrective than long-term detention in a school', and Cyril Burt approved of birching as 'a last [and] exceptional resort for some offences and for some offenders'. Many prisoners concurred in flogging's retention for violence towards staff, but wanted its judicial use extended to sex offenders.[33]

Most reformers, however, including members of the Howard League, were abolitionist. So too were a wide variety of others with experience of its imposition. Dr Maurice Hamblin Smith, an experienced prison medical officer, thought that its advocates were motivated by sadistic impulses and its use militated against the effective treatment of offenders.[34] So too did George Scott, the author of *The History of Corporal Punishment*.[35] Triston, a lowly prison officer, was positive that if those who clamoured for the 'cat' were once to see it administered they 'would never again advocate that human beings should be mangled by this barbarous instrument'.[36] On the other hand, Baden Ball, a humane and long-serving chaplain, thought stories of 'the sadistic pleasure taken in his job by the officer wielding the cat-o'-nine-tails' were nonsense, and its brutalising effect on those involved untrue. In his experience staff were as anxious as the prisoner to get it over, and often the lashes were laid on lightly or the flogging was curtailed.[37]

32   TNA, HO45/24535; Report (1929), pp. 9ff; Ruck, pp. 137f. The 1938 *Report of the Departmental Committee on Corporal Punishment* concluded that it was 'a far more certain deterrent for prison offences than for offences against the criminal law (para.72).

33   Charles Russell, *The Problem of Juvenile Crime* (Oxford, 1917), pp. 15f; Cyril Burt, *The Young Delinquent*, 4th edn (London, 1944), pp. 120–123; James Leigh, *My Prison House* (London, 1941), pp. 178ff.

34   'The Case Against Flogging', *The Spectator,* 8th September 1933. Ruck replied in 'Where Flogging is Justified', 15th September 1933. Smith reiterated his argument in 'Corporal Punishment for Cruelty', *HJ*, 4/1 (1st July 1934), pp. 15–18.

35   (London, 1938), pp.xixff, 194–239.

36   H.U. Triston, *Men in Cages* (London, 1938), pp. 189ff.

37   *Prison was my Parish* (London, 1956), pp. 161–166.

Its almost routine nature was illustrated by an account given by Dr Guy Richmond, the Portland medical officer in the 1930s. He had occasion to examine a boy who had been transferred from a local prison where he had been flogged with the 'cat' for assaulting an officer. The doctor found a lump on his breast and feared malignancy. Paterson came at once to investigate, and they concluded that the injury had been caused by the boy's body swinging on the triangle, as a result of which the whip had curved round his back and hit him on the chest. Alec immediately issued instructions that care be taken to ensure that in future the body be so secured as to prevent swinging on the impact of the lash. Writing in 1975, Richmond expressed incredulity that then 'we were able to discuss such details without proclaiming our disgust at such sadistic and revolting practices.'[38]

Judges such as Mr Justice Roche were won over by Paterson's lack of sentimentality and pragmatic realism.[39] They had every reason to have confidence in such a level-headed Commissioner whose judgment was never clouded by compassion. 'Where necessary', Harold Scott observed, 'no one could be more insistent on discipline or order than Alexander Paterson.' The tired label of 'sentimentalist' could not stick to him. Credibility with the judiciary was vital, and paid off.

A dramatic shift in the judicial attitude to borstal training came on 13th June 1932 when the Court of Appeal, in a number of conjoined cases of boys aged between sixteen and nineteen convicted on indictment, substituted borstal sentences for imprisonment. It did so after Baron Hewart, the newly-appointed Lord Chief Justice, requested that Paterson give evidence on the merits of the respective disposals for young people. As the appeal was by leave of the court and the appellants appeared in person without legal representation, it looks as though these rulings were stage-managed by the Lord Chief Justice to send out a strong message to the lower courts that borstal was preferable to prison, even

38   Guy Richmond, *Prison Doctor* (British Columbia, 1975), p. 35. A similar incident, relating to the birching of a nine-year-old boy left with weal marks on his stomach, led to the setting up of the Departmental Committee on Corporal Punishment in 1937. Two of the Prison Commissioners (Scott and East) gave evidence favouring retention for prison mutiny and serious assaults on officers, but wanted it abolished in borstals. It was rarely used and was not essential in the maintenance of discipline. Alec was not invited to contribute but he concurred, having become convinced that it was not justified for young offenders. The committee recommended the abolition of corporal punishment in the courts and borstals, but its retention 'as the ultimate sanction for serious offences against discipline in prisons'.

39   Roche would remain a great admirer of Paterson and of borstals, telling the House of Lords that the extraordinary success rate was 'a marvellous testimony of the system' (HL Debates, vol.131, col.349 (29th March 1944).

for first offenders.[40] Several other appellate judgments ruled that the term of detention, no matter how minor the offence, should be three years, just as Paterson had argued. Two years was needed for training and a year's remission was 'an important incentive to effort'.[41] The more judges appreciated that no-nonsense borstals under a no-nonsense Commissioner were striking at what were thought to be the root causes of youthful delinquency, the more miscreants they would send there. Borstal disposals increased year by year.

It was a mark of Paterson's initial success that by 1925 there was 'a general rise in prestige for borstal training.' The public and press were reassured. The judiciary, by and large, were being won over, and the few dissidents cajoled into submission.[42] Expansion could begin. Paterson would transform the borstal estate in number as well as nature, with a diversity of provision to cater for all, from the 'rougher types' to the 'trustworthy boys'. There was to be unity of purpose but no uniformity in means.[43]

To succeed he also needed the right subordinate staff. As in prisons, chaplains were integral to the regime and had the vital role of trying to make religion pivotal to the many youngsters who entered borstal with only the most basic understanding of Christianity or of other faiths. Every boy, however rudimentary his commitment, had to attend services. Reformation and religion were conjoined twins. As priests, chaplains took services and administered the sacraments; as preachers they enjoined repentance and rebirth; as pastors they befriended their charges and provided an ever-open ear and ever-empathetic counsel. As Bill Cottrell, the popular senior chaplain at Wormwood Scrubs, put it, they found 'great satisfaction' in helping others 'to get a grip on themselves and to give them courage and hope for the right ordering of their lives'. On the whole they were highly regarded.[44] And if effective, Paterson would defend them. On one occasion he refused to dismiss an unconventional padre who sometimes said things that ran counter to discipline and good order, but whose preaching touched the most obdurate. The pastoral role, the listening ear, was what Alec most admired and valued. When asked what he considered to be

40 *The Times*, 14th June 1932. One of the seven cases was reported: *R v Rankin*, 23, Criminal Appeal Reports (1932), 200. Hewart was educated at Manchester Grammar School and University College Oxford, and had been a prominent Liberal politician before his elevation.

41 *The Times*, 4th August 1925.

42 Hood, pp. 35f. Paterson was also on friendly terms with another influential legal figure: Sir Archibald Bodkin, the Director of Public Prosecutions.

43 'How England Handles the Young Offender', *op.cit.*, pp. 153ff.

44 W. Cottrell, 'The Prison Chaplain', *HJ*, 4/4 (July 1937), pp. 403–407. Even Louis Edward, who painted a fairly dismal picture of his borstal experience, depicted the chaplain in a favourable light (*Borstal Lives* [London, 1939], pp. 258ff, 318).

'the most potent factor in the betterment of an inmate, in typical British officer fashion he snapped out: "a good chaplain".'[45] He recalled 'a very truculent adolescent in a borstal institution on whom no form of punishment, dietary or corporal, had any effect.' The Commissioner asked a Canadian friend of his to intervene:

> The padre stayed for two hours in that cell with the impossible boy. Afterwards the lad worked hard, went back to his House and became a good leader or prefect. Like any amateur I wanted to know how the expert had done the trick. So I asked the lad what it was that the padre had said that had altered his attitude, and he answered simply, 'It was not anything he said, but something he was going to say; but he stopped short and said nothing'.[46]

Conversely, when a chaplain had cancelled a service without notifying the governor, Paterson advised the latter to write to the bishop about it, which he did to good effect. Good chaplains would not only minister to the trainees or prisoners but to the staff, as he explained to the Archbishop of York in an exchange of correspondence about their role and status:

> One of the greatest values of a chaplain is the spirit he breathes among the staff. In a quiet and unobtrusive way he gives them a spirit which they unconsciously infuse into the prisoners. I remember ... a fairly stiff prison officer [observing] 'the discipline in this prison has improved out of all knowledge since the new chaplain came'. It was interesting to find him congratulating the chaplain ... as a disciplinary asset.

Alec took the recruitment of full-time chaplains very seriously and a selection board was always convened in his own office when applicants were being interviewed.[47]

Other members of staff had a pastoral role to play. Matrons were a novelty when they were introduced into borstals in 1923. Ideally, they became mother-figures to the boys in this very masculine environment. They too were popular. Nor were disciplinary officers left out of the grand scheme. Rather, they were integral to it. As Alec told his colleagues:

> The House officer has become a very important part of the borstal system. He and his colleagues are members of the house board which meets every week to discuss questions of promotion etc. During part of the day he is in charge of the new boys who are cleaning the house, and during part of the

---

45   Joseph Schlarman, *Why Prisons?* (Illinois, 1937), p. 36.

46   Gordon, pp. 136ff; Alexander Paterson, 'The Prison Chaplain', *The Spectator*, 17th July 1947, p. 11.

47   Grew, p. 168; Letter of 30th December 1938 in Ruck, pp. 125–128. Paterson also explained to Temple that in order to prevent clergy becoming stale and to dissuade them from outstaying their usefulness chaplains were no longer appointed as pensionable civil servants.

day he is the sole officer in the House where 70 or 80 lads are having meals or playing games etc. He is therefore a man of parts and is chosen specially for this work, although, of course, he gets no additional pay for it. It frequently happens that after a man has been a House Officer for two or three years it is wise to remove him from those duties as he is apt to get a little stale, and to transfer him to a working party, bringing in another officer to take over his House duties and to gain experience.[48]

Ordinary prison officers were no longer ordinary, nor did they look the part. Uniforms were abolished in 1924, and custodial staff donned sports jackets and flannels, along with the dark blue, light blue and brown 'borstal tie', 'the co-lours of Oxbridge and Dartmoor'.[49] A gradual approach had been adopted in securing the transformation. Uniformed staff at one institution were asked to wear civilian clothing on weekends. When they saw that this change in dress 'brought no lessening of authority, it was easy to persuade them to abandon their uniforms permanently'. Officers at other borstals followed suit. This civil-ianisation indicated a transformation in their ethos as well as their role.[50]

Their ethos was that of a vocation and not just of a job. Staff were being professionalised in the highest sense. Character was key. Paterson thought that individuals with strong personalities and indomitable spirit, carefully select-ed, thoroughly trained, and dedicated to their vocation could overcome the shortcomings of anachronistic buildings, as it was 'men and not buildings' who would 'change the hearts of misguided lads'. To a large extent he was right, as he had been in Bermondsey when praising the dedicated teachers who com-pensated for the shortfall in educational provision. Prison officers and borstal housemasters alike should be adequately remunerated, but money must not be their motivation.

> Better an institution that consists of two log-huts in swamp or desert, with a staff devoted to their task, than a model block of buildings, equipped with-out thought of economy, whose staff is solely concerned with thoughts of pay and promotion.[51]

---

48 TNA, PCOM9/74.

49 The headmaster of a leading public school twice wrote complaining that the tie bore a resemblance to that of his former pupils, and implying that it would be de-meaning for them to be confused with borstal officers. Paterson took no notice of the first missive but replied to the second, assuring the headmaster that the Com-missioners had no objection to his old boys continuing to wear those colours (Wat-son [1969], pp. 71f).

50 William Healy and Benedict Alper, *Criminal Youth and the Borstal System* (New York, 1941), p. 62, n.6; Grew, p. 22.

51 Grew, p. 19.

Their role was the crucial one of 'strong men' helping, teaching and training 'weak boys', and they needed to have a triptych of qualities: 'a wise head, a kind heart, a firm hand.' They were to be moulders, not breakers. As the first of the borstal rules set down, they were to influence their young charges 'through their own example and leadership and by enlisting their willing co-operation'. They were a combination of 'mad saint, father confessor and Aunt Sally'.[52] All the staff, not just pastoral and vocational but custodial as well, were supposed to get to know their charges and use their initiative, a *volte face* from the normal role of the prison officer. Jack Gordon, who was at Feltham in the early 1920s, could 'not help admiring the borstal staff', and knew that they were following in Paterson's steps in 'revolutionizing lads' minds' by trusting them and leading them.[53]

After-care, the second part of training, was as significant as the first 'for it is not always easy to control a lad who is tasting again the wine of free life'. Alec insisted on integrating the two elements. From 1923 housemasters were given secondments to the Borstal Association so that they could learn its methods and review the progress of those who had already passed through its hands.[54]

In March 1929 Paterson, while busy with the annual Imperial Prison Course for overseas prison officials, proposed to his colleagues that principal officers in borstal institutions should be abolished. Of the three grades of 'subordinate officers', the principal officer was in the middle, below chief officers, and above officers. They were unnecessary and an anomaly in what had become 'much more of an educational institution than a place of detention' and in which 'the House' under a Housemaster was the focal point.[55] On this occasion Alec did not get his way and principal officers survived in the borstal system, although less in a supervisory capacity than as acting as assistants to housemasters.

This came on the cusp of the Great Depression which could have stifled all further attempts at reform on the simple grounds of economy. Yet it did not. Indeed, the high unemployment that ensued, while being a curse for discharged prisoners, proved a blessing for the prison service. It was looking for outstanding individuals, and with five to ten thousand applicants for the 120 vacancies to be filled each year, it was spoilt for choice.

Paterson knew that above all the success of his venture depended on leadership, leadership after his own image. Borstal governors who adhered to the more military model and strongly opposed 'the soft, sloppy, "sob-stuff"' that

---

52   Bernard Marchant, 'What is a Housemaster?', in Jack Reynolds and Ursula Smartt, *Prison Policy and Practice* (HMP Leyhill, 1996), pp. 4–5.

53   Grew, p. 24; Gordon, pp. 134f.

54   Alexander Paterson, 'Borstal Lads, III', *The Times*, 6th August 1925; *Principles of the Borstal System* (1932), p. 16; Hood, p. 183.

55   TNA, PCOM9/74.

was creeping in and which, in their view, was ruining the chances of making borstals effective as places of reform, were shunted off to prisons where Paterson thought their talents would be better utilised.[56] In their place he appointed a new breed of what he thought would be inspirational leaders. Some were young Oxford men who, before the war, had experienced life in Bermondsey or the East End. Some were fellow members of Toc H. Others he met by chance and encouraged to join in an idealistic venture. Grew was one. David Waddilove was another, but as he had no relevant experience, he was sent to spend time with the OBM before his first posting as assistant governor at Sherwood borstal. These young men were chosen by Paterson 'less as trainees than as disciples in a lay ministry of penal reform'. All would carry his vision of a decent, humane and reformatory prison service to whatever institution in which they were called to serve. In turn these early 'disciples' recruited like-minded subordinates. Paterson's unique contribution was not just in making changes but 'in finding and inspiring the men through whom the change was to work'.[57]

And not just men. In 1923 Alec poached a former colleague at the Ministry of Labour to be governor of Aylesbury girls' borstal and women's prison. This was the redoubtable Lilian Barker, a short, stocky, middle-aged woman with an exuberant energy, a huge personality and a stentorian voice. With an aversion to make-up, she wore a tweed suit, and kept her 'iron grey Eton crop' firmly encased in a pork-pie hat. 'Charming, kind, and cheerful,' she was 'possessed of great sympathies and a wonderful personality.' Always very direct, she could also come over as abrupt, or even abrasive. She once agreed that she had been called 'the rudest lady in the land', but added with a laugh, 'I'm not sure they meant lady, either.'[58] Importantly, she had a lot of relevant experience of social and educational work, and was an able administrator. Equally important, although common sense was more her sacred text than Holy Scripture, she was a devout Christian with a strong sense of duty and decided and vocal views on imprisonment: it should be curative not punitive. She took the job despite suffering a drastic drop in salary. She realised its importance, relished the prospect of working with Alec again, and knew that she would be given a free rein. He knew she would be 'mother, father, brother, sister, uncle and aunt to everybody'.[59]

Since its inception Aylesbury borstal had been housed in a disused institution for inebriates within the women's convict prison. It had been hoped to move it to buildings outside the austere walls, but this had never

56   Rich, pp. 96f, 105–108.
57   Hood, p. 109.
58   Cicely McCall, *Looking Back from the Nineties* (Norwich, 1994), p. 48; Gordon, p. 246; Gore, p. 100.
59   Gore, p. 166.

happened. Although prison and borstal existed side by side, were under one governor, and shared staff, there was no contact between the adult women – 'star-class' convicts convicted of murder or infanticide and others serving sentences of preventive detention – and the youngsters. All the girls deemed suitable for borstal disposal could be accommodated there and further provision would be made later, if needed.[60] Given that Aylesbury was the sole girls' borstal, classification was impossible, so first offenders were lumped in with recidivists, and soft girls with tough. Alec thought them so rough that if you struck them sparks would fly off. Barker's two predecessors had been rigid disciplinarians and the regime they had created was repressive, with too easy a resort to solitary confinement and even handcuffs and straight-waist-coats, as the report of the Prison Commissioners for 1921–1922 revealed. Those sentenced to two to three years in borstal for an offence that would merit two to three months in prison expected better than this. Resentment was building up among the inmates who, if they were united in anything, it was in hatred of the staff.[61]

Into this stepped Miss Barker, quite prepared to make an immediate impact and pick up the pieces thereafter. On the wall of her office she hung a plaque upon which she had inscribed words that encapsulated both her credo and that of Alec Paterson:

> O do not pray for easy lives,
> Pray to be stronger men and women.
> Do not pray for tasks equal to your powers
> Pray for powers equal to your tasks.[62]

Her methods 'were those of her generation and depended entirely on personality'. Finding the staff dispirited and the girls regimented, she cajoled the former to treat their charges as individuals, and gave the latter greater responsibility, the whole point of borstal training. Believing that the will to lead a good and useful life could never manifest itself in the unhappy and unfulfilled, she improved the quality of the food, the cut of the clothing, and the decor of the cells. Too much, too soon. The 'old guard' among the staff felt that their previous efforts were deprecated. They did not want to be pioneers in a 'wonderful experiment' but to go back to the old regimented ways. Gradually, by dint of personality, she won them over, if not to her way of thinking, at least to carrying out her plans, since she would brook no dissent. She cared deeply for her staff, and would let no one other than herself criticise them. They got used to her 'mood swings, the

---

60   Lionel Fox, *The Modern English Prison* (London, 1934), pp. 189f.
61   Gore, pp. 116f, 124. Moseley (pp. 94–105) referred to what he had heard and contrasted it with what he saw of Barker's 'Amazing Aylesbury'.
62   Scott, p. 92.

furious condemnation one moment and the slap on the back the next'. She was also kind to, and supportive of, the adult prisoners under her charge.[63]

The girls were harder to bring into line. Kindness could be interpreted as weakness. Reform and a relaxation of rules were repaid by revolt, when a number of girls on successive nights 'smashed-up' their rooms, an activity which had 'an addictive quality akin to cutting themselves'.[64] Others, having been given more freedom and trust, ran off. The Borstal Association, while noting that under Barker Aylesbury 'was alive – moving, not a valley of dead bones as so many girls' institutions, as contrasted with boys', seem to be', concluded that the changes had produced 'slackness', and found that the regime as it was currently constituted was unsuited to the needs of the inmates, many of whom seemed 'deficient in physique, intelligence and will-power'.

Barker took these comments to heart, learnt from her mistakes, and changed her approach to training – in style but not in purport. 'When I began there', she told the Young Offenders Committee, 'I was far too sentimental and soft; I find now that I get far better results from the girls ... by having a really strict discipline but with really a great deal of affection behind it.'[65] Her sentiments echoed those of her 'esteemed friend', Colonel Rich, who decanted many of his 'star-class' girls from Walton to Aylesbury 'to work out their salvation'.[66] Punishments, usually the loss of some privilege or spending time in the Spartan cells on 'D' Block inside the old prison, became more severe but were often imaginative and invariably just. They did not engender resentment, and rewards there were aplenty. Within a year it was a happy place. Flowers had grown in abundance, behaviour was good, and the staff understood how to go about their jobs. The purpose of training remained the same: to keep girls away from crime and to prepare them for the respectable womanly role they should lead on release, either as servants, shop assistants or housewives. They should have a place but know their place. This would be the Achilles heel of the borstal system: sometimes it incorporated assumptions and inculcated values that dated.

As the 'house system' had never been introduced into Aylesbury, there was a lack of the *esprit de corps* commonly found in boys' borstals.[67] Borstal girls were in any case somehow different from borstal boys. They were less enthusiastic, less able and less tractable, or so they were perceived. Consequently, they

---

63   McCall, *op.cit.*, p. 49. This half-admiring assistant housemistress also noted an occasional 'sadistic trait' which could produce 'a highly unstable atmosphere' (p. 51). A more admiring and longer-serving one did not (Mary Size, *Prisons I Have Known* [London, 1957], pp. 45ff).

64   Gore, p. 128f.

65   Quoted in Bailey (1987), p. 209.

66   Rich, p. 150.

67   Gore, pp. 71f; Vidler, p. 34.

did not benefit from borstal in the way boys did, or seemed to do. Barker did her best to change that. Keeping them constantly occupied in improving pursuits was key. Organised games became integral to the regime, as well as group discussions about the Christian faith and moral issues. Farm work was made readily available, along with training in the sort of skills appropriate for domestic service: laundering, gardening, cooking, needlework. But there were also brambling expeditions, picnics, holidays to Littlehampton, fancy dress parties, New Year's balls. Rapport between staff and their charges improved enormously, and Barker herself inspired both loyalty and devotion among her trainees. She took pains to get them good positions on discharge, told them they could write to her for advice, and took them back if they were recalled. She was a friend and confidante. She would invariably end her letters to them with 'always your friend', and she meant it. As one of her former charges appreciatively put it, 'we started as prisoners living in a prison and we ended as citizens living in a community. Miss Barker gave us responsibility and made us feel we had something to contribute; even expected us to make our own decisions.'[68] With her no-nonsense approach and constant refrain of 'my girls', she was a Miss Jean Brodie in her prime.

Alec Paterson took a great interest in Aylesbury and visited frequently. He and Lilian were two of a kind. Both were mavericks, both were extroverts, both were doers. They saw each other's faults all too clearly, and engaged in gentle rivalry, he fighting for the boys and she for the girls. Yet they respected each other's integrity and dedication. She could not help liking him for 'he had no "side", and was not concerned about his dignity.' On one of his visits when a tennis match was in progress, he wanted 'to have a bash'. As there were no shoes large enough for his feet, 'the Commissioner played in a pair of tartan socks with a hole in the toe.'[69]

In 1935 Harold Scott, another regular and appreciative visitor to Aylesbury, invited Barker to become an Assistant Commissioner with responsibility for women's prisons as well as for Aylesbury borstal. She was reluctant to take up the post – and her young charges were disconsolate at the news – but Scott persuaded her. The Home Secretary, Sir John Gilmour, almost put her off when he wrote saying that he felt that there was 'room for the advice of a woman on matters not only dealing with staff but also cooking and domestic economy generally'. She replied that while she was quite willing to visit the kitchens she had 'no intention of staying there'. Having made her point, she fulfilled the role until her retirement, just shy of seventy, in 1943.[70] She also remained director of the

---

68   Gore, pp. 161f; Report (1955), p. 4.
69   Gore, pp. 171f.
70   *Ibid.*, p. 208. Barker's immediate successor at Aylesbury was Molly Mellanby, a former Roedean housemistress who had had Scott's daughters in her charge. In turn

Aylesbury After-Care Association which she had created in 1928 when she separated girls from the increasingly moribund Borstal Association, and in which she found supervisors for the girls. In her new role, as in her old, her forte was people not food. The MP for East Hull, George Muff, who met this 'rather fearsome-looking' Assistant Commissioner at work, was surprised and impressed that she knew 'most of the women prisoners by their Christian names' and had a 'personal interest in them'. Her rapport with her colleagues was also close, and her opinions were valued. One of her first achievements in office was to decant the adult women still held in Aylesbury to Holloway. Her main disappointment was not being able to inaugurate an open borstal for girls.[71] Another world war put paid to that.

The 1929 Commissioners' report had envisaged a growth in the number of borstal institutions to cope with rising demand, especially as the courts, encouraged by the Commission, began giving minor offenders the 'benefit' of such a sentence. To the closed borstals of Rochester, Feltham and Portland would be added Camp Hill in 1931 and Sherwood in 1932, while innovatory open borstals sprang up everywhere. From 1923 Wandsworth housed a reception centre or 'sorting station' where the boys were given a medical examination, and assessed by volunteers who would interview them, read their school records, and visit their homes where possible. Once all the available information had been collated the lads would be classified and allocated to the appropriate borstal – Feltham for the 'physically and mentally defective' and neophytes, Portland for 'toughs and recidivists', and Rochester for those in between. Wormwood Scrubs adopted a dual role: it replaced Canterbury as the recall centre for those who broke the terms of their licence, and served as a correctional centre for those who seriously flouted the rules while serving their sentences. In 1931 the two London prisons switched functions, the reception centre moving to Wormwood Scrubs, and Wandsworth becoming the recall centre.

Just as borstal boys and girls varied enormously, so did the institutions themselves. Camp Hill took young boys with bad records, likely absconders who would at least have barriers to surmount and a sea to cross.[72] The ethos of Sherwood, created out of an old prison to house the more truculent, seemed at odds with everything Alec was progressing elsewhere. North Sea Camp, with its austere open-camp conditions, was ideal for the hardy but trustworthy outdoor types. Hollesley Bay Colony on the Suffolk coast introduced softer young men

---

she would replace Barker as Assistant Commissioner, while Victoria Bruce, the daughter of Lord Balfour of Burleigh, took over from her at Aylesbury.

71   HC debates, 4th June 1937, 5th series, vol.324, col.1351.

72   In 1937, while Joyce was governor, one of the boys, John Rowlands, murdered Lawrence Leech, an officer there.

to the joys of Arcadia, specialising in market gardening and dairy farming, and running the world's largest stud for Suffolk Punch horses. Because of its name and its beautiful seaside location, it was dubbed 'Holiday Bay'. It was one of the revolutionary 'open borstals', but it was not the first. That accolade went to Lowdham Grange.

CHAPTER 14

LONG MARCH TO LOWDHAM: 1930–1939

I am afraid you will say we have no discipline in borstal – All the lads talk to each other... At dinner they make a noise like the monkey house at the zoo ... They smile when they see the governor ... he knows all their names and pulls their legs. The officers play games with the[m] ... Discipline is invisible, not easily measured, spiritual not mechanical. Will you take fifty of your lads for a walk in the city with you, and will they all return? Can you send a dozen with an older lad to the Cathedral one Sunday evening? Will your officers take fifty away for a weekend camp in a field where they can run away at any moment? If a lad's mother is dying 200 miles away, can you send him home to see her and be sure he will of his own accord be back on Monday morning as promised? That is the measure of our discipline, and it is a strange thing as the English lad is a cussed animal.

Alexander Paterson

When Lionel Fox joined the Prison Commission in 1925, he found Alec placing in each of his colleagues' offices large cards with the words *'Borstalium quartum aedificiandum est'* (a fourth borstal must be built). It had become an obsession, as Carthage had been for Cato. He lobbied politicians and civil servants, and in memorandum after memorandum pressed his case. When five years later that *borstalium quartum* came into being, substituting self-discipline for penal discipline, it would embody 'all that enlargement of the spirit of borstal for which Paterson was especially responsible'.[1]

One day in early May 1930, Alec burst into his future chairman's room at the Home Office and issued 'one of his usual and abrupt and excited invitations':

We're starting a new borstal at Lowdham Grange in Nottinghamshire, and we're going to begin with a little experiment. Bill Llewellin, who's going to be the governor, will lead a party of forty boys on a route march from Feltham

---

1 TNA, PCOM9/55; *EPBS*, p. 336.

to Lowdham. They'll spend six days on the road, and will sleep in halls and
other places arranged by friends. Would you like to join them?

Harold Scott accepted the offer and 'never regretted it'.[2]

Paterson's vision for open borstals was fully shared by Alexander Maxwell
who, in 1928, had succeeded Waller, whose ill-health forced his resignation,
as chairman of the Prison Commission.[3] It was also supported by successive Home Secretaries, Conservative and Labour (despite some Labour MPs
demanding that local tradesmen be employed in the construction instead of
borstal boys).

Wanting to ease overcrowding in the borstal system, Paterson had been eager to secure a virgin site upon which the new philosophy of trust and training
could be put into practice, unrestrained by the debris of the past, and well away
from the prying eyes of the national press, who would seek only to disparage the
'pampering', especially in a time of severe economic depression. In Lowdham
Grange Alec had found what he believed to be the perfect spot. There were to
be no walls or fences to prevent escape, and while it was desirable for trainees
to interact with local host communities, it was essential that they did not steal
from them, damage their fences or maim their livestock. Public acceptance of
the experiment was vital. Conditions and facilities at Lowdham Grange would
be impressive, so press jibes would have some traction, but not sufficient to jeop-
ardise the enterprise.[4]

Alec personally interviewed 'individually and collectively' the nine staff
members, including the new governor, before they set out on the march. Their
calibre and that of the governor in particular was vital to the success of the enterprise. Should it fail, the progress of the borstal system would be retarded. In
Paterson's opinion, out of every hundred prison governors only five could run
a camp.[5] In William Llewellin he knew he had found just the sort of charismatic and Christian leadership needed. Indeed, Llewellin would prove to be
the 'outstanding disciple' who 'played a big part in making Paterson's theories

---

2   Scott, p. 69. In fact the march would take ten days.

3   Paterson had refused the offer of the post, the restraints of which he would have
     found insufferable. He would rather be a 'Commissioner at Sea' than one chained
     to a Whitehall desk.

4   See, for instance, 'He who doesn't get smacked' (*Sunday Pictorial*, 3rd July 1932),
     an article denouncing 'how naughty boys are treated by an indulgent State. Broad
     playing fields, a gymnasium, large open-air swimming bath ... some 350 youths and
     young men playing cricket, swimming or sparring in the gymnasium ... a stranger
     would take this as a public school.' Inevitably, it was reported, some parents hoped
     that their younger sons would soon join their siblings there ('Bad Boy's Paradise',
     Sunday Dispatch, 17th July 1932).

5   TNA, CO323/1344/7: letter, 31st October 1934.

work'.[6] He was an odd bird, a big, shy, solitary figure with a *pince nez* on the tip of his nose. While still at Oxford he had visited the OBM with Basil Henriques, and had met Alec there. After serving as captain in the Dorsetshire Regiment during the war, he went 'slumming' as a vagrant. Although he had felt a call to the priesthood, just before ordination he resiled. At Paterson's bidding, he joined the prison service in 1923, becoming first a housemaster at Portland borstal and, from 1925, deputy-governor of Feltham. Duty was his watchword and self-denying dedication his hallmark. Independently well-off, Llewellin for a long time never drew his salary, paid out of his own pocket for the first vehicle and lawnmower ever owned by the Prison Commission, and doubled the amount of money any inmate had saved for his discharge. He lived a life of great austerity, sleeping under canvas even when the boys were 'snugly housed in hutments', and eating the same food as that provided for them. He was available at all times, rarely going to bed before 3 or 4am. Breakfasting late on cold porridge and bread and margarine, he could be irascible at morning staff meetings. He expected no less dedication from his subordinates, but did not demand it of them. He merely, by his example and look of disappointment, made them feel guilty. As one admirer observed, 'he never imposed on others but evoked.' Not all of his subordinates warmed to him, some actively disliked him, but the boys under his charge generally revered him. He saw the best in them and brought out the best in them. He had a firm belief in human nature and in the 'sense of honour and loyalty inherent in every British boy'.[7]

He would put both traits to the test when, on 4th May 1930, along with eight members of staff and forty-four boys, all 'carefully selected volunteers' who over the previous six months had been trained 'in route marching and manners', he set out to walk the 162 miles from Feltham to Lowdham Grange near Nottingham. Llewellin decided that 'the pilgrimage' should begin on a Sunday, after 'the pioneers' had been fortified and their endeavour sanctified by a church service which Paterson, of course, attended, giving the full seal of official approval to this risky but rewarding undertaking. With the words of the final hymn, 'He who would valiant be', ringing in their ears, off they marched to the promised land, staff and boys all smartly attired in open-necked shirts and shorts, spreading the borstal gospel on the way. Although Alec had to leave them at Harrow, he would rejoin them the following Saturday. On 10th May Alec, with his wife in tow, found the marchers on the road from Market Harborough to Leicester. He also found Harold Scott, who

6   Scott, p. 77.

7   *Ibid.*, p. 76; 'Lowdham Grange – a Borstal Experiment', *HJ*, 3/4 (1933), p. 36. The boys reciprocated Bill's affection for them. In addition to letters, over the years he received so many visits from his former charges that he provided 'a bedroom for such in the old cottage, near Ploughman's Wood' (Report [1934], p. 67).

had joined them two days earlier. Alec brimmed with pleasure and pride, dispensed bananas, and gave 'an encouraging and inspiring talk'. He and Frank accompanied the party on the remainder of the way.

There was no need to impose discipline *en route*: 'the boys followed where Bill led.' They were cheered throughout by well-wishers and honoured by local worthies, an indication of public support for borstals and the optimism they had generated. The mayor of Granby 'raised a titter' by declaring that had he been younger he would have liked to be in their place. Passing boy scouts saluted their peers. Members of Toc H were out in force to organise accommodation and provide sustenance and entertainment, both on the march and after their footsore arrival on 13th May.[8] The Patersons and Scott left at 4pm, while 'the pioneers', after a hot bath and a substantial meal, bedded down in tents that had been erected for their use.

With them on the march had been Jack Gordon, who only wished that such an enterprise had been undertaken during his own time in borstal. He had gone to Feltham in 1923 as a sixteen-year-old for stealing a bicycle, and stayed for two years. To counter the criticisms made of borstals and the misinformation spread about them, he determined to write a book about his own experience. After he approached Llewellin, his former housemaster, about the project, he received a letter from Paterson suggesting they meet. They had in fact met once before at Feltham when Gordon had been talking to a Bermondsey lad, and the Commissioner, recognising the boy, had approached them. After discussing with Gordon the books he liked to read, Paterson had given some advice and assured him he would ask about his progress when next in Feltham. When this time they met, they did so as old friends. Over a chat and a smoke, Alec told him that he fully approved of his literary proposal, exhorted him to be frank and honest about what he wrote, offered him help in any way he could, and granted him permission to visit any borstal he wished. Gordon took him at his word. When he returned to his *alma mater* the governor himself put him up. As it was the sports day both Alec Paterson and Lilian Le Mesurier were there, chatting to the boys and their parents. Gordon was warmly received by staff and lads who were all pleased 'to see an old Borstalian in their midst who had managed to succeed as a result of his borstal training and who frankly admitted it'. He found Feltham much improved since his time. He went on to Rochester and Portland, both of which, despite their prison-like appearance, had 'an excellent spirit'. His final destination was Aylesbury, where he stayed with Miss Barker, who ran a 'splendid regime'. The culmination of his endeavours as recorded in the last chapter of his book was joining the 'pilgrimage' to the 'borstal without bars', Paterson's great inspiration.

8   Scott, p. 70.

Gordon was an outstanding example of what borstal could do for a wayward youth – 'it has lifted me from the dregs of humanity and given me ambition to rise in the right direction' – and he believed it could do the same for many others. He put pen to paper, and in a much-reviewed book (dedicated to Llewellin) produced the first autobiographical account of life as a borstal boy, and a potent plea to the public to 'support this system of curing young delinquents'.[9]

The march from start to finish had been a marvellous success, and for Llewellin 'one of the happiest experiences of [his] life'. His faith in the 'absolute loyalty of staff and lads' had been vindicated. It had been a risk, but one well worth taking. No one had absconded, all those granted a night's leave to visit their homes returned the following day, and a new relationship of interdependence had grown up between the lads and the staff. They were 'on the same side'. This transformative realignment was completely novel within a carceral setting.[10]

The day after their arrival at the Lowdham estate the enthusiastic team, still 'happy as sandboys' after 'a wonderful ten days', got down to work and began to build from scratch the fourth, and the first open, boys' borstal, achieving at last something Ruggles-Brise had merely envisaged. They did so under an agreement made with the National Federation of Building Trades, which had initially protested that criminals were taking jobs from law-abiding citizens, that the trade union would supply local craftsmen as instructors and supervisors. Nothing would stand in the way of, or be stinted on, what was to be 'an advertisement to the world of what borstal boys are capable of doing and of the progress and development of the borstal system for training young criminals into good law-abiding citizens.' The whole enterprise, from its inception to execution, demonstrated that 'young delinquents [could] be trained above crime and folly without walls or bars, without rigorous routine and ... without stern supervision.' 'Aim high' and 'stickability' were the watchwords.[11]

Lowdham Grange was to be something completely new, and totally different to anything that had gone before. It was, and would remain, the only purpose-built borstal. It had sloughed off any association with prison. There were to be no walls but open fields and woods, no wings but four Houses, no claustrophobic cells but dormitories with large windows that could be opened and closed at will. There was to be no slopping-out, no solitary confinement, no military parades, no stone-breaking. The work would be hard, but it was to be on construction, gardening or farming and would earn the labourers a little pocket-money. Educational and vocational classes were to be provided. Hobbies of all kinds and a wide variety of sports would be encouraged, and it was hoped that borstal boys would soon be

9   Gordon, pp. 190ff, 197f, 227–279.
10   LLGJ, 13th May 1930; Scott, p. 70.
11   Charles Cape's address to the 1936 Conference of Visiting Justices and Boards of Visitors.

competing against – and beating – football and cricket teams from nearby towns and schools. Meals would be taken at small tables and often shared with staff or visitors. Although all were there under the compulsion of the court, and miscreants could be moved back into restrictive confinement, the shades of the prison house had been largely dispelled. Such would be the future, but the staff and lads were already at work laying the foundations.

To cap it all, on 26th July an inaugural ceremony took place, with three hundred guests in attendance. Paterson was prominent among the many members of senior prison

FIGURE 25. With Clynes at Lowdham Grange, 1930

staff who were there.[12] These included Maxwell, a number of prison and borstal governors and a housemaster by the name of Gordon Stansfeld.[13] One foundation stone was laid by the Labour Home Secretary, John Clynes, who had replaced his Conservative counterpart, Joynson-Hicks, in June. Another was laid by Sir Evelyn Ruggles-Brise. He and Paterson had cemented their relationship.[14] In an address before the assembled guests, staff and boys, Clynes did not disappoint. He professed his faith in the 'inestimable worth of borstals ... the finest of our present-day state services', and expressed his conviction that the 'essence of borstal work is a profound belief in the ultimate goodness of the English boy'.[15] After the Home Secretary had left, the remaining guests 'inspected the site under the guidance of the officers, and the tents, gardens, rabbits, pigeons and farm animals under the

12   Although others were accompanied by their wives, Frank did not attend.

13   Later that year Gordon would return with his father for a visit (LLGJ, 2nd December 1930).

14   Despite their differences of approach Alec always acknowledged the debt he owed to the former chairman, presenting him with a framed picture of 'Boys in Portsmouth Prison' 'as a slight tribute to his Faith and Vision in delivering the Young Offender from the methods of earlier times'. Their correspondence was warm, they lunched together from time to time (TNA, PCOM9/55), and Alec presented leather-bound copies of Ruggles-Brise's *The English Prison System* (one of which I own) to friends.

15   Quoted in Lodge, *op.cit.*, p. 70.

guidance of the lads'. A gymnastics display was 'much appreciated'. Tea was then served in a marquee for the visitors, and in a tent for their chauffeurs.

For the first two years Lowdham remained largely a building site. Camp conditions required a new way of doing things for which the Prison Commission had no precedent. As the deputy governor, Charles Cape, appreciated:

> Time and again we happily found nothing to direct us, so that we were free to make our own decisions. That the Commissioners, knowing this state of affairs, played the Nelson game superbly, aware at the same time that ultimate responsibility rested on their shoulders, is the highest tribute I can and do pay them as enlightened and progressive administrators.[16]

The Commissioner upon whom this responsibility and accolade primarily fell was Alec Paterson. 'Safety first' was never his watchword. 'Who dares, wins' was.

Over the next few years Lowdham very much established itself on the carceral map. Paterson repeatedly visited. On the first anniversary of the march, he had to address the Housemasters' Conference at Gunthorpe Hall in Norfolk on his experiences in the United States. A few days later, however, he managed to attend a celebratory staff supper at the borstal itself, and was back again in July for the laying of the foundation stone of the first House when, 'to the pleasure and profit of those assembled', he spoke about 'the Borstal Idea'.[17]

Where some prison governors had to be cajoled, many prominent society figures from lord lieutenants, magistrates and chief constables to bishops and aristocrats (including Baden-Powell, the Chief Scout) clamoured to see something of this remarkable development in training young offenders. Indeed, scarcely a week went by without at least one visit from a dignitary or otherwise: on one occasion 'two young women in shorts and little else' arrived, wanting to look around. Alec encouraged guests from all over the world to see his proudest creation and most innovative project. For instance, as early as 19th June 1930 Llewellin recorded with pride that the Commissioner had accompanied 'thirty-one prison authorities from overseas to see and hear

---

16   C.T. Cape, 'Administrative and Other Experiences of a Borstal Governor', *Public Administration*, 19/1 (January 1941), pp. 61–65, at p. 62. Cape had previously served alongside Llewellin at Feltham.

17   LLGJ, 6th–7th and 13th May, 18th July 1931. Paterson was unable to attend the second anniversary celebrations as he was fully occupied with the aftermath of the 'Dartmoor Mutiny' and attending the trial in Princetown which lasted from 28th April to 13th May 1932. He returned in June for the opening of the administrative block, in May the following year for the third anniversary, and in June 1934 (with his wife) for the opening of the first House. He visited on many other occasions, as did his colleagues.

about the Lowdham venture'.[18] A month later Professor Edwin Sutherland of Chicago University's department of criminology visited; the following year yet another party of foreign penologists arrived; while the year after that saw Dr Fleming, medical advisor to the Scottish Prison Commission, Dr Marx, a Dutch judge, and Colonel F.A. Barker, Inspector-General of Prisons in the Punjab, all making inspections. Praise was universal, and cross-fertilisation was encouraged. There was an exchange of English housemasters and Danish prison officers whereby the former went to work in Söbysögaard, an institution opened in 1933 on the borstal model, while the latter worked in Lowdham.[19]

Llewellin was frequently asked to speak at meetings of Toc H, the Rotary Club, and Rover Scouts, or to address staff of Boots the chemist and students at University College, London. When Paterson was unable to fulfil a luncheon engagement with the National Council of Women, Llewellin seamlessly substituted. They spoke with one voice.

Meticulously, Llewellin kept records of all who passed through his hands. In red notebooks he recorded every boy's background history, progression through borstal, and response to after-care. These notebooks are no longer extant, but the governor's journal has survived, in a typed version and in English, not in the Greek he used for his desk diary.[20]

In the journal we discover that the neighbouring community was fully engaged to the extent that the South Notts Hunt held meets there, Mrs Pearson of Epperstone made a present of a drake and four ducks, Mr Stanley Bourne donated a billiard table, and 'The Friends of Lowdham' held whist drives and raffles to raise money for Christmas gifts for those lads who received none from home, and to supplement the festive dinner with raisins and almonds and cigarettes. On Christmas Day itself Mr Morley provided each lad with one packet of cigarettes, while Miss Madge Wills outdid him by providing two. Open days were held, attracting large crowds of visitors from the locality and beyond.

18   Throughout his prison career Alec was keen to show off his achievements. Notably, on a number of occasions between 1929 and 1938 he welcomed William Healy, an American expert on delinquency, to Britain to study 'the organization and operation of the borstal system'. As a result, Healy and Benedict Alper of the American Law Institute's Criminal Justice-Youth Committee produced the laudatory *Criminal Youth and the Borstal System* (New York, 1941). In their view it was 'justly renowned'.

19   Scott, p. 97.

20   Four pages of a photocopy of the governor's handwritten journal for June and July 1930 can be found in the Toc H archives in Birmingham. They contain many routine and a few substantial entries that are not in the typed journal in my possession. Llewellin also made films of Lowdham dating back to Christmas 1930 (LLGJ, 9th January 1935). They have been lost, although some of the photographs he took survive.

The involvement of Toc H was extensive and continuous throughout the year, its members helping with sports events, putting on social gatherings, holding hobby classes from beekeeping and pigeon-fancying to handicrafts, and even offering employment after discharge. The National Association of Boys' Clubs took a keen interest and both Henriques and Secretan visited Lowdham several times. Outside speakers were invited to address the boys on current topics, such as the League of Nations. The staff were encouraged to put on concerts in which they performed, and create a 'Study Circle' where they were soon reading Abraham Lincoln's speeches. Musical and dramatic societies put on performances, often with the participation of borstal boys. Whereas the Burton Joyce Amateur Dramatic Society put on '*The Dover Road* by A.A. Milne *for* the lads', when the Lowdham Grange Dramatic Society performed *The Pirates of Penzance* it was conducted by Cape, and had twenty-four boys in the chorus, one of whom would become a professional singer. The most prestigious was the D'Oyly Carte Opera Company's production of *HMS Pinafore*, in which some lads participated, and many more formed an appreciative audience.

There were setbacks. Although the boys were encouraged to pick blackberries on the estate lands, taking plums from Mr Whity's orchard was theft. But the locals on the whole were forbearing. When Mr and Mrs Sibert, whose shop had been broken into by a boy called Nolan, were invited by the governor to tea, they not only refused the money offered by the lads to make good their loss, but brought over 100 cigarettes for them. There were sporting defeats, such as when a team from Repton school thrashed the borstal boys at cricket. There was the occasional fatality, such as when George Smith contracted meningitis and died in Southwell Isolation Hospital. He was buried in Lowdham churchyard, a funeral attended by many of the boys as well as staff. Six officers acted as the pall-bearers. When Noel Ripley died suddenly from natural causes, the foreman of the coroner's jury assured his grieving parents 'that no lads in the land had more care and attention than those at Lowdham Grange'. There were absconders, two even making off in the governor's Daimler. A third was not so enterprising or successful as he was 'caught thirty yards from the gate hiding in a bed of nettles'. All sorts of reasons – or excuses – were put forward by escapees, including fear of dental appointments. There were transfers to Portland for miscreants, one boy being moved under instruction from the Commissioners 'owing to a clandestine meeting with a girl', another for 'congress with a sow', and a third for breaking into the bungalow of Mr and Mrs Lowater. Inevitably there were cases of 'gross indecency' between the boys, although the sanctions imposed for homoerotic expression were lighter than for heterosexual, let alone bestiality. Some experiments went awry, and Paterson ordered the discontinuance of the appointment of 'Houseboys'.

Yet 'in spite of a few disappointments', Llewellin considered that it would have been impossible to find 'a more loyal and enthusiastic staff and a crowd of lads with a finer spirit'. The high staff morale and the low failure rate supported his optimistic assessment. Of the 307 boys discharged from Lowdham between 1931 and 1936, only twenty-one were reconvicted in that period and six had their licences revoked. In a letter dispatched to the parents of each new arrival Llewellin assured them that their son had 'been given the privilege of being sent to Lowdham Grange for his borstal training'.[21]

Lowdham Grange was Paterson's pride and joy, and its success encouraged him to build upon it. For the right lads 'a year's hard work in a camp under normal conditions of life and work was better training than two years' residence in a walled institution'.[22] The idiosyncratic Llewellin had proved his worth, surpassing even the most optimistic prognostications, and Paterson relied on him to carry forward the venture.

On 6th December 1934 Paterson visited Lowdham to finalise the arrangements for Bill's next challenge, which was to establish an open borstal called North Sea Camp on the Lincolnshire coast. Paterson and Scott had spent much time trying to find a place which would provide unlimited heavy manual work with almost unfettered freedom. The one they had settled on was challenging and perfect. It was a bracing spot assailed by biting winds that would 'search out any weakness in those who had to work there' – boys and staff – 'but would steel those who stuck it out against any difficulties they might meet in later life.'[23] This was where Llewellin was to go.

The following day he broke the news of his imminent departure to his staff, reassuring them that, with Cape succeeding him, continuity would be maintained.[24] On 14th March 1935 Llewellin took his final leave of the place to which he had given so much, and with a Union flag presented to him by lads, made his way to Stafford prison. It had been reopened temporarily as a collecting centre for staff, inmates and stores, preparatory to the creation of the camp. From there, on 23rd May, the party of five staff and eighteen boys proceeded to march 110 miles to the site on the salt marshes at Freiston near Boston. On the pioneers' ten-day journey 'Toc H proved its ideals of fellowship and service to be not mere lip service' by providing food, accommodation and encouragement.[25]

21   Lodge, *op.cit.*, p. 103ff. This success rate would continue until its temporary closure at the outbreak of the Second World War when many of the boys were discharged to join the armed forces, and others were sent to Hollesley Bay.
22   *Ibid.*, pp. 107f. The average stay in Lowdham was fifteen months.
23   Scott, p. 76.
24   LLGJ, 6th–7th December 1934.
25   Report (1935), p. 73.

Although run on similar lines, and although populated by boys plucked from the same pool, this was to be a very different venture from Lowdham. It was almost a regression to a public works prison – without the walls or guards – as the boys who volunteered to go there lived a Spartan life, enduring cold and rain, and battling the elements as they set about reclaiming marshland in the Wash. If Lowdham with its playing fields was the Eton of borstals, then North Sea Camp with its bracing or harsh environment was the Gordonstoun. So onerous was it that it was the one borstal to which boys could elect not to go.

In their first summer the staff and boys lived in tents while they built permanent wooden huts. As the year progressed, the need for such windproof and rain-tight accommodation became all the more pressing. The North Sea coast could be unforgiving at any time of year but the months from October to April were the worst. Atrocious winters were the norm, but the weather was never too bad for work. And the work, though socially useful, was arduous, each boy digging and shifting twenty tons of mud every day. One particularly cold, wet and windy morning an officer, recently arrived from Feltham, brought a forestry party back to the assembly hut. Not only had he infringed Bill's rigid rule, but heresy! he was wearing completely different, and far more substantial, outdoor clothes than the boys. They were dispatched back to work; the officer was transferred. If the boys downed tools Llewellin, attired in shorts and an old anorak, picked up a shovel and started working himself. He shamed them into acquiescence. Coping with physical adversities would better prepare them for the pitfalls of life.

The Camp existed for more than a material purpose – the reclamation of land from the sea; it served a spiritual one – the 'reclamation of human waste'. Llewellin was quite open that there was 'a religious motive behind the whole thing'. Although not compulsory, prayers were said at the end of every evening, which 'the majority of the lads not only do not resent but welcome'.[26] As a leaving present to each boy he gave a New Testament inscribed with a quotation from 2 Timothy 2:3: 'Endure hardness, as a good soldier of Jesus Christ.' It has been rightly said that North Sea Camp was 'the inter-war summit of borstal training in open conditions. Here, at its most developed, was Paterson's conception of the likelihood of personal change through alteration in a boy's social environment.'[27]

The strain on the housemasters – there were no disciplinary officers – was even greater than on the boys. They were all bachelors and were expected to be. Borstal was their home, borstal was their family, and they would have had little time for any other. They worked a full day, taking roll-calls repeatedly and

26   W. Llewellin, 'The North Sea Camp – a Fresh Borstal Experiment', *HJ*, 4/3 (January 1936), p. 252–257; Address to the Conference of Visiting Justices and Boards of Visitors, 24th November 1936.
27   Bailey (1987), p. 238.

enduring the same hardships and gruelling conditions as their charges. This was followed by supervising classes or giving lectures in the evening. Most weeks the staff would work 'for fifty hours or more and think nothing of it', as Bill 'always worked more'. There was no privacy, as they slept in dormitories with the boys and ate meals with them as well. As there was no house system in place, each boy was meant to gravitate to the housemaster who shared his interests or with whom he particularly got on. Individualism was highly prized and each staff member specialised.

One in particular had a 'forceful effect on the regime'. The tall and athletic Barney Malone, the son of an Australian war hero who had died at Gallipoli, joined the service in 1930 at the age of twenty-two. His first posting was to Lowdham Grange, where his absolute dedication to the task endeared him to Llewellin, who took him to North Sea Camp as his second-in-command. This gave him the chance to use his great gifts of leadership and he became the driving force behind many of the experiments tried out there, 'and the full and varied educational programme which he devised gave many a lad his first insights into the meaning of citizenship'. An admirer of Kurt Hahn and his creation, Gordonstoun, Malone adopted many of the aspects of that school of hard knocks. He founded a troop of Sea Rovers, whose boat trips across the Wash gave an opportunity for outdoor adventure to borstal lads who had mainly come from cities and rarely, if ever, had seen the sea. Throughout the year and in any weather he led 'marsh runs', where he and the trainees wore bathing gear so that they could swim across the dykes. Only if the water was frozen were they spared the icy dip, if not the freezing wind. 'Barney never faltered; he inspired his colleagues and the lads with his own shining faith and devotion.' He led by example. He embodied manly virtues. He was hero-worshipped by the boys. All his endeavours would end with the coming of war, when Barney was the first borstal housemaster to join up. He would be killed in 1943 while fighting with the Scots Guards in Italy.[28] Llewellin's obituary of Malone ended thus:

> Borstal progress owes much to him and would have owed more had he returned after the war, renewed with vigour and enthusiasm, his somewhat over-critical mind mellowed by experience. Those who served with him have the memory of a loyal colleague and a tried friend, of noble ideals [with] the energy to translate [them] into action, but Barney's living memorial is in the lives of those lads – and those not a few – whom he led along the road of life from carelessness and crime to usefulness and happiness. They will remember him.[29]

28   Unpublished notes of a meeting with H. Kenyon, 1978.
29   *The Times*, 6th January 1944.

In Llewellin Alec Paterson had chosen well. This square peg could fit into several round holes. Unlikely as it seemed, he was the very model of a modern borstal governor. Like his leader, he believed that the 'two great weapons of moral training' were 'personal influence and the corporate spirit'[30] and tried to ensure that the institutions he ran would promote both. Many years later one of his junior colleagues, identified only as Alan, reminisced about one of the greatest influences in his life:

> [Llewellin] was a very shy man, no easy communicator, but somehow the absolute integrity and deep concern for what he was doing came across. He found it very difficult to talk comfortably to borstal boys – indeed with anyone it must have been very hard work for him. It was his habit ... to rush into his office just before noon, scan *The Times* quickly, pick out [some] current topics, go into ... the dining hall, sit with two or three boys at a table and solemnly go through the topics. One often wondered what the boys thought of it all, and yet he was massively respected and held in great, if somewhat awestruck, affection ... For all his carbuncles, and oddities he was a great man who wielded his authority with awareness, concern and reluctance.[31]

Despite his problems with social interaction and communication, the governor kept up a correspondence with several hundred of his former charges. He cared.

For many years Alec would read to new recruits at the training school a passage from a book written by an ex-borstal boy, 'as an index of what they might accomplish at a highly critical juncture in a lad's life, when he comes to us with all the soreness of injustice in his heart, and we want his goodwill and co-operation in the long and difficult process of his re-education.' The governor, Alec recounted, had wisely put one of his most imaginative officers in charge of the reception block. The lad 'gave a full resume of all he could remember of this officer's remarks to him, which had the effect of altering his whole demeanour and attitude to the prospect before him. He decided that the fellow seemed so decent that it was worthwhile giving the place a chance, and trying to co-operate with this system of training instead of fighting against it with all his boyish temper and truculence.' The moral was it paid 'to send the best men – apostles who are realists but not reactionaries – to help the beginners'.[32] Apostles were also disciples.

Alec had the knack of picking the right person for the job. When Llewellin left North Sea Camp, a governor of very similar ilk took his place. This was the wonderfully eccentric and exotically-named Sir Almeric Frederic Conness Rich,

---

30   *Principles of the Borstal System* (1932), p. 11.
31   It took Llewellin five years, and in the middle of a hectic car journey, to tell his subordinate that it was time to call him Bill. Alan 'rocked in his seat and could only answer "yes, sir"'. (Private communication).
32   *Over the Walls*, p. 35. This book may be *Borstalians*.

another oddball Paterson had enticed into the borstal service. Joining in 1932, he had first served under Llewellin at Lowdham. They were very much a match. He too was a devout Christian, utterly dedicated and completely indefatigable. He too found it difficult to communicate his ideas and so led by example. He too was very demanding of his staff, who found working with him exhilarating if confusing. He too identified entirely with his charges. He too imposed upon himself every hardship he expected others to endure. He slept in a cell even when in establishments other than his own. Further examples come from his time as the first governor of Huntercombe borstal. When he ordered a miscreant to scrub out the gymnasium or pick up flints from a field, he would get 'down beside him in dungarees to share the penitential task'. If he segregated a boy in a cell overnight, he would stay in an adjacent one 'to give moral support if needed'.[33] If Llewellin had to move on, who better to replace him?

In 1939 Llewellin was tasked with opening another borstal, this time in Usk. It had two parts. Unusually, given Alec's abhorrence at associating borstals with prison, the main building was the former Monmouthshire county gaol. As an annex, at nearby Prescoed, was a camp to which well-behaved trainees could be transferred. There they constructed huts and an outdoor swimming pool, and cleared land for cultivation. Llewellin of course joined in, helping one party of six boys push a heavily loaded cart up a slope until the summit was reached. 'Neither surprise nor gratitude was shown; it was evidently taken for granted that members of staff, even the superintendent, were interested in the completion of the construction work.'[34] Initially, 'Usk and Prescoed Camp' was to have a short life as it, like many other borstals after the outbreak of war, was closed. When it reopened in June 1940 it faced all the exigencies of wartime – shortage of services and recreational facilities, rationing, blackouts, movement of staff, and curtailed leave, while restricted travelling made it increasingly difficult for families to visit. Nonetheless the work carried on, transforming an old prison into a modern borstal, exorcising the carceral ghosts of the past.

One such ghost was the old Usk prison's most notorious inmate, who had arrived in April 1921, shortly before its closure. This was Harold Jones, who had been remanded there to await trial for the murder of two children, and, after conviction, returned pending allocation.

---

33   Terence Morris, 'British Criminology: 1935–48', *BJC*, 28/2 (Spring 1988), pp. 20–34, at p. 30, n.25; Louis Blom-Cooper, *The Penalty of Imprisonment* (London, 2008), p. 26; obituary in *The Times*, 1st July 1983.

34   William Healy and Benedict Alper, *Criminal Youth and the Borstal System* (New York, 1941), pp. 112f.

CHAPTER 15

THE ENIGMA OF HAROLD JONES: 1921–1941[1]

How little we know about the action of the mind and its reaction on
conduct, and how wildly we grope for the chain of causation

Alexander Paterson

In 1921, in the Monmouthshire town of Abertillery, eight-year-old Freda Burnell and eleven-year-old Florence Little were brutally murdered by a callous killer, so devious and plausible that he was acquitted of the first murder, allowing him to perpetrate the second seventeen days later. The murderer, Harold Jones, was only fifteen and of previous good character. While on remand he confessed to Percy Nash, the chaplain, that he had murdered Little. A few days later, on 17th September, he wrote down his confession. When he told Nash that he did not know why he had done it, the chaplain suggested he write down 'the reason for doing so was the desire to kill'. Again at Nash's prompting, on a separate sheet he wrote that he had murdered Freda Burnell as well. This time he gave no reason, perhaps because there was undoubtedly a sexual motivation behind that killing (and probably both). He later made a statement to his solicitor, admitting the second murder. He duly pleaded guilty, but being too young to hang, he was sentenced by Mr Justice Roche to detention during His Majesty's Pleasure, the juvenile equivalent of a life sentence.[2]

Jones was moved to the 'juvenile adult' section at Dartmoor. He proved so well-behaved that after a year he was transferred to Maidstone prison to serve the remainder of his sentence. The remarkable progress of this youth aroused Paterson's interest and he requested Jones's record with a view to re-classifying

1   The following is taken from two files in TNA: HO45/25417; PCOM9/742.
2   The judge was reluctant to accept so unusual a plea, but did so after hearing from defence counsel that Jones had been fully advised and had pleaded to preclude sentence being passed after his sixteenth birthday (11th January 1922). On the evidence conviction was inevitable so why risk your neck. Paterson and Roche would become acquainted and probably discussed the case.

279

him as a 'Star'. He was not alone in his interest. The case was notorious and attracted much attention. The medical profession had from the first been fascinated by this case of a boy who had twice killed children, and he was regularly seen by doctors eager to demonstrate or improve their understanding of 'sexual sadism' and 'the new science of psychology'.

In February 1922 the Dartmoor medical officer, Alexander French, reported that he had seen Jones frequently and gained his confidence. Jones had spoken 'unreservedly on all subjects [and] answered all [his] questions readily and with obvious veracity'. The doctor noted that Jones was well above average in intelligence (as indeed the books he kept in his cell and his later well-crafted petitions, beautifully written in fine copperplate, would confirm). When asked about his sexual history he made the telling remark that 'he has on only two or three occasions prior to his crimes thought seriously of attempting connection with small girls, but on each occasion did not consummate because he "thought better of it". French concluded that he seemed to have 'very little moral sense, and when his primary instincts are aroused his inhibitory power is almost nil and he becomes a slave to blind impulse'. He seemed 'quite without any remorse'. When asked why he had killed his victims he replied 'with facile smile "Oh! I don't know, it was just passion I suppose". When asked if he felt sorry, he replied, 'Oh yes, of course I am sorry. It was a grief to my mother.' He was most emphatic that, 'in neither crime, was he actuated by a sexual impulse or by simple lust.' The doctor was inclined to think he meant it, but believed that 'his morbid sexual impulses have taken the form of auto-indulgence, his criminal violence was a form of *"Furor Sexualis"*, and in the commission of both crimes he was subliminally driven by the impulse of lust, which being diverted by some sudden inhibition, was transformed into ordinary sexual fury.' As regards Jones's future, he opined that 'morally he is incorrigible (*qua* his proclivities) under any ordinary institutional discipline' but that he might respond to psychoanalysis and hypnosis. Harold Scott at the Home Office thought that if French was right in his diagnosis then the case was 'such a remarkable illustration of the subliminal self that from a merely scientific point of view it deserves all the attention it can get from psycho-analysts', but did not consider the expense of such intervention could be justified, especially so early in the sentence, and when decisions on eventual release could not be determined by the doubtful efficacy of a discipline still in its infancy.

Nonetheless, Jones's case papers were referred to Dr Sullivan, the medical superintendent at Broadmoor. He took a rather more sanguine view, although he was 'rather sceptical about the existence of any mental dissociation in this boy' and thought his denial of sexual motivation was 'merely a piece of face-saving pretence'. He had seen many such cases in Broadmoor and, although they were 'suggestive of permanent moral defect', they frequently appeared 'to be merely instances of retardation, developing normally in the long run'.

On 31st October 1923, at the request of the Commissioners, the then senior medical officer at Brixton, William Norwood East, examined Jones at Maidstone. He prepared a report five days later. While largely concurring with French, he noted that the two murdered girls and Jones's girlfriend were all considerably his junior in age, and disbelieved Jones's assertion that there was no sexual motivation behind the killings. The boy lacked 'an appreciation of the enormity of his crimes'. He concluded that 'both murders were due to sadism'. The young murderer was over-sexed with under-developed sexual restraints, a condition complicated by fetishism. Further, although 'solicitous concerning the welfare of his relations and friends' he showed no remorse for his actions and 'no apparent desire for any alteration in his condition'. Consequently 'psychoanalysis with its present uncertainties ... would probably be foredoomed to failure', and its effect could only be gauged 'by the enormously hazardous experiment of releasing the prisoner'.

So far, so bad, but these reports were written very early into his sentence when he was still a teenager and one at least had held out hope for the future. During the course of many years, with the inevitable maturation that adulthood brings, Jones could change considerably. In one respect at least he may have: his sexual orientation. In the prison department file a bizarre episode is recorded. In August 1927 Horatio Bottomley, a fraudster imprisoned in Maidstone, wrote an article for the *Weekly Dispatch* in which he referred to 'two bright specimens of humanity', the child-killer Harold Jones and his inseparable companion, another young murderer called Jack Hewitt.

> They work together in the same shop, they walk together at exercise, and they sit next to each other in Chapel. And they are known as the Romeo and Juliet of the prison. I have seen Jones in tears when Hewitt has spoken a cross word to him.

The innuendo was obvious, and the Commissioners were quick to react to its publication, asking the governor for his observations. In October Clayton confirmed that the two young men were both located in Howard House, worked together in the tinsmith's shop, drilled in the same squad and sat together in chapel, but he had never heard them addressed as Shakespearian lovers, and there was not the slightest suspicion that they were anything other than friends.

A month later Alec was noting in the Prison Commission minutes that 'this young convict was developing very favourably in the narrow limits of Maidstone, and should continue to improve for the next few years.' East agreed that there was no evidence that imprisonment had affected him adversely. He had developed mentally and physically in a satisfactory manner, and was bright, alert and intelligent. This was written in 1929 three days before Alec's note that Jones was 'honest and unassuming, and a wholesome influence among the other young convicts', assertions going beyond the doctor's assessment. This marked a professional disagreement between the two men, not a personality clash. Paterson and East were good friends and close collaborators.

In 1931 and 1932 Jones on two or three occasions petitioned for release. In the first petition, while acknowledging he had 'never before spoken of the crime for which [he] was convicted', he attributed it to 'temporary insanity'. He made no mention of the crime of which he was acquitted. In the second petition he asserted that he had learnt a great deal, technically, educationally and ethically, but he was 'now entering that difficult stage which is known to psychologists, most of whom admit that detention over ten years has a definitely deleterious effect mentally and morally on a prisoner.' He was 'absolutely confident' that he would pose no risk. Home Office officials were not convinced, and while one thought he ought to serve at least fifteen years, another thought 'it impossible to fix or even to suggest a date when it will be safe to release him'. They sought the views of both Paterson and East. In January 1933 East, by then head of the Prison Medical Service and a Commissioner, produced a short report. As required, he had seen Jones biannually, and had not altered his opinion of a decade before. He acknowledged that Jones was an 'excellent prisoner, well-liked by all who had dealings with him', but given his reluctance to discuss his problems or undergo treatment, it was impossible to know if 'the perversions associated with the two murders' were still present. Nonetheless he made a significant concession: it was his professional opinion that once Jones had served the full twenty years, he would have reached an age when any risk his release posed to the public would be 'acceptable'.

Two years later he was not so sure. As was his wont, he had asked Jones whether he thought it likely he would make a sexual attack on a girl or woman in the future. Jones had 'turned the question over in his mind' before answering that 'he did not think he would'. East was 'impressed with his reply which seemed genuine', in as much as it suggested a doubt, when he could have easily 'scoffed at the idea of the possibility of a future murderous attack'. 'Impressed' he may have been, but he also deemed the response so disturbing that the following year he viewed Jones's release with 'grave anxiety and should not be surprised if he committed another sex murder'.

Prison officials echoed this pessimistic assessment. Clayton, concurring with his chaplain and Dr Matheson, the medical officer, continued to have reservations. Having spoken to Jones many times over the years he had found him callous and untroubled by his crimes. He could see 'no hopeful prospects for Jones in the future'. He felt Jones was 'possessed of great cunning'. 'Cunning' was a word many staff attached to him.

Yet latterly others, and not just Paterson, would take a different view. One was a fellow prisoner in Maidstone: the well-educated and perceptive James Leigh. He knew the facts and the felon well. He found it hard to reconcile the man in his thirties with 'the boy who did these things', observing 'so may we change, to ourselves and others, over a span of eighteen years'. He suspected that this dichotomy 'trouble[d] and torture[d] Harold himself'. Prisoners are often cynical about their peers, but Leigh found 'no suggestion in his speech or actions of underlying cunning'. For the duration of his sentence Jones was a regular communicant, and Leigh thought his devoutness as 'unostentatious and genuine as his kindliness'. It could not be said 'that this one has not purged his offence against society: a sentence of eighteen years' penal servitude on a boy of fifteen, whatever his crime, does not err on the side of mercy.' He had done his time. He had matured and changed. He should be released.

> It may be that Harold does himself less than justice at the half-yearly inter-views with the senior medical officer: there may be a doubt in that official's mind whether the former sexual impulses have been finally suppressed. My own impression – and I have talked with him, and observed him … for many hours – is that the distortions of puberty have been spiritualized in the grown man to a benevolence which extends to all his associates, and is strong enough to be his pervading influence when he passes beyond the gate. But the responsibility for his release is not mine.[3]

In fact the medical officer had noted that Jones was 'more communicative than in the past' about his offences and their causes. In August 1938 Jones himself, for the first time in a petition for release, wrote of his 'wicked' crimes, the depravity of which filled him with 'self-hatred and disgust', and which he had no inclination to repeat. It was progress of sorts. Consideration was given to transferring him to the recently opened psychotherapeutic ward in Wormwood Scrubs so that he could be closely observed by Dr Hubert, but because he had served only seventeen years this did not happen, and shortly afterwards Hubert left the prison service.

Jones's fate came up for further discussion in May 1940 when he again pe-titioned for release to enable him to serve his country during the war. Both Paterson and East's recently appointed replacement as Commissioner, John Methven, were asked to contribute their views. Dr Methven, who had a reputa-tion for being a shrewd assessor of character, had over a period of fifteen years got to know Jones well. Although when he was governor of Maidstone he had found Jones 'at all times difficult to approach on the subject of his difficulties and crimes', he now had 'good insight into his condition'. While viewing such a course with some anxiety, he was inclined to advocate Jones's release and en-rolment in the army, where 'it may well be that in the dangers and excitement of active service he may find complete sublimation of his difficulties'. Paterson's conclusion was the same, but his contribution was revelatory. He too had seen Jones regularly throughout his sentence. Although it was not part of Paterson's 'province to discuss his offence with him, or the reasons which occasioned it, or

3   James Leigh, *My Prison House* (London, 1941), pp. 233–237.

his subsequent attitude towards it', Jones 'from time to time referred to it himself very simply and very openly'. In the previous year Jones had told the Commissioner 'something of the abhorrence with which he regards it, and in his own way had indicated that any curious feelings which he may have had in his early adolescence, have for some years past ceased to trouble him.' Why would this young man confide in Alec when he remained a closed book to most of the medical profession? It could be that the murderer had detected a soft touch. Or it could be that he found in Alec a sympathy or empathy that encouraged disclosure. Paterson himself suggested as much when he proffered the explanation Jones had given him: that while he had liked the medical officers who had sought to give him psychological help, he had 'tended to resent their enquiries and attentions'. The implication was that a less probing, more passive, approach was likely to win confidences. Maybe, or maybe he was being deceived. He prefaced his conclusions with a disclaimer:

> Personally, *as a layman and for what my opinion is worth*, I am strongly inclined to the view that he is as normal now as most fellows of his age, that further imprisonment is not likely to make him any more normal, and that if he is to return to the outside world sometime, it will be very much better that he should emerge from the routine of prison into the distraction of a European war. He will make a very fine soldier, and his experiences in the army should stabilise him effectively, besides giving him a very useful alibi which will help him cloak his previous history when he returns to a civil avocation after the war. I firmly believe that this is just the right time to licence him.

Both Commissioners, medical and lay, agreed that the war provided an opportunity to release potentially dangerous men whose aggression could be usefully directed towards the enemy, while being restrained by the self-discipline the army would instil.

The Home Secretary insisted he serve the full twenty years, but recommended he be moved to 'new surroundings where he could be under protracted observation by a skilled psychiatrist'. The former happened, the latter did not. He was transferred to Camp Hill. The chaplain there thought him completely normal, 'apart from a slight trace of mental immaturity', while the doctor noted that he showed 'no evidence of unsoundness of mind or psychoneurotic traits', his outlook and attitude to life being 'sound and sensible' and very different from when he was convicted. The testimony of prison officers who had known him for years was the same. He invariably worked and behaved well, never got into fights, and showed insight and self-control. Good behaviour within the confines of an all-male prison, however, was not necessarily an indication of how he would behave towards girls or women in the outside world.

At the end of July 1941 Paterson wrote yet another revealing report. He verged on denigrating the views of 'prison medical officers', pointing out that their expertise was still rudimentary. Singularly few cases of sadistic crime had come within their purview, and consequently 'their opportunities for diagnosis, treatment and prognosis [we]re correspondingly scant'. They had to rely on the writings of others who practised on the Continent rather than on their own clinical experience. He was right about their limited expertise in that the study of sexual psychopathy was in its infancy, and little was known about its causes or course, or 'whether a man of thirty-six is or is not likely to behave as a boy of sixteen behaved', the main reason given for his continued detention. This was an area where 'experts' had not yet established an unassailable dominance in the field. In 1949, long after his retirement, East himself acknowledged that 'criminology has hardly reached the dignity of a science, and psychiatry has scarcely attained the high estate of maturity.' His published essays represented 'some of the stepping stones' over which he had 'travelled towards a better understanding of crime and criminals' and were the product of 'hardly earned experience' throughout his professional life.[4] Doctors, if in the dark, were at least grappling with the issues, and learning on the job. Scientific progress was being made, albeit slowly.

In contrast Alec was 'a layman', an amateur, although he saw himself as an expert in the make-up of adolescent boys, an expertise gained in Bermondsey. In addition, he trusted his own judgment and intuition. Why not? East himself had emphasised that 'the study of criminal personalities is an art as well as a science.'[5] Paterson, agreeing, took flight. Many 'healthy boys' exhibited a form of sadism, he wrote, but it was 'invariably evanescent'. If Jones 'were one of that small unhappy group of sadistic perverts who can only find gratification in rape and death, some indication of this would have been apparent in the last twenty years' when he had been 'under close and constant supervision, but neither in manner, speech or habit has anything been disclosed'. Furthermore, while 'it is common knowledge that when a deep-seated perversion is by the limits of environment deprived of realisation, some other abnormality of mind or conduct will manifest itself', there was 'no suggestion of such a thing in the development of Jones from boyhood to manhood. Few have had so smooth and easy a passage on what is for many a stormy track. There have been no jerks or violent reactions.'

Why Paterson took such an interest in this lifer in particular is hard to fathom, unless he reminded him of Jimmy Jones who had killed a woman and gone to Dartmoor, or because his case was uniquely challenging to his belief in the reclaimability of all. But take an interest he did, seeing Jones frequently throughout his sentence, and, like those many others in whom he took an

4   Norwood East, *Society and the Criminal* (London, 1949), pp. 1, 91. Although East included many case studies, that of Jones was not among them.
5   *Ibid.*, p. 1.

interest, finding redeeming qualities and predicting better times. As ever, even when faced with a double child-murderer, he could write no one off. Yet laudable empathy transitioned into questionable admiration.

> It has fallen to me to be the only person to be in regular contact with him since three months after his conviction, and I have watched his growth with deep interest, and marvelled at his patience. At times without any question or prompting he has spoken of his crime, punishment and future openly and sensibly. He has never lied or snivelled. The war will give him his opportunity. If as 'Harry Jones' he can be specially enlisted in the Royal Engineers, he will give good service, and should someday be the father of happy children.

Jones could put the past behind him, or, as sceptics would have said, brush it under the carpet.

Not so Methven, Paterson's new ally. He had recently talked to the killer about his crimes and he had told the doctor of his abhorrence of them. Whether this new openness to a medical professional had been prompted by Paterson we can but surmise. As a result Methven believed that Jones 'had outgrown any sadistic tendency he may have had', and agreed 'with Mr Paterson that neither in manner, speech nor habit has anything sinister been disclosed'. Acknowledging that 'the crimes he committed and the circumstances surrounding them quite properly arouse[d] apprehensions in the minds of those charged with the responsibility of releasing him', yet he felt that the time had come. Although 'some anxiety must attend his release, I believe from my knowledge of the man that the risk of him committing further crime is negligible'.

Release was finally authorised, and Alec was asked to supervise it. Just before it took place Jones was moved to Wandsworth prison so that he could be interviewed once more by the Commissioner. The meeting regarding arrangements for discharge took place on Friday 21st November 1941. Jones was destined for the army, after a short stay with his sister in Slough. A small amount of money was made available to him by the Central Association, which Alec had approached on his behalf. Jones was released on licence in early December, Alec collecting him at the prison gate and driving him off to begin his new life in Slough.[6] It is not certain if he did enlist (and if he had, given his notoriety, it would have been under a pseudonym), but he survived the war, married, and was never reconvicted nor returned to prison.[7] He died in 1971.

---

6   HL Debates, 28th April 1948, vol.155, col.510.
7   Grew (pp. 156f.) asserted that after leaving prison Jones 'served his country well as a volunteer in the services, and now can be truly said to be a reclaimed life'. The governor had known Jones in Maidstone and doubted he would ever be safe to release, but changed his mind after seeing him in Wandsworth.

In two articles Professors Brookes and Wilson have criticised Paterson for being 'cavalier' and 'overstepping the mark' in his ardent championing of Jones despite the opinions and objections of prison staff and of his colleague, Norwood East.[8] In a BBC documentary, *Dark Son*, released in January 2019, Wilson went much further, asserting that Jones remained a 'cold and cunning killer' for the rest of his life. This theory was based on the then unexplored speculations of a local historian, Neil Milkins, that Jones had been responsible for a number of unsolved murders. First in time was the 1946 killing of the twelve-year-old Swansea schoolgirl, Muriel Drinkwater, who had been raped and shot twice. Yet in May 2019 Jones was conclusively exonerated when the DNA from semen found on her coat was found not to be his. Later there were the 'Jack the Stripper' killings of adult prostitutes in 1960s Hammersmith, the area of London where Jones was by then living with his wife and daughter. The documentary re-examined these 'cold cases', and named Jones the most likely perpetrator. Yet the victims were all much older than the two we know he did murder, and the men seen with them were in their thirties and driving vehicles, whereas Jones was in his late fifties, did not own a car and may not even have had a licence. At the time the prime suspect was Mungo Ireland, a Scottish security guard who lived nearby. He committed suicide in March 1965, after which the killings ceased. Thus, while there is speculation, there is not even a *prima facie* case that Jones did anything other than what the Commissioners had hoped.

If Jones led the blameless life of an 'unassuming family man' after his release, which his fellow prisoner had predicted, his daughter thought he had, and so far as we know he did, then that release was justified. If he did kill again, it must be remembered that given that he had served twenty years, normally the maximum term of a life sentence and unique for one sentenced as a teenager,[9] that release had been refused earlier not to reduce risk but to minimise public outcry, and that there was scientific uncertainty, Jones would have been granted his freedom anyway, no matter who the Commissioners were. Further, when he was freed it was with the concurrence not just of Paterson but of Methven too, while East had long before countenanced such a denouement. The difference between Paterson and the medical experts was more of degree than substance. While East had conceded that after twenty years the risk attendant on release should be manageable, and Methven exhibited 'some anxiety' in recommending

8   Michael Brookes and David Wilson, 'Making sense of the sexual sadist between the wars: the case of Harold Jones', *Journal of Forensic Psychiatry and Psychology*, 22/4 (2011), pp. 535–550; 'A Child Killer and Interwar Penal Policy Tensions', *HJ*, 52/2 (May 2013), pp. 132–143. The authors are mistaken in that Jones was not initially held in Usk *borstal*, mis-spell Methven as Methvan, seem unaware of Leigh's account, and accessed the Prison Commission file but not the Home Office one.

9   No lifer had been detained for more than twenty years since 1907.

it, Paterson was more enthusiastic in advocating it. He did not proffer his opinion unsolicited; he was repeatedly asked for it by the Home Office. He did not bamboozle or bully others into acceding to his view. He did not secure the release of Jones against the wishes or even reluctant acquiescence of his colleagues. They concurred. And the final decision was not theirs, but that of the Home Secretary, considering their opinions, but not bound by them.

Nor was this Paterson's only intervention on behalf of a life-sentence prisoner. Another instance was in the summer of 1926 when he paid a visit to Liverpool prison, where Mary Size was lady superintendent. Size had, like Paterson, been an elementary school teacher in her youth, and although she had joined the prison service in 1906, she was very much in tune with the changes brought in during his benevolent despotism. She mentioned a lifer called Sally who had served fourteen years for the murder of her lover, and asked him if he thought she would ever be released. Alec enquired about Sally's conduct, examined her record, and wanted to know if she had relatives or friends who could give her a home. Snapping his notebook shut, he sat awhile, silently pondering, before leaving the prison without further mention of her case. A few months later the Home Secretary notified the prisoner that she would be released early in 1927.[10]

In short, the Harold Jones case was not the exception but the norm.

10   Mary Size, *Prisons I Have Known* (London, 1957), pp. 81ff.

CHAPTER 16

VOYAGE OF DISCOVERY: 1931

Each country gets in the end the prison administration for which it is prepared to pay, and that administration is in turn decided by the degree to which the interest of the average citizen in the matter has been aroused.

Alexander Paterson

At the tail-end of 1930 the Patersons set sail aboard the *SS Mauritania* bound for America, where Alec was to spend four months inspecting the penal and reformatory institutions of the United States. He was the first of his office to visit that country since Ruggles-Brise in 1897. The trustees of Rocke-feller's Bureau of Social Hygiene made it possible, but it was Edward Cass, the general-secretary of the American Prison Association, and Sanford Bates, the first director of the recently formed Federal Bureau of Prisons, who planned his tour.[1] Both hosts had adversely compared the rising crime and incarceration rate in America with 'England's emptying prisons', and hoped that Paterson's incursion would be the catalyst needed to change public and political opinion in the United States, and inspire a different approach to criminal justice.

On the week-long voyage to New York Alec had done his homework, reading various reports as well as Charles Dickens's *American Notes*.[2] During his stay he too would take copious notes of all he saw and heard. They would become the factual basis of what he would write, which would be more an extended essay than a civil servant's report.

He gave a copy of *The Prison Problem of America* to his sister, who had 'made possible this journey to a strange place' (presumably by subsidising it financially as expenses never covered Alec's costs), and another to his wife, on which he

---

1   Alec first met Bates in 1925 when the latter was visiting English prisons.
2   It gave Paterson particular satisfaction to see the beginning of the demolition of 'The Tombs', the remand prison of New York, the 'honeycomb of horror' which had so appalled Dickens ninety years before ('Salute the Prison Officer' [unpub-lished, c.1946–1947]).

had inscribed 'To Frank, the best fellow-traveller in a big world'. She would accompany him on many of his trips, thus resolving in part the conflict of loyalties
between service and family.[3] But only in part, for as a result of these conjugal
excursions their only child, Margaret, from her earliest years would be sent off
to stay with Aunt Dodo in Bowdon or with Uncle Willis at his holiday home
in Wales. She was the infant and adolescent casualty of their marital collaboration.[4] Alec and Mrs Jellyby had something in common.[5]

His subsequent report took a long time to write, 'principally because it is
difficult to criticise without offences and to praise without patronage.' The
published version was hard-hitting but it was more measured than the original.
Sensible of the political sensitivities in the Anglo-American relationship, and
wishing to be as accurate and fair as possible, Alec had sent the draft to three of
his American colleagues for comment and correction. These were Bates, Cass
and the eminent criminologist, Thorsten Sellin. In return he received lengthy
replies which enabled him to revise and amend the published text.[6] Even in its
final form he was conscious that he may have been 'opinionated throughout'
and 'too censorious at times'. He justified both. Opinion based on fact enabled
him in the first chapter to set forth 'very resolutely certain principles of penal
administration', while a 'shade of exaggeration may sometimes be allowed if it
will help to rivet attention, foment indignation and stimulate action.'

In it we find the clearest statement of his penal philosophy, and an early
expression of his great penal maxim: 'Men come to prison *as* a punishment,
not *for* punishment ... It is the length of sentence that measures the degree of

3   Alec wrote that 'having joined the Service, it must be your first care, and loyalty to
     its claims upon you must override all other considerations. Should you find com-
     pliance with these claims involving you in doing something less than your duty to
     your wife and family, if you wish to remain in the Service, you must put its claims
     before those of family ... This is a hard saying, but the tradition behind all real ser-
     vice is that the claim of community is greater than that of kin' ('A Highway Code',
     [unpublished and undated typescript]).
4   In 1933 Margaret would be enrolled in a privately run school at Caversham. She
     remained bitter about being farmed off to boarding school in term-time and to her
     aunt in the holidays. She craved her distant father's approval, which she found hard
     to gain. She never claimed ill-treatment, but neglect. Her cousin Tony later told her
     children that Alec had really wanted a son. That is entirely probable, though given
     his lifestyle and commitments, any son of his would have been neglected as well.
5   Mrs Jellyby, in *Bleak House*, was a philanthropist so obsessed with setting up settle-
     ments in Africa that she neglected her own home, spouse and children.
6   TNA, PCOM9/80. *The Prison Problem of America* (HMP Maidstone, n.d.) was
     widely disseminated at home and abroad. Each borstal received seven copies and
     a thousand were sent to the American Prison Association, despite initial problems
     with the authorities about the importation of prison-manufactured goods.

FIGURE 26. Father and Daughter, c.1932

punishment, and not the conditions under which it is served.' While he recognised that when dealing with hard facts we cannot afford to be soft, he reiterated that when we are also dealing with human beings we 'cannot allow ourselves
to lose hope'. Against these principles, he judged what he saw in the States. As
'a keen observer and cogent critic', he approached the prisons of America determined 'not to be ruled by sentiment, nor unduly attracted by the theories of too
exact a science', but in the hope 'that a sense of humour and a belief in human
nature' might lead 'a little closer to the truth'.[7]

7   *Ibid.*, Preface, pp. 9–15; Negley Teeters, 'The Prison Systems of England', *JCLC*,
     41/5 (1951), pp. 578–589, at p. 579.

He would need a sense of humour as he immersed himself in what was not one national system as in England but forty-nine different systems. Each of the forty-eight states had their own way of doing things, and then there was the federal system that dealt with offenders against federal law. In four months he inspected ninety penal establishments, interviewed officials and consulted experts. He found that 'fatigue marches with bewilderment as the visitor seeks in a single week to absorb minutiae of administration in one State, and in the following week plunges into the varying method and point of view maintained by the neighbouring State.'[8] The federal prisons were few in number and widely dispersed, making classification difficult, inspection arduous, and after-care exiguous. In addition to the state penitentiaries there were county gaols 'scattered throughout the States', each maintained in its own arbitrary way, free from all inspection, subject to no standards, and almost all 'smelly and disorderly Hells':

> Hard words about prisons were written by Charles Dickens eighty years ago; more bitter still were the graphic notes of John Howard a hundred years before. The vitriol of the former and the indignation of the latter are still not out of place today in trying to depict the horrors of an American County Gaol. Young and old, virtuous and depraved, innocent and double-dyed, are thrown into closest association by night and day. For the most part they spend the whole day in idleness, reading tattered newspapers or playing cards, herded in cages, devoid of proper sanitation with little chance of exercise or occupation. The smell of these places is foul, their whole suggestion is infamous; their effect on the young or innocent can only be deplorable. There they sit and lounge and lie this day, rotting in foetid air, and though all agree that these things are unspeakably evil, yet they continue from year to year, and the public conscience is not sufficiently aroused to demand a cleansing of the stable.

On one occasion when Paterson was addressing a gathering of county prison staff he read aloud from Dickens's *Notes*, 'punctuating each paragraph with the simple query, have things changed?' The embarrassed hush said it all. The only hope of improvement was if each state took control of its local gaols and made them 'an organic part of its penal system'.[9] He did not rub it in that England had done this half a century before.

Even then, the problem of staffing would remain. Political patronage dictated the appointments of prison wardens and prison guards. Many were former police officers or sheriffs. Rarely were they of the right character or expertise, and those who were might be ousted from office after an election. In one prison

8   *PPA*, p. 27.
9   *Ibid.*, pp. 29–33; 'Salute the Prison Officer', *op.cit.*

the warden experienced some difficulty in finding his way around, and some of the inmates were under the impression that Alec was in charge. Women wardens were the exception.

> There are to be found women of vision and strength, competent, charming and conciliatory to staff their reformatories for women and girls. No country in the world can reveal a finer group. They live above the level of politics, they convince the States in which they serve, and as a rule no upheaval of government can shake their position. Infinite are their difficulties, and infinite therefore their patience. They read and think, they are women of taste and education, they lead the world today in that difficult domain of a woman's prison.[10]

Wardens of both sexes came in for the same criticism as in England. Either the regimes they ran were tyrannical, or dangerous prisoners were being molly-coddled. For Alec, having the best staff able to use their initiative over a prolonged period to ensure continuity was far more important than infrastructure. Inspiring wardens were invaluable, but good subordinate staff were indispensable, 'the pivot on which any system turns'. To get 'sentries who will beat the bounds, or bullies who will beat the prisoners', was cheap. To find those who by force of personality and leadership would exercise control and inspire emulation was a lot more expensive. But money was always short when it came to prisons.

There was a further problem relating to funding: cash was more readily available for tangible benefits than intangible goals. In the United States, 'if a choice is to be made between providing an expensive apparatus for the hospital and an organ for the chapel, between central heating and a central library, the decision is inevitable. The plumber and the surgeon prevail always against the priest and teacher.'

He was highly critical of the methods employed in the state reformatories for young offenders. The buildings had the appearance of a prison where the lads lived in a honeycomb of steel cells, were drilled in vast companies, and the individuality of each was known to none. 'The genius of the country', he said, 'lies rather in handling the remorseless detail of a great organism, and in the cold-bloodied reduction of human action to a scientific system, than that subtle art of education which defies all charts and diagrams.'[11]

Work, 'the most deterrent and the most reformative feature of prison life', was a problem becoming a crisis. In many state prisons the workshops were in the hands of outside contractors who profited from 'an inexhaustible pool of cheap labour'. It led to 'the grossest forms of sweated labour; it impose[d] on grown men the most useless type of work, wholly unrelated to their previous or

10   *PPA*, p. 42.
11   *Ibid.*, p. 38; 'U.S. Way with Crime', I, *The Times*, 10th July 1931.

subsequent calling'; and it resulted in exploitation and abuse. Where the states made provision, the authorities were equally inadequate to the task of providing employment in the overcrowded system. 'If there are not cells enough for all, there is not work enough for all.'[12] In every prison there were 'working parties where ten men drift through the day doing the work of two'. In one penitentiary Paterson found 2,000 inmates wholly idle, immured in their cells for most of the time. At the other extreme trusted inmates were given the most extraordinary jobs, from unlocking gates to censoring fellow-prisoners' letters. Such a prisoner 'passes in and out of the gate within a few feet of a loaded rifle, but the Warden calls him Joe'. This 'strange mixture of firearms and familiarity [was] difficult to translate to another country'.

Religious provision was inadequate. It was the scarcity of chaplains rather than their quality that was the issue. In county gaols no services were held, and no chaplains ministered. In others there were no full-time clergy, and services took place only on Sundays. Ministers were not allowed to enter the cell of the condemned, but had to offer what comfort they could through the bars. In contrast medical provision was first-class, and well-equipped hospital wings the norm. 'From this', Alec commented, 'it may be inferred that in America as in other countries, the state has a greater regard for the care of the body than for the invisible and less measurable duty of caring for the human soul.'[13]

Although Alec found little of the physical training that was becoming so much part of the English system, and not much by way of education, secular or religious, generally prisoners in America were better dressed and better fed than those in England. Meals were communal, the menu was more varied, and additional items could be purchased from the commissary. Costs, of course, were commensurately higher.

He also visited many of the penitentiaries in the United States. Although nowhere in his report does he identify them, in his other writings he mentions two by name, both of which were seriously overcrowded, and prone to violent eruptions and brutal suppression. The first was Joliet, the Illinois state penitentiary, which he visited one Saturday morning just before a jail-break occurred in which three of the escapees were gunned down by the guards. The second was the Leavenworth federal penitentiary near Kansas City. It had been subject to an uprising the previous August in which several convicts were wounded and one was killed.[14] In the 'big top' or 'the hothouse' as it was colloquially known, he was introduced to Robert Stroud,

---

12   *PPA*, p. 80.
13   *Ibid.*, pp. 82, 89.
14   Clarence Peterson, 'Prison Officers' Training Schools', *JCLC*, 22/6 (1932), pp. 895–898.

a remarkable man of misplaced talents, who had side-stepped the electric chair half a dozen times because capital punishment had been abolished in that State, and he was serving a series of cumulative sentences, totalling 150 years. He had surrounded himself with cages of canaries and had devoted the first ten years of his almost endless captivity to a study of the dietetic problem of canaries in captivity. He had written a thesis on the problem and gave me a copy of the result of his researches. I was fain to entitle my copy 'A prisoner cares for other prisoners, *Laus Deo*'.[15]

One thing the Commissioner did notice was the great difference between the cell-blocks of English and American prisons. In England each prisoner in his cell could see something of the outside world and taste some fresh air. The disadvantage was that officers on patrol could not readily see into the cells unless they accessed the spy-hole in the door. The reverse was true in America. Cells had grilled gates so that officers patrolling the corridors had every inmate under observation day and night. On the other hand, prisoners could see nothing beyond the bars but the interior of the prison. Paterson asserted that they should be allowed to look 'upon that little tent of blue which prisoners call the sky', and granted some privacy – to shut the cell door behind them, and feel free from constant observation and intrusion. He had been particularly appalled, and 'expressed [his] feelings in no uncertain terms', by a remand prison for women where he found that 'each had to live for weeks behind a grilled gate through which all her most intimate actions and movements could be observed by patrolling officers.' So far as security was concerned the American system of cell-block building was easily superior to the British, as indeed had been the case with the penitentiaries of the nineteenth century when each prisoner was confined in silence to a single cell and allowed no interaction with others. The demands of security, however, should not subvert those of humanity.

In one regard, America was far in advance of England: sanitation. By federal law 'every cell in an American prison is fitted not only with a toilet flush, but with running hot and cold water day and night.' He hoped that before long in England cell sanitation would be revolutionised, but recognised that 'as is true in so many matters, it is almost entirely a question of money, and the tax-payer does not always pay very gladly for the comfort of the prisoner.'[16]

In America overcrowding was the bugbear that militated against all attempts to make prisons truly reformative. The inexorable rise of the prison population was the cause. This factor alone was responsible for so many of

15   *Over the Walls*, p. 29. Stroud was imprisoned in Leavenworth from 1912 until 1942, when he was transferred to 'The Rock' in San Francisco Bay. A film about 'The Birdman of Alcatraz' was made in 1962.
16   *Over the Walls*, p. 38.

the deficiencies Alec had highlighted, and was due to a variety of interrelated factors: the Great Depression and Prohibition; inhibitions being eroded while temptations proliferated; more offences being created by the legislature; more crimes being committed by drivers and drinkers and drug addicts; more offenders being sentenced to imprisonment; the duration of sentences increasing; and the reluctance of some authorities to grant early release on parole. There were 250,000 prisoners in 4,000 penal institutions. Even this provision was insufficient. One prison with 800 cells had to house over 2,000 men. Workshops were converted into dormitories, beds were put in corridors. A grim parallel upon which he drew was his wartime experience of seeing field hospitals in France where the wounded lay on stretchers for hundreds of yards outside the huts designed to shelter them. In such cattle-pens classification – that vital tool for differentiation – was impossible; contamination – that scourge of all carceral institutions – commonplace; and character-training – that Holy Grail of rehabilitation – out of the question. Overcrowding was 'inimical to good prison administration' and undermined every rehabilitative endeavour. The same was true of the provision for juvenile and adolescent offenders: the excessive population of the majority of state schools (for under-sixteens) and of state reformatories (for sixteen- to twenty-five-year-olds) undermined all attempts at individualised treatment or training. If such conditions obtained in England 'many of our fundamental principles would be obliterated by such pressure upon space.'[17]

When in California he addressed the Oakland Forum at the city's Ebell Hall, he informed his audience of his findings and strictures. He did not mince words. American prisons were 'terribly overcrowded, and either the number of prisoners should be reduced or the space for them increased'. The former course was the better. Paterson was alive to the peril of increasing the penal estate. In some states prisons 'containing 6,000 indestructible cages of steel were being built'. This presented a real danger, 'harness[ing] the administration of justice to the method of imprisonment'. 'There is nothing so terrible about these new prisons as their permanence', and 'as long as the cages are there the courts will fill them.'[18] All those under twenty-one, women, drug addicts and 'mental defectives', should be dealt with other than in a carceral setting, while prisons should be a training school for character. 'Criminality', he said, was 'caused by children being born in overcrowded slum conditions.' They are sent to overcrowded schools, have nowhere to play but on the streets, and after minor infractions of the law which in England would result in fines, probation or borstal, are incarcerated in the county jails and forced to associate with older, far more experienced criminals in an environment of enforced idleness. 'As nurseries of crime

17   *PPA*, pp. 16–26, 109ff.
18   'U.S. Way with Crime', II, *The Times*, 11th July 1931.

and cesspools of degradation the county gaols [were] unsurpassed.' Learning nothing good inside, and finding it hard to get employment on release, the young reverted to crime and further imprisonment.

But Paterson gave praise where praise was due. 'The charm of uniformity [did] not exercise the same grip throughout America', and, although classification according to race still predominated, many states had resorted to classifying prisoners according to their dangerousness, and confining them with the amount of security proportionate to the risk. Some states had adopted the policy of low-security prisons for first offenders and others deemed suitable.

Best of all, California, Massachusetts, Washington DC and New Jersey had set up camps where '200 men or more, many of them recidivists and some with long years to serve, live simply in wooden huts, working on the reclamation of land, the construction of new roads, or the afforestation of a bare hillside.' There they have 'the bearing of pioneers [and] undergo a training far more appropriate to their future than the slow and meticulous regime of prison life.' An after-care officer in San Francisco had told him that it was far easier to place and keep in employment those who came to him from prison camps than from cells in 'the Big House'. In this respect America had made 'a great contribution to the penal problem', one that Alec was determined to emulate in England.[19]

As regards women the United States was also a trailblazer. In several areas and notably in the federal administration they had abolished imprisonment and instituted cottage reformatories where women and girls lived and worked in small units, knew 'neither walls nor wire as an enclosure', and experienced a 'remarkable feeling of corporate life and individual growth'. Those in charge of them had 'the light of heaven in their eyes and their feet firmly grounded in common sense.' America was 'teaching the world that a woman's prison is an anomaly, that it is unnecessary and misplaced'.[20]

The American system 'did not make bad people into good *prisoners*', but nor did it make 'prisoners – good or bad – into good *citizens*'. There had been some hope that the innovative ideas of the celebrated penal reformer and prison governor, Thomas Mott Osborne, would have taken root, but since his death in 1926 the application of his principles had been 'losing rather than gaining ground'. He was a maverick. On two occasions he posed as a prisoner in order to experience life behind bars, and during his governorship of Sing Sing he habitually entered the prison yard unarmed and unescorted. He established a system of internal self-rule called the 'Mutual Welfare League', and quickly won the enthusiastic support of guards and prisoners. For so brave an experiment to succeed required an exceptional personality, and when he resigned, amidst acrimony, it was greatly curtailed. Consultation on welfare and recreation was

19   *Ibid.*
20   *Ibid.*; TNA, CO323/1344/3: letter, 31st October 1934.

one thing, but prisoners, it was thought, should have no say on the discipline or governance of a prison. 'It was feared – with some justification – that gangsters would rig any election.'[21]

Osborne was not the only kindred spirit Alec found in America. There were many others who shared his views, and some his passion. Sanford Bates was first among these, and he would testify of his friend that 'perhaps some of the most valuable acquaintances that American penologists ever made occurred during his visits to America.'[22] The benefit was mutual, as Paterson was the first to admit. Most significantly, one of his most celebrated innovations in England – the 'prison without walls' – was inspired by the Virginian prison camp to which Bates had taken him, and his surprise that the chauffeur who drove them to the station was a convict who then had to make the return journey unescorted.

Other than that, Paterson's most abiding memory of his visit was 'the freedom and friendliness of speech and the abounding welcome and goodwill shown by all ranks of her prison services.' To visit America, he declared, was 'to discover kindness everywhere'. He remained confident that 'a country whose human material is so fine, with charity as wide as her prairies, and courage that strides from sea to sea, will in time solve the problem of her prisons.'[23] Such confidence was misplaced.

In July 1931 he wrote two articles for *The Times* on American prisons, but had to do so as 'a correspondent' since the Foreign Office considered them too outspoken and insisted on anonymity. A letter to *The Times* did bear his name and official designation. In it he defended the federal authorities from an unjust accusation that they tolerated barbaric conditions in children's prisons. In fact, as he pointed out, there were no children in federal prisons, and even in the federal reformatory of Chillicothe the youngest offender was over the age of sixteen. This intervention won the approbation of Bates.[24] In September *The Annals of the American Academy of Political and Social Science* returned the favour by publishing an article by him on 'English Prisons'.[25] Alec was also willing to speak about American prisons, one instance being on 14th November 1932 when he addressed the National Council of Women.

---

21   Rudolph Chamberlain, *There is No Truce: A Life of Thomas Mott Osborne* (London, 1936), pp. 283–303.

22   Sanford Bates, 'Anglo-American Progress in Penitentiary Affairs', in Manuel Lopez-Rey and Charles Germain (eds), *Studies in Penology* (The Hague, 1964), pp. 30–41, at p. 30.

23   'U.S. Way with Crime', II, *op.cit.*

24   *The Times*, 9th July 1931; Letter to Dorothy, 23rd July 1931; TNA, PCOM9/80.

25   Vol.157, pp. 164–173.

For the rest of his career he would maintain close contact with his American colleagues, and would do what he could to assist them in their reformist endeavours. When William Woodward asked for advice about the Oregon state penitentiary at Salem, Paterson suggested to the Home Office that it would be preferable for him to reply personally as 'our friends in the US very much appreciate a personal rather than a purely formal response to such requests.' When the Roman Catholic Bishop of Peoria, Joseph Schlarman, came to England in 1936 on a fact-finding mission on behalf of Henry Horner, the Governor of Illinois, he was afforded every courtesy by the man he thought was chairman of the Prison Commission. Schlarman was duly impressed by the continuity provided by a centralised administration uncompromised by political appointees, the careful selection and thorough training of officers, the relatively small prisons, the individualisation of treatment, and above all by the borstal system. His report incorporated extensive quotations from Paterson himself.[26]

Meanwhile back home Alec traversed old ground when penning the introduction to Hubert Secretan's *London Below Bridges*. Secretan, another Toc H member and the current warden of the OBC, described Bermondsey as it then was, somewhat different from what it had been before the war. Homes were better, schools improved by greater leadership and less regulation, and parents more engaged in the education of their children, but as Alec observed, 'there was still waste in South London because human personality is starved in spirit and cramped in growth by the crudeness of its environment and the scarcity of leaders.' The year ended in tragedy, casting a shadow over days of happy memory. In December 1931 Gordon Stansfeld drowned in Burma. He was twenty-eight.

'The Doctor's son had gone from the Dragon school to Repton and from there to Hertford College, Oxford to read medicine. He was the main inspiration behind a club of Oxford men pledged to befriend those in Bermondsey. He was determined to go there and live. Abandoning medicine, he took a job as a clerk in the Bank of England, all the while devoting his attentions south of the river. He had a 'genius for friendship, quiet, deep and undemonstrative' and 'regardless of all hours the coffee stall and street corner knew him as an understanding friend, to whom you could say anything at any time.' Alec, however, had other ideas and lured him away to take up a post as an assistant housemaster at Rochester borstal. Reluctantly he acceded and, in Paterson's estimation, 'in a few years grew to be a housemaster of most unusual power'. The lads accepted him. He was so obviously empathetic 'they almost forgot he was also

26   Joseph Schlarman, *Why Prisons?* (Illinois, 1937).

an uncompromising leader. The staff accepted him, at first aghast, afterwards attached and bewitched.' In 1931 there were moves afoot in Burma to establish a training school for young offenders. Someone from England should go out and take charge, and Alec knew the man. In the spring Gordon set sail. In a few months he reorganised the school at Thayetmyo, and placed it on a solid foundation. As he who had dispatched him to so dangerous a post later wrote:

> He made a great beginning in Burma, set a standard and began a tradition. But on a dark day in December, after nine months, he pursued a runaway boy to the Irrawaddy, took to the water in chase, was caught in a fishing-net and was drowned. He died on duty, as he had lived.[27]

A Burmese friend of Gordon's, Sawson Ba, died alongside him. On the anniversary of their deaths 500 boys of the school would assemble round the graves to lay flowers and salute their fallen comrades to the notes of the 'Last Post'. Characteristically, Stansfeld's father, by then seventy-seven, wrote to Paterson offering to go out at once to take his son's place until another governor should be appointed. Alec was deeply touched but understandably felt unable to accept the offer. On 3rd January 1932 a memorial service was held at Bermondsey parish church. The doctor and his disciple met there once more, united in grief.[28]

Change proved unstoppable. It would survive the death of one of its brightest stars, and it would survive an explosion within the prison estate.

---

27   'Father and Son', *The Times*, 10th September 1934.
28   Baron, p. 133. 'The Gordon Stansfeld Thanksgiving Fund' was set up by Alec to provide more clubs for Bermondsey boys and opportunities for Oxford men to work among them. One of the houses at Lowdham Grange was renamed Stansfeld House in his memory.

CHAPTER 17

FROM DARTMOOR TO BERLIN: 1932–1935

Paterson's status, influence and adroitness ... proved stronger than ... the drama of an event which remains unique in English prison history, the Dartmoor mutiny.

J.E. Thomas

When in January 1932 a wave of unrest affected the prison estate, even this blow to public confidence over the direction of penal policy did not derail the impetus for reform. The 'Dartmoor Mutiny' as it was called was the most serious incident by far. 'Mutiny' was a word much in vogue and had been used of the action taken by sailors in the Royal Navy when they went on strike at Invergordon in September 1931. The economic slump was biting deep, spreading discontent. The nation was queasy.

Dartmoor, the most isolated prison in England, was suffering from neglect as well as from budgetary cuts occasioned by the depressed state of the country. Staff reductions accompanied rising prisoner numbers. As a convict prison it was a receptacle for serial offenders who had committed crimes of varying severity. Many were recidivist pests. Others were more dangerous, characterised or caricatured as 'young, determined and adventurous' gangsters. All added to the 'quota of discontent'.[1] The new governor, Stanley Roberts, was an unusual appointment. He had risen from the ranks, and, more pertinently, he had no prior experience of convict prisons. In his eight months in office he had increased both security and labour productivity. For some time the prison had been simmering, and in the week prior to the mutiny there had been an attempted escape and an officer slashed with a razor blade. Roberts asked Major Lamb, the Senior Assistant Commissioner, for permission to call on police assistance if necessary. Permission was given, and Colonel Turner, Lamb's colleague who knew Dartmoor well, rushed there to advise and assist. On Sunday 24th January the place erupted in an orgy of destruction and violence, during which officers and

---

1   Baden Ball, *Prison was my Parish* (London, 1956), p. 122.

prisoners were injured (some by other prisoners), records were burnt, and the administrative block was gutted by fire. It culminated in an assault on Turner, who was rescued by the intervention of a convicted murderer called George Donovan.[2] The riot was quelled. No one was killed. No one escaped.

Paterson arrived at the scene the following morning to take charge. So early was it when he detrained that he had to hitch a ride on the pillion-seat of a newsboy's motorcycle to get to the prison. Although order had been restored with the timely assistance of armed police, he arranged for additional prison officers to be despatched to the prison, and requested the temporary deployment of troops around the perimeter. He addressed the Dartmoor staff in their club, complimenting them on their conduct and assuring them of their jobs. He also took statements from them and issued a short, factual press release which played down the incident but did little to quash rumours.[3]

Alec knew that this untoward event would be used by those who had opposed the reforms of the previous ten years and were determined to bring them to an end. If those already implemented were to survive and the impetus for further reforms was to be maintained, he would have to be in Dartmoor in person to choreograph the response. At this he was adept. An inquiry into the disturbance was quickly set up under Herbert Du Parcq. A noted Liberal who had written a four-volume biography of Lloyd George, his interest in prisons was long-standing, and had recently increased when he joined the Home Secretary's Committee on Persistent Offenders. He was to be assisted in Dartmoor by none other than Alec Paterson. They were not only old friends from their Oxford Union days but had recently become reacquainted when Alec gave evidence before that same committee. While there is no evidence that he was instrumental in Du Parcq's appointment to the inquiry, it is quite possible. On the afternoon of Tuesday 26th Alec arranged for a car to convey the judge from Tavistock railway station to the prison. That evening they set to work.

Held in private, the whole investigation lasted only three days, during which dozens of witnesses were interviewed, including prison staff, police officers and convicts, and more than a hundred statements were taken. Some prisoners suspected of involvement in the disturbances were interviewed by Du Parcq and Paterson in their cells. So many referred to Baden Ball, the Church Army evangelist, in their defence that Alec informed him that the prosecution would not

---

2   In 1928 Donovan and two others had been sentenced to death for killing an elderly Brighton man. Their graves had been dug, the scaffold tested, and the executioners had been about to undertake their deadly task when reprieves came through.

3   Guy Richmond, *Prison Doctor* (British Columbia, 1975), p. 26; A.J. Rhodes, *Dartmoor Prison* (London, 1932), pp. 238–243.

call him to give evidence in the trials that would ensue, but the accused might.[4] The subsequent report, written within two days, placed the blame on a number of factors. Salient among them were mistakes made by the governor; the singularity of the 'dismal, bleak and demoralising' prison itself; political agitators who had been singing 'the Red Flag'; and a number of dangerous 'gangsters' who had 'great powers of evil', exiled as they were to so isolated a place.[5]

Riots and unrest were often blamed on internal agitators ('bandits', 'gangsters') or external subversives (academics, communists, social scientists), rarely on conditions, whereas in reality leaders tended to arise as a result of disturbances rather than before them. In an early example of its kind, it was also suggested by the newspapers and other pundits that young prisoners who had seen the 1930 American jail-break film, *The Big House*, had taken their inspiration for a mass mutiny from it. But a mass mutiny could only come about when an inmate community had been formed, able to communicate, able to congregate, and, when conditions were intolerable and grievances ignored, able to take concerted action. Such a thing would have been impossible under Du Cane's regime. It was a product of reforms which, however necessary or desirable, had compromised the ability of discipline officers to exert control and gave prisoners the opportunity to conspire if they could not escape.[6]

Nonetheless, Du Parcq specifically dismissed the idea that it was the emphasis of the Prison Commission on 'humane and reformative treatment' (which isolated Dartmoor had largely eluded – such 'small reforms' as had been made being no more than a 'few drops of rain in a vast Sahara'[7]) that had led to the trouble. He also denied that prisoners had any substantial grievances, which in Dartmoor of all places was stretching credibility. Perhaps it was at Alec's prompting that he also scotched the notion that it was dangerous to allow authorised visitors – mainly Rotarians and members of Toc H – to enter cells unaccompanied by wardens. Du Parcq concluded that they had a 'humanising and reformative influence', and it would 'be lamentable if these efforts were stopped or suspended'. Critics, unconvinced by what they saw as a self-serving whitewash, blamed lax discipline, 'caused by prisons being converted into a species of "homes" or "institutions"' where there were 'too many concerts and too

---

4   Ball, *op.cit.*, p. 138. Ball, a firm admirer of the 'resolution and vision' of the 'new reformers', had first met the Commissioner when he was interviewed by him for the post of assistant to Dartmoor's chaplain. With Alec's encouragement, he was ordained in 1936 and returned as chaplain. He would remain on the Moor for a further twelve years (pp. 121f, 145–148).

5   Cronin, p. 122.

6   *Ibid.*, p. 118; Rich, pp. 46, 276; J.E. Thomas, *The English Prison Officer since 1850* (London, 1972), p. 159.

7   Grew, p. 66.

many comforts'. The *Prison Officers' Magazine* blamed the Commissioners for staff reductions, and demanded a curb on 'the so-called reformer type', since 'borstalizing in prisons will not do'.[8]

It was significant that Du Parcq, in acknowledging 'the great assistance given to me by Mr Alexander Paterson', added that he had 'scrupulously abstained from any endeavour to influence my judgment'. This disclaimer came in response to criticism in the press that Paterson's role was compromising the impartiality of the inquiry since he himself, as 'the senior Commissioner' (which he was not), was 'to some considerable extent responsible for the system in force' (which he was), and that under his benevolent regime 'prisons have been turned into homes of rest where the dangerous criminal has been given far too much opportunity to conspire.'[9] Despite the denial, it would have been odd indeed if an individual as knowledgeable about prison matters as Alec and with a personality as persuasive as his did not influence Du Parcq, although all that would be needed would be a gentle push in the right direction. They were *ad idem*. Fortunately, none seemed aware of their long-standing friendship. In the event the report was largely accepted as an impartial assessment that incidentally exonerated the prison reformers.

Roberts, suffering a nervous breakdown, was 'ordered to rest', and relieved of his responsibilities.[10] His temporary replacement soon became permanent. This was Alec's superior from his army days, Major Pannall, the then governor of Camp Hill borstal, and a strong proponent of the treatment of prisoners on modern reformative lines. There was to be no repression, and no return to Dartmoor's dark past. Yet the prison was not closed, as many of the rioters had been hoping.[11]

The decision the previous November to reduce the number of prisoners in Dartmoor, a leader in *The Times* supporting 'the humane tendencies in prison administration' against their detractors, and the existence of the Persistent

<hr>

8   *Report by Herbert Du Parcq, K.C. on the Circumstances Connected with the Recent Disorder at Dartmoor Convict Prison* (HMSO, London, 1932); Alyson Brown, *Inter-War Penal Policy and Crime in England* (Basingstoke, 2013), pp. 44–47; Rich, pp. 47ff, 275–279; Thomas, *op.cit.*, pp. 160, 165. The *Magazine* was consistently opposed to reformative changes, especially when they seemed to elevate the needs of prisoners over those of staff.
9   *Daily Mail*, 28th January 1932.
10 This was no ruse. Roberts wrote to Maxwell from a hotel in Swansea reassuring him that he and his wife were feeling much better for the change of air (Letter, 11th February 1932).
11 The World's News Theatre, the first London cinema to show a film of the disturbance, engaged Jacobus Peters Van Dyn, a recently released Dartmoor inmate, to describe his experiences. He maintained that the mutiny was an attempt to get Dartmoor closed for good, the physical conditions there militating against any ameliorating efforts made by the authorities (*Morning Post*, 30th January 1932).

Offenders' Committee, provided further public reassurance and insulated the Commissioners to some degree from any backlash. Alec was well aware of the criticism that this riot and other unrelated disturbances had unleashed. Much had arrived at his door, predominantly in the form of 'hate mail', with one notable exception.

> The writers were largely anonymous. Many were clearly mad and others abusive, a few had axes to grind and a panacea for every ill. Among the strange medley was a small book from Mr John Galsworthy, containing a selection of his sketches and stories, and on the fly leaf he had written 'with many thanks for all you have tried to do' – the only word of encouragement in a welter of reproach. It was typical of his imagination that, when he read of the trouble, he should guess that the storm would break around the head of the man the Home Office had sent there.[12]

This was all the encouragement he needed. For Paterson, determined to press on with transforming the prison system, Dartmoor would provide the impetus not the brake. In particular it would give a boost to the other end of the spectrum: borstals. If they succeeded in their redemptive task, then convict prisons would be redundant.

On 13th April an article on 'Youth and Crime' appeared in *The Listener*. It was an attempt by Alec to reach and influence a wide audience. With a rising crime rate among the young, it was very much a defence of the borstal system in the face of public scepticism. Poverty, envy, and lack of direction and stimulus were largely responsible for the waywardness of the young. Deprivation in the North, and in the South an appetite for luxury goods beyond the means of the 'excited children of the War', were to blame. Harking back to his Bermondsey days, Paterson believed that the solution lay in providing smaller classes and larger playgrounds in elementary schools, more open spaces and hostels for hikers, and encouraging school leavers to join a club, Scout troop or the Boys' Brigade, all of which 'enjoined self-discipline'. For some of those not deflected from acts of criminality, corporal punishment was the 'most effective and scientific remedy', for others probation. For those who could not be diverted from detention the choice was prison or borstal. For Alec it was no choice at all. He had seen 'lads walking round the exercise yard' of a prison, and marked 'the furtive and defiant expressions on their faces'. Young prisoners today, hardened criminals tomorrow! Fortunately, magistrates had recognised that it was 'better to make the restless lad in his teens stretch himself in a borstal institution than to bottle him up in a prison cell'. His claim that three quarters of those who had undergone borstal training would not re-offend was open to question, but his

---

12   *Over the Walls*, p. 11; 'Doomed to Dartmoor', *The Spectator*, 17th January 1947, pp. 9f.

FIGURE 27.
Alec and Tubby in the Lake
District, 1933

assertion that while failures were publicised successes remained silent was not. There was no need for despair. There was need for a helping hand from the general public.[13]

This was similar to the appeal for popular engagement that he had made in *Across the Bridges*. Nor was it restricted to youths. The 'lively and intelligent interest of Commissioner Paterson' in harnessing the goodwill of the citizen proved a major factor in the expansion of prison visiting by volunteers. He penned the booklet for prison visitors, and wrote about them in the *Prison Journal*. Not only did his friends in Toc H take avidly to visiting, but many others were keen to be involved. By 1928 the number of volunteer workers – including teachers – in some prisons was almost as great as the number of official staff. Volunteers were closely vetted, and invited for a year, at the end of which the invitation could be renewed or revoked. Failures there would be, but the 'net gain' was considerable. The isolated felt less isolated, the outcast

13   In similar vein the Prison Commission in 1932 published *The Principles of the Borstal System*, the clearest and fullest expression to date of Alec's ideals, and four years later a reassuring circular on 'Borstal Training', written by Alec, would be issued by the Home Office and printed in full in *The Magistrate*, September–October 1936, p. 1062.

less forlorn. Hope for the future could be nurtured, and often a visitor would take a lively interest in the prisoner on release, helping find suitable accommodation and calling upon friends to provide employment opportunities. Prison visitors were seen as another great success. Harold Scott largely attributed the 25 per cent fall in the prison population between 1930 and 1935 to their work. Improved behaviour also resulted: in 1935, for the first time, the Commissioners could report that there was no case of corporal punishment in any of their prisons, local or convict.[14]

D artmoor, with its unique problems of geography and history, was an aberration, but it was also a demonstration of what could befall if the reform movement was truncated. For a man on a mission the disturbances were not the result of the changes but evidence that the changes had not gone far enough. He had the full backing of the other Commissioners, and in particular of Scott, their recently appointed chief, who stood up to the new Home Secretary, Sir John Gilmour, who had been 'well primed by critics of prison reform', and won him over. Gilmour would prove a true convert.[15] This was an era when Tories could become liberals. And so the Commissioners continued on the same path, the incline less steep, the summit in sight.

The proponents of reform were as vocal as its detractors. Alec, who had nothing to hide, welcomed and encouraged their work, and provided access to the penal estate. The Howard League went on the offensive and, echoing Paterson's viewpoint, proclaimed that 'the main criticism to be levelled against modern prison administration is not that there is an excess of leniency but that there is stagnation'.[16] Roy and Theodora Calvert, the anti-capital punishment campaigners, rushed into print with The Lawbreaker, a cogently written riposte to those blaming reforms for the chaos. Borstals in particular garnered glowing appraisals. Le Mesurier, an old ally, proved to be one of borstal's fiercest defenders and doughtiest champions. In Boys in Trouble, published prior to 'the mutiny', she extolled borstal as a 'high endeavour … one of the really remarkable and interesting institutions born in this country in the twentieth century', a 'living thing, growing and changing from year to year, dynamic, not dead and static'.

14   Report (1928), p. 30; The Magistrate, July–August 1936, p. 1040. 'The Prison Visitor in England', Jail Association Journal, 2/1 (January–February 1940), pp. 10ff.
15   Scott, p. 75. Gilmour would give his full backing to North Sea Camp, entering 'the plan with gusto' and accepting that the boys 'would be held not by bolts and bars but by the leadership of the governor and his staff' (TNA, HO45/20190/658284/1-3).
16   Gordon Rose, The Struggle for Penal Reform (London, 1961), pp. 175f; The Times, 8th February 1932.

Her chapters on borstal mirrored Alec's views, especially in the call for more such institutions to allow a larger intake and more effective classification. His influence is everywhere evident: hardly surprising since he had read the book in manuscript, corrected some passages, and added a laudatory preface.[17] Jack Gordon was the most obscure contributor but perhaps the most persuasive advocate since he wrote with all the authority and authenticity of having been a borstal boy. Borstal had been his salvation and, like any convert, he was fanatical about it. He wanted to dispel the myths about it that were propagated by the press and believed by the public, and which were retarding its progress. He specifically took on the 'Dartmoor detractors' and the aspersions of Colonel Rich. *Borstalians* was the result.[18] Then there was a more restrained commentator, an Indian barrister called Satyabhushan Barman. He wanted to examine the borstal system with a view to providing a practical manual for its further development in his homeland. In conducting his researches he was provided with every possible assistance, advice and encouragement from 'the outstanding authority on the borstal system'. In 1934 the results were published in *The English Borstal System*, another book for which Alec wrote an introduction. It provided a detailed account of its history and the law undergirding it, before considering the individual institutions in all their variety. The author was patently impressed by what he had seen, and his book, one of the earliest delineations of the borstal system in its entirety, did much to promote it.

The weightiest support for Alec's endeavours both in prisons and in borstals came not from a book, but in a lecture delivered by the Archbishop of York. On 19th March 1934 Alec attended Gray's Inn for a meeting chaired by Viscount Sankey, the Lord Chancellor. It was the first Clarke Hall lecture. Sir William Clarke Hall had incarnated the Patersonian ideal. As president of the juvenile courts his firm but sympathetic approach was designed to gain the confidence of those brought before him by treating them as individuals who were not to be condemned outright, but to be 'strengthened and given a fresh chance'. Probation and borstals, he believed, could do just that, provided that the latter

17   *Boys in Trouble* (London, 1931) was on Alec's reading list for the officers' training school. In the second edition Le Mesurier added a chapter praising the Criminal Justice Bill which would have put Alec's policies on a statutory basis. The 'fruit of long travail' was the 'goal to which innumerable eyes are looking'.

18   Hood (p. 177, n.5) claims that Gordon's real name was Wright and that *Borstalians* was 'ghosted by a journalist'. I have found nothing to verify these assertions, and Hood merely states it was 'information provided through personal contact'. Ghost-written or not, and even if under an assumed name, the book was authored by an ex-borstal boy who had benefited from the experience.

were reformatory and not penal. After his death in 1932 a Fellowship was established 'to commemorate his name and propagate his methods', with Charles Duncombe, the young Earl of Faversham, as chairman of a nine-strong executive committee.[19] Both Henriques and Paterson were members.

That evening Alec heard William Temple speak for less than an hour to a receptive audience. With concision and clarity the archbishop rendered his summation of the ethics of penal action comprehensible and convincing to all who heard him. In limpid prose he perfectly reflected the views of his old friend sitting near him on the podium. Temple's aim was to co-ordinate the theoretical principles undergirding punishment.[20]

Punishment ought to be distinguished from revenge, Bacon's 'wild kind of justice', whereby individuals exacted vengeance for wrongs done to themselves or their family or property. Punishment was imposed by the community, or the state on its behalf, on those of its own members who, by breaking the criminal law, had offended not just against the individual but against the social order itself. Under what principles should it act? 'The essence of punishment, as distinct from revenge, [was] the reaction of a community against a constituent member, not of one member or group of members against another.' The community had three interlocking and indivisible interests to consider but in an order of priority: the maintenance of its own integrity 'upon which the welfare of all its members depends'; the interest of the individual members generally; and the interest of its offending members. If the last was neglected, any 'action taken loses its quality of punishment and deteriorates into vengeance'.

Deterrence was the primary means by which the state protected itself and its members. It was 'scarcely better than a regrettable necessity', and if its sole aim was to dissuade others from offending it would offend against the Kantian maxim that no one should be treated as a means but always as an end. If it also persuaded the individual to change for the better it could be morally justifiable so long as it remained subordinate to other elements in penal action.

Retribution, for some the essential element in punishment, at least treats offenders as moral agents who get their 'just deserts'. Even in its most vindictive form it had an ethical superiority to mere deterrence. By inflicting suffering on those members guilty of criminal acts the community was defending its own integrity. While it was bound to inflict pain on criminals it was under an equal obligation to treat them as members who had lapsed into crime but might, and must, be restored to the community against which they had offended.

19   Herbert Samuel's foreword and Sankey's introduction to William Temple, *The Ethics of Penal Action* (London, 1934), pp. 8, 11ff. The Fellowship would last until 1959.
20   At a practical level, Temple expressed the hope of living to see the creation of a Ministry of Justice with responsibility for all aspects of the trial and treatment of offenders. It came into being in 2007, sixty-three years after his death.

The reformative aspect of penal action must 'never take such forms as to destroy the retributive and deterrent elements'. The fact that certainty rather than severity was the main source of deterrent efficacy was relevant since much could be done to address the disciplinary needs of criminals without 'depriving our action of its deterrent quality'. The process of reintegration could not be advanced by fear, which merely performs 'the sacrilegious office of making virtue odious'. Fear might induce temporary compliance; it could not ensure ready and lasting assent. Indeed it could make matters worse, especially in the case of those within whom resided the greatest hope of reclamation: the young, in whom 'the potentialities [were] actually greater than the actualities'. Flogging juvenile delinquents was likely to turn them into criminals bitter against a 'stern and hostile' state intent on mere vengeance. No penal system was just that failed to ensure that rehabilitation was one of its ethical obligations. In sum:

> Retribution is the most fundamental element in penal action, and Deterrence for practical reasons the most indispensable, yet the Reformative element is not only the most valuable in the sympathy which it exhibits and in the effects which it produces, but is also that which alone confers upon the other two the full quality of Justice.

Retribution, deterrence, reformation: these three, but the greatest of these is reformation. Paterson could not have put it better himself, and his own maxim that 'prison is the punishment, not for punishment' is one with which Temple concurred.

It was not, however, a sentiment shared by the new German National Socialist government which had reversed reformist moves and reinstated a stern regime where prisoners obeyed or were broken. Before the Nazi takeover, Alec had recommended to the IPPC an 'arrangement of visits by a group of prison officials from one country to another'. Such an exchange was warmly approved, as was his suggestion that it should begin with 'a friendly interchange of knowledge between the prison authorities in England and Germany'. As a result ten officials came to England in June 1934. Alec, out of his own pocket, paid for an interpreter and transport. He also arranged accommodation in a Toc H house. The delegates toured many penal establishments, listened 'patiently to lectures, asked many thoughtful questions, engaged in discussion and exchanged experiences'.[21] Their visit was a success, and was repaid in September when Scott took a party of prison staff to Germany.

21   TNA, HO45/20458.

Alec was not included, presumably because he had visited Germany before and would do so again, and there was no need for two Commissioners to go on the same trip. A further factor may have been his forthrightness. Targeting the twin totalitarian regimes of Russia and Germany, he had denounced the 'cruelty and brutality, masked or unmasked' pertaining in some countries' prisons, and had no compunction in declaring 'that certain practices are directly contrary to the dictates of humanity, and should not be tolerated under any circumstances in a civilized community.' Had he gone on the visit he would have questioned the limitations placed on the delegation. It was not to investigate the treatment of political prisoners nor see concentration camps. Its remit was 'strictly limited to an examination of the methods of treatment of the ordinary prisoner'. In any case he would have been appalled by what he would have seen in the civil penal estate. 'The jackboot rule of whip and cosh' was very much in evidence. When the British party was shown round the new Brandenburg convict prison, they observed that discipline was maintained in the chapel by having a machine gun mounted behind the altar screen, not the sort of 'discipline' of which Alec would approve. Nor would Scott, who 'could only speculate on the character of the people who had thought out this devilish arrangement'. But where he considered 'comment within the bounds of courtesy was impossible', Alec, despite his customary 'delicacy of the diplomat', might have found such restraint in such circumstances intolerable.[22]

He would soon see at first-hand how the Nazis operated. In August 1935 he was one of the official British delegates to the 11th International Penal and Penitentiary Congress, held that year in Berlin.[23] The venue had been set in happier

---

22 Memorandum to the IPPC, in Ruck, pp. 155, 159; *German Prisons in 1934* (Maidstone prison, 1936), pp. 7, 82; Clayton, p. 158f; Scott, p. 95. In his report Scott recorded his 'feeling of depression' when he left Brandenburg, noting that 'in the elaboration of an efficient machine emphasis was so clearly laid on the purely deterrent side of imprisonment that the individuality of the prisoner had disappeared.' By way of relief was the *Städtisches Landerziehungsheim Struveshof*, a colony near Berlin for neglected and delinquent children. It operated much like an open borstal, having 'a soul of its own' and possessing 'both ideals and idealists'.

23 See Simon van der Aa (ed.), *Proceedings of the XIth International Penal and Penitentiary Congress held in Berlin, August 1935* (Bern, 1937), the official, unctuous account; Polwarth and Paterson's seven-page report of 19th November 1935 to the Home Office (TNA, HO4520458); Hermann Mannheim, *The Dilemma of Penal Reform* (London, 1939), pp. 67–74; William Forsythe, 'National Socialists and the English Prison Commission: the Berlin Penitentiary Congress of 1935', *IJSL*, 17 (1989), pp. 131–145; Richard Wetzell, 'Nazi Criminal Justice in the Transnational Arena: the 1935 International Penal and Penitentiary Congress in Berlin', in Stephen Skinner (ed.), *Ideology and Criminal Law* (Oxford, 2019), pp. 77–104.

times, when the Congress had met in Prague five years before.[24] Then Paterson's proposed minimum rules for the treatment of prisoners, having been presented by a German delegate, Erwin Bumke, were widely discussed and largely applauded. Bumke, a key exponent of Weimar-era penal reform whom Alec had first met at the London Congress, had sat with him on the sub-committee that had revised them. At the urging of this seemingly progressive jurist, the German invitation to host the next Congress had been accepted.[25] In the interim, a lot had changed on the international map, and nowhere more so than in Germany. Such was the disquiet that there was a flurry of letters to the Secretary of State and the Prison Commission, and in July 1934 a deputation attended the Home Office, imploring Alec to try to postpone the Congress or change its venue.[26] He considered that neither was practicable, and in any case 'the better policy was to go to Germany and do what we can to foster and encourage the sound opinions which exist among a great number of German people on penal questions'. His view mirrored that of the Home Secretary and Foreign Office officials.[27] He also knew that any such proposal would be vetoed by Bumke, the then president of the IPPC, and by the pro-German Dutch Secretary-General, Simon van der Aa. At a meeting at its headquarters in Berne the following month (which Alec attended) the Commission confirmed that the Congress would go ahead as planned.

The atmosphere of Berlin was very different from that of Prague. The Congress was to be a showcase for the Nazis, and they did everything they could to ensure its success as they defined it. They politicised it. Packing it was a prerequisite. Even without a boycott by some bodies such as the Howard League, the Germans would have easily predominated. Their 436 delegates far outnumbered all the others put together and 'were under orders how they should vote'.[28] Jackboots were preparing to stamp on Oxford brogues. On the evening of Sunday 18th August, a reception was held for the delegates. The following morning the Congress opened in the Kroll Opera House, the seat of the Reichstag since the fire of 1933, a fitting setting for what would be political theatre. A bust of Hitler was prominently displayed and swastikas festooned the building. Bumke presided. From the viewpoint of its hosts the objective of the Congress was not penal reform as hitherto understood, but to unveil before a receptive

24 Mrs Paterson accompanied her husband to Prague but not to Berlin.
25 Arthur Gardner, 'The Tenth International Penal and Penitentiary Congress at Prague, 1930', *HJ*, 3/2 (September 1931), pp. 83–85; F. Emory Lyon, 'Tenth International Prison Congress', *JCLC*, 21/4 (1931), pp. 499–503.
26 The Archbishop of Canterbury was one correspondent, and questions were asked in Parliament.
27 TNA, PCOM9/195; HO45/20458/553922/35.
28 Polwarth and Paterson, *op.cit.*, p. 4.

international audience the latest innovations in German penal practice and criminal justice, to 'enlighten foreign legal elements dismissive and hostile towards the new Germany', to defend Nazi policies from critics abroad, and to win all the votes.[29] During the preliminary and plenary sessions the delegates were subjected to interminable lecturing and hectoring by a number of Nazi luminaries, most notably the Justice Minister Franz Gürtner, the jurists Roland Freisler and Hans Frank, and the Reich Minister of Propaganda, Joseph Goebbels.

Gürtner, in an emollient opening address, tried to camouflage the extent of the rupture with the recent past by emphasising the close connection of much of the thinking in Germany with that of other countries, by speaking of the need for humanity to accompany the 'order, subordination and obedience' required of prisoners, and by asserting the value of education, especially 'in the case of young prisoners still capable of being trained'. On subsequent days Freisler, Frank and Goebbels, 'fanatical exponents of the principle of reprisal and intimidation', made no such effort to mollify or deceive. Beneath a veneer of history and philosophy merciless and murderous was their mantra. Liberalism and its cult of the individual had been conquered. The nation was a 'higher organism than the individual, with its own rights and its own laws'. The National Socialist state harboured 'no humanitarian scruples so far as the criminal is concerned', and was determined to cleanse the criminal element from the body politic. They – like Gürtner – divorced Nazi 'true justice' from legality. New laws would be retrospective and any 'offence against the demands of the national life', even if not proscribed by law, was punishable as a wrong. Judges, replacing the maxim *nulla poena sine lege* (no punishment without law) with its inversion, *nullum crimen sine poena* (no crime without punishment), should 'manufacture' new definitions of crime to fit the case. The rights of the individual were subordinated to 'the Volk's right to life' and the Nazi state embodied the Volk. Protection of the race was the supreme law. Frank demanded an 'international anti-criminal front' aimed at Russia, not for its 'show-trials' which the Nazis grudgingly admired, but for fomenting insurrection in the West. Dissenting intellectuals and subverting Communists were as culpable as ordinary criminals and would pay the price. Those placed into 'protective custody' were confined indefinitely without charge, trial or right of appeal. 'What did it matter', asked Dr Goebbels in his culminating address, 'if a few thousand individuals hostile to society are taken into custody so that life may be restored to a people numbering sixty-six millions?' The main duty of the prison service was to punish prisoners, and that of the state to eliminate incorrigibles. To prevent reoffending, to eradicate the criminal bacillus, recourse would be made to sterilisation, castration and

29   Nikolaus Wachsmann, *Hitler's Prisons* (Yale, 2004), p. 369.

euthanasia.[30] This policy of 'vengeance and extermination' was counter to all
that Alec held dear. He was determined to show that the polite applause the
speakers received 'should not be taken to imply universal agreement'.[31]

The German delegates, adhering *en bloc* to the Nazi position, would support all these assertions and vote accordingly on the resolutions put forward
in the four 'sections' in which different issues were deliberated. Members of
the Gestapo 'sat insolently at the back of the rooms, smoking and chattering
while speeches were being made'. While compromise or even agreement could
be reached over the agenda items in three of the 'sections' (indeterminate detention for public protection, for instance), there would be total impasse in the one
Alec attended and which Sanford Bates chaired. Section II ('Administration')
dealt with a number of key issues, the most important and contentious being
the education and reformation of prisoners. On all matters it was known that
the British position was furthest removed from the German, no more so than
on these two. Repression and selective indoctrination rather than universal education or training were Nazi priorities.

Before the discussion began on these points disgruntled delegates from
Belgium, Denmark, Holland, Norway and Sweden converged on the hotel
where the British delegation was staying, and requested that Paterson take the
lead in opposing any resolution maintaining that the first and main duty of
the state was to punish the imprisoned. This would controvert the whole *rai-
son d'être* of the IPPC.[32] He took up the challenge, roping in the Americans as
allies. Some, such as Bates and Cass, were old friends, and all shared his views.
With thirty and twenty-seven delegates respectively, the British and Americans formed the largest groups after the Germans, but their combined representatives could never outvote them in either plenary or section. To surmount
this difficulty, they and the other dissidents hatched a co-ordinated plot to
foil the Nazis over what was generally considered to be the most important
question before the Congress. Their plan was played out over the following
days in Section II. Paterson in particular had to be careful, conscious that he

30 The British delegation would vote against all three. Euthanasia had some English
    supporters. George Bernard Shaw proposed it for dangerous incorrigibles (Preface
    to Sidney and Beatrice Webb, *English Prisons under Local Government* (London,
    1922), pp.xxviii–xxxiv), as did a contributor to *The Spectator* (6th February 1932, p.
    17). Eugenics, despite its native origins, never achieved serious traction in England.
    Just as well. There was a short step from eugenics to euthanasia.
31 Polwarth and Paterson, *op.cit.*, p. 4; Aa, *op.cit.*, p. 454; A.G. Dickson, 'Justice
    in Germany', *The Spectator*, 6th September 1935, pp. 10f; Geoffrey Bing, 'The
    International Penal and Penitentiary Congress, Berlin', *HJ*, 4/2 (September
    1935), pp. 195–198.
32 Alec Paterson, 'The Present Policy of the Prison Commission', *The Magistrate*, No-
    vember–December 1938, p. 141.

could not compromise his official position as a representative of the British government or cause diplomatic embarrassment. He could clandestinely subvert but not overtly condemn.

As soon as the *rapporteur*, a Dutch Nazi jurist called Muller, had delivered his report to the section, Alec was first to his feet to make 'a few slight amendments to the conclusions'. What he proposed was a complete rewriting of them by substituting the declaration that the first aim of the prison system was to educate and reform, and this should apply to all the imprisoned, even the seemingly intractable. He was immediately seconded by a Norwegian prison director, and supported by Cass and Lewis Lawes of the American delegation, and many others.[33] While some Germans leapt to Muller's defence, the majority remained 'silent, true to type as fanatical exponents of the new justice, determined to detect and vote down any concession to humanitarian feeling'. They were not participants but tools. They had the numbers. And they had allies.[34] One Nazi jurist, Karl Waldmann, did interject, enraging many of the foreign delegates by describing concentration camps as 'educational institutions' for making anti-social elements into useful citizens.

Amidst the rancorous exchanges Bates appointed a committee including himself and Alec as well as Dr Muller and two advocates of repression. Remarkably they came up with a resolution which, while omitting all reference to 'humanitarianism', endorsed 'the education and betterment' of all prisoners. Yet it had been a hard-fought compromise and Alec had only agreed to it with the proviso that he would seek to amend it when it was presented to the section. There he proposed omitting the second paragraph, which still implied that the major purpose of imprisonment was the imposition of punishment, and inserting a new one asserting that no one should be excluded from the prospect of betterment. A similar but stronger amendment, proposed by a Belgian delegate acting in cahoots with Alec, was overwhelmingly defeated on individual votes,[35] but was narrowly won when Bates conveniently yielded to a demand in accordance with Article 17 of the Regulations of the Congress for a vote by country, ten voting for, nine against. He declared the amendment carried, but such was the uproar from the Germans that he kicked the issue into the long grass by leaving the final decision on which method of voting should count to the Bureau of the Congress. It never was decided. Paterson's amendments were never put to the vote. No resolution was passed. The chasm could not be bridged. It was the only occasion in the Congress when this occurred. Every other resolution – even

33   Lawes was the much-celebrated Warden of Sing Sing.

34   *The Times*, 21st November 1935; 'Prison Reform or Reaction?', *The Spectator*, 23rd August 1935, p. 3.

35   One of the six British delegates broke ranks and voted 'no', as did one of the nine Americans. Their names are not recorded. All 121 Germans opposed.

that on sterilisation and castration – had been passed in section by roll-call and adopted by acclamation in the main assembly, even though, as one participant put it, 'the opposition represented at least half of the civilised world.' On the most important issue, however, that had not happened. The Germans fumed. Others fumed for different reasons, and before the close of the final plenary session some foreign delegates walked out. While the Nazis and their supporters proclaimed the success of the 'great Berlin Congress', for others it 'dissolved in acrimony and bewilderment'.[36]

At a meeting of the IPPC on the last day of the Congress (24th August) Alec, in an attempt to rein in the worst excesses of totalitarianism, proposed 'that a "black list" should be made of certain practices which should never under any circumstances exist in any country, and certain others which should only exist in exceptional circumstances'. The Commission would not countenance this. It further decided, against the opposition of Paterson and Bates, that the next Congress should be held in Rome in 1940.[37]

Alec was one of eighty foreign delegates who accepted an invitation to spend a week's study-tour of prisons. Bumke, Freisler and Gürtner accompanied the party. Everything was laid on for them: special trains, buses and coaches, the finest hotels, lavish receptions, the best wines and liqueurs, folk-dancing in Bavaria, operatic performances in Dresden, and a concert in Leipzig. In between the junketing were tours of several carefully selected prisons where well-nourished prisoners provided musical entertainment. The Germans took great pains and spared no expense to 'dispel myths' and portray the new Reich in the best light. All went according to plan until the outside world intruded on this idyll. The hosts became aware of articles critical of the Congress being published in *The Times*.[38] They cajoled their guests into making public their appreciation. Partly under pressure, but more out of loyalty to a man he had long respected and whose erstwhile views he had shared, Alec wrote to *The Times* defending the reputation, conduct and integrity of Dr Bumke, who during his five-year presidency of the IPPC had been a 'loyal friend and colleague to us all'. On 31st August, the day after the letter was published, Alec gave an address at the final reception in which he effusively praised Bumke for his many years of service. The Commissioner was wrong in his assessment of the man and had been proved wrong about attending the Congress.[39] The Germans had remained obdurate in their views, and were delighted

36   TNA, HO45/20458; Bing, *op.cit.*, p. 198; Aa, *op.cit.*, preface, pp. 205, 227–231.
37   It would not be reconvened until 1950, when all threat from Nazis and Fascists had been removed, although the severe damage done to the reputation of the IPPC by its past associations could not be repaired and ultimately led to its demise.
38   19th, 20th, 22nd, 24th August.
39   Whatever he might have been in the past, Bumke had sold his soul. He retained his position under the new regime and joined the Nazi Party in 1937. Responsible

by their propaganda coup in holding 'the great Berlin Congress'. Back home Paterson confirmed this assessment when he told the Home Office that no German delegate dared oppose the Nazi viewpoint and that the Congress had indeed been subverted into an exercise in propaganda.[40]

His sojourn in Germany meant that Alec could not attend the funeral of the man who had founded the borstal system, and been the very first British representative to attend a Congress. He had died on the day the 1935 Congress began. He was borne to his last resting-place by six senior prison officers. Among the large wreaths was a bunch of flowers 'to the memory of a humane man, Sir Evelyn Ruggles-Brise KCB. He saved me from the cat. Convict No 2148.'[41] Inscribed during his lifetime on the gateway of Borstal were the words that would become his epitaph, words that Alec would use to preface his booklet on *The Principles of the Borstal System*:

> He determined to save the young and careless from a wasted life of crime. Through his vision and persistence, a system of repression has been gradually replaced by one of leadership and training. We shall remember him as one who believed in his fellow men.

After a month at home, Alec returned to the Continent as part of the English delegation to the Assembly of the League of Nations in Geneva. Although Italy's aggression against Abyssinia absorbed most of the time and energy of the delegates, there was still quite a lot of attention paid to penal matters, and prison reformers found a more conducive atmosphere in which to discuss their views and share their concerns than in Berlin. Paterson played a major and successful part in pressing the League to adopt the Standard Minimum Rules for the Treatment of Prisoners. On 25th September the Assembly passed a resolution condemning practices contrary to those rules. It was a principled stand, but the League was impotent against 'governments who rely on cruelty'.[42]

---

for a number of unjust and racially motivated verdicts, he committed suicide on Hitler's birthday, 20th April 1945. Another of the British delegates, Geoffrey Bing, had a similar opinion of him but took a dim view of his role. 'The real tragedy of the Congress', he wrote, 'was to see Dr Bumke [giving] a semblance of respectability and decency to proceedings that had neither respectability nor decency' ('The Nazi Way with Prisoners', *The Times*, 21st November 1935). In the same article Bing praised Paterson for 'leading the opposition in showing the Germans that the Western nations would never abandon the principle of humane treatment'.

40   TNA, HO45/20458/553922/52
41   Shane Leslie, *Sir Evelyn Ruggles-Brise* (London, 1938), p. 209.
42   Letter from Margery Fry, *HJ*, 4/7 (September 1935); TNA, PCOM7/61-2; 9/141; Enid Jones, *Margery Fry* (Oxford, 1966), p. 182.

CHAPTER 18

STRANGE NEW WORLD: 1937

> On the door that leads to the prison
> Is written in chalk this verse;
> 'Tis here the good man turns bad man,
> And the bad man changes to worse.
>
> *Blanco Fombona*

The British government was disinclined to so rely. In the face of the labour unrest which had beset the Caribbean over the previous two years, laying bare the risks posed to imperial control by mass unemployment and poverty, the Colonial Office wished to accelerate its new strategy of development and welfare. And so, at the end of 1936 Paterson was despatched from England to visit and report on the penal and reformatory establishments of the British colonies in the West Indies and South America. Frances accompanied him on this opportunity for a holiday, albeit a working one for Alec.[1] Their voyage over the Christmas and New Year period was pleasant and relaxing, one of cocktail parties, deck games, dinners at the captain's table, and much opportunity for reading. There was one curious incident when two flying fish landed aboard and were duly skinned and hung up to dry. Alec named them 'Hitler' and 'Mussolini'.

On 6th January 1937 they docked in Kingston, Jamaica, their first port of call. The next day Alec was off to Spanish Town to inspect St Catherine's prison and its 'juvenile-adult' section. Thereafter he went to Port Royal, and to Stony Hill on the outskirts of Kingston to see a juvenile reformatory. To Alec's surprise there were very few adolescent offenders in either. He also visited country police stations and a vocational training school. In between there was the usual round of dinner parties, tennis matches ('poor show on our part'), and rubbers of bridge ('lose heavily'). Bizarrely, Alec and Frank were invited to a dance in the yard of Kingston penitentiary. Frank also attended a 'priceless' meeting of a committee which organised the sewing class in the women's block, during

---

[1]   Frank kept a diary of their trip upon which most of the following account is based.

FIGURE 28. Sailing to the West Indies, 1937

which she was asked if she was 'High Class Anglican'. Unperturbed, she accepted an invitation to look round the prison herself, where she saw 'sixty not very
prepossessing women', one of whom was in the hospital wing having been 'terribly burnt by boiling water thrown over her by a "bad girl"'. The 19th of January
was a day of striking contrasts in Alec's schedule. He was away early in the morning to witness an execution in Spanish Town, resulting in his recommending
the erection of a new scaffold. In the evening he attended a meeting of Toc H
to discuss the possibility of starting a boys' club in Kingston. He completed his
report on 1st February.

The following day he and Frank embarked on the *Lady Rodney*, bound for
Bermuda. *En route* it berthed briefly in Nassau in the Bahamas before arriving
at Hamilton, Bermuda's capital, on 8th February. Apart from sight-seeing, Alec
took his wife to Nonsuch island to see a residential institution for young offenders. They were also shown an old slave prison at Salter's School.

After a week they departed on the *Lady Hawkins* for Barbados. On the way
the ship docked at St Kitts, where they spent a day on the islands, but they did
not go ashore when they reached Nevis 'as there is no prison there and not very

much to see'. On the 20th they disembarked at Antigua. There Alec was asked to meet a killer whose crimes he treated with some levity:

> He had murdered once or twice outside, and proposed to continue his tire-some practice within the prison. After fifteen minutes of conversation and ob-servation it was clear that he was primarily a musician rather than a murderer. He pleaded guilty to a passion for the flute, and the obvious solution of his acclimatisation to prison discipline was to send a warder to his island home and bring back his flute, and allow him to play in his cell till his fellow pris-oners began to insist that they now had the power and right to murder him.[2]

After this odd encounter, the Patersons attended a reception given in their honour at Government House. Back on board, the next stop was Montserrat, where Alec did go ashore as there was a small jail that had recently been re-built. To his dismay this had been done on Victorian lines, without any con-sultation with England about modern designs. The following morning they reached Dominica. Alec breakfasted on board early so that he could visit the jail. Then, passing by Martinique, they reached St Lucia in the Windward Is-lands. Alec made straight for the jail as they had to re-embark at 10pm. Bridge-town, Barbados, was the next stop, where they were escorted to Government House. Alec spent the afternoon in the prison. On subsequent days he visited various schools and a girls' reformatory. The final leg of their journey began on 28th February when they boarded the *SS Scarpenia* bound for Trinidad.

They arrived off Port of Spain the next day. After they had checked in to the Sand Hotel, Alec was off to the prison. He was back for pre-prandial drinks with an old army friend, Humphrey Gilkes, a former lieutenant in the 21st Battalion of the London Regiment, who had the distinction during the Great War of being one of only four men awarded a third bar to his Military Cross. While working in the Colonial Medical Service Gilkes had been posted to Trinidad as director.

Although left to her own devices a lot of the time, Frank did accompany her husband on some of his visits. They went together to the Church Army's Rose Hill Institution for delinquent girls run by Captain Williams and his wife. Williams took the Patersons to visit a potential site for a new young offenders' institution. They also went to an orphanage 'for little dark lads from 0-16'. It was 'rather an attractive place' and 'very uninstitutional'. Despite his busy schedule Alec still managed to play squash or tennis from time to time, swim in the sea, and take part in a hockey match between prison officers and the police, which the latter won. He and Frances were also wined and dined by their friends ev-ery evening and sometimes played post-prandial bridge or roulette. After one such dinner on Monday 15th March with Robert Johnstone and his wife, their hosts drove Alec to the harbour so that he could get a boat for Tobago, only to

2   *Over the Walls*, p. 29.

discover that, although he was supposed to return to the mainland the following evening, the next passage back was not until the Thursday morning. Frank
stayed with the Johnstones until her husband returned. When he did, he was so
tired that although they went to dinner with their hosts they made their excuses
and retired early.

On the evening of 24th March the Patersons boarded a police launch which
took them to the *Lady Hawkins*, which was to set sail for British Guiana at 2am
the following morning. Twenty-eight hours later they docked in Georgetown,
the capital of the colony. Alec was particularly pleased to see the prison labour
camp in the interior of the colony, as he had advised the local authorities on this
three years before.[3] As usual Frank saw very little of Alec during the day, but he
was back for the inevitable lunches, dinners and cocktail parties held by a number of local worthies, including the chief justices. Their social round was even
more hectic than Alec's business schedule.

Before he left England Alec had made arrangements to visit Cayenne, the
capital of French Guiana, and its penal colony. The latter was situated both on
the mainland and on three offshore islands, the most notorious of which was
Devil's Island. The islands could be reached only by a hazardous sea journey. He
had overcome French reluctance to ferry him across by cabling 'British Commissioner prefers rough seas and small boats'. He got his way. After finishing his
official duties in British Guiana, and on holiday, he set sail on a French steamer
carrying Senegalese troops and recaptured convicts to the penal colony.[4] Warmly welcomed by the governor, Monsieur Veber, he was given access to everything
and everywhere he wanted to see, and was even allowed to interview in private
any inmate he wished. One was a French journalist who had been tried and
sentenced in 1917 as an enemy to his country for publishing an article in which
he wrote that 'the carnage [of Verdun] had outstripped any conceivable limits of
sense and decency'. He had served twenty years and was desperate for a pardon.
Alec, conversing as best he could in his schoolboy French, spent Good Friday
walking round the island with this 'admirable man'.[5] On the same day he visited
a dying leper and had to kneel in order to hear what he said. As Alec rose from
his knees, the leper stretched out his disfigured hand.

---

3   TNA, CO323/1344/3: letter of 31st October 1934. This letter was considered to
     be of such value that it was sent to other British colonies in the Caribbean and
     beyond.

4   Alexander Paterson, 'Devil's Island', *The Spectator*, 20th June 1947, p. 10; TNA,
     PCOM9/81.

5   Preface to William Douglas-Home, *"Now Barabbas..."*. I have been unable to iden-
     tify this journalist.

For a moment I shrank back. Then I said to myself, if you cannot shake hands on this Good Friday with a dying leper, how can you hold out your hands on Easter morning to receive the Bread of Life?[6]

That Easter Sunday Alec, by happy chance, bumped into a remarkable young man with whom he would long remain in touch. This was Charles Palpant, an officer in the French Salvation Army. They spent the day together at the little homestead where Palpant grew flowers and vegetables, and cultivated souls. His hospitality was simple: a slice of seed cake and a bottle of lemonade. For Alec it was an Easter communion he would never forget. He mused that where 'thousands of French criminals had to go to Guiana to learn what hell was like, I had to go to Cayenne to know what Christ was like'.[7]

Paterson had tried to dismiss from his mind all preconceptions, and expected to find that much of what he had read and heard was greatly exaggerated. Some was. The material conditions, while Spartan, were adequate, the food simple but good, the guards (anachronistically called *porte-clefs*) not prone to brutality. Yet he was appalled by what he experienced, and while he could not make a public statement neither could he remain silent. He conferred with the governor, who concurred in his observations, and acting on his advice Alec wrote to Monsieur Andrieu, the Director of Penal Administration, the very official who had secured permission for him to visit the penal settlements in the first place. In a long letter Alec laid his feelings bare.

> The spiritual despair of perpetual banishment among some thousands of them afflicted me more sorely than anything I have ever known ... To see these battalions of men, sentenced without hope to die in a limbo of the tropics, not mercifully in an instant under the sure blade of the guillotine, but yielding drop by drop of blood to the merciless mosquito, is enough to shake the sternest heart. They look straight ahead with those staring eyes and see nothing. They move as men who have been long in Purgatory and know only that Hell awaits them. Through camp after camp, barrack after barrack, tier upon tier, we were met sometimes with a few curt words of defiance or despair, sometimes with a wailing torrent of accusation and appeal, and always with those recurrent words that spell damnation – *doublage* – *libéré* – *en perpetuité*. It was but a procession among ghosts who are not allowed to die. They have lost faith in God, in France and in themselves.

There was nothing in 'the muddy waters of Guiana ... to elevate the mind or raise the morale'. Inevitably 'the bad gr[ew] worse, and mutual corruption of every sort serve[d] to bestialise those who need to be civilized'. After serving their sentence, men had to do '*doublage*', the same number of years, during which they

6   Vicar's letter, St Paul's, Wimbledon Park, September 1954.
7   Paterson, *op.cit.*

were supposed to earn the money for their passage back to France. This period was more deadly than the prison time, because they received no food nor housing at all, and employment was almost impossible to find. Emaciated, listless, they awaited death in jungle or swamp, and an anonymous grave. Slowly killing men in this way was worse than speedy execution. Was it not sad that under the flag of France the word *libéré* should be so grievously misused?[8]

This letter, a resolution passed, at his instigation, by the IPPC[9] during their meeting in Berne at the end of 1937, the report he hand-delivered to the Ministry of Justice in Paris the following Easter, and the ensuing conversations with officials had the cumulative effect of persuading the French government to pass a law ending the despatch of criminals to Guiana, and ultimately to repatriate those already there. Amongst much back-tracking and shilly-shallying it would take a decade to close the place down. In the interim, most of his ameliorative suggestions were put into practice, and with the outbreak of the Second World War some of the convicts were repatriated to take part in the war effort in Europe. Alec would wryly observe that it took 'the inferno of a European war to rescue men from the inhumanity of peace'.[10]

Fortuitously, back in British Guiana, he and Frank played tennis with a man whose father, a count and a killer, had been sent to Cayenne. He had escaped, settled in Demerara, 'married an aboriginal Indian, founded a timber business, and provided the colony with very useful sons.' On 1st April the couple attended a concert put on by the local militia in the Georgetown Botanic Gardens. Alec also visited the industrial school for juvenile delinquents at nearby Onderneeming.

On 20th April they embarked on *SS Ingoma*, which was bound ultimately for England but would stop off at a number of islands before crossing the Atlantic. On the voyage Alec had plenty of time to compose his report for the

---

8   TNA, PCOM9/81: letter, 19th June 1937 (an earlier draft of which was reprinted in Ruck, pp. 149ff). Alec had waited several weeks before writing, 'lest judgment be swayed by sentiment'. The Foreign Office expressly approved the sending of this 'very touching letter'.

9   Report (1936), p. 47.

10   'Devil's Island – the End of the Story', letter from Charles Germain, the Director of Penal Administration, French Ministry of Justice, to Lionel Fox, 20th October 1950, reprinted in Ruck, pp. 183ff; 'Prison in Wartime – and After', *HJ*, 13/2 (July 1941), pp. 12–16, at p. 15; 'Devil's Island', *op.cit.* Alec was so enraged by a decision in November 1938 to revive transportation for certain recidivists and those serving preventive detention that he cancelled a planned visit to England by French prison officials. They would be heavily criticised for perpetuating transportation, and he could not expect his friends and colleagues 'to entertain those who still co-operate with its existence' (TNA, PCOM9/81). Devil's island would not be closed finally until 1953.

Colonial Office.[11] When their ship finally arrived in the Thames on 10th May they were met by their daughter Margaret and by the ever-faithful Tom Angliss. As they drove through London they noticed that the streets were bedecked for the coronation of George VI two days later.

In addition to the official report, Alec wrote a summary called 'Crime in the West Indies' for *The Metropolitan Police College Journal*.[12] Both show their age, at times lapsing into stereotypes, yet his acumen still shines through:

> Sixty per cent of the crimes of the West Indian Negro are against the person, because he is excitable, and forty per cent against property because he is lazy. The anopheles mosquito lies at the root of the worst of his troubles. It breeds in the coarse grass that grows as quickly as the human beard in these hot places. To mitigate the onset of malaria, this grass is perpetually in the process of being cut or chopped or 'bushed', and every West Indian wishing to seem industri-ous must carry everywhere with him a cutlass for this purpose ... the Negro, when he has what he is pleased to call a 'contention' and wishes to put a finer point on his argument, uses his cutlass for the purpose. Officially the offence is 'wounding', but in prison parlance it is always referred to as 'chopping'. The arm of the law tests the edge of the cutlass, and in accordance with its sharp-ness awards a sentence varying from six months to ten years.

Jealousy, inflamed by cheap rum, led to murder, and 'more are killed for love than for loot'. Most thefts were of a neighbour's fruit and vegetables, and the of-fence was so rife that it attracted penalties 'reminiscent of poaching and witch-craft'. 'A man may still be flogged for stealing an unripe banana.'

> The average thief is the Negro who does not earn enough to buy the smart shirt he fancies or the rum that will make him feel big. Subconsciously aware that his grandparents were slaves upon the soil, he revolts with sullen obsti-nacy against work on the land, and without skill of hand or power of pen drifts into a town that has neither need nor rum for him. There follows the overcrowded cabin, the street corner with its easy temptation and then the prison cell. His inhibition is often weakened by malaria, which saps the mor-al fibre as much as the physical stamina, or by the smoking of *gangia* [sic], a common grass so accessible as scarcely to be counted a secret vice.

Alec believed that West Indian criminals were the product of overcrowding, il-legitimacy, indolence, illiteracy and unemployment, all legacies of slavery. East Indians, predominant in British Guiana and growing fast in Trinidad, were very

---

11   *Report of Mr Alexander Paterson on his visits to the Reformatory and Penal Estab-lishments of Jamaica, British Honduras, The Bahamas, the Leeward and Windward Islands, Barbados, Trinidad and Tobago, British Guiana in five months of sunshine between 20th December 1936 and 10th May 1937* (TNA, CO859/72/13/14).

12   3/2 (Autumn 1937).

different. Industrious and uncomplaining, 'their crimes are those of personal violence, the sudden outburst of revenge, long-harboured behind an inscrutable
mask.' They were model prisoners, and rarely recidivists. The Portuguese were seldom in trouble, and the Chinese only for smoking opium. Yet overall there was
little serious crime. Smuggling was as prolific as it was profitable, but most offences were petty, such as cycling with no light or letting an 'unconfined goat' obstruct
the highway. Alec foresaw, however, that with an economic downturn, and a rise
in population, things could easily change for the worse. As indeed they did.

So far as the imprisoned were concerned the public showed 'bland, un-
questioning indifference or even hostility'. There were the usual jibes that
criminals were better off inside prison than out, and had no 'desire to co-operate with the authorities' in their rehabilitation. In fact, prisons were purely
punitive and were inadequately funded.[13] There was no desire to lavish money
on reprobates – all the more so, perhaps, when the taxpayers were predominantly white and the reprobates black. Prison officials, especially those who
had attended Home Office courses or had come with borstal experience in
Britain, such as William Shillingford, the recently appointed Director of Ja-
maican Prisons, took a more enlightened view, but were hampered by such
opposition until it was gradually won over by such reforms as were instituted.[14]
Although all the administrations were sympathetic, they needed the backing
of public opinion to splurge money when strapped for cash. This made for
makeshift remedies. In most colonies it was left to the superintendents and
officers of the Salvation Army to provide help on discharge. The latter also
undertook such probation work as there was.[15]

Paterson recommended a contraction of the prison estate and that other
methods, as effective but less expensive, should be deployed. These were probation for minor offences and offenders, fines in lieu of which distraint of property or unpaid labour should be imposed, hutted camps where first offenders
could grow crops or undertake public works, and a complete overhaul of industrial schools for juveniles, which should be concerned with training, not profit,
and where discipline should be 'co-operative rather than resistive'. Less of the
cane, more of the caring.[16]

13   *Ibid.*, p. 3.
14   S.J. Hogarth, 'Prison Reform in Jamaica', *HJ*, 3/1 (September 1930), pp. 52–55. In
     October 1941 T.S. Simey reported that since 1937 some of Paterson's proposals had
     been implemented, but there was still much left undone (TNA, CO859/72/13).
15   Terence Morris ('British Criminology: 1935–48', *BJC*, 28/2 [Spring 1988], pp. 20–
     34, at p. 24, n.14) mistakenly states that Paterson signed the visitors' book at the
     Salvation Army Reformatory for Boys at Baking Pot, British Honduras *in 1934*. It
     was 1937.
16   Report (1937), pp. 4–10.

Again, he urged proper classification, and – 'the root and crown of the whole matter' – the careful selection and adequate training of prison officers, many of whom were venal and unfit for promotion. He suggested that a training school for new recruits from the whole of the West Indies be established at the prison on Carrera Island off the coast of Trinidad.[17] He even appended a reading list, including works by Jeremy Bentham, John Howard, Thomas Mott Osborne, Sanford Bates, William Norwood East and Cyril Burt and his own report on American prisons.[18] Full-time chaplains able to do much more than just take hurried services should be appointed. More doctors were needed, as well as 'a peripatetic psychologist', since there was no provision for the mental health of prisoners in any of the colonies. Prisoners should be put to productive and profitable work but not exploited as free labour by officials. Education classes and physical training should be encouraged, as should the involvement of prison visitors. When it came to the question of 'European prisoners', he thought that they should be differentiated from the others, not, he claimed, on racial grounds, but on medical ones, in that a too drastic change in diet and environment might adversely affect their health. In such circumstances a doctor should be able to recommend adjustments in diet, bedding, clothing and employment. Paterson should have been aware that this would amount to decidedly better treatment for white prisoners than for black. All the while the English Commissioner was conscious that 'the prison is not a desert island in the community', and that 'the system developed at home could not simply be imposed on a country where the problems of life are so utterly different.'

17 Such a school was established, providing two-month elementary courses for junior officers, while some senior staff were sent on the overseas course run by the Home Office.

18 It is not surprising Paterson included Burt, whom he may well have known from their Oxford days since they were exact contemporaries and studied the same subject. Burt went on to work in a Liverpool dockland settlement, before becoming an eminent psychologist. His *Young Delinquent* (London, 1925) leant academic credence to Alec's views. It emphasised the multiplicity of factors behind youthful criminality. Heredity was not one. Poverty and its attendant evils had a part to play but much more significant were discordant family relationships and defective discipline. The problem of delinquency was inseparable from child welfare as a whole, and the court must 'regard not the offence, but the offender'. The aim must be not punishment, but treatment and 'educative training', and the target not isolated actions but their causes. Before passing sentence 'such authorities should have access to all available information about the individual delinquent and have expert help from a variety of sources.' Specifically, Burt urged that 'institutions for the delinquent should continue their laudable development towards a less uniform organization and a less repressive code' (4th edn, pp. 610f). What greater endorsement could Alec have wanted?

After praising the friends and colleagues whom it was 'as hard to leave as impossible to forget', he ended with a personal vignette:

> At a breakfast given to schoolchildren, a small Indian boy of 14 was with the greatest difficulty persuaded to say a word of thanks ... With greater frankness than is usually shown on such occasions, his first halting sentence 'we are very grateful to Mr Paterson for coming today and making a speech' was, after a nervous pause, followed by 'We hope he will come again someday and make a better speech'.[19]

Out of the mouths of babes and sucklings!

19   Report (1937), p. 37. Fearing upsetting some of the officials Paterson considered important to keep onside, the Colonial Office declined to publish the full report. It did dispatch copies to the governors and senior prison officials and visiting justices. It also circulated a bulletin on the principles of penal reform. Paterson criticised the latter for being dated and parochial (TNA, CO859/72/13).

CHAPTER 19

POLICY, PROGRESS AND THE ONSET OF WAR: 1938–1939

> The reformation of the offender has become in recent years the keynote of the administration of justice.
>
> *Report of the Committee on the Treatment of Young Offenders*

> Personality is at its best the expression of a spirit wherein a desire to serve has earned the power to lead.
>
> *Alexander Paterson*

In September 1938 Paterson provided the preface for the posthumously published *Notes of a Prison Visitor* by Major Gordon Gardiner, one of the first lay visitors at Wormwood Scrubs. For the previous sixteen years the policy of the Commissioners, recognising the deleterious effects of confinement on the personality, had been to invite 'men of goodwill to visit prisoners weekly in their cells'. More than 600 had taken up the challenge. Gardiner's notes from the years 1922 and 1923 were of 'inestimable value in giving a picture of the inside of a prison that is without the bias of too close a perspective' – unlike the accounts written by ex-officials and ex-prisoners. Unusually, ready consent had been given for them to be published. Unusual the publication may have been, unpredictable it was not. The *Notes* were confirmation of the great claims that the Commissioners had made for the scheme, all the more compelling for coming from the early years of prison reform. The more public awareness of prisons and the Commissioners' policies, purveyed by 'objective outsiders' such as the author, the better.[1] Prison visitors were even encouraged to push for change, particularly in respect of boy prisoners. In March

---

1   Two other prison visitors he encouraged into print were T. Whyte Mountain and Albert Crew. Both produced books for popular consumption: *Life in London's Great Prisons* (London, 1930) and *London Prisons of Today and Yesterday, Plain Facts and Coloured Impressions* (London, 1933) respectively – describing in pastel

1935, 'with the consent and full cooperation of the Commissioners', they had conducted an inquiry into their lot. It had found that there were over 300 of them, a third of whom were first offenders. Provision for them was poor, contamination inevitable, but 'one salient fact emerged: the Prison Commissioners were doing all they could against overwhelming odds.'[2]

A few days after Gardiner's book was published Alec addressed a group of women magistrates on 'the present policy of the Prison Commission'. He reiterated his three points. The cardinal one was 'to treat the offender as an individual, as a separate and distinct personality, quite different from every other one who is in our charge.' He quoted Temple's maxim that 'no man is a criminal and nothing else.' There was 'always something else – the person he was when he was not committing crime ... even a bad penny has two sides to it'. That other side was what most concerned the prison service. The second point was the need for classification to prevent contamination and differentiate training. Borstals were leading the way in this. After careful assessment boys were assigned to one of eight institutions on the basis of their trustworthiness, degree of criminality and intelligence in the hope that they would encounter no one more depraved than themselves and would receive the sort of training most appropriate to their needs. He confidently predicted that 'what is true of borstal today' would become true of prison in the future. The third point was that imprisonment was the punishment. It was not the duty of prison staff to inflict further punishment but to train prisoners in habit, mind and character. Chaplains on their parochial round, salaried teachers or well-educated outsiders taking evening classes, tutors instructing in useful trades, volunteers paying regular cell visits – all were integral to this.

He then turned to the international role of the Prison Commission in promoting penal reform. It had always played a major part in the IPPC and had received visits from and exchanged visits with foreign dignitaries and authorities. But its impact and influence had been most profound within the prison services of the British Empire, where increasingly 'our English prison service is coming to be regarded as the parent' of them all. For eleven years the Home Office had hosted a two-week summer school for twenty or more representatives from all parts of the British Empire. There they were introduced to the principles undergirding prison policy in England and, it was hoped, would enter into the spirit of that policy. It seemed to be so, as increasingly the Prison Commission was asked to nominate staff to go to the farthest points of the globe as 'penal missionaries'. In particular borstal housemasters had been sent

---

hues the prisons of the metropolis, and advocating the sort of ameliorations Alec wanted to make.

2   Watson (1939), pp. 91f.

to Burma, Uganda and British Guiana to inaugurate borstals, and another was soon to go to Ceylon for the same purpose.[3]

G reat progress had been made from what was a pretty low base, but it was imperfect, and inconsistently applied. Money was short. Implementation was patchy. Cicely McCall, a psychiatric social worker who joined the prison service, in her 1938 exposé, *They Always Come Back*, complained that women and girls were neglected in the reform process. For a year she worked as an assistant housemistress in Aylesbury borstal under Miss Barker, before being posted to Holloway prison in 1936. Boys, she noted, were getting a better deal in borstal – better staff, better facilities, better trade-training, better after-care. Indeed she looked with envy at the sense of purpose exuding from Lowdham Grange and contrasted it with the provision for girls at Aylesbury. She found that conditions in Holloway remained largely untouched, with inadequate medical provision, poor clothing, worse food and petty rules persisting. Too many of the old ways endured, and the old attitudes:

> One of the reasons why the attitude of the average officer towards the women in her charge is unimaginative is lack of training; and another is that the whole prison system tends to deaden spontaneous humanitarian impulses. This is not primarily the officer's fault. The deadening of all spontaneity is an insidious malady in most institutions, and the older staff, already steeped in institutionalism, set the tone for the juniors. Before many years have passed an officer forgets how to speak naturally to a prisoner.

Pay for prisoners, pioneered in 1929, took almost ten years to reach Holloway, and women officers were on the whole of a lower stamp and less imaginative than their male equivalents. McCall was unique. In this period lowly housemistresses did not write books, let alone ones criticising the Commissioners and mirroring the issues raised in inmate accounts. She was letting the side down. Nor was she entirely fair, as both the numbers of women prisoners and of prisons holding them had gone down.[4]

Reservations apart, and however variously applied, reforms continued. For Alec it was the 1930s that was the roaring decade. Success seemed enduring and inevitable, and successes kept coming. On 4th June 1937, in a debate on the

---

3   *The Magistrate*, November–December 1938, pp. 140ff; Alexander Paterson, afterword to the second edition of Le Mesurier's *Boys in Trouble* (London, 1939), p.xvi.
4   Cicely McCall, *They Always Come Back* (London, 1938), pp. 55, 58, 69, 183ff; Report (1936). McCall was not of lowly status. Her father was both a knight and KC, and she had matriculated at St Hugh's College, Oxford.

civil service estimates, members of the House of Commons clamoured to heap praise on the 'far-seeing' Prison Commissioners for their startling success with borstals, 'undoubtedly and beyond question the very finest remedy for the child who is down and out', and for the experimental adult regime and the prison officers' training school at Wakefield which they had set up. The latter produced 'men radiating a new influence and a new spirit throughout our prisons.' 'For years', one MP said, 'the Prison Commissioners have been the best of prison reformers.' Equally, members recognised that the good work being done was gravely hampered by the obsolete prison buildings with which they had to contend. Politicians of all parties not only approved of what the Commissioners were trying to achieve, they recognised the obstacles in their way and wanted to remove them. Indeed it was fully anticipated that Pentonville, Reading and Oxford would close. Paterson doubted 'whether we shall ever build another walled establishment for penal purposes in this country'.[5]

In the 1930s, with its excess of optimism, plethora of pliable youths and surfeit of exceptional governors, self-sacrificing housemasters, and custodial staff who had imbibed Paterson's charisma, borstals in particular had reached the apogee of success. For all the tabloid griping (and sometimes justified criticism), they proved to be a penal experiment that actually worked, at least when political bipartisanship reigned, social mores were conducive, and the right staff were in place. These found working in borstals both rewarding and inspiring, which cannot be said for many initiatives in the prison service. A large number of young people benefited from them: some gained literacy; others learnt trades and became employable; and many who experienced borstal training praised it. Only a minority became recidivists. Borstals had exceeded all expectations, surmounted all challenges, and become an integral, and the most innovative, part of a great movement for penal transformation.

The Prison Commissioners believed they had found the secret of ending recidivism and hoped that they could soon begin closing many of their prisons. That hope was buttressed by political consensus. In 1937 Samuel Hoare became Home Secretary, the most radical since Churchill. Like Margery Fry he was of Quaker stock, but Hoare, unlike Margery, was in lineal descent from the great reformer herself. He was also, unlike Margery, a Conservative, albeit with a strong liberal streak. To master his new brief, he toured prisons and talked to staff, something few Home Secretaries had ever done. When in Paterson's company Hoare visited Dartmoor, he was convinced by the human wrecks he saw there that short sentences led to recidivism and that probation, approved schools and long periods of corrective training were needed, very much Alec's agenda. 'Nervous, assertive, transparently sincere', Paterson, 'the new man with the new ideas of treatment',

5   HC debates, 5th Series, vol.324, cols.1315–1351.

FIGURE 29. Alec relaxing on the cusp of complete success, 1938

transmitted to the Home Secretary much of his own 'crusading fervour'.[6] For once there was an excellent story to tell about prisons and Hoare believed that the time to tell it had come. He agreed that there should be a fundamental change in penal methods. Determined to force a major criminal justice bill through within his own term of office, Hoare wasted no time.

Wanting to sweep 'away ... the remnants of Victorian melodrama ... that looked at the treatment of crime principally from the angles of retribution and deterrence', he approached the issue 'from the angles of prevention and

6   Viscount Templewood, *Nine Troubled Years* (London, 1954), pp. 228–235.

reformation'. With the aim of curtailing and ultimately extinguishing imprisonment for adolescents, and protecting society from persistent pests, Hoare put forward a comprehensive Criminal Justice Bill which 'gathered up the fruits of thirty years' experiment, experience, criticism and reflection'.[7] The harvest was ready, 'drilled and cultivated by skilled men and women', and he would 'cut and winnow it'. The Bill would have enacted many of the proposals of the departmental committees which had festooned the previous quarter century, and in particular those of the Young Offenders Committee. *Inter alia*, it would have abolished penal servitude, prohibited imprisonment for all under sixteen years of age, removed the power of magistrates to sentence those under twenty-one to prison, and placed restrictions on the higher courts. Corrective detention for adults between twenty-one and thirty and preventive detention for the older would have been introduced. For young offenders, remand homes, attendance centres and residential hostels called Howard Houses would have been set up as an alternative to custody, and the use of borstal under the new sentence of 'borstal training' would have expanded.[8]

Apart from that restricting corporal punishment to prison offences, the most contentious proposal, and one advocated both by Maxwell (by then Under-Secretary of State at the Home Office) and Paterson, had been to empower magistrates' courts to commit offenders directly to borstal. The hope was that this would reduce the use of short prison sentences; the fear was that they would impose borstal detention in cases for which non-custodial options were more appropriate. Faced with opposition from the Labour Party, the Howard League and the Magistrates' Association, Hoare backed down and withdrew the proposal, substituting the provision relating to magistrates' sentencing powers. Maxwell and Paterson, however, were successful in opposing the introduction of short-term borstals which they believed would be merely punitive, 'in effect a system of boys' prisons' perpetuating all the evils of imprisonment.

To provide the necessary infrastructure for the new dispensation, Hoare also proposed both a major prison building programme, which would have replaced relics such as Pentonville, Holloway, and above all Dartmoor, and the establishment of the psychotherapeutic prison recommended by Norwood East and

7   Cicely Craven, 'The Trend of Criminal Legislation', in Leon Radzinowicz and J. Turner (eds), *Penal Reform in England* (London, 1946), pp. 18–32, at p. 29.
8   The idea behind attendance centres originated with Paterson. Giving evidence before the Persistent Offenders' Committee, he had acknowledged that borstal and probation would not do for all, least of all for minor first-time offenders, and recommended 'the deprivation of leisure as a means of dealing with the troublesome adolescent' who had broken a by-law or failed to pay a fine but whose future should not be jeopardised by 'the dislocation or stigma of such a sentence' (Ruck, p. 60). They were, in effect, compulsory boys' and girls' clubs with added chores.

William Hubert, the psychotherapist who since 1934 had done much valuable work in Wormwood Scrubs. All was set for the greatest transformation of the prison system in a hundred years.

The draft legislation 'was essentially an expression of Paterson's aspirations'.[9] It met with widespread support in Parliament and in the press. His agenda was to be given statutory approval, laying the foundations for future progress. Yet it was not to be. The imminence of war with Germany scuppered the Bill in its very last stages, along with the long-awaited replacement of defunct prisons.[10] These were huge blows and hugely frustrating.

Not that Alec sat around moping. He was increasingly busy both at home and abroad. There was international interest in what was going on in England and increasing appreciation that it was world-leading in penal reform. Recognised as the towering force behind this, Alec, the 'prison wallah', was much in demand. In April 1938, for instance, a report of the Canadian Royal Commission recommended a restructuring of the penal system along English lines, having found none better.[11] Centralised control under a prison commission of three members should be instigated, and 'an outstanding prison authority from England, preferably Mr Alexander Paterson ... should be invited to come to Canada to counsel and advise on the reorganisation of the prison system in order to give practical effect to the recommendations contained in this report.' He had welcomed the Commissioners to England the previous

9   HC debates, 30th November 1938; Playfair, *op.cit.*, p. 177.
10   Hugh Klare in Manuel Lopez-Rey and Charles Germain, *Studies in Penology* (The Hague, 1964), p. 113. The 'East-Hubert Institute' would have to await the opening of Grendon in 1962. Holloway survived until recent years, while Pentonville (along with many other Victorian prisons) remains operational to this day. It has recently been announced that Dartmoor is to be axed, but the blade has yet to fall. Herbert Morrison, the wartime Home Secretary, mused that perhaps it would have been better if all the old prisons had been demolished by the Germans, a sentiment shared by one of his department's civil servants, Lionel Fox.
11   Similarly, in 1935 the Inspector-General of Prisons in Ceylon, after attending the course for overseas prison staff officers and studying recruitment, concluded that 'the careful method of selection and the comprehensive system of instruction and training ... have resulted in the personnel of that service being the finest in the world, and has furnished the best type of machinery whereby the needs of modern penology and the policies of the Commissioners are capable of intelligent appreciation and efficient and enthusiastic execution' (Report [1935], p. 44).

July and had clearly impressed them.[12] If the invitation ever came, he was unable to take it up at that time. He did, however, go elsewhere.

From March to June 1939, with Frank in tow, Alec embarked on an extensive inspection of the prisons and 'other delinquency services' of the East African dependencies of Kenya, Uganda, Tanganyika, Zanzibar, Aden and Somaliland. For some time, the Colonial Office had been concerned about the state of the prisons and the number imprisoned in its territories, and began pressing local administrations to enact reforms in keeping with good practice in the mother country and the rehabilitative emphasis emanating from it. African prisons were amongst the worst. A 1936 report of the Ugandan Prison Commission had concluded that in the protectorate there was 'not a prison which should not at once be condemned'. Apart from the accommodation being deplorable, the buildings were insanitary and a fire risk. In twenty years nothing had been done to provide proper treatment for young offenders. Although Paterson's report on Burma and Fox's *The Modern English Prison* were well-known to officials, they had little influence.[13] Uganda was far from unique.

First stop on the itinerary was Aden. The Patersons spent only a few days there but nonetheless Alec made one recruit. He got into conversation with an army sergeant sitting on a wall outside the Anglican church. As a result of this serendipitous encounter in Aden that soldier would become a housemaster in England.

Shortly after their arrival in Kenya, Alec attended the first conference of the East African Prison Commissioners, all of whom he knew from the home service. It was held in Mombasa on 28th April and was followed by a dinner for the five attendees. The report of the proceedings (which Alec co-wrote) showed a consensus to move in a more reformatory direction. The Commissioners proposed that prison camps for both Europeans and Africans be established, 'lunatics' and 'tax-defaulters' be kept out of prisons, long-sentence prisoners be allowed to play football, money be provided for education within prisons, and the carrying of rifles by warders be phased out. So useful had the inaugural conference been that Alec later recommended to the Colonial Penal Administration Committee that they be held regularly not just in East Africa but in other parts of the Empire.[14]

In his exploration of Kenya Alec found that what was lacking were alternatives to imprisonment, such as probation and unpaid work schemes. What was not lacking were prisons: they were proliferating. Kenya incarcerated a far greater

12   Report (1937), p. 45; *The Times*, 19th July 1937.
13   Julius Lewin, 'Uganda's Prison Problem', *HJ*, 4/4 (July 1937), pp. 409f.
14   TNA, CO859/19/8.

proportion of its population than any other British colony in East or Central Africa.[15] There was little provision for after-care. Above all, more should be done for the young. Just as in England, the first moves to a reformatory system had begun with adolescents. Founded in 1907 a few miles north of Nairobi, Kabete reformatory remained for thirty years the sole institution dedicated to the detention of male juvenile offenders. They were employed in farm work and the manufacture of cheap furniture and household implements for settlers. It had already been criticised for being totally ineffective in reforming inmates. In Swahili it was known as *jaili watoto* (children's jail). Indeed it was more a prison than a school with 'little, if any, reformation and quite inadequate education'. It was ripe for change. A 1933 report on 'the applicability to Kenya of methods pursued in borstals and other reformatory schools in England' led to legislative action. The author, Sydney La Fontaine, who, like many colonial administrators, was imbued with a 'strong sense of obligation to the welfare of indigenous people', had toured borstal institutions at home to determine whether 'African human nature' was amenable to a similar reformative policy. He concluded that it was, and that Kabete should become a training school, similar to an English borstal, for delinquent boys aged between fourteen and nineteen.[16] The Paterson blueprint should be imported. It was, and in January 1935 Commander William Harrison, a housemaster from Portland and another of Paterson's recruits, became superintendent. Two years later a similar state-run school for children up to the age of sixteen was opened at Dagoretti. At least for juveniles, Alec found, some things were progressing. Others were not. He deplored the promiscuous use of the cane to discipline children in Kenyan prisons, describing it as a 'barbarous weapon for the beating of small boys', mitigated by the fact that most warders were too humane to use a stick more than a quarter of an inch in diameter.[17]

In Tanganyika he spent a day in a small up-country district gaol. Accompanied by the District Commissioner, Alec 'wandered round the hot prison yards, the hotter kitchen, and the still hotter bathroom, and heard applications and complaints that prisoners and warders had to make'. On emerging from the prison, as the gate closed behind him, he paused for a moment in bewilderment.

15   Daniel Branch, 'Imprisonment and Colonialism in Kenya, c.1930–1952: Escaping the Carceral Archipelago', *International Journal of African Historical Studies*, 38/2 (2005), pp. 239–265, at p. 248.

16   Chloe Campbell, 'Juvenile Delinquency in Colonial Kenya 1900–1939', *Historical Journal*, 45/1 (March 2002), pp. 129–151, at pp. 136f, 143ff; Paul Ocobock, *An Uncertain Age* (Ohio, 2017), pp. 137–157; Leonard Kercher, *The Kenya Penal System* (Washington, 1981), p. 35. In 1933 the upper age limit was set at eighteen, in 1935 at twenty-one.

17   TNA, CO912/4: *Report on a Visit to the Prisons of Kenya, Uganda, Tanganyika, Zanzibar, Aden and Somaliland* (1939), p. 15; Ocobock, *op.cit.*, pp. 114–136.

The keyhole was on the outside of the gate. Not only could it be unlocked by somebody outside the prison, but the prison could be left empty of staff but full of prisoners. 'Warders', he told his colleague, 'should never be given this chance of leaving a prison, with all the men locked up inside the walls.'

> There may be fires or fights or other contingencies. These prisoners are human beings, whose safety, security and well-being are entrusted to you by the courts. They cannot be left lightly by bored or weary warders, locked up for the night like dogs in a kennel, or umbrellas in a cloakroom. The unvarying prison rule is that there shall always be two gates to every prison, and that each can only be opened by the gate-keeper, who is stationed day and night in the space be-tween them. It is also axiomatic that to prevent a rush, inward or outward, the two gates shall never be opened at the same time. This is all very tiresome and doctrinaire to the average man, but very elementary to the 'prison wallah'.[18]

He deplored the fact that at night prisoners were accommodated in dormito-ries. The worst had been constructed before the Great War in the capital Dar-es-Salaam, when Tanganyika had been German East Africa. The Germans had built a massive open structure where over 1,000 prisoners slept on mats. Alec hoped that his representations to the local government and the Colonial Office would play a part 'in the abandonment of this miserable maelstrom of vice and venality'. The lot of women was the worst. Few in number, widely dispersed, and forced to live in prolonged isolation or promiscuous association, they were an easy prey to depression or contamination. 'To remedy these real injustices to women' the small wards in the county prisons should be closed and their occupants gathered in 'one or two central gaols' where they could work outside under light security.

One aspect of African prisons he did enjoy was visiting them just after day-break for 'the dawn chorus':

> In many other countries the visiting official would be greeted with snores or snarls, but in East Africa, as he enters, fifty or a hundred prisoners rise to their feet, and there is a universal chorus of 'Jambo, Jambo' from every angle.

Years later he named his 'very cheerful yellow kitten "Jambo" in memory of our friends in the East African prisons' although he never succeeded in teaching him 'to welcome the dawn with the same cheerful shout'.[19]

This interlude apart, his subsequent report was both a vivid depiction of East African prisons and an excoriating indictment of them. Laxity, inertia and exploitation were their salient features. Probation, that vital alternative to in-carceration for minor offenders, and after-care, so important for rehabilitation,

18   *Over the Walls*, pp. 12ff.
19   *Over the Walls*, p. 36. Jambo remains a widely used Swahili greeting.

were wholly inadequate or totally absent. The use of African prisoners as 'a convenient supply of free labour' was a disgrace:

> Hence arose vast workshops where hundreds of prisoners performed mechanical and repetitive operations in the manufacture of strange articles for which there was a market. Thus a thousand natives might engage in the making of boots for army and police, though on return to their villages they would never see a boot again in their lives.

Senior officials were abusing their position by using prisoners as unpaid gardeners or servants. He denounced the 'insidious fallacy that lurks behind the employment of prisoners – the conception of their labour as a convenience to the more privileged members of the community'. 'Under such a system', he thundered, 'everything becomes subordinate to the question of profit.' Profit, or paying its way in hard economic times. All other aspects of imprisonment, including reformation, were secondary to this. While there was no ill-treatment, brutality or trafficking, there was no physical or mental training, and 'only sporadic instances of spiritual training'. There had been one experiment of value. A restriction on the use of corporal punishment over the previous decade had changed it from being the most common form of punishment to being the least, while during the same period assaults on staff had reduced and the conduct of prisoners improved. Paterson welcomed this development, 'as it would be unfortunate if it were widely held that whipping is the only instrument of justice that follows the British flag.'[20]

The quality of subordinate staff also exercised him. Poorly paid, inadequately trained, and of dubious quality, African warders were 'the heart of the problem'. While security was lax, and walls were crumbling, wardens were unnecessarily armed with guns when mounting guard over or drilling prisoners who showed little inclination to escape or even cause trouble. The problem of staff was not irresolvable, if those of calibre could be recruited. In Uganda that was already happening, with graduates of Makarere College joining the prison service as assistant gaolers. They were the right sort, 'humane and good at sport'.[21]

The multiplication of penal institutions, especially in Kenya, had to be reversed: 'He who builds a prison digs a hole. A hole fills up in time.' The first to go should be that in Mombasa, located within the walls of a fort built by the Portuguese in 1595. As it was 'not suitable in site or construction for its present purpose', it should be turned into a museum, Alec suggested.[22]

Once again, the Colonial Office had misgivings about publishing his report, some senior officials worrying that such an exposé of the state of East African

---

20   Report (1939), pp. 17ff.
21   *Ibid.*, pp. 6ff.
22   *Ibid.*, p. 33.

prisons was unwise, especially during wartime, others deprecating those aspects they conceived to be 'trivial' or 'flippant' and which were more likely to annoy than convert their readership to 'his sound views'. With Paterson's consent some offending passages were omitted, but as he objected to any alterations in wording these were not made. A hundred and forty copies of the expurgated report were then circulated to the relevant colonial governments. As a result, many of the recommendations (in particular cost-neutral or cost-cutting ones such as prison camps) of this 'St Paul of prison reform'[23] were implemented throughout East Africa, despite wartime exigencies and prisons having low priority.[24]

His idiosyncratic approach aside, Alec was held in high regard by the Colonial Office and his services remained in great demand. A similar tour of the prisons of West Africa, planned for 1940, had to be postponed owing to the critical stage of the war, but remained a live possibility.

Great Britain declared war on Germany on 3rd September 1939. Undeterred, Alec remained determined to fulfil an engagement overseas. He had been invited by the American Prison Association as the IPPC representative to attend its congress, to see for himself the most recent penal developments, and to give the speech at the closing dinner. On 7th October he embarked for New York across what had become a much more dangerous ocean. It was too risky for Frank to accompany him this time. Due to 'the vicissitudes of weather and war' he did not arrive until the second day of the conference, where he was received with a standing ovation.[25] He spoke at most of the general sessions and sectional meetings. There was dinner on the 16th attended by the mayor of the city and the governor of the state. There was a luncheon three days later which was addressed by Eleanor Roosevelt, who by her words and presence gave prison reform a quasi-regal blessing. Alec, who was seated beside the First Lady, told her about the work of the IPPC.

There was also time to visit prisons. Alec looked with envy at the penitentiaries recently constructed at Lewisburg in Pennsylvania and Wallkill in New York State. With their Norman cloisters, leafy quadrangles, libraries and collegiate aspect, they were far superior to the 'great gaols of frozen ugliness' conceived in the Victorian age. They reminded him 'of the most beautiful schools and colleges anywhere in the world'. America, he concluded, 'had brought beauty into the prison without shame or apology, and it is to America that the prison-builders of Europe must go for inspiration, as they once

23   So called by a reviewer in *The Magistrate*, May–June 1939.
24   TNA, CO859/19/8.
25   TNA, PCOM9/83: Paterson's report.

went to Pennsylvania for isolation.'[26] Further, he was well aware that the President had poured money into the federal prisons – he had written an article on it.[27] When the delegates visited Sing Sing, they were joined again by Mrs Roosevelt. At the splendid culminating banquet in the Hotel New Yorker in Manhattan, Paterson addressed the gathering on his beloved borstal system, which had already come in for much praise in the United States. After his speech it would receive even more.[28]

Having spoken to Bates and Cass about the danger that American funding of the IPPC might cease, Alec travelled to Washington to lobby on its behalf. He met Chief Justice Charles Hughes and Associate Justice Owen Roberts of the Supreme Court, James Bennett, Director of the Federal Bureau of Prisons and an official delegate to the Berlin Congress, various members of Congress, and another friend of his, G. Howland Shaw, Director of Personnel at the State Department. He pressed upon them the importance of continued funding.

On 4th November Alec embarked on the Cunard liner *Scythia*, bound for England. He had been away for twice the time anticipated, but was delighted by the visit, gratified by his reception, honoured to be asked to speak, and confident that his lobbying in Washington had had its effect. It was worth the effort – and the expense. To keep up appearances, he had had to subsidise the trip out of his own pocket. Penal activism did not come cheap.

O n 17th December 1939, appropriately enough a Sunday, an era ended with the death of John Stansfeld. He was buried in his parish of Spelsbury, but on 13th January the following year a thanksgiving service took place in Bermondsey parish church. Archbishop Temple could not be there, but Alec was, along with many others. Clifford Woodward, by then Bishop of Bristol, delivered the address. Afterwards the whole congregation streamed across Tower Bridge Road for tea in the Old Boys' Club. It was a fitting send-off, one that 'the Doctor' would have deprecated for its extravagance.

Meanwhile Alec's domestic life had been temporarily disrupted. Frank and Margaret went to stay with relatives in the country at the start of the war. They

---

26 Alexander Paterson, 'Prisons in Wartime – and After', *HJ*, 13/2 (July 1941), pp. 12–16, at p. 15; 'Privileged Prisoners', *The Spectator*, 15th August 1947, p. 11.

27 '$14,000,000 allocated for Repair and Construction of Federal Penal and Correctional Institutions', *Federal Probation*, 2/3 (3rd July 1938), pp. 26ff.

28 'How England Handles the Young Offender', *Proceedings of the Annual Congress of the American Prison Association* (1939), pp. 149–157; *New York Times*, 21st October 1939. There were also calls to emulate his involvement of lay people in penal reform – see his article 'The Prison Visitor in England', *Jail Association Journal*, 2/1 (Jan–Feb 1940), pp. 10ff.

soon returned to Christchurch Terrace, where they would remain throughout the worst of the blitz, even after it had been badly shaken during the bombing of the nearby Royal Hospital.

It was just as well Frank came home since there were a lot of guests staying with them, including German nationals who should have been interned.

CHAPTER 20

WAR WORK: 1939–1943

> The war has put the prison clock back almost to 1922.
> *The Howard League*

The expansion of the borstal system at home and abroad, the success of innovative schemes at Wakefield and elsewhere, the gathering together of exceptional governors, housemasters and officers, the increasing involvement of a sympathetic public, and the legislative imprimatur that would be provided when the Criminal Justice Bill became law, all heralded a golden age for reformers. But the war came, reining in the steady progress which until then had 'generated unalloyed admiration throughout the world'.[1]

The structure erected during the inter-war years was undermined, not so much by German bombs, but by other effects of the war.[2] Two thirds of trainees were discharged, many of whom, along with many of the staff, joined the armed forces. The loss of the latter was particularly damaging. They were the standard-bearers of the reform movement, and had laboured hard to create a tradition that would endure. All gone! So too were some of the institutions. Five were taken over in full or in part for use by the War Office or for adults decanted from urban prisons. Some suffered. While both Rochester and Feltham were hit by bombs, Portland, because of its location, fared the worst, being repeatedly subjected to bombing and machine-gunning by the Luftwaffe, which damaged buildings and killed or wounded several boys. Their comrades got their revenge when one of the planes crashed and the lads, rummaging through the wreckage, made off with the pilot's ear as a trophy.[3] Overcrowded and under-manned, borstals were unable to provide the same quality of training as heretofore. In addition, war-work took precedence over everything, and borstal boys and girls

---

1   Radzinowicz, p. 397.
2   A detailed account of the effects of war, upon which the following is based, was given in the Commissioners' Report for 1939–1941 (published in 1946), pp. 5–19.
3   Guy Richmond, *Prison Doctor* (British Columbia, 1975), p. 39; Vidler, pp. 58ff.

were not exempted. Life for them would be taken at a brisker tempo. As the war progressed the number of young offenders increased and they seemed more difficult and disturbed, an aberration occasioned by the turmoil, disruption of family life, and privations of wartime, or so it was thought. As training was in retreat, birchings as well as committals to prison were on the increase. It was assumed that with victory things would gradually return to normal, borstal would be resurgent and its success consummated.

Prisons also suffered.[4] Bristol, Manchester, Hull, Cardiff and Swansea were damaged during air raids, Liverpool most seriously. For his actions when it was bombed its governor, James Holt, was awarded the OBE, while J. Meehan, a female officer who single-handedly extinguished an incendiary which had lodged in the roof of a wing, won the George Medal. With the exception of Wormwood Scrubs,[5] the London prisons were all victims of the blitz, perhaps mistaken for factories. Brixton escaped major damage. Holloway suffered more. Pentonville, the worst affected, was hit on several occasions, culminating in an incendiary attack on 10th May 1941 which resulted in seventeen people, staff as well as prisoners, losing their lives. Wandsworth likewise was repeatedly bombed. Grew described the destruction and havoc wreaked by three German planes on one such occasion, although, because of a well-drilled procedure whereby each night the prisoners (other than the few on fire-watch duty) were kept locked in their virtually bomb-proof cells with strict instructions to observe the black-out, there was no fatality.[6] Alec was on the scene within the hour. Even when surveying the badly damaged reception block, his sense of the absurd never failed him:

> In a thousand pigeon-holes were the private clothes and property of a thousand prisoners. The bowler hats which betokened the last days of respectable freedom were dirty and misshapen. The weighing scales of the medical officer had stuck obstinately at zero, as though the enemy had determined that even our smart London thieves should be of no weight or account.[7]

He remained upbeat. Guest speaker at a Howard League luncheon in February 1940, his chosen topic was 'Prison in Wartime and After'.[8] First the bad news.

---

4   For an assessment of prisons during wartime see Mark Benney's compilation of prisoner accounts, *Gaol Delivery* (London, 1948). Between August 1942 and March 1944 conscientious objectors detained in Wormwood Scrubs, and spared the bombs, produced *The Flowery*, an underground 'Conchie' review. It took its name from Cockney rhyming slang for a cell: 'flowery dell'.
5   In February 1944 its luck would run out when incendiary bombs fell on it.
6   Grew, pp. 115, 118–122. Paterson had told Grew: 'London will either be the safest place in the country, or the most hellish.'
7   *Over the Walls*, pp. 25f.
8   *HJ*, 13/2 (July 1941), pp. 12–16.

Economic retrenchment had meant the postponement of a new prison for women and a new borstal for girls. The advent of aerial warfare had necessitated the evacuation of several prisons and borstals and the dispersal or discharge of thousands of inmates, since nothing was 'so inhuman as to cause a man to be at the same time under fire and under constraint'. For those remaining, the black-out had curtailed working hours and evening programmes. The danger was that 'the whole period of the war may, in itself, be a sort of blackout', so far as prisons were concerned, a 'period of paralysis and stagnation' during which 'the machine just tick[ed] over' and no forward advance would be made.

But the war also provided opportunities. Prisoners worked harder, knowing that they would be paid for their efforts and that those efforts were part of the war-effort; 'star class' prisoners were decanted from Wakefield to open conditions at Lowdham Grange and from Wormwood Scrubs to the open-air and relaxed regime at Camp Hill; and women were moved from Holloway to Aylesbury. To provide the necessary space for evacuated prisoners, 1,700 lads had been discharged within forty-eight hours of the declaration of war. Not all were suitable for the armed forces or work in munitions factories, but less than 15 per cent had been re-convicted in the following six months. Best of all, in Alec's opinion, the war had brought about what he had long desired: the removal of all borstal boys from Wormwood Scrubs to a non-penal institution in the countryside. They were all taken to Feltham borstal for the duration, or until their transfer or discharge. He ended on a note of optimism. After hostilities had ceased, as a result of the experiments that they had been forced to make and the risks they had to run, the consensus would be that the problem of imprisonment would be seen as part of wider social problems. The Colonial Office had recently set up a Social Services Department and all matters relating to prisons fell within its remit. So should it be at home. No one should any longer view the prison administration as just 'a tiresome little side-show'.

He was too sanguine. The Second World War changed everything as he predicted, but not for the better. Worst of all, unlike during the Great War, the number of the imprisoned began to increase substantially.

War brought other and novel duties for this versatile Commissioner. Reports of collaborators in Norway and France fuelled fears in Britain that enemies lurked within. There were some home-grown Nazi sympathisers, of course, such as Oswald Mosley and his Fascist League, but foreign nationals fleeing to this country to escape persecution were unlikely to aid the perpetrators. For a time, hysteria overrode reason. No chances would be taken, and orders went out to 'collar the lot'. 'The lot' included thousands of innocents, many of whom were actively opposed to Hitler and his murderous regime.

The internment of these mainly Jewish refugees from Austria and Germany continued apace. Many 'enemy aliens' spent time in prisons – Reading gaol had been refurbished by thirty boys from Feltham borstal and reopened for their reception[9] – or in hastily prepared camps before being deported to Canada or Australia.

For others, at the instigation of Paterson, the temporary destination would be the Isle of Man, pending their ultimate disposal. The first 823 prisoners arrived on 27th May 1940, native Nazi supporters detained under Defence Regulation 18B mixed in with Jewish 'enemy aliens' and other refugees from Germany. By August there were some 14,000 men, women and children interned on the island. While conditions were on the whole very good, with food fresh from farm or sea, intellectual life was spectacular owing to the conglomeration of scientists, artists, writers and musicians who ended up there, including three violinists who would subsequently form three quarters of the Amadeus String Quartet. A camp 'Extension University' was established which had the most highly qualified student contingent in the world. Alec went to see for himself, accompanied by the teenage Margaret who, during the sea-crossing, was allowed to sleep in the captain's cabin. Alec soon realised that the vast majority of the detainees were the harmless victims of the crisis. Within a year most of the Jewish internees had left, being allowed to enlist, or asked to assist in the war effort. Their experience left little bitterness as they understood that at the time the British were merely taking necessary precautions.[10]

Having sorted out the domestic issue Alec was asked by the newly appointed Home Secretary, Herbert Morrison, to undertake a special mission to Canada to explore the extent of national sympathies among the deported Germans and Italians held there, and determine who should be released and, if they so desired, repatriated to Britain to help in the war effort.[11] The British government had a guilty conscience. In a two-week period in mid-1940 almost a thousand

9   William Healy and Benedict Alper, *Criminal Youth and the Borstal System* (New York, 1941), pp. 161–164. During daytime the boys restored the interior, and were then allowed to spend their evenings in the town.

10   H.A. Schlossmann, 'Internment Life', *The Spectator*, 29th November 1940, pp. 8f; Rene Elvin, 'Isle of Forgotten Man', *The Spectator*, 28th March 1941, pp. 9f; Cheryl Kempler, 'Imprisoned on the Isle of Man: Jewish Refugees Classified as "Enemy Aliens"', *B'Nai B'rith* (19th September 2016), pp. 1–12.

11   One was Frederick Friedlander, a brilliant mathematician, born in Austria but from the age of sixteen resident in England. He was enrolled in Latymer School, and won a scholarship to Trinity College Cambridge. In May 1940 he was interned briefly on the Isle of Man before being sent to Canada. He was elected a Fellow of Trinity in October 1940. After a letter of protest in *The Times* pointing out that his skills were needed in the war effort and that the actions of Trinity were more sensible than those of the government, he was released and returned to his *alma mater*

men and boys had been hastily transported across the Atlantic. Fathers and sons had been separated. Jews, German POWs and Nazi sympathisers had been thrust together. Personal belongings had been lost in transit or pilfered on arrival. The internees were housed behind barbed wire and machine guns in hastily constructed camps. They were all supposed to be so dangerous that it was not safe to leave them in England, but to General Panet, Director of Internment Operations, 'the shy professors and the perky schoolboys' seemed unlikely 'allies for determined parachutists'.[12] He wanted their status changed to 'refugees' and their guards removed. But the Canadian government wanted assurances from the home government that they were not in fact as dangerous as they had been described. An official should be dispatched from England to separate the sheep from the goats. Paterson was chosen as 'a man who would combine human sympathy with a realistic appreciation of the claims of national security'.[13]

Leaving Liverpool on 7th November 1940, he arrived in Halifax, Nova Scotia, ten days later. His early encounter with Colonel Stethem was dispiriting. He was Panet's replacement, but a man of very different character. Having kept Alec waiting for forty minutes while he dictated a letter and made a private phone call, he launched into 'a tirade against refugees and Jews and voluntary agencies'. Tactless, abrasive, and lacking in compassion, he was ill-suited to the role he filled.

Alec spent his first week in Ottawa, making contact with government departments and then touring the camps. It was the first of several tours. Lack of empathy or imagination was commonplace. In one of the camps, an Austrian youth approached him about his younger brother, a student at Leeds University who had tried to commit suicide rather than be interned. He survived but was struggling with internment. Alec arranged for his transfer to an Italian camp near Montreal where he could apply for a visa to join his parents in South America. Unhappily at the camp, while the Italians were retreating in Libya, he had made some boyish boast about Germans being better soldiers than Italians. This remark was overheard and reported to the general commanding the district. Instead of being allowed to emigrate to Brazil, he was labelled a dangerous Nazi,

---

(*The Times*, 12th and 25th October 1940; Miriam Kochan, *Britain's Internees in the Second World War* [London, 1983], p. 64).

12   British soldiers guarding internees had been told they were parachutists. When Neville Chamberlain's dentist pointed to elderly rabbis and asked if they looked the part, he was told 'they are disguised'. Thereafter, however, the soldiers referred to them as 'porridge-chutists'.

13   The following is from Paterson's *Report on Civilian Internees sent from the United Kingdom to Canada during the unusually fine summer of 1940* (July 1941, TNA, HO215/30). First-hand accounts from Jews interned in Canada may be found in Kochan, *op.cit.*, pp. 93–96.

and was to be transferred to a Nazi camp. Alec went to where he was held and took soundings. The sergeant-major and some other Jewish refugees spoke up for him, while the medical officer said that such a transfer could lead to another suicide attempt. Alec, convinced the boy was no Nazi, wrote to the general and the order was rescinded.

Three quarters of the internees were Jews. Anti-Semitic comments were frequently made by those guarding them. Alec drafted the following order, which the general signed:

> Canada is a free country, where different races have contrived to make a great nation where every man is free to worship as he pleases. It has been brought to my notice that personnel in the Prisoners of War (11) Camps have on occasion been heard referring in a contemptuous way to the fact that those in their charge are of the Jewish race and faith. This practice is unworthy of a free Canadian and will cease forthwith.

Alec was bemused and angered by the bureaucratic ineptitude and inefficiency he found everywhere. Those in charge of the camps never visited them. Writing letters was *de rigeur*, as was delaying their transmission. It was only after several months that he persuaded commandants and adjutants to use the telephone, 'contrary to the rule, but in accordance with common sense'. Regulations were often absurd, and punishments for infringing them draconian. A boy who hung out his wet towel to dry (rather than unhygienically but tidily folding it up and placing it between sheet and blanket on his bunk) was sent to the cells for seven days and was required to scrub the same unused floor thrice a day. Towards the end of his punishment, he was provoked by the chiding of a guard to say, 'You'll be a general one day.' For this 'boyish impudence' he spent a further two weeks locked up. One commandant told Alec that he had received a written order that whenever he went within the wire he must be accompanied by two guards with fixed bayonets. In some camps the wearing of 'a derogatory and ridiculous circus outfit' was mandatory. It was all so dehumanising.

For some months Alec forbore from making official criticisms on what he had found, since that was not one of the objects of his being sent there. 'But the easy, comfortable policy of silence and appeasement' could not be maintained after a winter visit to one camp. He was introduced to a shy seventeen-year-old German. When Alec asked him to read a document, he replied that he had broken his spectacles and, although he had money, could not get them repaired. No one would help. For five months he had been unable to read a book or newspaper, or even the letters sent to him by his mother. 'That night', Alec stated, 'the policy of appeasement came to an abrupt end.' He would have forfeited his own self-respect if he failed to comment on 'such callous negligence'.

Accordingly, he called upon Dr Coleman, the Under-Secretary of State, to inform him that on his return to England he would be making trenchant criticisms of what he had seen, but would prefer to make them known to the Canadian government first. Coleman encouraged him to write freely, and on 26th April Alec presented both his scathing report and the remedy: to differentiate refugees legally and physically from prisoners of war by creating new, separately administered camps for the former. Within a week Coleman informed him that the government had accepted all he had written, and would put his recommendations into effect. Within another week implementation began. Alec suggested Colonel Fordham, who was then in charge of a Nazi camp, as Commissioner of Refugee Camps. He had impressed Alec 'as a man of wide sympathy, strong character, and most charming personality', very different from Stethem, who would be left in charge of the dwindling number of internees. Alec had found far more sheep than goats, and had managed to separate them.

But for the sheep their pasture was uncertain. Many were desperate to go to the United States, where they had relatives and job prospects. But the Americans were unwilling to take them, partially out of a belief that the British were foisting on them undesirables, partially out of prejudice. Alec observed that 'latent but potent was an anti-Semitic bias, rarely admitted, rarely missing'. As hopes faded, Alec 'felt a great responsibility for their distress'. Wherever he went in Canada he was pursued with letters, telegrams and telephone calls from their friends in the States. Christmas Day found him in New York and, returning from church to his hotel, he encountered in the lobby groups of parents waiting for him, and beseeching him to send their children back to them. In the face of American opposition, and despite lobbying in Washington, Alec was powerless to help. In all he visited the United States on four occasions to try to persuade the authorities to accept internees. To small effect.

Returning internees to war-torn Britain was a different matter. A considerable number wanted to enlist in the auxiliary Pioneer Corps as 'the King's Most Loyal Enemy Aliens', doing what they could to defeat their Nazi oppressors. In the absence of dossiers or intelligence on them, it fell to Alec to do the sifting, and determine who would be fit for return to Britain and release. Alec admired the fact that many of these aspirants had university degrees, but none asked whether he could be considered for a commission. He took a self-confessedly liberal approach, especially towards those who he feared would suffer a 'genuine breakdown if they stayed any longer under the rigid and unimaginative regime of Canada'. As a result, he dispatched many hundreds back to Britain, some of whom would be interred there for the duration. Frequently he prolonged an interview to allow the applicant time to regain composure and smoke a cigarette. 'So the time passed.' One of the returnees told Barkis: 'Mr Paterson came among us like an angel from heaven.' Even when Alec could hold out no prospect of early release or repatriation, 'his courteous patience and interest' proved a comfort.

The fate of the boys concerned him the most. They had had their education at school or university curtailed, and their prospects blighted. They grew 'fat and flabby, slack and lazy'. Life was ebbing. They sickened. As one wrote, 'un-fathomable darkness gazes into nought.' In the case of one sick boy, he arranged for his transfer to England to receive medical treatment. Despite the numbers with which he had to deal he never lost sight of the individual. Until the ado-lescents could be released Alec proposed substituting school discipline for mili-tary, and replacing officers with technical instructors, very much along the lines of how he had transformed the borstal regime.

Italians proved the most difficult to sieve. Some were Jews, some were Fas-cists, many were ice-cream sellers from Glasgow. Most wanted to sit out the war, avoid a dangerous sea-crossing, and 'sell ice-creams to the winners'. Internees of all nationalities with the requisite skills or expertise were easier to free since, after Alec's intercession with the Minister of Supply, the Canadian government agreed to employ them in munitions factories or research.

The rapport he built with staff was noted, and it grew as the months passed. He often dined with them in their mess and joined in their leisure-time. He won their trust, just as he had that of their superiors, and of the internees. On his last visit to a camp, twenty men were booked to see him, but a hundred others turned up to say goodbye. Officers too expressed regret at his parting.

The reforms he was instrumental in introducing and the winnowing he accomplished did 'a great deal to restore British credit'. The Canadian High Commissioner wrote to Morrison to express 'the warmest praise of the tact and co-operation with which Mr Paterson approached a difficult problem'. The Home Secretary averred that he 'could not have sent a better man', and was de-lighted that 'his outstanding qualities ha[d] won the confidence of the Canadi-an Government and its officers'. Alec set sail to return to England on 6th July 1941. On the voyage he penned his 'enjoyably racy' *Report*. In a letter of thanks, Morrison told Alec that he regarded it 'as a most valuable and important State Paper', its value enhanced because it was 'so human a document'. It was the finest report he ever wrote and, suffused with indignation and compassion, reads well to this day. Within a month of his return Alec was back on the Isle of Man to resume his sifting work there.[14] To better the lot of those still detained he had Tom Angliss appointed Liaison and Welfare Officer for the Internment Camps. For this work Tom would be awarded the MBE in 1946.

'Enemy aliens' on the Isle of Man and in Canada were only two of his wartime concerns. From 1941 he acted as director of the Czechoslovakia Refugee Trust, devoting his attention in particular to the social welfare of children and young people orphaned or separated from their parents. In June 1942, ever willing to adopt unconventional means, he suggested that he might be able to help British

14   *The Times*, 19th December 1940; Baron, 'Across the Bridges', *Four Men* (London, n.d.), p. 38; Gordon Hawkins, *Alex Paterson: an Appreciation* (privately printed, n.d.), p. 23.

prisoners of war being held by the Japanese, if allowed to contact his former colleague and penal reformer, Dr Akira Masaki, with a view to visiting Japan in his capacity as vice-president of the IPPC. The Foreign Office expressed 'grave objections' to this proposal and, with good grace, he did not pursue the matter. Paterson was also made a member of the War Office committee set up to examine military detention centres – 'glass-houses' as they were called – and make recommendations. He was the only civilian on the committee, and also the only member who had ever been an ordinary soldier, shouldered a rifle or been inside a guardroom. After hearing evidence, and visiting a number of military prisons and detention barracks, he was convinced that the main problem was absenteeism, and that the Army was facing the same dichotomy that had beset the prison system: to inflict such pain and misery as to deter the miscreant and others so tempted, or to retrain and return the lapsed 'to his unit as a man who had improved so much in calibre and experience that he might well be considered ripe for promotion'. Alec was of the latter view. As a result of the inquiry, new establishments known as 'Young Soldier Training Units' were set up and, when a new Inspector-General of Military Prisons was required, Lieutenant-Colonel W.H. Beak, who as commanding officer of the Sowerby Bridge detention barracks 'had done all in his power to transform it into an educational establishment for the retraining of indifferent soldiers', was appointed. It seemed that instead of 'glass-houses' there were to be military correction establishments, whose object was to transform the indifferent into the exceptional. Alec, as a former 'squaddie', was all too glad to see the military authorities moving in the same direction as the civil. His direction.[15]

In April 1939 the Prison Commission had moved its headquarters from Whitehall to Baker Street. Not for long. In October 1940 it took up residence in Oriel College, Oxford. Whenever Alec was there, he was granted permission to stay in his old college, an unusual concession and a testament to the regard with which he was held by his *alma mater*. Beveridge being Master may have helped. Alec's presence might have been less welcome had the dons known of his habit of smuggling in his wife under cover of the blackout for illicit night-time assignations. As ever he was popular with the young, one student remembering him as being 'extremely kind and helpful to many of the undergraduates'. He appears in a College group photograph taken in June 1943, just before the Commission returned to London. On 6th October 1943 he was elected an Honorary Fellow of the College.[16] It was his proudest

15   'The Glass-House Goes', *The Spectator*, 4th April 1947, p. 10.
16   Attlee had been similarly honoured on 23rd April 1942.

FIGURE 30. The soon-to-be Fellow in the middle of the front row, 1943, by permission of the Master and Fellows of University College Oxford

moment, and would mean much more to him than his later knighthood. Frances preferred the latter.

Oxford might be his base camp for almost three years, but his work and inclination would frequently take him back to the danger zone of London. One such occasion was in February 1943 when, despite incessant air raids, both he and Lilian Barker travelled there for Mary Size's farewell presentation. Due to ill-health, she had retired the previous August after thirty-six years in the prison service, for thirteen of which she had been deputy-governor of Holloway. Barker had nurtured her early career at Aylesbury, and Paterson had long been her inspiration. Neither would miss the occasion because of a few bombs.[17]

---

17   Mary Size, *Prisons I Have Known* (London, 1957), p. 140. Barker retired two months later.

There was another significant change in 1942, but one that brought with it no disruption but continuity and reinforcement. Lionel Fox became Chairman of the Prison Commission. He would be Alec's fourth and last superior, and he too would be enthralled by his 'world-renowned' colleague. They had worked closely together between 1925 and 1934 when Fox, a Home Office civil servant, had been secretary of the Commission. Over those years, as he frankly acknowledged, Paterson 'had helped him tremendously in shaping his own thoughts and opinions on the difficult problem of prison management'.[18] Throughout his book on *The Modern English Prison*, Fox had replicated much of his then superior's vision as to how it should develop, quoted extensively from *The Borstal Book*, the precursor to *The Principles of the Borstal System*, and echoed his concerns about the continuing imprisonment of the young, antiquated infrastructure and inadequate funding. Once again, with such a chairman as Fox, Alec could work with his back covered.[19]

18 James Bennett, 'Ahead of his Time: Memories of Sir Lionel Fox', in Manuel Lopez-Rey and Charles Germain (eds), *Studies in Penology* (The Hague, 1964), p. 42.

19 In 1952 Fox would publish *The English Prison and Borstal Systems*, in which he described the prison system as it was shortly after Alec's demise, and provided a stout defence of the whole reformatory project with which he was identified.

CHAPTER 21

WEST AFRICA AND MALTA: 1943–1944

The Colonial Office may claim to be the only department that has solved the housing problem, for it has indeed provided a hole for every pigeon that flies its way from any corner of the earth. In one of these well-occupied holes may be found a report of mine in which it is asserted, originally perhaps, by way of independent epigram, but ultimately I fear, by way of epitaph, that among the European population a colonial prison is commonly regarded as a familiar joke and a public convenience.

Alexander Paterson

In 1943 Alec was able to make his long-delayed visit to the West African colonies. The only extant letters to his daughter date from this time. In the first, written from his rooms in Oxford, he told her that he and her mother were much looking forward to her confirmation, which was to take place on Friday 5th March.

A month later the Colonial Office approached Alexander Maxwell, who was by then Under-Secretary of State at the Home Office, with a view to 'poaching' Alec for a secondment to report on the penal administration and welfare services of Nigeria, Gold Coast, Sierra Leone and Gambia, recommend improvements, and discuss his findings with the respective governors. He was also to make proposals for borstals, juvenile courts and other youth services, and address the problem of prostitution and the welfare of girls in the larger towns. Apart from their appetite for social welfare in the colonies, the British wanted to demonstrate to the world that, unlike the Nazis, they took the rights and welfare of prisoners seriously. He was the obvious candidate. In 1936 he had been instrumental in setting up the Colonial Office's Advisory Committee on Social Welfare, upon which both he and Margery Fry sat. The following year he was appointed to its newly established Colonial Penal Administration Committee, and chaired its Juvenile Delinquency sub-committee, tasked with considering 'the question of juvenile delinquency in the Colonies and Dependencies with a view to its prevention and proper treatment'. In addition, he had visited many colonial prisons 'in his holidays and otherwise', and with his extensive knowledge, and unique 'combination of idealism with practicality', had produced reports which had inspired progress and showed administrators how it could be achieved. Arrangements were made for the payment of his salary and the all-important preservation of his pension rights.

The trip would be for six months, or more if he insisted on going by sea, as indeed he did. The Prison Commission was less than enthusiastic at losing him for so long, fearing that in 'the sphere of policy' the gap could not be filled and 'the Chairman ... embarrassed from time to time by his absence'. That absence would be exacerbated by the fact that Dr Methven had to devote much of his energy to government duties, and that the vacancy left by the retirement of Major Lamb in 1940 had not been filled.[1] The latter, at least, was rectified in May by the appointment of James Holt as Assistant Commissioner responsible for staff issues. There were ten governors senior to Holt, but only two potential rivals for the post: Dr Matheson and Major Grew. Although their junior, he secured the promotion.[2] In mid-June William Waddams, secretary to the Commission and Assistant Commissioner, was appointed *pro tem* to Alec's position, which would soon be vacant. In a letter written from the Prison Commission on 17th June, Alec told Margaret of his sorrow at not being at home for her half-term, but his pleasure that she would be company for her mother. The following day he arrived at Liverpool docks to take passage for Africa.

A fortnight later, he disembarked at Freetown in Sierra Leone. Over the following week he carried out extensive inspections. He also contracted malaria, resulting in hospitalisation for three weeks, and disrupting his schedule. Upon his apparent recovery he flew to Gambia for a few days. After that he was given permission by the French authorities to cross the Côte D'Ivoire to the Gold Coast. From there he made his way via Togo and Dahomey to Nigeria, reaching Lagos on 26th September.

He was warmly welcomed by Lieutenant-Colonel Victor Mabb, the Director of Prisons, and other members of the Labour, Police and Prisons Department, all of whom were keen on an injection of new thinking. Alec came bearing the gifts that they had specifically requested: boxing gloves. Nigeria was bereft of them. The British Council would pay since boxing was included 'in its conception of cultural activity'. By visiting numerous departments, completing innumerable forms, and giving guarantees, Alec had finally secured them, although 'it would have been easier to take out a case of guns!' It was worth the trouble since both Mabb and he believed that boxing gloves were the best substitute for weapons.[3] They also believed in nurturing local talent, be it in

1   TNA, HO45/21687: letters, 2nd, 16th, 17th April 1943.
2   *Ibid.*: letter, 11th May 1943.
3   'Privileges' (unpublished and undated typescript).

the backstreets of Bermondsey or in the African bush. In his subsequent report Paterson praised the director for being the first European official in the whole of West Africa to promote an African to the post of Assistant Superintendent of Prisons. After this consultation, Paterson set out on a tour of inspection of government and native administration prisons in both northern and southern provinces. In each he interviewed officials and gathered as much information as he could on the condition of prisoners and the regimes under which they lived.

He spent several days in Lagos's Broad Street prison, observing and talking to staff and inmates, including a condemned man who had gone on hunger strike the day before his execution. One evening when he entered the gates he was surprised to see, sitting at a rickety table, 'a major in the British Army playing cribbage with a lance-corporal, both in uniform, equally at ease.' They stood up, one that he might salute, the other that he might shake hands. The superintendent hastened to explain that the major was an army welfare officer who had learned that a soldier was in prison on some minor charge and subjected to solitary confinement since it was the rule that European prisoners should not associate with Africans. The young man, thousands of miles from home, was utterly alone day and night. So the officer attended the prison every evening to play cribbage with him. Alec mused that the lance-corporal might never have gone there, if the cribbage-playing major had been his commanding officer rather than his prison visitor. Alec was scathing about how the prison was used as 'the handyman of the European community'. 'White folk', while dismissing it as 'playing no useful part either in the deterrence, punishment or reform of the evil-doer', exploited it as 'a very present help in time of trouble'. Toy trains and teddy bears, shoes and coats, anything and everything, were brought into the prison for repair, and colonial officials deposited their furniture and other household belongings there when they were posted away.

> They have brought all their 'loads' and the prison will store them safely till they call for them in two or three years' time. The prison superintendent will accept them, knowing that it is part of his job to do so, and that he in due course will have to store his own 'loads' when his next transfer is announced. This 'left luggage office' business is an annoying feature of his life, for this accumulation of baggage opens the door to much pilfering, or accusations of theft, and furthermore there is always the grim certainty that one or other member of the family will reappear in the course of the next year or so, and ask leave to open one of the trunks and extract a fur coat or a summer frock that is badly needed in a different climate. So does the prison become a convenience to all concerned.

To all concerned – except the prisoners![4]

4   *Over the Walls*, pp. 14–18.

After a fortnight in Lagos, he set out on an arduous tour of the hinterland. On 11th November he wrote to his daughter from 'somewhere in Nigeria', wishing her a happy Christmas. He was writing in a room crawling with earwigs, some of which had got inside his shirt and shoes. Far worse than earwigs were mosquitos. He suffered three more bouts of malaria, one necessitating a further week in hospital in Kaduwa. Of this malady and the toll it had taken on his health, he makes no mention to Margaret. By the end of the year he was completely exhausted and longing for home.

Once again duty intervened. In January 1944, on the point of leaving for Sierra Leone to discuss his *Report on the Penal Administration and Welfare Services* with the governor there, Alec received a telegram from the Secretary of State for the Colonies. This time it was the deplorable state of affairs in Malta that demanded his attention. Allegations had been made by Captain Strologo, a British officer sentenced by a Maltese court to thirteen months' imprisonment for the unlawful arrest of a civilian, about the conditions under which servicemen were confined in Corradino prison on the outskirts of Valetta. Inadequate nourishment, insect infestation, insomnia induced by having to sleep on hard boards, and the insanitary habits of the Maltese prisoners were just some of his vividly depicted complaints. The Governor, Field Marshal Lord Gort, believed that 'the whole prison service in Malta require[d] a thorough overhaul'. He was determined to act, but wanted authoritative advice first from someone with up-to-date knowledge of modern prison administration. A recognised expert was needed and who better than Paterson? Although he was not to participate directly in the official inquiry into Strologo's strictures, Alec was asked to 'look into conditions generally and advise'.[5]

Maxwell worried about the impact that this might have on 'such a willing camel as Paterson who is far from robust and has had a bad time in West Africa.' He was 'the type of man who would kill himself in the public service without any regard to personal or family considerations.' In words of some prescience he observed that 'this could prove the last straw'. Although 'not quite fit', and able to decline if he felt any doubt about his capacity to stand the strain, the willing camel was 'unwilling to forego an opportunity to help', and resolved to go. A medical consultation in Freetown a week later put paid to that, at least for the time being. Reluctantly Paterson informed England that he would first have to return home to recuperate. He reassured Maxwell that he would take advantage of the long sea journey to recover his health and write reports. He hoped he would be able to visit Malta later.[6] During the voyage back he did indeed write a number of reports, finishing them in March 1944.

5   *Ibid.*; TNA, ADM178/355B.
6   TNA, CO859/118: letters, 19th and 21st January; telegram, 22nd January; memo, 26th January; telegrams, 27th January and 8th February 1944.

One was *Social Welfare in the Gold Coast*.[7] In this short, pithy report, Alec expressed his incredulity at the colonial government's aspirations for a 'giant scheme of post-war reconstruction'. Combining under 'its benevolent umbrella' an extensive programme of house building and town planning, the provision of such utilities as water, electricity, sewage and hospitals, and the expansion of educational and social programmes, it was a rewriting of the Book of Genesis 'with the Beveridge Report as an appendix'. It would be a 'new Heaven and a new earth'. But this was at the expense of present, pressing needs for juvenile courts, probation officers and hostels. Prostitution and malnourished school-children were major problems requiring prompt action. The appointment of native women as welfare officers was essential, but they needed training, pref-erably in Africa. Although seven Gold Coast students had been enrolled in the London School of Economics, they were all men. All efforts at social improve-ment, however, were undermined by the prevalence of bribery in all walks of life. Dealing with this enemy of good governance and making modest but im-mediate improvements in social welfare provision should take priority.

In *Crime and its Treatment in the Colony and Protectorate of Nigeria*, Paterson made rather different observations.[8] He derided the contemptuous and erroneous views that Africans were not stigmatised on release or that they preferred prison with its food and lodging to their own homes in the bush or village. Officials must abandon such notions and establish penal goals aimed at the reformation of char-acter. He blamed British officials for 'the absence of a well-rounded and coherent penal policy'. 'If the prisons of Nigeria', he wrote, 'are at the end of the war to be so recast as to become effective engines of deterrence and training, the first changes must start with the administrative machine at headquarters.' Mabb should have sufficient staff to assist him, and three inspectors who would visit distant and iso-lated prisons and report back. Despite the fact that the native authorities seemed incapable of running their prisons on modern lines, he advocated the employ-ment and promotion of Africans to senior posts in the government system, which in turn should take over the running of native administration prisons just as had happened to local prisons in Victorian Britain. The old, overcrowded prison in Lagos should be closed, and a new one for recidivists opened. Most importantly, prison camps for first offenders, some long-term and life sentence prisoners, and women should be erected, and far more recourse to non-custodial disposals for those committing minor offences should be made. Chaplains and teachers should be employed to instruct prisoners, and social workers to supervise and assist them on release. He deplored the time-wasting futility of the prison work provided, and deprecated the use of chains and other restraints on 'lunatics', frequently without reason, and invariably without a record being kept.

7   TNA, CO859/123/1.
8   TNA, CO554/132.

Chaining and flogging prisoners should cease, lepers should be sent to leper colonies and lunatics should get proper care and treatment. Paterson was alarmed by the growth in crime among the young, and warned that if the government failed to take effective measures to reduce recidivism, crime would increase, and juvenile delinquents would, in time, 'form the hardcore of habitual criminals'. He urged the authorities to find some other means of dealing with delinquents than locking them up for short terms, and recommended the establishment of juvenile courts and training schools, the deployment of welfare and probation officers, and the building of hostels for urban delinquents. He advocated the creation of a welfare department to 'take the field against poverty, overcrowding and cruelty' and to implement new policies for dealing with juveniles.[9]

His report was not universally well received by officialdom in Nigeria. One district officer thought his recommendations largely impracticable. Another purported to be shocked that a humanitarian should advocate longer sentences, harder work and a more restricted diet. A third, while recognising that the report contained a number of original ideas, said it was 'spoilt by some glaring inaccuracies and inconsistencies and by a misplaced attempt at humour'. Officialese was not a style Paterson would ever adopt. Worst of all, some of what he was recommending would give prisoners benefits that law-abiding citizens lacked – a regurgitation of the age-old 'less-eligibility' argument.[10] Better provision for juveniles, frequent inspections, the opening of a training school for staff, proved more welcome suggestions.

London was a different matter and it had the ultimate say. And what it said was dictated by Paterson. At his bidding, to bring fresh thinking into Nigeria, the Colonial Office appointed David Faulkner, the director of the Approved School at Enugu, as the social welfare officer, the first such appointment in the British Empire. It also ordered the Nigerian administration to implement Paterson's recommendations, and submit plans for the post-war development of the prison system.[11] These instructions were carried out just after the war ended, to Alec's gratification.

When he finally set foot on English soil in March 1944, he was so enervated that he contemplated resigning on his sixtieth birthday. He sent a letter to that effect to Maxwell. Both Maxwell and Fox were insistent that Paterson stay on to help in the post-war reconstruction of the prison and borstal systems. They could not conceive of carrying on, let alone succeeding, without

---

9   He made no mention of borstal training (which was not inaugurated until 1958).

10   Tosin Abiodun, 'A Historical Study on Penal Confinement and Industrial Life in Southern Nigeria 1860–1956' (Texas PhD dissertation, 2013), p. 283.

11   Laurent Fourchard, 'Lagos and the Invention of Juvenile Delinquency in Nigeria, 1920–1960', *Journal of African History*, 47 (2006), pp. 115–137, at p. 130.

him, nor could they 'find a successor who [would] make anything like the same contribution' as he made to the public service.[12] He relented. Duty first.

Back in harness, Malta called. In May Sir George Gater, the Under-Secretary of State for the Colonies, reiterated the request that Paterson visit Malta, and wondered if he could call on Gibraltar 'for a day or two' to inspect the prison and give advice to the administration. In Malta, in addition to 'reviewing the prison administration and the arrangements for the treatment of offenders generally', he was asked to provide a confidential report on the politically sensitive question of whether Maltese prisons 'under existing conditions' were suitable 'for the confinement of British servicemen'. Paterson professed himself well enough to undertake these important assignments. Indeed they were deemed such a priority that an exception was made to a recently imposed travel ban. Before leaving, at his request, he was provided with the Admiralty file containing Strologo's allegations and the responses to them.

In June he set sail for the 'George Cross Island'. It had been reduced to rubble by years of Axis bombing and was in dire need of reconstruction. While it had been much touched by weapons of modern war, it had been little touched by developments in modern penal administration. Punishment was the priority, privileges scant, visiting severely restricted. Meanwhile R.J. Ransley, who was spending time in England observing how Paterson's ideas had worked there, had recently been appointed Director of Prisons with the avowed intent of bringing Maltese prisons into line with those of the United Kingdom. He would use his discretionary powers to modify the regime along Patersonian precepts, but there was only so far he could progress without legislative action. That would not come for several years.[13]

On arrival Alec wasted no time. He may have met Gort, although the governor was only in Malta for a few days while Paterson was there. He certainly inspected the approved school which held eighty young offenders, many of whom had pilfered food and most of whom had absent fathers. He interviewed each of them individually and in private. He could see that the provision made for the boys was inadequate, especially in the areas of recreation, education, cleanliness and after-care.

But it was Corradino, the main prison in the colony, that occupied the bulk of his time. Once again, the gates bemused him as they were the wrong way round: the grilled one was on the outside – as was its keyhole – the solid

---

12   TNA, HO54/21867: letters, 30th May and 12th June 1944.
13   Sandra Scicluna, *The Prison in Malta 1850–70 and 1931–51* (University of Leicester PhD, 2004), p. 165.

timber one on the inside. For security purposes they should be immediately exchanged and the gatekeeper should have his keys secured by a chain to his belt. Within, he found 240 men and women incarcerated, far more than before the war, which had brought the desperation of hunger and the opportunity of looting from bomb-damaged buildings. Most were under the age of thirty. Many were first offenders. All were interviewed. He spent ten hours one Sunday interrogating each of the fifteen British prisoners. Their combined testimony indicated that food was monotonous and unappetising to the English palate, bugs were ever-present, Maltese officers, who were generally smaller than their charges, were prone 'to assert their superiority in a petty way', and overcrowding was discomfiting. However, when he asked the superintendent 'whether, in view of the way in which men had to be crowded together in the cells and dormitories, he had any trouble about unnatural offences', prompt was the reply – '"No, sir. The priests won't allow it"'. Alec observed that 'while the casual scientist, with his somewhat superficial criticism of Catholic theology, is blaming this church for its over-generous contribution to the prison population, we of the prison service are paying our tribute to the power of the priest, rejoicing that he is nearly always on our side and has acquired a control we have not yet achieved.'[14]

Alec's *Report on the Treatment of the Offender in the Maltese Islands* was published in August. Concerning Corradino he upheld the criticisms made by the inmates, but noted that remediable steps were being taken and was confident that Ransley, on his return from England, would establish 'modern standards of cleanliness and discipline'. Practical measures to eradicate or alleviate other problems could meanwhile be taken. Changing the gate layout was one. Another was to pay staff weekly rather than monthly to prevent warders getting into debt at the end of the month and falling prey to corruption. Cooking could be improved if prisoners who had been in the catering trade were put to work in the kitchen. Educational provision was inadequate. A full-time teacher should be employed, and literacy classes and weekly lectures put on. More visiting rooms were needed and visits should be booked in advance. There should be a comprehensive dossier for each inmate. All these measures would be both cheap and effective.

More positively, Gozo, a small island off the north coast, was an ideal location for prison camps. Paterson proposed that a camp for forty or fifty adult first-offenders be created out of an RAF base. This would ensure that servicemen could be moved out of Corradino, a measure not otherwise appropriate since Corradino was not 'wholly unsuitable' for them as Strologo had asserted, and it would 'seriously wound Maltese opinion' if the British were treated differently from the indigenous population. In addition, another camp of

14   *Over the Walls*, p. 44.

similar size should be erected nearby, where young delinquents could work on the land or learn navigation.

In an additional, confidential and unpublished report which he sent to the Secretary of State for the Colonies, Alec went way beyond his normal expertise and took up issues relating to the governance of Malta.[15] He advocated a more culturally sensitive approach to the native population, but to allay mutual suspicion and ensure the perception of a fair trial it was preferable for service personnel to be tried by court-martial whenever possible and that those sentenced to more than twelve months' imprisonment should be transferred back to England under the Colonial Prisoners Removal Act 1884, the cost being borne by the United Kingdom. Rightly, this had not been sanctioned in the case of Captain Strologo, whose offence was more serious than Alec had first supposed. It was not merely one of 'unlawful detention'. The 'haughty and arrogant' officer had 'beaten up' a ten-year-old boy he had arrested, not only in the street but back in the guardroom as well. It was that 'flagrant assault' which had enraged public opinion. He had ridden 'roughshod over the civil liberties of a friendly nation'. Alec happened to be in the Union Club when the decision of the Privy Council allowing Strologo's appeal came through. While those in uniform were jubilant, civilian officials were dismayed.[16]

So far as Corradino was concerned Alec was sceptical about the means by which complaints were handled. They were always referred to the governor or the medical officer. The former was too busy to consider them in detail; the latter too dismissive. He was also 'notoriously idle and incompetent', even failing to diagnose tuberculosis in a seventeen-year-old English soldier who was like to die as a result.

> The doctor's only claim to efficiency was that by now 'he knew all the prisoners' tricks', and whether prisoners lived or died, he was content so long as he had made malingering a shade more risky.

Alec recommended – and secured – his removal, while the return of the sick soldier to England was expedited. Paterson's restrained strictures on the prison, confirmed as they were by the new governor, Lieutenant-General Sir Edmund Schreiber, had their effect. Although a number of improvements were made immediately, it was not until 1948 that far more sweeping changes were introduced.[17] 'The Paterson Era' began in Malta only after its begetter had died.

15   *A Report to the Secretary of State for the Colonies on some aspects of the Government of Malta, with some recommendations for the well-being of the colony in the future* (August 1944, CO859/118).

16   The judgment, handed down on 19th July 1944, found that the Maltese court had erred in law.

17   TNA, ADM178/355B: letters, 17th October and 19th November 1944.

On 24th July he set sail for Gibraltar, arriving the following day. He would stay not 'for a day or two' inspecting the prison as proposed, but for over two weeks, writing his reports on Malta, and recuperating from the strains of an arduous twelve months. Then England.[18] Although he did not know it, Gibraltar would be his last venture for the Colonial Office.

18 Being back home when William Temple died, it is likely Alec attended his funeral in Canterbury Cathedral on 31st October.

PART IV

CROSSING THE BRIDGE: 1945–1947

CHAPTER 22

PICKING UP THE PIECES: 1945–1946

Only a living organism, well based in good tradition and procedure, sustained by the loyalty and devotion of its constituent members, and informed by a corporate 'will-to-win', could have adapted itself to meet and bear the incessant and manifold stresses to which the Service was exposed during the war; and this was never more manifest than in 1945 when, despite the cumulative fatigue of years of overstrain in all sections of the staff, the Prison Service finally staved off defeat in its long battle.

Report (1945)

In 1945 a political revolution took place. Despite his triumph over Hitler, Churchill could not triumph over Labour, which came to power in July with a landslide victory. Clem Attlee became Prime Minister. By this time the Labour Party, under the leadership of Alec's chum, had shed any lingering revolutionary aspirations and its 'class-war' pretensions, and opted for social cohesion and democratic socialism. By so doing it reflected what Paterson, an erstwhile radical Liberal, had long espoused. He also knew that a Labour administration would reintroduce a version of his much-coveted Criminal Justice Bill. Alec voted Labour, while Frank remained true blue to the last.

In the immediate post-war period there was much for Alec and his colleagues to do picking up the pieces and replenishing the losses. It was a time of exceptional difficulty for the Commissioners. The end of hostilities, far from bringing any respite to the over-strained and under-staffed prison service already entangled in a complex of urgent problems, brought still more difficulties. In particular, the highest daily population since 1914, due mainly to a doubling of the number of women prisoners and a dramatic increase of committals to borstal, had led to overcrowding and bottlenecks. The old Victorian prisons had a stay of execution. Instead of being demolished they were patched up.[1]

Alec was still a repository of fresh ideas. He discussed with Grew, who had moved to Wormwood Scrubs in February 1945, the possibility of using 'D' Hall for senior-stage 'stars' exclusively. Within the walls they would have almost complete freedom of movement between 7am and 9pm – 'practically "open" conditions in a close-security prison'. Like so much else, it was not to be. He also lobbied hard for the retention of state-run Howard Houses in any new legislation. He was overruled in favour of probation hostels under voluntary management.[2]

It was the revival of his beloved borstal system that taxed him the most, and engaged his remaining energy. The Second World War had dealt the maturing system a blow far more severe than the First, destabilising borstals by removing experienced and dedicated staff, some of whom would be killed, and others never return. It had also 'bitten far more deeply into the emotions and instincts of the young'. During the war there had been a marked spike in juvenile offending, and after it the number sent to borstal increased sharply. Many of them were 'restless, reckless and seemingly rootless' and prone to abscond. Their ready recapture did not seem to deter others since, as Alec put it, 'youth is not embarrassed in its optimism by others' lack of success.'[3]

With the demand for places rising, Alec wasted no time in repairing the damage, reviving his dream, and adding to his empire. He took to the lecture circuit, speaking in schools and colleges, hoping to inspire another generation to devote themselves to the unfinished and now fractured reformatory task. Sometimes when he was invited to speak, he would decline any offer of hospitality, pleading a previous engagement for supper with an ex-prisoner.[4] With such dedication and determination, the old Pied Piper could still enrapture the young. Twenty-six-year-old Michael Gale, straight from the fighting, was one who heard him speak. As a result, he became a borstal housemaster and went on to have a long career in the prison service, yet another of that remarkable band of young men and women who constituted 'Paterson's light horse'.

Alec also went into print, being the prime mover behind the publication of *Prisons and Borstals*, an 'authoritative statement of policy and practice in the administration of prisons and borstal institutions in England and Wales'. The pamphlet, 'pleasantly presented (with photographs)', was aimed not just at the magistracy and judiciary, but at the general public, and its message was that 'the conception of "training" as the governing principle of the prison regime' was

1   Report (1945), pp. 5, 10, 57; Scott, p. 86.
2   Grew, p. 137; Bailey (1987), p. 294.
3   'Privileges' (unpublished and undated typescript); Report (1945), p. 47.
4   *Chester Guardian*, 8th November 1947.

well-established and generally accepted.[5] The problems to be solved concerned method rather than principle. Cicely Craven found 'a great deal of sincerity in this exposition', but detected that the Commissioners realised the folly of much of the system for which they were responsible. They had reduced the prison estate since 1922, and they had produced in Lowdham Grange, North Sea Camp, Hollesley Bay and Wakefield open borstal and prison camp experiments that were world-beaters. But the old unsuitable buildings remained, as did many of the old ways, from 'slopping out' to sewing mailbags. Lack of money was largely to blame, but so too was lack of imagination on the part of some.[6] This could never be said of Alec Paterson.

The Commissioner sprang into action, hoping to regain the pre-war momentum. Former army camps and government-owned country houses were commandeered to provide extra spaces and opportunities. In late 1945, while provision was being created in Durham and Exeter prisons for girls' closed borstals, East Sutton Park, an Elizabethan manor house in Kent, was transformed into the first open borstal for girls. There they would be trained in 'housecraft' and 'poultry and rabbit-keeping'. The first governor, Elsie Hooker, yet another in the Paterson mould, served there from 1946 until her retirement in 1963, refusing promotion. Motivated by her Christian faith, she ran the country house as though it were a home for a large family.[7] Alec saw for himself what he called 'this most modern institution for adolescent delinquent girls', as well as the most beautiful, and wrote an article defending it against its traducers, who were carping about pampering criminals.[8] Margery Fry was equally impressed. The borstal system, with its new additions, seemed to be fast recovering its standing.[9]

Also, in 1946, Askham Grange was converted into the first women's open prison, which Mary Size was brought from retirement to run. In the same year Latchmere House, the first borstal allocation centre with no connection to a prison, and the open borstals of Gaynes Hall, Huntercombe, Hewell Grange, and Gringley, were all up and running. There was one backward step when part of Dartmoor prison was designated a closed borstal. This was a recourse born

5   Report (1945), p. 6.
6   *HJ*, 7/1 (July 1946), pp. 64f; Craven's colleague, Margery Fry, echoed these sentiments in *Arms of the Law* (London, 1951), pp. 137f.
7   Report (1946), pp. 58f. Joanna Kelly, 'Elsie Hooker', in Neale, pp. 79–89.
8   Alexander Paterson, 'Privileged Prisoners', *The Spectator*, 15th August 1947, p. 11.
9   Fry, *op.cit.*, p. 135. In Fry's not uncritical opinion, borstals 'at their best' represented 'the most hopeful achievement of our penal institutions'. She knew how badly they had suffered during the war and was encouraged by their rapid resurgence, and by the fact that the principles upon which they were founded were being extended to the adult estate in the training centres at Wakefield, Leyhill, Sudbury and Askham Grange (p. 162).

out of necessity, but it caused controversy as it again associated borstal with prison, and stood for a 'moral contamination and social isolation', totally at variance to 'the reformative ideals on which training had been developed in the open institutions before the war'.[10]

Borstals were a unique part of the rehabilitative landscape. Their post-war resurgence also suggested that they were an indelible part. It would take time for the system to recover its old *élan*. Paterson, with his usual vim, had begun the process, but his time was short and he was irreplaceable. Gradually, however, things seemed to be back on course and the institution seemed still to be a supreme success. With Lionel Fox in charge, Alec could withdraw with confidence that his work would continue.

Despite his failing health, from March to May 1946 Alec was busy on Commission business on the Continent. In particular, he travelled to Berne for a meeting, over which he was to preside, of the IPPC executive committee to be held there on 24th April, the first such gathering since before the war. By this time Fox, who had accompanied him as an observer, was increasingly concerned for his colleague's well-being. Back in England, Fox intervened with the Colonial Office, discouraged direct contact, and opened up an alternative channel of communication.[11] But the damage had been done. Years of arduous work and constant foreign travel had taken their toll on Paterson's health and would hasten his demise.

In August, on his way to Berne, the newly elected president of the IPPC, Sanford Bates, spent a few hours with the Patersons in London. Despite a recent stroke from which he had not yet recovered, Alec exuded 'the same indomitable optimism' that had been the hallmark of his career. His moral and political compass remained intact. The last resolution he wished to submit was one condemning the outrage of the concentration camps, and he sent a message warning against proposals to subsume the IPPC's work within the structure of the United Nations, a move that could lead to its own extinction.[12] Bates had no doubt that, but for his infirmity, it would have been Paterson who would have been elected to his position. He had, after all, been vice-president since 1938 and acting president since 1943. In his inaugural address Bates paid handsome tribute to his absent colleague for the service he had 'rendered to the cause of penological progress in the world'. Rarely had he 'encountered a personality as rich and useful' as that of Alec, whom he considered to be one of the 'great and

---

10   *The Times*, 26th November 1945.

11   TNA, CO859/118: letter, 28th June 1946.

12   Thorsten Sellin, 'Lionel Fox and the International Penal and Penitentiary Commission', in Manuel Lopez-Rey and Charles Germain, *Studies in Penology* (The Hague, 1964), p. 198. The IPPC held its last Congress in August 1950 before being dissolved in December by the UN, which duly incorporated its functions.

potent inspirations' of his life.[13] To Bates's satisfaction, the delegates made his friend '*Président d'Honneur*'.

Alec's health was deteriorating fast, and it was noted at the Home Office that although he had recovered sufficiently to resume some of his duties, he was unlikely to be able to cope with the arduous full-time work of the Commission. Alec was of the same mind, and in August he once more broached the idea that he retire in 1947. In a letter to Maxwell he said that 'in the true interest of the service' he should expedite his departure so that Fox could appoint, as he was anxious to do, a vice-chairman. So long as he filled one of the Commissioner's posts that would be difficult.[14] Yet he was reluctant to retire when he discovered that his period in Burma would not count towards his twenty-five years of pensionable service. To get a full pension he would have to stay on until June 1947.

Staying on so long was out of the question, but another possibility arose that could mutually benefit him and the service he loved. The Home Office was reluctant to lose him, as an effusive internal memorandum emphasised. With 'a unique power of getting his ideals translated into practical form … almost all the best features introduced into our prison and borstal systems during the last twenty years' had been due to Paterson. An impressive speaker and writer, he had recruited and inspired most of the best staff at home and encouraged some of them to take up posts in the colonies. He had 'instituted and kept alive' an invaluable prison visitors' scheme, and had become 'a friend and advisor not only to numerous prisoners, especially young ones and borstal boys, but to numerous members of every grade of staff, and by personal contacts has exercised a remarkably far-reaching influence.' Given that 'his work has been of quite exceptional value both to the English prison service and to those of many other countries', he should be offered a part-time post, initially for three years, with a salary of £750 per annum. Maxwell hoped to retain his services on these terms.[15]

Alec appreciated the offer as otherwise his pension would have been insufficient to enable his daughter to complete her training as a property manager. Before he retired, he tried to persuade his old friend John Watson to take his place. Over lunch at the Oxford and Cambridge Club Alec asked him if he would care to succeed him in the Prison Commission. Watson did not know if Alec was being his usual maverick self or acting in conjunction with the Home Secretary. In any case he declined.[16]

New Year's Eve was Alec's last day as a Commissioner. On 10th January 1947 there was a farewell dinner held in his honour at the Connaught Rooms. Sir Alexander Maxwell delivered the tribute:

13   Typescript in the family archive.
14   TNA, HO45/21687, letter, 8th July 1946.
15   TNA, HO45/21687, letter from Maxwell to Wilson Smith, 26th July 1946.
16   Watson (1969), p. 72.

FIGURE 31.
Alec and Frank shortly
before his death

The number of large and bold changes that have been effected during [Paterson's tenure] is very striking. The war has been a great hindrance to progress, yet present-day conditions in the prisons are considerably in advance of what they were in 1922 when Paterson became a Commissioner. Great as has been his contribution to progress in this country, his work has not been confined to England. Through the International Penal Commission ... his influence has been effective in many countries ... One of the sources of his power is his faith in human nature. To him the important thing is not what a man has done or is doing, but what he is capable of becoming. He has kept alive, despite all the disappointments inevitable in work of this kind, his belief that even the most unpromising of human beings can be influenced for the better, and it is this faith that has given his work its great strength.[17]

There was an accolade to ease his passing. Attlee put his name forward for a knighthood in the New Year's Honours list.

'Utterly worked out in body and mind', Alec did not fare well in retirement. He was on a downward trajectory. He suffered a second stroke which meant he found it hard to walk unaided, and rendered his behaviour increasingly erratic. When on 28th January 1947 his wife and daughter accompanied him to Buckingham Palace to receive the knighthood, they tried to persuade him to accept their assistance. He refused the offer in brusque terms, protesting that he did not need any help to kneel before his sovereign. On that occasion Alec was proved to be right, and unaided Sir Alec made it back to his seat, much to Frank's and Margaret's relief.[18]

He would still assiduously attend his local church (where he was a church councillor), or St Paul's Cathedral, but would sometimes stand up in the middle of the service and stumble out. He would also wander off on his own, and Frank

17   Grew, pp. 212f.
18   *London Gazette*, Issue 37868, 31st January 1947, p. 558.

would contact the devoted Tom Angliss, his comrade-in-arms, who since 1939 had been ensconced with his wife in nearby Hammersmith, to ask his help in finding Alec and returning him safely home.[19] It was a sad and swift decline. Margaret felt this particularly as she had hoped to get to know her father better in his retirement.

In order to supplement his meagre pension Alec persisted in writing articles on all sorts of subjects from vitamins to prison reform, although it was Frank who polished and typed them up. He wrote a preface for William Douglas-Home's play, *"Now Barabbas…"*, praising it for reaching a far wider public than could ever be effected by official reports, and for engaging sympathy and interest in the plight of the prisoner. Never before had a Prison Commissioner so dramatically endorsed an ex-prisoner's account of life inside, let alone invoke it in his aid. Douglas-Home was no ordinary prisoner, but came of aristocratic stock, was educated at Harrow and Oxford, and during the war had been an army officer. Court-martialled for refusing to attack a town full of civilians, he had served eight months in Wormwood Scrubs and Wakefield. Paterson would have done the same. They had much in common.

Alec also composed several pieces for *The Spectator*, the editor of which was his acquaintance from their university debating days, Henry Harris.[20] Although he never completed his sequel to *Across the Bridges*, he left a draft of the first hundred pages of *Over the Walls*, and parts of it were incorporated into these articles.[21] In 'Privileged Prisoners' he stoutly defended the policy of giving to a few delinquents more than could be afforded for 'many more virtuous'.

> We are generally dealing with unformed adolescents from broken homes, who have had no friend or faith in the years before they came into our care, and we can never entirely remove the handicap of their early years or expunge

---

19   Tom married a widow, Ida Redfern, in 1939. They remained childless. She died almost six years before him. On his own death in 1971 he bequeathed £500 to the OBC.

20   The articles were 'Doomed to Dartmoor' (17th January); 'The Glass-House Goes' (4th April); 'Approved – and Why?' (17th April); 'Transport the Gunman?' (22nd May); 'Devil's Island' (19th June); 'The Prison Chaplain' (17th July); 'Privileged Prisoners' (15th August); 'The American Court' (12th September). Harris, under the *nom de plume* Janus, would write Alec's obituary (14th November 1947).

21   Although undated, its content reveals that it was written in 1946–1947. As it progresses it shows the decline in his powers that his niece told me she had witnessed in his latter days. His wife amended and typed up his articles and was probably responsible for typing this fragment. The typescript, corrected in pencil, is still in draft form, and unfinished, breaking off in the middle of chapter 3. While adding little to our understanding of his penal principles, these last reflections fill in gaps in his biography, or add colour to it.

the stigma that conviction has cast upon them. They have had a poor start, and the law has branded them. Whatever we do we shall find it almost impossible to give them the chance others had to become the men and women God meant them to be.

He turned on its head the doctrine of 'less-eligibility'. Delinquents were usually deprived, and the deprived should be more eligible and not less. It was 'the very spirit of his life's work'.[22]

Appositely, the last thing he wrote, and which was published posthumously, was the introduction to the report of the Borstal Association for 1947. In it he summed up the great advance he did more than any other to bring about:

The borstal institution was little more in reality than a boys' prison ... as nearly akin to prison as dog-racing is to horse-racing ... Between the two wars borstal entered into its second stage. The Prison Commissioners took a risk which no architect of any repute could possibly have approved. They changed completely the foundation of a young structure barely one storey high ... They refounded borstal on educational rather than military discipline, asked the borstal officers to serve in mufti rather than uniform [and] established the house system ... A very remarkable body of nearly a hundred borstal housemasters came into being. They came from anywhere and have gone everywhere. I am proud that many of them were friends of mine, some of them the best friends I ever knew.

He saw himself as but one among many, even if he had been *primus inter pares* in the development of 'one of the great Christian adventures of British education ... a chain of very happy uphill schools where the stronger men want to help and teach and train the weaker boys' – a cross between 'Riley College' and Gordonstoun. No one should be discounted: 'the borstal boy, right or wrong, weak or foolish, nuisance or danger, is still a British boy.'

In February 1947 the OBC celebrated its jubilee. There was a thanksgiving service in Bermondsey parish church at which Archbishop Fisher preached. It was followed by a great reunion of 'old boys' – many of whom were now old men – in a school hall where they were addressed by Clem Attlee, who had motored there from Manchester, driving through wind and rain to do

---

22   B.C. Hamilton, 'The Borstal System', *Queen's Quarterly*, 56 (Kingston, Ontario, 1st January 1949), pp. 367–374, at p. 373. Hamilton was one of the many within the Empire who had seen the borstal system in operation in the mother country. He thought its contribution to English penological practice immeasurable, and 'by no means confined to the age group for whom the system was devised'.

so. Two key figures were absent. John Stansfeld was dead, and his right-hand man, Alec Paterson, was dying. As retiring president, he had intended giving a farewell address during the service, but he was too frail to attend, let alone speak.[23] The names of the missing, 'the Doctor' and 'Pat', passed many a lip. It was the end of an era.

23   *The Times*, 12th February 1947.

CHAPTER 23

DEATH, COMMEMORATION, LEGACY: 1947 AND BEYOND

Though the Prison Service can claim at least its fair share of legendary figures, Alexander Paterson stands out head and shoulders among them. Without doubt he exerted there some of the most civilizing influences of the twentieth century, perhaps of all time, and he will long be remembered as one who above all loved and understood his fellow mortals ... It was truly said of him ... that he 'vitalised our penal system with the values of humanity'.

Hayes and Penn

To say today that a man, and still less an adolescent, cannot be made fit for freedom in the conditions of captivity, is to utter a platitude. But it was Paterson who first said it, and who went on saying it until we had all come to accept its truth.

Time and Tide, 18th August 1951

Alec Paterson died on Friday 7th November 1947 at his home in Chelsea. The cause of death, as certified by Dr R.L. Symes, was myocardial degeneration and arterio-sclerosis. He had just failed to reach his sixty-third birthday. His wife had been unstinting in her care of her ailing husband,[1] and Barclay Baron assiduous in his attendance. He was at his friend's bedside in his last hours.

I knew this was goodbye. He was breathing quietly in the sleep from which he would not awake. Already he was in sight of the last Bridge, which each one of us must sooner or later cross alone. On the other side, it seemed, the trumpets were sounding to welcome a servant of the King of that Country where new tasks are given to those who kept faith with Him.[2]

---

1   TNA, HO45/21687: letter from Anne Daley of 2 Christchurch Terrace.
2   Baron, 'Across the Bridges', *Four Men* (London, n.d.), pp. 30–40, at p. 40.

If there were indeed many mansions in His Father's house, then Alec's new task would surely be to turn one into an open borstal to train those imprisoned in Purgatory.[3]

There was widespread sorrow at his passing, and an opportunity for obituarists to out-do themselves in apotheosizing 'one of the greatest prison reformers'.[4] He had become the third person in the Holy Trinity of penal reform, alongside John Howard and Elizabeth Fry. Once again, Maxwell eulogised the 'practical idealist whose grasp of reality was as firm as his aspirations were lofty', and to whose 'imagination and inventive force almost all the schemes of penal reform which have been developed in the last twenty-five years' can be attributed.

> Alexander Paterson will be affectionately remembered in the Home Office and the Prison Service as an honoured leader who won loyalty and devotion not only by his intellectual gifts, his zest and driving energy, his humanity and sympathetic understanding of men and women of all types, his wisdom, wit and humour, but by his ever-present sense of life's high ends. The many activities of his crowded official career were lifted above the common level by the intensity of his faith and vision ... He was fertile of constructive ideas as he was powerful to kindle enthusiasm ... Disciples who have caught some measure of his spirit are working in many distant parts of the world ... His friends are to be found in every walk of life, among the great and the humble, among the Bermondsey lads who followed him into the 22nd Queen's in 1914, among prisoners and borstal boys. To few men in our time has it been given to touch so many lives so deeply for good.[5]

Fox added his own encomium:

> Out of all his rich contribution to the revolution in the spirit of our prison and borstal systems, perhaps the part which above all bore the stamp of Paterson's personality was his insistence that it is through men and not through buildings or regulations that this work must be done; his flair for finding the right men to do it; and his ability to inspire them with his own faith.[6]

---

3   This would fulfil the prophecy of Louis Edward, who had been in Rochester in the 1930s, and written *Borstal Lives* (London, 1939), each page of which was headed 'There are Borstals in Heaven'.

4   *The Times*, 10th November 1947.

5   *The Times*, 19th November 1947. Alan Paton concurred. He wrote of his regret at not meeting the man who had 'revolutionised the borstal institutions by attracting into the service a new breed of men and women, from the navy and the army and the church and the legal, medical and nursing professions' (*Towards the Mountain* [Oxford, 1980], p. 264).

6   *EPBS*, p. 74.

Certainly Paterson had overseen a considerable improvement in prison regimes, but above all he had brought about a transformation in the attitude and aptitude of staff, and in the aspirations of the errant young. He also brought friendship, as Maxwell was not alone in asserting. His old friend Attlee wrote, 'if his truest memorial is to be sought, it will be found in the hearts of many hundreds of men and lads who had the good fortune to come under his influence and enjoy his friendship.' For his faithful disciple, Benjamin Grew, it was Paterson's personal qualities that endured – 'his modest and Christian approach to his fellow-men, his many acts of kindness, and his gift for friendship.'[7] Perhaps the most moving testimonial to this comes from a former prisoner who had served five years' penal servitude. He recalled how, when he was wallowing in bitterness, self-pity and self-justification, a stranger entered his cell:

> He sat down quietly on my stool and talked casually but gently about my case, about my predicament, and above all about my attitude to life as it now appeared. At first I thought he must be a cleric in mufti – the scholarly face and urbane manner were in keeping. His attitude was so simple, direct and devoid of moral judgment or prejudice, and his comments so penetrating and yet sympathetic, that I began to feel a new hope and a new courage. His sudden incursion did not solve any of my difficulties nor did it revolutionise my outlook, but from that time I began to see beyond the implications of the law and the conventions of society, that my real problem was an inner one and that my most difficult conflict was with myself. The familiar landmarks around which I had built my life – family, friends, the laws and customs of my fellow men – were things in which I had completely lost faith. A new standard of values had to take their place and it was to a large extent the genius of Alec Paterson that he was able, without enunciating any particular doctrine or philosophy, to demonstrate the value to a man like me of direct human sympathy; and in doing so to make life appear bearable and comprehensible once more.

> My friendship with Alec Paterson lasted up to his death, and never fell below the intimacy and identity of feeling established at our first meeting. After my release we often met, either at my lodgings or his house. The relationship was entirely personal: we never discussed prison topics or personalities. He was never a Prison Commissioner to me, and there was neither patronage on his part nor diffidence on mine.[8]

Friends such as this would flock to pay their respects to the man for whom they had such affection.

7   Ruck, p. 7; Grew, p. 213.
8   Quoted in Gordon Hawkins, *Alex Paterson: an Appreciation* (privately printed, n.d.), p. 23.

The funeral was held on 11th November at his parish church, Christ Church. At the request of the widow there were to be no flowers or mourning but 'thankfulness rather for the inspiration of his life'. The latter injunction was better honoured than the prohibitions. The Bishop of Gloucester, Clifford Woodward, presided, and a bugler from the 22nd Battalion (The Queen's) attended to sound the Last Post. Alec's body was cremated, and on 27th November his ashes were interred alongside his parents' in the graveyard of Hale Chapel, near Bowdon. He had come home at last and come home for good.[9] His wife was his sole beneficiary. He bequeathed her a meagre £2,500. He never managed to save much money. Indeed he estimated that he spent from £200–£300 annually on carrying out his duties, 'perhaps at times a little quixotically, but always ... in the interests of the public service.'[10]

The first commemoration of his life took place appropriately enough in his old, beloved college. It was an intimate Oxford 'family affair'. A service was held in the chapel on Friday 14th November, conducted by the Master, John Wild. During the war he had been chaplain and vice-master and so knew the Honorary Fellow well and admired him. One of Alec's articles was read instead of a sermon. In a way it was a sermon, a sermon and a summation of his life. It was about a 'giver':

> He has not chosen an easy life, proceeding without jolt or worry past the measured milestones to a punctual haven. Rather has he thrown himself in faith and fun upon the great bosom of the world, believing that if he does his best to serve, his life will be abundant. Poverty or wealth may come upon him ... it matters little. Those who have seen both poor and rich know that happiness has its own coinage, its own brand of butter and champagne ... Fame will, perhaps, leave him in merciful obscurity, and his recreations will be unknown to the readers of *What's What*. But he will gain a knowledge and a love of man past measure; he will have friends wherever he treads, and though tired and disillusioned, empty in pocket and sore of foot, he will learn that the eternal gifts come only to those who in their turn have given all they have.[11]

On the morning of 24th November, a grander memorial service was held in St Martin-in-the-Fields at which Alec's family, friends, colleagues and admirers gathered to celebrate his life and work. Woodward officiated, while Attlee read the passage on the Last Judgment from St Matthew's Gospel, including the line, 'I was in prison and ye came unto me.' The congregation sang the hymn, 'Thy way, not mine, O Lord', and heard a rendition of Psalm 15, 'Lord, who shall

9   Frances would join him there when she died in 1977.
10   TNA, HO45/21687: letter, 8th July 1946.
11   'Give or Get', *THJ* (November 1924).

FIGURE 32. RIP

dwell in thy tabernacle....? Even he that leadeth an uncorrupt life, and doeth the thing that is right, and speaketh the truth from the heart.'

But the service Alec would have appreciated most was held that evening at St Mary Magdalene, attended not only by the family and Tom and Barkis, but by a host of Alec's former Bermondsey boys, men of all ages, who packed out the church. After hymns, the OBC prayer, and a reading of the parable of the Good Samaritan from St Luke's Gospel, Woodward preached, reminding the congregation, if reminding they needed, that Bermondsey was blessed in having had two born leaders and compelling personalities in 'the Doctor' and Alec. It was impossible to describe Alec's character, but two qualities stood out: humility and courage. He was 'lowly in his own eyes, never sought the limelight', and the description he had given of Gordon Stansfeld as 'one who chose to lead from the middle of the crowd' was equally applicable to him. There was nothing of the dictator in him. He had a genius for friendship. Wherever he went he found friends; wherever he went friends followed. His courage was both physical and spiritual, and enabled him to persist in the face of difficulties and discouragements. He always soldiered on. He never sacrificed principle for pragmatism. In similar tenor, and perhaps to even greater effect, one of his 'old boys' tearfully gave thanks 'for the memory and example of Alec Paterson, for his whole life, for all that he did to uplift the fallen, to uphold the weak, to make each one of us feel that we had a part to play and a work to do.'

> Here in the Bermondsey that he loved and served so faithfully, we think of him especially as the good neighbour of Wolseley Buildings, the teacher of Riley Street School, the comrade of the 22nd Queen's, the leader in club and camp and sport; as one who built with courage and imagination upon the Doctor's foundations. We give thanks, each one of us, for the ways in which he has touched our lives, for his friendship, his firmness of purpose, his laughter, and his lightness of touch.

The Stansfeld Club Prayer (which Alec had composed) followed, enjoining each congregant to be 'the master of himself, and the servant of others'. The club hymn, 'Father who hast made us Brothers, binding us to set us free', made the resounding finale.[12]

A t home and abroad he was memorialised.
    In March 1948 Lionel Fox, as vice-president of the IPPC, paid another handsome tribute to one 'who had vitalised our penal systems with the values of humanity'. Since his appointment in 1922 his 'vision, faith and practical

---

12   Orders of service provided by the family. The hymn's words were written by Barkis.

idealism' had breathed new life into the reformatory movement to which he had given so richly. He was, as he himself had said, 'a missionary not an administrator', and had never sought nor wanted to be chairman of the Prison Commission, but had inspired all the holders of that office. The revolution in the spirit of the English prison and borstal systems that had marked the years between the wars 'was, in essence, the spirit of Alec Paterson'. Perhaps such change would have come through others, but who else could have found 'men through whom the change was to work, and inspired them, as he did, with the faith to make it work'. This was his unique contribution, and his spirit would live on in them. 'One may well ask whether any one man has had a knowledge at once so deep and so wide of the condition of man in captivity.'[13]

Tubby Clayton had a plaque to Paterson erected in his bomb-damaged church,[14] while his words, 'O Lord, help us to be masters of ourselves that we may be the servants of others', were engraved on the wall of the chapel of the International Peace Garden in North America. Sidney Ruck published a compilation of his papers in *Paterson on Prisons* in 1951. Clem Attlee, at the request of his widow, wrote the preface.[15] In July of the same year Ronald Wright broadcast on the BBC, and then published, a number of 'short impressions of certain great men who are not as widely known as they ought to be'. One was Alexander Paterson, whose true greatness was to be found in his 'almost deliberate obscurity'. He sought no fame but earned it. He was 'an Apostle of the second chance', and his 'greatest memorials' were to be found 'in the lives of men to whom he gave the second chance'.[16] The following year Sir William Hamilton Fyfe gave another radio talk about Paterson, whom he aptly described as 'a peculiar kind of Christian [who] habitually practised what he seldom preached.'[17] His friend Sanford Bates would delineate him as one of the great names in prison reform, 'a gallant soldier, a brilliant sociologist and a conscientious public servant' who 'began to put into practice many of the ideals of his great predecessors.'[18] *The Spectator* confidently predicted that his 'tireless reformative zeal as a Prison Commissioner [would] not soon be forgotten'.[19]

13   Report (1947), pp. 6f.
14   This was seen by Katharine Draper at her wedding on 24th October 1953 on the wall left of the altar in the restored aisle. It has since vanished.
15   Attlee Papers, MS Attlee, dep. 116, fol.74.
16   Ronald Wright, *Great Men* (London, 1951), pp. 28–32.
17   'Retribution or Reform', 2nd January 1952.
18   Sanford Bates, 'Anglo-American Progress in Penitentiary Affairs', in Manuel Lopez-Rey and Charles Germain (eds), *Studies in Penology* (The Hague, 1964), pp. 30–41, at p. 30.
19   R.H. Cecil, 'The Crowded Prisons', 13th August 1948, pp. 8f.

Moves were afoot for some durable commemoration. Both the Archbishop of Canterbury and the Prime Minister wanted to sponsor a public appeal in his memory. A committee was set up under two veterans of the 47th Division, Benjamin Allsop MC and R.L. Bradley MC, the latter a lieutenant in the Bermondsey Battalion who, like so many others, had been enticed by Alec into the prison service. The aim was to raise £50,000 for a fitting memorial to ensure that Paterson's example was emulated and his influence perpetuated. Erstwhile colleagues such as Fox and Methven, and several old friends including Barclay Baron OBE and Tom Angliss MBE (as they by then were), formed the executive committee. On the recommendation of John Wild, Master of University College, and Hubert Secretan, chairman of the OBC, they aimed at something that would 'assist Oxford men or others to acquire the experience necessary for a career of personal service at home or overseas, to assist Bermondsey men and boys who have shown promise and need help to fulfil it, to assist men and women to prepare themselves for work in the prevention and treatment of crime, and in exceptional cases to assist ex-prisoners and borstal boys who, despite their past record, are exercising a real influence for good.' The Home Secretary made an appeal on the radio which so moved the inmates at Sudbury prison that they donated a sixth of their weekly earnings to the memorial fund.[20] The outcome would not be a statue but the funding of a number of young people to train in club leadership or undertake university courses in social science, and the creation of a small park, little more than a large playground for children, out of a bomb site in Bermondsey, opened by Clement Attlee in October 1953. Paterson would have approved.[21]

O ther than a park, the most fitting memorial was the passing, with bipartisan support, of Labour's Criminal Justice Act of 1948. It largely enacted the earlier Conservative government's proposals, even though one of Paterson's cherished measures from 1938 – Howard Houses – had been dropped, and the purely deterrent Detention Centres – 'boys' prisons' or 'glasshouses' of which he would have disapproved – had been added.[22] Although falling

20 *Derby Evening Telegraph*, 3rd June 1949.
21 *The Times*, 28th October 1954. He would also have been pleased that one of the Houses at Lowdham Grange was renamed Paterson House in his memory.
22 This was as a result of the Lord Chancellor's intervention. William Jowett was in favour of imprisoning the young so long as they were kept apart from adults. He was in favour of a 'Children's Prison' – which 'no doubt the prison Commissioners would want to call a "rest home"' – where children should be subjected to 'the most stern and rigorous discipline' rather like the public school of old. Having to make do with 'detention centres', he continued to rail against the Prison Commissioners,

further short of his ideals than the 1938 Bill, the new Act placed further restrictions on the use of imprisonment, always his primary aim. Paterson's decisive impact on the legislation was acknowledged at the time. In November 1947 Chuter Ede, the Home Secretary, in moving the second reading of the Bill, had expressed his deep regret that one of the leaders of prison reform, nationally and internationally, should have died just before it came before the House. In a continuation of the debate on the following day Cyril Osborne, the Conservative MP for Louth and a member of Toc H, associated himself with the Home Secretary's tribute, and said that 'this Bill is a true memorial to his work. Nothing would have rejoiced his heart so much as the clause dealing with young offenders and borstal.'

Even during the debate, the invocation of his name could cause disarray. It arose out of that most contentious of issues: capital punishment. Nothing aroused greater passions. Abolitionists hoped that a clause erasing the one remaining relic of purely retributive punishment would be inserted in the Bill. It was not to be, as the divided Cabinet compromised. There would be no abolition clause, but members could try to insert an abolitionist amendment. It was a derogation of responsibility. It was more than that. Without government backing there was little hope of any amendment surviving, especially in the Lords. At the second reading on 27th November 1947 the Home Secretary made matters worse by stating that the government was in favour of retention, but would leave the ultimate decision to a free vote in the House. In December abolitionist MPs decided they would not press for complete abolition but would submit an amendment for a five-year suspension, hoping that a more limited provision would secure greater support.

On 14th April 1948, when the House of Commons was considering the proposed amendment at the report stage of the Bill, Alexander Paterson, the 'great humanitarian', was much quoted as stating that death was preferable to the inhumane effects of prolonged imprisonment. He was an ace in the hands of the retentionists. If a moral crusader could countenance the continuation of the penalty, the most sensitive consciences would be salved. Reginald Paget, the Labour MP for Northampton, at the very end of the sitting, electrified the members by informing them that before his death Sir Alexander, given the vast improvement in prison conditions, had changed his mind, joined the Society for the Abolition of Capital Punishment and become a subscriber to that society. Cheers erupted throughout the House at this pronouncement, and the amendment narrowly passed. Opponents of it (which included Attlee) were

'high-minded men of great humanity' whose judgment he profoundly distrusted. They had rendered prison life so tolerable that it had ceased to have a deterrent effect (TNA, HO45/21951/884452/99, Jowett to Ede, 28th February and 19th March 1947).

convinced that Paget's revelation had influenced a significant number of members on a matter of conscience. Mr Marlowe, for instance, was one who had been 'very shaken', and had 'wavered'.

Chuter Ede made his own inquiries and reported his findings to the House. The Society denied that Paterson had ever been a member or a subscriber, and there was 'no public record of any statement by Sir Alexander Paterson subsequent to his evidence before the Select Committee on Capital Punishment contradicting the view he then gave'.[23] Ede repudiated the idea that those were official views expressed for the Home Office and not Paterson's personal opinion. 'Anyone who knew him', the Home Secretary continued, 'would know that if any Department had asked him to give evidence not in accordance with his own personal views, they would not have succeeded.' Outrage and acrimony ensued on the floor of the House as other members made furious attacks on Paget. Earl Winterton, the MP for Horsham, condemned him for making 'a statement that was absolutely baseless about someone who was a great personal friend of mine, whom I, like everyone who worked with him, honour, and who is not here to answer for himself'.[24]

Paget admitted he had misread a note that had been handed to him in the course of the debate, but insisted that while Paterson could not as a civil servant join the Society and had not subscribed to it in monetary terms, he did in fact subscribe to its aims. The note, he said, had come from a Mr Dawtry, who for many years had been one of the principal officers of the Prisoners' Aid Society. Before he transferred to the National Council for the Abolition of the Death Penalty he had talked to Paterson, whom he knew well, and had received his assurance that, the alternative for which he had pleaded having been provided, he now supported abolition. For that alternative, 'a form of imprisonment that does not rot and destroy the soul', Paterson, of course, had been largely responsible. This assertion of a 'death-bed recantation' failed to satisfy Paget's critics, especially as he would not disclose the note, and some demanded a new vote on the issue.[25]

The Bill was then sent to the House of Lords. In the debate on the amendment, Paterson's name was again prominent. Lord Roche, who knew him well, and Viscount Simon, who was acquainted with him, denied that he had made

23   As the Society had ceased to exist by 1914, both sides must have been referring to the National Council for the Abolition of the Death Penalty which was created in 1925 and merged with the Howard League in 1948.

24   Edward Turnour, 6th Earl Winterton, as holder of an Irish peerage was not disqualified from sitting in the Commons. He and Paterson were contemporaries at Oxford.

25   HC debates, 16th April 1948, 5th Series, vol.449, cols 1090, 1306f. On this whole debate and its consequences see Harry Potter, *Hanging in Judgment* (London, 1993), pp. 142–152; Bailey (2019), pp. 249–272.

any *volte face* on the issue of capital punishment.[26] The amendment would have been lost in any case, but its overwhelming rejection by the Lords may be explained in part by this 'clarification'. Securing his posthumous approbation if not the final nail in the coffin was the icing on the cake. The impact of the moral stature of Alexander Paterson on a debate of conscience was obvious and considerable. It was also deeply ironical. The failure to get suspension, let alone abolition, was the first setback in two decades for the reform movement he had championed, and his name and reputation had been successfully deployed on the side of retribution and reaction. It marked the turning of the tide.[27]

Nonetheless, the Lords approved the rest of the Bill's measures and, after further parliamentary manoeuvres, the Criminal Justice Act, shorn of any provision on the death penalty, received royal assent in July 1948. It was an epitaph for the man who had bestrode the inter-war penal stage like a colossus. It was also the first statute since 1898 that affected the administration of the prison system. Although less radical than the abandoned pre-war Bill, it provided something of a coherent code for the treatment of young offenders and recidivists, and enacted many of Paterson's ideas. At long last 'borstal detention' was replaced with 'borstal training', bringing the nomenclature into line with the long-established ethos, and the redundant additional designation of Directors of Convict Prisons was removed from the Prison Commissioners. These were merely a cosmetic tidying up, matching the language to the reality. Similarly, the redundant terms 'hard labour' and 'penal servitude' were abolished. In future only sentences of imprisonment could be imposed. More significantly, the use of the 'birch rod' and 'the cat-o-nine-tails' was prohibited for all prison offences other than mutiny and 'gross personal violence' on staff. Preventive detention was revived for 'incorrigibles', repeat offenders over thirty, while younger recidivists would be subject to a new sentence of 'corrective training'. In both cases the length of sentence was determined not by the severity of the crime but the supposed need for public protection or the supposed efficacy of training – classic examples of sentence-inflation for the sake of providing 'a benefit', either to the individual concerned or to society at large or to both. Most importantly, no one under fifteen could be sent to prison and, unless there was no alternative, nor could anyone under twenty-one, the hope being that alternatives would soon be in place to make the dream of decarcerating all young people a reality.

The 1949 Prison Rules, drawn up as a result of the Act, had as great an impact, enshrining Paterson's belief in the reformation of offenders. At the beginning was the statement that would define the very ethos of the prison estate

---

26 HL debates, 2nd June 1948, vol.156, cols 113f. It is uncertain whether he had. In 1937 he had written, 'I have seen many men put to death in many countries and in many ways, and known that these things must be' (TNA, PCOM9/81).

27 Bailey (2019), pp. 252f.

FIGURE 33. The National Treasure © National Portrait Gallery, London

for years to come, or at least give lip-service to it: that 'the purpose of training and treatment of convicted prisoners shall be to establish in them the will to live a good and useful life, and to fit them to do so.' This declaration was embossed on every prison gate. In modified form it persists to today, though on the prison service website 'law-abiding' – a lower aspiration – has replaced 'good'. As recently as 2018 the Justice Secretary, David Gauke, wrote that it 'was only by prioritising rehabilitation that we can reduce reoffending, and, in turn, the numbers of future victims of crime'.[28] The Paterson spirit is still at the heart of public pronouncements about prisons, even if his name is largely forgotten.

So how much did Alexander Paterson achieve, and what is his legacy? Does he have one, other than the lip-service paid to maxims? Prisons still persist, the walls have been strengthened rather than cast down, conditions remain degrading, prisoner numbers have rocketed, overcrowding gets ever worse, security tighter, and any international consensus around the rehabilitative ideal that existed in the inter-war years and thereafter has quite gone. Penal optimism, one of his great attributes, is rarely in vogue.

When Paterson first came on the scene the times were propitious. Unusually, there was a growing worldwide movement in favour of prison reform. Penologists, politicians of all persuasions, and the general public backed it. The press blew hot and cold, publishing exposés, publicising failures, but on the whole accepting the reformatory ideal. Many highly motivated individuals were prepared to offer help to those in custody and on release. Yet every prison reformer comes up against almost insuperable problems. Alec certainly did. Old buildings inadequate for a new purpose, senior staff chary of reform, and too little time to consolidate gains were some he encountered. Above all, financial constraints bedevilled all attempts at major change. The prison service is a Cinderella among government departments. At the best of times it is left hungry, at time of dearth it is left to starve. The early years of the 1930s saw the Great Depression, the later rearmament. What could have been achieved with adequate, let alone lavish, funding we shall never know. What was achieved, despite all exigencies, was nonetheless remarkable. Du Cane's era was well and truly over. A 'great relaxation' had occurred.[29] Paterson made bricks with little straw. Had he but more – more time, more money, more tranquillity – he would have built to last.

---

28   In a speech reproduced in Mark Leech (ed.), *The Prisons Handbook 2018* (High Peak, 2018), p. 20.

29   W. Forsythe, *Penal Discipline, Reformatory Projects and The English Prison Commission, 1895–1939* (Exeter, 1991), p. 211.

Much of what he did has crumbled with time, but the spirit which animated him and others persists in the carceral ether, or at least still haunts the cell-blocks, corridors and chapels of our prison estate. Alec and his colleagues believed that the best form of prison reform was to close prisons. That they could not do, but they could try to empty them by creating open borstals for the young and open prisons for adults. Get them out, not keep them in. Wakefield and Maidstone demonstrated that some Victorian prisons could serve a new purpose. All the Commissioners' other efforts with the remaining estate were little more than palliative, but better than nothing and perhaps all that could be achieved. Alec hoped that, through the success of the borstal system, if he could reduce or eradicate recidivism then the need for prisons would recede and those that remained, like those in the past, could be closed, not replaced. If more could have been achieved, blame cannot stick to Alec and his colleagues.

Paterson's era, his 'reign', was a high point that has never been equalled, let alone surpassed. His period in office was the third and last time in English penal history that a concerted effort was made to put prisons at the forefront of crime reduction. The first was the age of the penitentiaries when religion was deployed to induce repentance within semi-monastic surroundings. The second was the Du Cane imperium of undifferentiated, rigid, and savage repression, deterrence being predominant. The third began with the tentative reforms of Ruggles-Brise and culminated in the radical ones of Alec Paterson. Not only did he bring a completely fresh impetus to the problem of how to cut crime and deal with criminals, he realised much of what he imagined, and convinced the public and politicians that this approach was the right one. By his assiduous concern for public opinion, by the talks he gave and the articles he wrote, and by encouraging his 'light horse' to do the same, he proved a significant force in shaping it.[30] Where he led others followed. He created a consensus. For the first time reform took prime place. For the first time experimentation was valued. For the first time the emphasis was not on prisons and the criminals they kept in or let escape, but on borstals and the hope they brought.

Borstals were his greatest legacy, and their demise, if he had lived to see it, would have been his greatest regret. They grew out of optimism and a faith in human nature. In the 1930s borstals dominated the carceral scene, and the expectation was that the lessons learned there would be transplanted into the entire prison estate and the successes they enjoyed would be replicated. While we do not know how things would have progressed had war not intervened, we can say that progress was retarded and momentum lost. Despite Alec's efforts in the short time he had left, and the efforts of Fox and others, the prison system's upward trajectory had stalled and levelled off. It would begin an inexorable

30   Why he never appeared on the BBC Home Service remains a mystery.

decline, culminating in disillusion with the rehabilitative project, the death of borstals and the ever-growing prison estate of today.

Did his approach then merely provide a plaster for a gaping wound? Was it too centred on individuals and not enough on the society that spawned them? Paterson knew that to reduce criminality it was necessary to eliminate poverty, improve housing, enhance educational provision, and ensure full and worth-while employment. These were of primary importance, but were long-term po-litical aims. What he would not countenance was leaving the current casualties untreated while waiting for a cure for the disease. He also knew that a myriad of other factors lay behind individuals' offending, such as bad parenting, neglect, abuse, mental instability, and lack of self-esteem. They required personal inter-vention to put right, and that intervention could be put in place immediately if the resources were available and the right personnel could be found.

Was he constrained by being part of the establishment? It has often been said that Paterson's ability to find like-minded individuals to implement the chang-es he effected was even more important than the changes themselves. Had he worked outside the system, as some critics thought he should, he would have been powerless to recruit the personnel or effect the changes he did. In addition, had he failed to gain the backing of his colleagues he would have been rendered impotent. As Maxwell said, 'the far-reaching reforms ... were the work of the Commissioners as a team but they sprang from Paterson's constructive imagina-tion, and it was through his influence on the prison staff that the new methods were carried out with understanding.'[31] For many years after his death people still joined the prison service, inspired by his vision.

Alec wanted to put himself out of a job. His aim was to abolish prison, by finding other ways to protect the public. Give probation first, training second, and only if all else fails imprisonment. It should be the last resort and a diminish-ing resource. The first part of that statement is still reflected in current sentenc-ing practice whereby non-custodial alternatives – fines, probation, community service – are usually imposed before custody is contemplated. The big differ-ence is that 'training' is now the preserve of a specifically custodial setting – we have 'training prisons' and inmates in young offenders' institutions are known as 'trainees'. Lip-service is still paid to rehabilitation, albeit within a carceral set-ting and in the context of an expanding prison population. His maxims, that 'men come to prison as a punishment and not for punishment' and that the task of prisons was to enable offenders to lead 'good and useful lives', still echo, but with lessening sonority, and little traction. What seems to be lacking is his mis-sionary zeal, his vision, his dedication, his risk-taking. Those are the attributes once more needed if the prison system is to be extricated from the slough of

31   Hawkins, *op.cit.*, pp. 25f.

despond in which it has languished for fifty years. Once encouraged, innovation is disparaged, and risk-avoidance has become the cardinal virtue.

In any other arena he would have shone and gained greater fame and honour. His achievements were not confined to his work as a Commissioner of prisons. They straddled his Oxford days, his years in Bermondsey, and his role in the Great War and in Toc H. His legacy lived on in those lives he had touched. That was reward enough. He did not seek self-aggrandisement. That was his strength.

In his advocacy of prison reform, he proved to be one of a select group who might be considered as genuine innovators. He influenced a real change of penal perspective, at home and abroad. Twenty years after his death it could still be asserted that the 'blast of fresh thinking' that Paterson directed at penal problems was his most enduring monument.[32]

Would that it was so today. Since the 1960s, reaction, not reform, and risk-aversion, not risk-taking, have been the hallmarks of our prison system. It is well that Alec did not live to be a hundred or he would have witnessed the casual destruction of his beloved borstals in 1983 and their replacement by 'boys' prisons' – Young Offenders' Institutions. It was a poignant and disheartening moment when in 1997 the bulldozers demolished the buildings so carefully constructed at Lowdham Grange, to make space for a high-security prison. His creation was crushed, and despoiled. The eclipse of all he inspired is a major reason for his own eclipse. So what does he leave us? Imagination, faith, determination, daring. We need, in all walks of life, more 'practical idealists', dynamic exponents of purposeful optimism.

The evangelical imperative that drove him is no longer dominant in public life, but appeals to humanitarian or philanthropic impulses can still be made. Getting those of an idealistic bent to join the prison service at all levels, to see it as a vocation and a challenge where they may be stimulated and supported is imperative. Initiative, imagination, risk-taking, and even eccentricity are needed. Politicians are risk-averse and prone to pass the blame onto officials. Ever since 1963, when they seized control of the prison department, it has been in crisis. We need rather to go back to the semi-autonomous leadership that was the essence of the Prison Commission. Give the prison system autonomy and let experimentation be encouraged. An official with vision, dedication and determination, with like-minded staff to assist, and the bipartisan backing of government and opposition could have, as in Paterson's case it did have, a transformative effect on the prison system.

As the 'patron saint of the prison department' he would be the obvious choice, although in competition with Howard and Fry.[33] Howard, in his exposé

32   Michael Wolff, *Prison* (London, 1967), p. 72.
33   The attribution was used by *The Spectator* as late as 17th December 1965, but ('Out on Parole', pp. 3f.) had been coined much earlier.

of prison conditions, did much to change them. Fry, by her example and with her influence, did much to ameliorate the lot of prisoners. Paterson, with his energy, imagination, and power as a Commissioner, did much to make rehabilitation central to the prison system. Like Fry, he found in his faith 'an irresistible impulse towards activity'. Like Howard, dedication to ceaseless activity killed him. His name is still invoked in prison circles by those in the know. Recently an imagined 'super-enhanced' prison, functioning like a 'secure college', and operating on a hundred-per-cent education and training model, was named HMP Paterson by the radical arts organisation, Rideout's Creative Prison Project. Alec would have approved of the concept if not of the name: the word 'Prison' should not adorn any reformative institution associated with him. He wanted to tear down walls, not grow ivy on them.

As an outstanding example of how much can be achieved in a short time and with small resources, he should be an inspiration for future generations. In Browning's words he was

One who never turned his back
But marched breast forward – never doubted
Clouds would break; never dreamed
Though right were worsted wrong would triumph.[34]

He was one of whom it can rightly be said: he lived a good and useful life. Good and useful lives leave a benign legacy. His did.

34   Robert Browning, 'Epilogue'.

Bibliography

Material relating to Paterson can be found in the Home Office, Prison Commission, Colonial Office and War Office deposits in The National Archives.

Aa, Simon van der (ed.), *Proceedings of the XIth International Penal and Penitentiary Congress held in Berlin, August 1935* (Bern, 1937).

Abiodun, Tosin Funmi, 'A Historical Study on Penal Confinement and Industrial Life in Southern Nigeria, 1860–1956' (Texas PhD dissertation, 2013).

Allen, Fletcher, 'The Wakefield Scheme', *The Humanist* (February–March 1925), pp. 3–8.

Ashley, Percy, 'University Settlements in Great Britain', *Harvard Theological Review*, 4/2 (April 1911), pp. 175–203.

Atter, Nigel, *In the Shadow of Bois Hugo* (Solihull, 2017).

Attlee, Clement, *The Social Worker* (London, 1920).

——, *As It Happened* (Kingswood, 1954).

Bailey, Victor, *Delinquency and Citizenship: Reclaiming the Young Offender 1914–1948* (Oxford, 1987).

——, *The Rise and Fall of the Rehabilitative Ideal 1895–1970* (Oxford, 2019).

Ball, Baden, *Prison was my Parish* (London, 1956).

Balshaw, Charles, *Stranger's Guide and Complete Directory to Altrincham, Bowdon, Dunham, Timperley, Baguley, Ashley, Hale, and Bollington* (Altrincham, c.1850).

Barman, Satyabhushan, *The English Borstal System* (London, 1934).

Baron, Barclay, *Once Upon a Time* (unpublished memoir, 1942).

——, *The Birth of a Movement* (London, 1946).

——, 'Give or Get', *THJ*, XXV, 7 (July 1947).

——, *The Doctor* (London, 1952).

——, *One Man's Pattern* (London, n.d.).

——, *Four Men* (London, n.d.).

Batchelor, Peter and Christopher Matson, *VCs of the First World War, The Western Front 1915* (Stroud, 1997).

Behan, Brendan, *Borstal Boy* (London, 1958).

Bell, Stuart, *Faith in Conflict: The Impact of the Great War on the Faith of the People of Britain* (Solihull, 2017).

Benney, Mark, *Low Company* (London, 1936).

——, 'Borstal as it might be', *The Spectator*, 5th March 1937, pp. 10f.

——, *Gaol Delivery* (London, 1948).

Bing, Geoffrey, 'The International Penal and Penitentiary Congress, Berlin', *HJ*, 4/2 (September 1935), pp. 195–198.

——, 'The Nazi Way with Prisoners', *The Times*, 21st November 1935.

Birkmire, Alexander and Henry Michelmore, *Toc H at the Crossroads* (private circulation letter 1928, Toc H archives).

Blake, Wallace, *Quod* (London, c.1928).

Blom-Cooper, Louis (ed.), *Progress in Penal Reform* (Oxford, 1974).

——, *The Penalty of Imprisonment* (London, 2008).

Blythe, Ronald, *The Age of Illusion* (London, 1963).

Booth, Charles, *Life and Labour of the People in London* (London, 1902).

——, *First Series: Poverty*, 3/II, *London Children*.

——, *Third Series: Religious Influences*, 4, *Inner South London*.

Bowdon History Society, *Bowdon and Dunham Massey* (Stroud, 1999).

Branch, Daniel, 'Imprisonment and Colonialism in Kenya, c.1930–1952: Escaping the Carceral Archipelago', *International Journal of African Historical Studies*, 38/2 (2005), pp. 239–265.

Brockway, Fenner, *Bermondsey Story: The Life of Alfred Salter* (new edition, Stroud, 1995).

Brookes, Michael and David Wilson, 'Making sense of the sexual sadist between the wars: the case of Harold Jones', *Journal of Forensic Psychiatry and Psychology*, 22/4 (2011), pp. 535–550.

——, 'A Child Killer and Interwar Penal Policy Tensions', *HJ*, 52/2 (May 2013), pp. 132–143.

Brown, Alyson, *Inter-War Penal Policy and Crime in England* (Basingstoke, 2013).

Brown, Ian, 'A Commissioner Calls: Alexander Paterson and Colonial Burma's Prisons', *Journal of Southeast Asian Studies*, 38/2 (June 2007), pp. 293–308.

Brown, Malcolm, *Imperial War Museum Book of the Western Front* (London, 1993).

Burt, Cyril, *The Young Delinquent* (London, 1925, 4th edn, 1944).

Campbell, Chloe, 'Juvenile Delinquency in Colonial Kenya 1900–1939', *Historical Journal*, 45/1 (March 2002), pp. 129–151.

Cape, C.T., 'Learning a Trade: a Borstal Experiment in View', *HJ*, 4/4 (July 1937), pp. 406–409.

——, 'Administrative and Other Experiences of a Borstal Governor', *Public Administration*, 19/1 (January 1941), pp. 61–65.

Carr, William, *University College* (London, 1902).

Cecil, R.H., 'The Crowded Prisons', *The Spectator*, 13th August 1948, pp. 8f.

Chamberlain, Rudolph, *There Is No Truce: A Life of Thomas Mott Osborne* (London, 1936).

Chapman, Guy, *A Passionate Prodigality* (Leatherhead, 1990).

Chapman, Paul, *A Haven in Hell: Talbot House, Poperinghe* (Oxford, 2000).

——, *In the Shadow of Hell* (Barnsley, 2001).

Churchill, Winston, *The World Crisis*, 5 vols (Folio Society, London, 2007).

Clayton, Gerold, *The Wall is Strong* (London, 1958).

Clayton, P.B., *Tales of Talbot House* (London, 1919).

——, *Plain Tales from Flanders* (London, 1929).

——, *Earthquake Love* (London, 1932).

——, *The Smoking Furnace and the Burning Lamp* (London, 1934).

——, *The Compass* (September 1937).

——, 'Dick Sheppard, in Thanksgiving: a Sermon', *THJ* (December 1937).

Collingwood, R.G., *An Autobiography* (Oxford, 1939).

Coppard, George, *With a Machine Gun to Cambrai* (London, 1980).

Corns, Cathryn and John Hughes-Wilson, *Blindfold and Alone* (London, 2001).

Cottrell, W.L., 'The Prison Chaplain', *HJ*, 4/4 (July 1937), pp. 403–407.

Crew, Albert, *London Prisons of Today and Yesterday, Plain Facts and Coloured Impressions* (London, 1933).

Crockford's Clerical Directory.

Cronin, Harley, *The Screw Turns* (London, 1967).

Cross, Rupert, *Punishment, Prison and the Public* (London, 1971).

Crossley, E.K., *He Heard from God* (London, 1959).

Dahrendorf, Ralf, *A History of the London School of Economics and Political Science 1895–1995* (Oxford, 1995).

Darwall-Smith, Robin, *A History of University College, Oxford* (Oxford, 2008).

Daunt, Marjorie, *By Peaceful Means: The Story of Time and Talents 1887–1987* (London, 1989).

David, Saul (ed.), *Mud and Bodies: The War Diaries of Captain N.A.C. Weir* (Barnsley, 2013).

Dickson, A.G., 'Justice in Germany', *The Spectator,* 6th September 1935, pp. 10f.

Dickson, Alec, 'Technical Assistance and Idealism: Misgivings and Mistakings', *British Association for the Advancement of Science*, no.55 (December 1957), pp. 177–185.

Doyle, Arthur Conan, *British Campaigns in France and Flanders 1914–1918*, 6 vols (London, 1916–1920).

Eagar, Waldo McG., *Making Men: The History of Boys' Clubs and Related Movements in Great Britain* (London, 1953).

East, William Norwood, *Society and the Criminal* (London, 1949).

Edward, Louis, *Borstal Lives* (London, 1939).

Edwards, David, *F.J. Shirley: An Extraordinary Headmaster* (London, 1969).

Elvin, Rene, 'Isle of Forgotten Man', *The Spectator,* 28th March 1941, pp. 9f.

Field, Frank, *Attlee's Great Contemporaries* (London, 2009).

Fletcher, John, *A Menace to Society* (London, 1972).

Forsythe, W.J., 'National Socialists and the English Prison Commission: The Berlin Penitentiary Congress of 1935', *IJSL*, 17 (1989), pp. 131–145.

——, *Penal Discipline, Reformatory Projects and The English Prison Commission, 1895–1939* (Exeter, 1991).

——, 'The Garland Thesis and the Origins of Modern English Prison Discipline: 1835–1939', *HJ*, 34/3 (August 1995).

Fourchard, Laurent, 'Lagos and the Invention of Juvenile Delinquency in Nigeria, 1920–1960', *Journal of African History*, 47 (2006), pp. 115–137.

Fox, Lionel, *The Modern English Prison* (London, 1934).

——, *The English Prison and Borstal Systems* (London, 1952).

Fry, Margery, *Arms of the Law* (London, 1951).

Fyfe, William Hamilton, 'Retribution or Reform' (transcript of a radio talk, 8th January 1952).

Gardiner, Gordon, *Notes of a Prison Visitor* (Oxford, 1938).

Gardner, Arthur, 'The Tenth International Penal and Penitentiary Congress at Prague, 1930', *HJ*, 3/2 (September 1931), pp. 83–85.

Gee, T. and J.H.S. Wild, 'Social Work in London', *University College Record, VII* (1979).

Goldman, Lawrence (ed.), *Welfare and Social Policy in Britain since 1870* (Oxford, 2019).

Goodwin, Reginald, 'A Matter of Faith' (Toc H archives, 1973).

Gordon, Jack, *Borstalians* (London, 1932).

Gore, Elizabeth, *The Better Fight: The Story of Dame Lilian Barker* (London, 1965).

Goring, Charles, *The English Convict: A Statistical Study* (London, 1913).

Gowdey, R.J., 'Borstal Methods', *The Spectator*, 3rd September 1937, pp. 8f.

Graves, Robert, *Goodbye to All That* (Folio edn, 1981).

Grew, Benjamin, *Prison Governor* (London, 1958).

Gutman, Sidney, *Seven Years' Harvest: An Anthology of The Bermondsey Book 1923–1930* (London, 1934).

Hall, Harold Fielding, *The Soul of a People* (London, 1898).

Hamilton, B.C., 'The Borstal System', *Queen's Quarterly*, 56 (Kingston, Ontario, 1st January 1949), pp. 367–374.

Hankey, Donald, *A Student in Arms* (London, 1916).

——, *A Student in Arms*, 2nd Series (London, 1917).

——, *Letters* (London, 1919).

Harcourt, Melville, *Tubby Clayton: A Personal Saga* (London, 1953).

Hardcastle, Marjory, *Halfpenny Alley* (London, 1913).

Hawkins, Gordon, *Alex Paterson: An Appreciation* (privately printed, n.d.).

Healy, William and Benedict Alper, *Criminal Youth and the Borstal System* (New York, 1941).

Henriques, Basil, *Indiscretions of a Warden* (London, 1937).

Hetherington, Andrea, *Deserters of the First World War* (Barnsley, 2021).

Hill, Billy, *Boss of Britain's Underworld* (King's Lynn, 2008).

Hobhouse, Stephen, *Forty Years and an Epilogue* (London, 1951).

Hobhouse, Stephen and A. Fenner Brockway (eds), *English Prisons Today* (London, 1922).

Hogarth, S.J., 'Prison Reform in Jamaica', *HJ*, 3/1 (September 1930), pp. 52–55.

Hood, Roger, *Borstal Re-assessed* (London, 1965).

Horne, J. (ed.), *State, Society and Mobilization in Europe during the First World War* (Cambridge, 1997).

Hyde, Montgomery, *Lord Alfred Douglas* (London, 1984).

Ingham, Alfred, *Altrincham and Bowdon* (London, c.1897).

Iremonger, F.A., *William Temple* (Oxford, 1948).

Jones, Enid, *Margery Fry* (Oxford, 1966).

Joyce, C.A., *By Courtesy of the Criminal* (London, 1955).

——, *Thoughts of a Lifetime* (London, 1971).

Kempler, Cheryl, 'Imprisoned on the Isle of Man: Jewish Refugees Classified as "Enemy Aliens"', *B'Nai B'rith Magazine*, 19th September 2016, pp. 1–12.

Kent, John, *William Temple* (Cambridge, 1992).

Kercher, Leonard, *The Kenya Penal System* (Washington, 1981).

Kipling, Rudyard, *The Irish Guards in the Great War*, 2 vols (London, 1923).

Knapp, H.H.G., *Reports on the Prison Administration of Burma*, 1921.

Knepper, Paul, 'Falling crime rates: What happened last time', *Theoretical Criminology* (2014), pp. 1–18.

Kochan, Miriam, *Britain's Internees in the Second World War* (London, 1983).

Koven, Seth, *Slumming: Sexual Politics in Victorian England* (Princeton, 2004).

Le Mesurier, Lilian, *Boys in Trouble* (London, 1931).

Leech, Mark (ed.), *The Prisons Handbook 2018* (High Peak, 2018).

Leigh, James, *My Prison House* (London, 1941).

Leslie, Shane, *Sir Evelyn Ruggles-Brise* (London, 1938).

Lever, Tresham, *Clayton of Toc H* (London, 1971).

Lewin, Julius, 'Uganda's Prison Problem', *HJ*, 4/4 (July 1937).

Llewellin, William, 'The North Sea Camp – A Fresh Borstal Experiment', *HJ*, 4/3 (January 1936), pp. 252–257.

——, 'The Prison Chaplain', *HJ*, 4/4 (July 1937), pp. 403–407.

Llewellyn-Smith, H., 'The New Survey of London Life and Labour', *Journal of the Royal Statistical Society*, 92/4 (1929), pp. 530–558.

Lockhart, J.G., *Cosmo Gordon Lang* (London, 1949).

Lodge, Jeremy, *Lowdham Grange. Borstal!* (Nottingham, 2016).

Loewe, L.L., *Basil Henriques* (London, 1976).

Lopez-Rey, Manuel and Charles Germain, *Studies in Penology* (The Hague, 1964).

Louagie, Jan, *A Touch of Paradise in Hell* (Solihull, 2015).

Lyon, F. Emory, 'Tenth International Prison Congress', *JCLC*, 21/4 (1931), pp. 499–503.

Macan, R.W., *Religious Changes in Oxford During the Last Fifty Years* (Oxford, 1918).

Macartney, Wilfred, *Walls Have Mouths* (London, 1936).

McCall, Cicely, *They Always Come Back* (London, 1938).

——, *Looking Back from the Nineties* (Norwich, 1994).

MacGill, Patrick, *The Great Push: An Episode of the Great War* (London, 1917).

Mannheim, Hermann, *The Dilemma of Penal Reform* (London, 1939).

——, *Social Aspects of Crime in England Between the Wars* (London, 1940).

Manual of Military Law, 6th edn (HMSO, London, 1914).

Marrot, H.V., *The Life and Letters of John Galsworthy* (London, 1935).

Maude, Alan (ed.), *The History of the 47th London Division, 1914–1919* (London, 1922).

Maxwell, Richard, *Borstal and Better* (London, 1956).

Mearns, Andrew, *The Bitter Cry of Outcast London* (London, 1883).

Merrow-Smith, L.W., *Prison Screw* (London, 1962).

Morris, Terence, 'British Criminology: 1935–48', *BJC*, 28/2 (Spring 1988), pp. 20–34.

Moseley, Sydney, *The Truth About Borstal* (London, 1926).

Mountain, T. Whyte, *Life in London's Great Prisons* (London, 1930).

Moynihan, Michael, *God on our Side: The British Padre in World War I* (London, 1983).

Neale, Kenneth (ed.), *Prison Service People* (Newbold Revel, 1993).

Nickson, Charles, *Bygone Altrincham* (Altrincham, 1935).

Ocobock, Paul, *An Uncertain Age: The Politics of Manhood in Kenya* (Ohio, 2017).

Official History of the Great War:

——, *Order of Battle of Divisions, Part 2A* (London, 1936).

——, *Military Operations: France and Belgium, 1915, Battles of Aubers Ridge, Festubert, and Loos* (London, 1928).

——, *Military Operations: France and Belgium, 1917, The Battle of Cambrai* (London, 1948).

Old Bailey Proceedings Online.

Ormerod, George, *History of Cheshire*, 3 vols, 2nd edn (1882).

Osborne, Thomas Mott, *Society and Prisons* (New Haven, 1916).

Page, Leo, *The Young Lag* (London, 1950).

——, *Sense and Sentimentalism* (1961, provenance unknown).

Parker, Linda, *A Fool for Thy Feast: The Life and Times of Tubby Clayton, 1885–1972* (Solihull, 2015).

PATERSON, ALEXANDER, 'The Tyranny of the Classics', *Oxford Chronicle*, 1st May 1903.

——, 'The Lonely Way', *Oxford Chronicle*, 15th May 1903.

——, 'Oxford's Financial Troubles', *Oxford Chronicle*, 22nd May 1903.

——, 'A Varsity Novel', *Oxford Chronicle*, 23rd May 1903.

——, 'East London in Oxford', *Oxford Chronicle*, 5th June 1903.

——, 'Undergraduate Expenses in Oxford', *Oxford Chronicle*, 12th June 1903.

——, 'An Exponent of Rational Christianity', *Oxford Chronicle*, 12th June 1903.

——, 'The Slums of Oxford: An Evening in a Tramps' Lodging House', *Oxford Chronicle*, 27th November 1903.

——, 'Out of Work in Oxford', *Oxford Chronicle*, 27th November 1903.

——, 'Children and the Child', *Fratres*, VII (December 1907), pp. 5–8.

——, *The Doctor and the OMM* (Oxford Medical Mission, London, 1910).

——, *Across the Bridges* (London, 1911).

——, Introduction to Marjory Hardcastle's *Halfpenny Alley* (London, 1913).

——, *War Diary 1914–16* (unpublished).

——, *Letters 1914–19* (unpublished).

——, 'To Those Who Love Their Fellow-Men', Preface to *Letters of Donald Hankey* (London, 1919).

——, *German Prisons, 1922* (Maidstone prison, 1923).

——, 'Give or Get', *THJ* (November 1924).

——, *A Report of Visits to some Belgian and Dutch Prisons and Reformatories in the Autumn of 1924* (Maidstone prison, 1925).

——, 'Borstal Lads', *The Times*, 4th, 5th, 6th August 1925.

——, 'A Scheme for the Redistribution of Prisoners among the Prisons of England and Wales submitted to his colleagues by a Commissioner at Sea' (unpublished, November 1925).

——, 'A Borstal Camp in Burma', *Rangoon Gazette*, 8th March 1926.

——, *Report on the Prevention of Crime and the Treatment of the Criminal in the Province of Burma* (Rangoon, 1927).

——, 'The Apprentice to Crime', *Police Journal* (1st January 1928), pp. 139–148.

——, *Report of an Inquiry into a Series of Assaults committed by Prisoners upon Officers at Wandsworth Prison during 1929* (HO45/24535).

——, Introduction to Hubert Secretan, *London Below Bridges* (London, 1931), pp.xi–xiii.

——, 'U.S. Way with Crime', *The Times*, 10th, 11th July 1931.

——, 'English Prisons', *The Annals of the American Academy of Political and Social Science* (September 1931), vol.157, pp. 164–173.

——, *The Principles of the Borstal System* (Maidstone prison, 1932).

——, 'Should the Criminologist be Encouraged?', *Transactions of the Medico-Legal Society*, 26/1 (1932), pp. 180–200.

——, 'Youth and Crime' (*The Listener*, 13th April 1932), pp. 517f.

——, *The Prison Problem of America* (Maidstone prison, 1934).

——, 'Father and Son', *The Times*, 10th September 1934.

——, 'Borstal Training', *The Magistrate*, September–October 1936, p. 1062.

——, *Report on his Visits to the Reformatory and Penal Establishments of Jamaica, British Honduras, The Bahamas, The Leeward and Windward Islands, Barbados, Trinidad and Tobago, British Guiana in Five Months of Sunshine between 20th December 1936 and 10th May 1937* (TNA, CO1937).

——, 'Clubs for Boys: Guiding the Adventures of Adolescence', *The Times*, 30th September 1937.

——, 'Crime in the West Indies', *The Metropolitan Police College Journal*, 3/2 (Autumn 1937).

——, Preface to Gordon Gardiner's *Notes of a Prison Visitor* (Oxford, 1938).

——, '$14,000,000 allocated for Repair and Construction of Federal Penal and Correctional Institutions', *Federal Probation*, 2/3 (3rd July 1938), pp. 26ff.

——, 'The Present Policy of the Prison Commission', *The Magistrate*, November–December 1938, p. 141.

——, 'The Triple Alliance', *PJ* (April 1939), pp. 72–74.

——, Afterword to the second edition of Le Mesurier's *Boys in Trouble* (London, 1939).

——, *Report on a Visit to the Prisons of Kenya, Uganda, Tanganyika, Zanzibar, Aden and Somaliland* (1939, TNA, CO912/4).

——, 'How England Handles the Young Offender', *Proceedings of the Annual Congress of the American Prison Association* (1939), pp. 149–157.

——, 'The Prison Visitor in England', *Jail Association Journal*, 2/1 (January–February 1940), pp. 10f, 43, reprinted in *Prison Journal*, 20/2–3 (1st April 1940), pp. 51–54.

——, 'Prison in Wartime – and After', *HJ*, 13/2 (July 1941), pp. 12–16.

——, *Report on Civilian Internees sent from the United Kingdom to Canada during the unusually fine summer of 1940* (July 1941, TNA, HO215/30).

——, *Report on Social Welfare in the Gold Coast* (March 1944, TNA, CO859/123/1).

——, *Report to His Excellency the Governor of Nigeria on Crime and its Treatment in the Colony and Protectorate* (1944, TNA, CO554/132).

——, *Report on the Treatment of the Offender in the Maltese Islands* (Malta, 1944).

——, *Report to the Secretary of State for the Colonies on some aspects of the Government of Malta, with some recommendations for the well-being of the colony in the future* (August 1944, TNA, CO859/118).

——, *Prisons and Borstals* (HMSO, London, 1945).

——, *Over the Walls* (unpublished, c.1946–1947). Transcript to be found at (https://dhjhkxawhe8q4.cloudfront.net/boydell-and-brewer-wp/wp-content/uploads/2021/11/15102344/Alexander-Paterson-Online-Appendix.pdf).

——, Preface to William Douglas-Home's *"Now Barabbas ..."* (London, 1947).

——, 'Doomed to Dartmoor', *The Spectator*, 17th January 1947, pp. 9f.

——, 'The Glass-House Goes', *The Spectator*, 4th April 1947, p. 10.

——, 'Approved – and Why?', *The Spectator*, 17th April 1947, p 10.

——, 'The Problem of the Young Gunman', *Evening Standard*, 15th May 1947.

——, 'Transport the Gunman?', *The Spectator*, 22nd May 1947, p. 10.

——, 'Devil's Island', *The Spectator*, 19th June 1947, p. 10.

——, 'The Prison Chaplain', *The Spectator*, 17th July 1947, p. 11.

——, 'Privileged Prisoners', *The Spectator*, 15th August 1947, p. 11.

——, 'Salute the Prison Officer' (unpublished, August 1947).

——, 'The American Court', *The Spectator*, 12th September 1947, pp. 9f.

——, 'A Highway Code' (unpublished, 1947).

——, 'At the Gates of Brixton Prison' (unpublished, 1947).

——, 'Prison: The Great Illusion or the *Tertium Quid*' (unpublished, 1947).

——, 'Privileges' (unpublished, 1947).

——, Introduction to *The Report of the Borstal Association*, 1947.

Paterson, Arthur, *John Glynn* (London, 1907).

——, *Our Prisons* (London, 1911).

Pepys, Samuel, *Diary*, ed. Robert Latham and William Matthews, 11 vols (London, 1970–1983).

Peterson, Clarence, 'Prison Officers' Training Schools', *JCLC*, 22/6 (1932), pp. 895–898.

Pevsner, Nicholas, *The Buildings of England: Cheshire* (London, 1971).

Phelan, James, *Jail Journey* (London, 1940).

Pinney, Thomas (ed.), *The Letters of Rudyard Kipling, 5, 1920–1930* (Iowa, 2004).

Playfair, Giles, *The Punitive Obsession* (London, 1971).

Potter, Harry, *Hanging in Judgment: Religion and the Death Penalty in England from the Bloody Code to Abolition* (London, 1993).

——, *Shades of the Prison House: A History of Incarceration in the British Isles* (Woodbridge, 2019).

Quinlan, Maurice, *Victorian Prelude* (Columbia, 1941).

Radzinowicz, Leon, 'The Evolution of the Modern Prison System', *Modern Law Review* (Oct. 1939), pp. 121–135.

——, (with J. Turner) (eds), *Penal Reform in England* (London, 1946).

——, (with Roger Hood), *History of English Criminal Law, Vol.5: The Emergence of Penal Policy* (London, 1986).

Reason, Will (ed.), *University and Social Settlements* (London, 1898).

Report of the Departmental Committee on the Treatment of Young Offenders (HMSO, London, 1927).

Report from the Select Committee on Capital Punishment (HMSO, London, 1931).

Report of the Departmental Committee on Persistent Offenders (HMSO, London, 1932).

Report by Mr Herbert Du Parcq, K.C. on the Circumstances Connected with the Recent Disorder at Dartmoor Convict Prison (HMSO, London, 1932).

Report of the Departmental Committee on Corporal Punishment (HMSO, London, 1938).

Reports of the Commissioners for Prisons and Directors of Convict Prisons (HMSO, London, 1922–1948).

Reynolds, Jack and Ursula Smartt, *Prison Policy and Practice* (HMP Leyhill, 1996).

Rhodes, A.J., *Dartmoor Prison* (London, 1932).

Rich, Charles, *Recollections of a Prison Governor* (London, 1932).

Richards, Andrew, *The Flag: The Story of Revd David Railton MC and the Tomb of the Unknown Warrior* (Oxford, 2017).

Richmond, Guy, *Prison Doctor* (British Columbia, 1975).

Richter, Melvin, *The Politics of Conscience* (London, 1964).

Rose, Gordon, *The Struggle for Penal Reform* (London, 1961).

Ruck, Sidney (ed.), *Paterson on Prisons* (London, 1951).

——, 'Where Flogging is Justified', *The Spectator*, 15th September 1933.

Ruggles-Brise, Evelyn, *The English Prison System* (London, 1921).

——, *Prison Reform at Home and Abroad* (London, 1924).

Schlarman, Joseph, *Why Prisons?* (Illinois, 1937).

Schlossmann, H.A., 'Internment Life', *The Spectator*, 29th November 1940, pp. 8f.

Scott, George, *The History of Corporal Punishment* (London, 1938).

Scott, Harold, *Your Obedient Servant* (London, 1959).

Secretan, Hubert, *London Below the Bridges* (London, 1931).

Simhony, Avital and David Weinstein (eds), *The New Liberalism* (Cambridge, 2001).

Size, Mary, *Prisons I Have Known* (London, 1957).

Skinner, Stephen (ed.), *Ideology and Criminal Law* (Oxford, 2019).

Smith, Maurice Hamblin, 'The Case Against Flogging', *The Spectator*, 8th September 1933.

——, 'Corporal Punishment for Cruelty', *HJ*, 4/1 (1st July 1934), pp. 15–18.

Snape, Michael, *The Back Parts of War: The YMCA Memoirs and Letters of Barclay Baron, 1915–1919* (Woodbridge, 2009).

Springhall, John, *Youth, Empire and Society* (London, 1977).

Statistics of the Military Effort of the British Empire in the Great War 1914–1920 (HMSO, London, 1922).

Steele, Tommy, *Bermondsey Boy* (London, 2006).

Stow, John, *A Survey of London* (1603), 2 vols (Oxford, 1908).

Stratta, Erica, *The Education of Borstal Boys* (London, 1970).

Teagle, Frances and John Midgley (eds), *The Unitarian Congregation in Altrincham 1814–1997* (Dunham Road Unitarian Chapel, 1997).

Tebbutt, Melanie, 'Questioning the Rhetoric of British Borstal Reform in the 1930s', *Historical Journal*, 63/3 (June 2020), pp. 710–731.

Teeters, Negley, 'The Prison Systems of England', *JCLC*, 41/5 (1951), pp. 578–589.

Temple, William, *The Ethics of Penal Action* (London, 1934).

Templewood, Viscount, *Nine Troubled Years* (London, 1954).

The 23rd London Regiment 1798–1919 compiled from contributions by former officers of the Regiment (London, 1936).

Thomas, J.E., *The English Prison Officer since 1850* (London, 1972).

Triston, H.U., *Men in Cages* (London, 1938).

Vidler, John, *If Freedom Fail* (London, 1964).

Wachsmann, Nikolaus, *Hitler's Prisons* (Yale, 2004).

Ward, Mrs Humphry, *Robert Elsmere* (London, 1881).

——, *A Writer's Recollections* (London, 1918).

Ward, R.H., *The Hidden Boy* (London, 1962).

War Diary, 47th Division, 142nd Infantry Brigade, London Regiment, 22nd (County of London) Battalion (The Queen's), 2 vols (Uckfield, 2015).

Watson, John, *Meet the Prisoner* (London, 1939).

——, *Which is the Justice?* (London, 1969).

Webb, Beatrice, *My Apprenticeship* (London, 1926; Cambridge, 1979).

——, *Diary, ii, All the Good Things in Life 1892–1905* (London, 1983).

Webb, Paul, *Ivor Novello: Portrait of a Star*, revised edn (London, 2005).

Wicks, H.W., *The Prisoner Speaks* (London, 1938).

Williamson, Benedict, *"Happy Days" in France and Flanders* (London, 1921).

Wolff, Michael, *Prison* (London, 1967).

Wood, Stuart, *Shades of the Prison House* (London, 1932).

Wright, Ronald, *Great Men* (London, 1951).

INDEX

Numbers in bold refer to illustrations and their captions.
Individual English prisons are listed alphabetically by names, but borstals are listed under Borstal Institutions. The dates of their opening and closing are given.